CONCISE COLLEGE TEXTS

CRIMINAL LAW AND PROCEDURE

OTHER BOOKS IN THIS SERIES:

Civil and Criminal Procedure, by J. R. Lewis (1968)

Landlord and Tenant, by J. R. Lewis and J. A. Holland (1968)

Labour Law, by C. D. Drake (1969)

Estate Duty in England and Wales, by A. Douglas Lawton (1970)
(Adapted from *An Outline of Estate Duty in Scotland* by G. Herbert
Brown and John M. Halliday)

D1579392

AUSTRALIA
The Law Book Company Ltd.
Sydney : Melbourne : Brisbane

CANADA AND U.S.A.
The Carswell Company Ltd.
Toronto

INDIA
N. M. Tripathi Private Ltd.
Bombay

ISRAEL
Steimatzky's Agency Ltd.
Jerusalem : Tel Aviv : Haifa

NEW ZEALAND
Sweet & Maxwell (N.Z.) Ltd.
Wellington

PAKISTAN
Pakistan Law House
Karachi

CONCISE COLLEGE TEXTS

CRIMINAL LAW
AND
PROCEDURE

by

I. G. CARVELL, LL.B.
*Of the Middle Temple and Midland Circuit,
Barrister-at-Law
A Member of the Board of Management of the
College of Law*

and

E. SWINFEN GREEN
*Of Lincoln's Inn, Barrister-at-Law
Formerly a Member of the Board of Management of the
College of Law*

LONDON
SWEET & MAXWELL
1970

Published in 1970 by
Sweet & Maxwell Limited of
11 New Fetter Lane, London
and printed in Great Britain
by Northumberland Press Limited
Gateshead

SBN Hardback 421 06130 8
Paperback 421 06120 0

PREFACE

THERE exists already a number of good and established works on criminal law, some of which deal also with criminal procedure. Nevertheless, during the years in which we have been teaching these subjects, mainly to students who have been preparing for the Bar and Law Society's examinations, but also to candidates for the London LL.B. examinations, we have come to feel the need for a new and comprehensive outline written with these professional examinations particularly in mind. Our main object, therefore, has been to produce a practical book which will be found adequate for the Law Society's examination in criminal law and for the Bar examinations in criminal law and criminal procedure, but which can also be used by police officers and others who are seeking a comprehensive introduction to these important subjects. In addition, we hope that the book will provide a sound foundation for the more academic study entailed in degree courses, in which it is only too easy to lose sight of the wood for the trees if the main outlines of the subject have not been firmly grasped.

The original concept of this book was that of the second-named author, and he wrote the original text of the chapters on criminal law, while the chapters on criminal procedure were written by the first-named author. However, through extraneous circumstances and the unexpected delay caused by the many statutory changes which have occurred during the last two years, the task of incorporating these changes into both parts of the book fell to the first-named author. Nevertheless, the proofs have been checked and agreed by us both and we jointly accept responsibility for the whole.

We have endeavoured to state the law as it stood on January 1, 1969, but we did anticipate certain impending changes, including those made by the Magistrates' Courts Rules 1968, and we have been able to incorporate a few of the more recent cases at the proof stage. One important Bill which came too late for inclusion in the text but which will, when it becomes law, effect a number of important changes (particularly in relation to criminal procedure) is the Children and Young Persons Bill. This Bill, if it reaches the statute book in its present form, will mean, *inter alia*, that it will not be possible to charge a person with an offence, except homicide, by reason of anything done or omitted while he was a child. This will not mean that a child who has attained at least ten years of age

v

will not be able to commit a criminal offence except homicide, but it will mean that it will not be possible to charge him with it by criminal process. Instead, the child may be brought before a juvenile court by civil process and if he is, *inter alia*, guilty of an offence [and in need of care or control which he is not otherwise likely to receive][1] then the court will be able to make (*a*) an order requiring his parent or guardian to enter into a recognizance to take proper control over him (provided his parent or guardian consents) or (*b*) a supervision order (which will place him under the supervision of a local authority) or (*c*) a care order (which will commit him to the care of a local authority) or (*d*) a hospital order within the meaning of Part V of the Mental Health Act 1959 or (*e*) a guardianship order. In the case of a young person, moreover, it will only be possible for a qualified informant (*e.g.*, a police officer or an officer of a local authority) to lay an information (which will have to be in writing), and this will also be subject to certain other specified conditions. Further, a young person will have to be tried summarily for all indictable offences (except homicide and certain other grave offences) and for all hybrid offences, and a young person will not be able to claim trial by jury under section 25 of the Magistrates' Courts Act 1952. Alternatively, it will be possible to bring a young person before a juvenile court by civil process in the same manner as a child and the court may then either make one of the orders already mentioned or bind the young person over to keep the peace or to be of good behaviour. In addition, the minimum age for borstal training will be seventeen (except that it will sometimes be possible for a young person aged at least fifteen to be removed from the care of a local authority to a borstal institution), the minimum age for a probation order will also be seventeen, it will no longer be possible for a court to make a detention centre order or an order committing an offender to the care of a fit person, and the Home Secretary will have the power to issue an order stopping the sending of offenders to approved schools.

We wish to record our thanks to the following of our colleagues at the College of Law: to Mr. W. E. D. Davies for his assistance in the preparation of the index, to Mr. B. M. Dickens for reading the proofs of the chapters on criminal procedure and, in particular, to Mr. P. G. Chiswell for his assistance and advice in the preparation of the chapters on criminal law.

I. G. CARVELL
E. SWINFEN GREEN

---

[1] It is possible that the need for this additional requirement will not appear in the Act.

CONTENTS

PART 1

CRIMINAL LAW

PART 2

CRIMINAL PROCEDURE

Contents

TABLE OF CASES

TABLE OF STATUTES

xxvii

TABLE OF RULES

PART 1

CRIMINAL LAW

Chapter One

NATURE OF A CRIME
CLASSIFICATION OF CRIMES

Nature of a Crime

THOSE forms of conduct which the law recognizes as wrongful fall into two principal classes, *viz.*, civil wrongs and criminal wrongs. Civil wrongs are mainly breaches of contract and torts (such as trespass against land, personal assault and libel); these give rise to civil proceedings, usually with the object of obtaining damages. Criminal wrongs, such as murder, theft and burglary, give rise to criminal proceedings, the object of which is usually the punishment of the offender: a good working definition of a crime is that it is an act or omission forbidden by law on pain of punishment.

Conduct is often both criminal and tortious. For example, of the torts mentioned above, personal assault and libel are criminal as well as tortious, whereas trespass against land generally is not. As a rule, if an act is both a tort and a crime, criminal and civil proceedings may be taken in respect of it, concurrently or otherwise. There are, however, a few exceptions. For example, if summary proceedings are taken in a magistrates' court by or on behalf of the person aggrieved for a common assault, or for an aggravated assault upon a boy who is not over fourteen or any female, and the court grants a certificate of dismissal of the proceedings, or the accused suffers the punishment inflicted upon him by the court, the accused is released from all further proceedings, civil or criminal, in respect of the same cause (Offences against the Person Act 1861, sections 44, 45). In this case, therefore, if the person aggrieved wishes to take civil proceedings in respect of the assault, he must be careful not to bring a criminal prosecution first.

Classification of Crimes

There are various ways in which criminal offences may be classified. Of these we may notice three.

3

(1) *Indictable, summary and hybrid offences*

From the point of view of procedure, criminal offences may be divided into indictable, summary and hybrid offences. These terms are fully explained in Chapter 27 and a very brief treatment will suffice here. Indictable offences are those which may be tried on indictment, *i.e.* by a jury at assizes (including the Old Bailey and the Crown Courts at Liverpool and Manchester) or quarter sessions: this is the only category known to the common law, and it includes all the most serious offences. A summary offence is one which the statute creating it provides shall be triable summarily, *i.e.* by a magistrates' court. A hybrid offence is one which the statute creating it provides shall be triable summarily or on indictment. It will be observed that statutory offences are indictable offences unless the statute creating the offence puts it into one of the other two classes.

(2) *Felonies and misdemeanours*

Before the Criminal Law Act 1967 all offences were either felonies or misdemeanours (treasons were technically felonies, although for convenience they were often regarded as forming a separate category). A felony was an offence conviction of which at common law had automatically involved forfeiture of the offender's property, or an offence which had been made a felony by statute. All other offences were misdemeanours. Thus, broadly speaking, the more serious offences were felonies and the less serious misdemeanours. This was not altogether true, however; for example, simple larceny was a felony and punishable with a maximum of five years' imprisonment, whereas fraudulent conversion was a misdemeanour but punishable with a maximum of seven years' imprisonment (these crimes are now covered by the offence of theft).

Section 1 of the Criminal Law Act 1967 has abolished this classification, which was clearly unsatisfactory, or at least it has abolished all distinctions between felonies and misdemeanours (section 1(1)). It is possible on the wording of the section to argue that the classification remains and all offences are still felonies or misdemeanours, but there is now no distinction between them. Moreover, section 12(5)(*a*) of the Criminal Law Act 1967 provides that "any enactment creating an offence by directing it to be felony shall be read as directing it to be an offence." Nevertheless, treason is to be treated as a separate category of offence (*ibid.*, s. 12(6): see Chap. 21).

There were a number of procedural differences between felonies and misdemeanours, and, though section 1(2) of the Criminal Law Act 1967 provides that, subject to the provisions of the Act, on all

matters on which a distinction has previously been made the law
and practice in relation to all offences shall be the law and practice
applicable at the commencement of the Act in relation to misdemeanours, it is necessary to know of the major differences in order
to understand many of the older cases. Nevertheless, many of the
differences had been abolished by statute before 1967, for example,
the automatic forfeiture on conviction of felony was abolished by
the Forfeiture Act 1870. The main differences immediately before
the Criminal Law Act 1967 were:

1. The rules as to parties were different. In the case of felonies
there could be a principal in the first degree, a principal in the
second degree, an accessory before the fact and an accessory after
the fact, while in the case of misdemeanours there could be no
accessory after the fact and the other parties were all called principals (see Chap. 5).

2. There was a rule in relation to felonies only, known as the
rule in *Smith* v. *Selwyn* (1914), that a civil action could be stayed
by the court if it clearly appeared to be an action in respect of a
wrong which was also a felony and the proceedings were against
the felon himself by a person directly injured by the felonious act,
unless a criminal prosecution had already been brought or some
good reason could be shown for the failure to prosecute.

3. The offences of misprision of felony and compounding a felony
did not, as the names imply, extend to misdemeanours. These
offences have, in fact, been abolished, but similar offences still
apply in relation to treason (see Chap. 20).

4. There were procedural differences, including differences as to
powers of arrest. As a general rule an accused could only be
arrested without a warrant for arrest having been issued if the
offence was a felony. See now the classification into arrestable and
non arrestable offences, below.

5. Disqualification from public office followed a conviction for
felony if the convicted person was sentenced to more than twelve
months imprisonment. There were no corresponding provisions for
misdemeanours.
   Although all distinctions between felonies and misdemeanours
have now been abolished, in view of the difficulty in understanding many of the older cases without knowing whether the offence
was a felony or a misdemeanour, this fact is still indicated through-

out this book by the insertion of (f) or (m) after each offence. Moreover, the term "a common law misdemeanour" had acquired a technical meaning and indicated that the offence was one for which there was no fixed maximum punishment, although on appeal a sentence would be reduced if considered to be excessive (see *R. v. Morris* (1951), C.C.A.; *Verrier* v. *D.P.P.* (1967), H.L.; and see Chap. 44). The former common law misdemeanours are therefore indicated in this book by the term "common law offence (m)."

(3) *Arrestable and non-arrestable offences*

By section 2(1) of the Criminal Law Act 1967 an arrestable offence is any offence, or attempt to commit any offence, for which the sentence is fixed by law (*e.g.*, murder, see Chap. 7) or for which a person (not previously convicted) may under or by virtue of any enactment be sentenced to imprisonment for a term of five years. In addition, certain other offences have expressly been made arrestable offences (*e.g.*, taking a conveyance without authority: Theft Act 1968, s. 12(3)). Otherwise, however, an offence is a non-arrestable offence. The classification of arrestable and non-arrestable offences is not therefore synonymous with that of felonies and misdemeanours.

As a general rule an accused may only be arrested without a warrant if he has committed, or there is reasonable cause for suspecting that he has committed, an arrestable offence (see Chap. 30), but the classification of offences into arrestable and non-arrestable offences is also of importance in relation to certain particular crimes. Thus, for example, as we shall see (Chap. 26), it is an offence under section 4 of the Vagrancy Act 1824 for a suspected person or a reputed thief to loiter with intent to commit an arrestable offence.

Chapter Two

SOURCES OF THE CRIMINAL LAW

THE basis of the criminal law (as of the law of contract and tort and land) is common law, *i.e.* judge-made law. Some of this law has been codified, *e.g.* in the Offences against the Person Act 1861. In modern times statute has become increasingly an original source of criminal law. Parliament meets much more frequently and for longer sessions than it did during the formative period of the common law. In consequence, in the nineteenth century the view gained wide acceptance that the judges would no longer exercise their old power to create new crimes, but would leave it to Parliament to do so as necessary. (See, *e.g.*, *R.* v. *Price* (1884), in which Stephen J. refused to hold it criminal to cremate a dead body instead of burying it.) *Nulla poena sine lege* was felt to be the correct principle. However, this view did not commend itself to the judges of the Court of Criminal Appeal in 1932 in the case of *R.* v. *Manley*, and in this case the court cited as still representing the law a dictum of Lawrence J. in *R.* v. *Higgins* (1801): "All such acts or attempts as tend to the prejudice of the community are indictable." (The Court of Criminal Appeal was abolished and its jurisdiction transferred to a Criminal Division of the Court of Appeal under the Criminal Appeal Act 1966, s. 1. The new court, however, has substantially the same powers as the former Court of Criminal Appeal. See Chaps. 28 and 41.) This seemed to be a clear assertion by the judges of their old power to recognize conduct as criminal which had not previously been declared to be so, and this in fact they did in *Manley's* case. In that case one Elizabeth Manley had falsely reported to the police that she had been attacked and robbed by a man whose description she gave. She was charged with a common law misdemeanour on the ground that she had caused a public mischief by wasting the time of the police and putting innocent members of the public in peril of arrest. Her conviction was affirmed by the Court of Criminal Appeal. Hence was born the crime now known as "public mischief" (see also now the offence of giving false information, Chap 20). But in *R.* v. *Newland* in 1953 the then Court of Criminal Appeal criticized the wide grounds upon which

7

the court had founded its decision in *Manley's* case, and Lord Goddard, the Lord Chief Justice, expressly stated his opinion that new crimes could be created only by statute. However, more recently in *Shaw* v. *D.P.P.* (1962) the House of Lords has shown a different disposition. In particular, Lord Simonds in that case said: "I entertain no doubt that there remains in the courts of law a residual power to enforce the supreme and fundamental purpose of the law, to conserve not only the safety and order but also the moral welfare of the state, and that it is their duty to guard it against attacks that may be the more insidious because they are novel and unprepared for."

It is still an open question, therefore, whether today the judges still have power to create new crimes.

Chapter Three

THE TWO ELEMENTS OF A CRIME

AT common law, with few exceptions, every crime is compounded of two elements, *viz.* a certain *actus reus* and a certain *mens rea.* That is to say, the crime consists of some form of conduct accompanied by a certain state of mind on the part of the doer. Both the conduct and the mental element differ from crime to crime and can be ascertained only by studying the definition of the particular crime as it has been evolved by the judges over the years; thus, as Stephen J. said in *R. v. Tolson* (1889), C.C.R., with reference to *mens rea,* "The definition of every crime contains, expressly or by implication, a proposition as to a state of mind."

Actus Reus

Actus reus may be defined as conduct that causes an event which it is the policy of the criminal law to prevent. For example, in a case of murder the *actus reus* is conduct which causes the death of a human being in circumstances in which it is the policy of the criminal law to prevent such a killing (homicide is not always unlawful, as will be seen later).

Actus reus may consist of a positive act or of an omission to act. However, an omission to act is sufficient only when it constitutes a breach of a duty to act imposed by law. The common law does not usually impose such duties, being content with negative prohibitions. However in the following cases (*inter alia*) the law does impose such a duty, so that in these cases an omission to act may found criminal liability.

(1) Parents are under a legal duty to take proper care of their children until they are old enough to look after themselves. This duty extends to the provision of food, clothing, shelter, medical attention and general care, and the duty rests upon both parents (*R. v. Watson and Watson* (1959), in which both parents were charged with manslaughter by reason of their failure to call a doctor to their

scalded child). If the duty imposed by the law is not fulfilled, conscientious objection (*e.g.* to the use of medicine) is no defence (*R. v. Senior* (1899), C.C.R.). On the other hand, rather strangely, it has been held that an expectant mother does not owe a duty of care to her unborn child, so that if the child dies in consequence of the mother's failure to make proper arrangements for her confinement, the mother cannot be convicted of any form of unlawful homicide (*R. v. Knights* (1860)).

(2) One who undertakes the care of another who is unable to look after himself properly, *e.g.* by reason of sickness or old age, is under a legal duty to take proper care of that other person (*R. v. Marriott* (1838)).

(3) One who undertakes work upon the careful performance of which the safety of others depends is under a legal duty towards those others. For example, in *R. v. Lowe* (1850) the accused was in charge of a colliery engine, the management of which he delegated to an inexperienced lad, through whose incompetence in the management of the engine a miner was killed: the accused was held to have caused the death.

(4) There is a duty to report to the police the commission of treason of which one is aware: failure to do so is known as misprision of treason and is a common law offence (m). (See Chap. 20; and see also the offence of "concealing offences.")
    It may be mentioned that it is quite common for Acts of Parliament to create offences of omission. These often take the form of requiring the citizen to supply information, *e.g.* to the income tax authorities.

Causation
    A person will not be held criminally liable unless his conduct can fairly be regarded as having caused that event which it is the policy of the criminal law to prevent. This gives rise to the very difficult problem of causation. The judges cannot be said to have evolved any scientific principles on this subject, and are very much guided by their sense of fairness in the individual case. The following propositions, however, may safely be made:

(1) The mere fact that the accused's conduct was not the sole cause of the event in question will not necessarily exempt him from responsibility. For example, in cases of homicide (in which these

problems generally arise) if A unlawfully wounds B, and this wound ultimately leads to B's death, A will generally be considered to have caused the death, even if B in all probability would not have died but for errors in treatment made by doctors or nurses who were doing their best to save B from the consequences of A's action, or if B would probably not have died but for some mistake which he himself made. For example, in *R. v. Smith* (1959), C.-M.A.C., the accused had unlawfully wounded the deceased, who probably would have recovered if he had been kept still and warm: the wound would then in all likelihood have healed. In fact, the wounded man was twice dropped on the ground on the way to a medical reception station: at the station his condition was misunderstood and he was given artificial respiration. These mistakes prevented the wound from healing, and the wounded man died from haemorrhage. The accused was held to have caused the death.

In another oft-cited case, that of *R. v. Holland* in 1841, the accused had unlawfully wounded the deceased, who was advised to submit to the amputation of a finger, but refused. The wounded man died in consequence of blood poisoning, but probably would not have done so if he had agreed to the amputation. The accused was held responsible for causing his death. (It is conceivable, but unlikely, that the decision would be different today, because, of course, the risks of surgical treatment were much greater in 1841 than they now are.)

(2) On the other hand, the court may hold in particular circumstances that, although an event would not have occurred but for what the accused did, it would not be just to hold him responsible for causing that event, because in the light of other contributory factors the accused's act must be regarded as too remote. For example, in *R. v. Jordan* (1956) C.C.A., the accused had inflicted an unlawful wound upon the deceased, who died eight days after admission to hospital, by which time the wound had largely healed. Two medical experts gave evidence that the cause of death was pneumonia, which had been brought on by two errors in treatment, *viz.* the continued administration of the drug terramycin after the patient had shown himself intolerant to it and the intravenous injection of wholly abnormal quantities of fluid. In these circumstances the Court of Criminal Appeal considered that it would not be fair to hold the accused responsible for causing the death. But in *R. v. Smith* (*supra*) it was stated that the facts of *Jordan's* case must be regarded as wholly exceptional.

The law may perhaps be summarized by saying that the accused's conduct must have been a substantial cause of the event, but that it need not have been the only cause. Thus if two motorists are driving in opposite directions in the middle lane of a three-lane highway, and neither will give way to the other, it may well be that whichever of the motorists is killed the survivor will be guilty of causing death by dangerous driving: his conduct was a substantial cause of the death despite the fact that the other was equally blameworthy (see *R. v. Gould* (1963)).

Another factor which must be considered in relation to causation is the question of *contributory negligence*. This has arisen, in practice, in cases of homicide, and the general rule is that it is no defence to a charge of homicide that the victim contributed to his own death by his own negligence. Thus in *R. v. Swindall and Osborne* (1846), the two accused entered into a race between themselves and drove dangerously along a public street. It was held that they were guilty of causing the death of a pedestrian who was struck and killed, and that it was no defence that the pedestrian had contributed to his own death by his own negligence. Nevertheless, the victim's conduct may be relevant in deciding whether the conduct of the accused was in fact the cause of his death. In *R. v. Swindall and Osborne*, the accused would not have been guilty if they could not have avoided the accident even if they had been driving with proper care (*R. v. Dalloway* (1847)). In these circumstances, the dangerous driving of the accused would not, in fact, be the cause of the victim's death.

Mens Rea

As has been mentioned, an act or an omission does not of itself constitute a crime at common law: it must be accompanied by a particular mental state. As the old common law maxim has it, *actus non facit reum nisi mens sit rea* (an act does not make a man guilty unless his mind is guilty). In this connection three mental elements require consideration, which we may designate *voluntas*, foresight and specific (or ulterior) intent. In modern usage the term "*mens rea*" is normally applied only to the last two.

(1) *Voluntas*

The accused must have acted voluntarily in the sense that he was not at the time subject to certain forms of duress, which we shall consider later. Again, a person will not be held responsible for actions over which he had no conscious control, as with the actions of a sleepwalker, or the reflex action of a person who is suddenly attacked by a swarm of bees. (See the discussion of Automatism in Chap. 4.)

(2) *Foresight*

A person will not generally be held responsible for an occurrence unless he foresaw that his act would, or might, cause that event. This requirement of foresight may be satisfied by intention or by recklessness. Intention indicates the state of mind of one who foresees a consequence of his conduct and desires to produce it, or who foresees that his act is morally certain to have that consequence. Recklessness indicates the state of mind of one who foresees that his conduct will probably have a given consequence, but who does not desire to produce it. (These, at least, are the senses in which these terms are generally employed.) It is the requirement of foresight that gives rise to the general defence of mistake in criminal law, because a person's mistake with regard to the surrounding facts may conceal from him the probable consequences of his act. (See Chap. 4 for this defence.)

Negligence, in the sense of failure to attain to a certain standard of care prescribed by law or in the sense of culpable inadvertence to consequences (as where a driver has his mind on other things and knocks down a pedestrian in consequence), is not generally sufficient to found criminal liability at common law, although frequently sufficient for statutory offences, *e.g.*, careless driving (see Chap. 25). The common law offence of manslaughter is an exception; for this gross negligence suffices (see Chap. 7).

(3) *Specific (or ulterior) intent*

By this is meant some intention in addition to that which is immediately involved in the commission of the act. For example, the definition of burglary (in one of its forms) requires that the accused should enter a building *with intent to commit, inter alia,* theft (see Chap. 17). A specific intent of this kind is by no means always found in the definition of a crime.

Mens Rea in Statutory Offences

It is a question of construction of the particular statutory provision whether any, and if so what, *mens rea* is required for a statutory offence. (For this purpose the term *statutory offence* means an offence *created* by statute, and does not include common law offences which have been codified by statute.) This means that the court must decide what the intention of Parliament was upon the point, having regard to the language of the statute as a whole and the few aids to construction outside the statute which the courts permit themselves. For example, the courts allow themselves to have regard to the legislative history of the enactment; it may be found that previous statutes dealing with the same matter expressly required some element of *mens rea*, whereas the present statute is absolute in its terms, in which case that is some indication that Parliament no longer requires *mens rea* as an ingredient of the offence. But the courts do not permit themselves to have regard to the debates in Parliament during the passage of the enactment.

Not infrequently a statute expressly requires some element of *mens rea*, *e.g.*, by the use of such expressions as "knowingly" and "with intent to defraud". But even if the statute is absolute in its terms, *i.e.*, it is silent with regard to *mens rea*, the court may still hold that some form of *mens rea* is necessary. It is not possible to lay down any hard and fast rules as to the view which the court will take in a particular case, and the courts' attitude has varied in different periods, but the following are some of the factors which have weighed with the courts in decided cases:

(1) There is a presumption that some form of *mens rea* is required, *i.e.*, the court approaches its task of construction with a bias in this direction. For example, in *Brend* v. *Wood* (1946), D.C., Lord Goddard C.J. said: "It is of the utmost importance for the protection of the liberty of the subject that a court should always bear in mind that, unless a statute either clearly or by necessary implication rules out *mens rea* as a constituent part of a crime, the court should not find a man guilty of an offence against the criminal law unless he has a guilty mind."

(2) Where the object of the statute is to regulate the conduct of a trade or business, the presumption is easily rebutted, and in such cases the courts have often held *mens rea* to be unnecessary. For example, in *Cundy* v. *Le Cocq* (1884), D.C., on a charge against a licensee of unlawfully selling intoxicating liquor to a drunken person, contrary to section 13 of the Licensing Act 1872, it was held no defence that the licensee did not know that the customer was drunk. Offences of this kind are sometimes known as quasi-criminal, or administrative, offences. There are several justifications for eliminating the requirement of *mens rea* in such cases. For example, if *mens rea* were required it would often be difficult for the prosecution to secure a conviction and the mischief at which the statute is aimed would not be suppressed. Moreover, the imposition of strict liability at least has a tendency to keep the trader on his toes. In

the words of Dean Roscoe Pound: "Such statutes are not meant to punish the vicious will, but to put pressure upon the thoughtless and inefficient to do their whole duty in the interest of public health or safety or morals" (*The Spirit of the Common Law*, p. 52, quoted in *Reynolds* v. *G. H. Austin & Sons* (1951).) Another example where it has been held that *mens rea* is not necessary is in relation to certain statutory offences concerning drugs, because of the necessity to curtail or prevent the drug traffic (*R.* v. *Warner* (1968), H.L.), but the courts will not construe all offences relating to drugs as absolute offences (*Sweet* v. *Parsley* (1969), H.L.).

(3) The court will seldom construe a statute as imposing, or seeking to impose, upon the citizen the task of achieving the impossible or near-impossible. Thus, it may be stated as a general principle that where the statute requires the performance of an act, ignorance of the circumstances which give rise to the duty to perform that act will generally be a defence. For example, in *Harding* v. *Price* (1948), D.C., the accused was charged with failing to report to the police an accident involving his motor vehicle, contrary to section 22 of the Road Traffic Act 1930 (now the Road Traffic Act 1960, s. 77). It was held a defence that the accused did not know that the collision had occurred: the vehicle which he was driving was a mechanical horse with a trailer attached to it and it collided with a stationary car, but owing to the noise made by the vehicle the accused was unaware of this occurrence. This case was a strong one because section 22 re-enacted a similar provision in the Motor Car Act 1903, which, however, had used the word "knowingly" in the definition, so that the omission of that word from section 22 was some indication that Parliament did not intend knowledge to be a necessary ingredient of the offence. Again, in *Sherras* v. *De Rutzen* (1895), D.C., a licensee was charged with supplying liquor to a constable on duty, contrary to section 16 of the Licensing Act 1872. It was held a defence that the licensee believed the constable to be off duty, because he had removed his duty armlet before entering the premises. If such a defence were not allowed it would be virtually impossible for licensees to avoid infringing the provision in question. This also was a strong case, because in another sub-section of the same section the word "knowingly" appeared, whereas it was absent from the sub-section under which the licensee was charged. Day J. expressed the view that in such circumstances the omission of the word had the effect of casting upon the accused the burden of proving absence of knowledge, but this view has not commended itself to later judges (*e.g.*, Devlin J. in *Roper* v. *Taylor's Central Garage* (1951)), and the better view would appear to be that, when

mens rea is necessary for an offence, the burden of proving the *mens rea* is always upon the prosecution, unless the statute provides to the contrary.

It must not be supposed that the court will never construe a statute in such a way as to impose criminal liability for involuntary conduct. For example, in the remarkable case of *R. v. Larsonneur* (1933), C.C.A., the accused was held rightly convicted of an offence under the Aliens Order 1920, in that she, being an alien to whom leave to land in the United Kingdom had been refused, was found in the United Kingdom, despite the fact that she had been deported from Ireland and had been brought into the United Kingdom in the custody of the police. In this case there was an absence not only of *mens rea,* but even of *voluntas.* The justification for such a construction no doubt was that the purpose of putting the woman in prison was not so much punitive as to give the authorities control over her until arrangements could be made to deport her elsewhere.

(4) *Mens rea* is rarely held to be unnecessary where the offence is of a serious character, although the offence of causing death by dangerous driving is an exception (see Chap. 7).

Vicarious Liability

(A) At Common Law

By vicarious liability is meant liability for a wrong committed by another which one has *not* authorized. In the law of tort there is a general doctrine of vicarious liability, in that a master is civilly liable for a tort committed by his servant in the course of his employment: it is no defence to the master that he has not authorized the servant to commit the wrong, or even that he has expressly forbidden him to do so. In the criminal law, on the other hand, the general rule is that there is no such vicarious liability (*R. v. Huggins* (1730)). There are, however, a few exceptions:

(1) Public nuisance
A master is criminally liable for a public nuisance committed by his servant in the course of his employment. A public nuisance, broadly, is interference with public rights, *e.g.,* obstruction of a public highway.

(2) Criminal libel
At common law a master is criminally liable for a libel published

in his newspaper. Now, however, by the Libel Act 1843, section 7, the master is not liable unless the libel was published with his authority or in consequence of his negligence. *Vicarious* liability, therefore, is now limited to cases of negligence.

(3) *Contempt of court*

At common law a master is vicariously liable for contempt of court committed by the publication of matter which is likely (it need not be intended) to prejudice the fair trial of any pending legal proceeding. This common law offence (m) is remarkable not only by reason of the vicarious liability that exists for it, but also by reason of the fact that *mens rea* is not necessary: for example, it is no defence that the accused did not know that such legal proceedings were pending. Thus, in *R*. v. *Odhams Press Ltd*. (1957), D.C., the "Criminal Investigation Department" of a popular Sunday newspaper, in ignorance of the fact that proceedings had already been instituted against him, published allegations that a certain person had committed criminal offences. The proprietors were held guilty of contempt of court. (See also *R*. v. *Evening Standard Co*. (1954), D.C.) Now, however, by the Administration of Justice Act 1960, it is a defence for the accused to prove that, having taken all reasonable care, he did not know and had no reason to suspect that proceedings were pending or imminent; and the mere distributor of a publication is given a defence of innocent dissemination, *i.e.*, he has a defence if he proves that having taken all reasonable care he did not know that the publication contained any such matter and had no reason to suspect that it was likely to do so.

(B) *Statutory Offences*

It is a question of construction of the particular statutory provision whether Parliament intended to impose vicarious liability, *i.e.*, as with the question whether *mens rea* is required for a statutory offence. the intention of Parliament must be gathered from a consideration of the statute as a whole and those few external aids to construction that the courts permit themselves. Where the offence does not require *mens rea* in the actor, and the statute is concerned to regulate the conduct of a trade or business, vicarious liability generally exists. Most of the licensing offences for which *mens rea* is not required fall into this category. But even if *mens rea* is required in the actor the court may hold the master vicariously liable. For example, in *Mousell Brothers* v. *L. & N. W. Railway* (1917), D.C., a company was held rightly convicted of having given a false account of goods consigned for carriage on the railway with intent to avoid payment of tolls, contrary to section 99 of the Railway Clauses Consolidation Act 1845. The goods had been falsely described by a servant of the company on the instruction of the company's manager; the manager had formed the fraudulent intention, and it was held that this was sufficient to affect the company with liability. A still more remarkable case was that of *Allen* v. *Whitehead* (1930), D.C., in which the proprietor of a refreshment house was held guilty of knowingly permitting prostitutes to meet together and remain in the house, contrary to section 44 of the Metropolitan Police Act 1839, although in fact the proprietor had no such knowledge. He had delegated the management of the premises to a manager and the manager had the necessary guilty knowledge. It was held that this knowledge had to be imputed to the master, and this despite the fact that he had expressly warned his manager not to allow prostitutes to congregate on the premises. This decision has not escaped criticism, and in *Vane* v. *Yiannopoullos* (1965) the House of Lords held that the general principle must be that the word "knowingly" excludes vicarious liability. Two of the five law lords in that case were, however, prepared to accept that an exception exists in licensing cases where the licensee has delegated the management of the premises; the other law lords either doubted the supposed exception or preferred to express no opinion. In *Vane's* case the licensee held a conditional licence which permitted the supply of intoxicating liquor only with meals. A waitress to whom the management of the premises had not been delegated supplied liquor to customers not taking meals. But it was held that the licensee could not on this account be held guilty of knowingly supplying liquor in breach of the conditions of his licence, as he had not authorized the waitress to commit the offences, and he himself had no knowledge of them.

In any event, a master will not be held vicariously liable for an *attempt* to commit a statutory offence (*Gardner* v. *Akeroyd* (1952), D.C.), or on a charge of *aiding and abetting* the commission of such an offence (*Ferguson* v. *Weaving* (1951), D.C.). (For aiding and abetting see Chap. 5.)

Words requiring Mens Rea

As has been mentioned, a statute not infrequently uses words which expressly require some form of *mens rea*. Several of these expressions, such as "maliciously" and "with intent to defraud," we shall come across later in connection with particular crimes, and their meaning will be considered then. We may here notice one or two expressions that we shall not meet again.

"Wilfully." The courts have sometimes given a very narrow interpretation to this word. For example, in *Horton* v. *Gwynne* (1921), D.C., it was held no defence to a charge of unlawfully and wilfully killing a house pigeon, contrary to section 23 of the Larceny Act 1861, that the accused thought the pigeon to be a wild pigeon. He had intentionally killed a bird that was in fact a house pigeon, and that was all that the word "wilfully" required. It was not, said Darling J., as if he had shot at a crow and killed a pigeon unintentionally. (See also *Cotterill* v. *Penn* (1936), D.C. (belief that the bird was wild and about to attack defendant's crops also no defence).)

Again, an act may be done "wilfully" even though the accused honestly thought that he had a right to do the act. For example, in *Wells* v. *Hardy* (1964), D.C., the accused was held rightly convicted of wilfully taking fish from private water, contrary to section 24 of the Larceny Act 1861, although he honestly thought that he had a right to fish there. (*Cf. Cotterill* v. *Penn, supra.*) On the other hand, in *Eaton* v. *Cobb* (1950), D.C., a motorist was charged with wilfully obstructing the free passage of the highway, contrary to the Highways Act 1835, s. 72, on the ground that in opening his car door he had knocked a passing cyclist off his bicycle; but he was held to have a defence in that before opening the door he had looked in his rear mirror and failed to notice the cyclist, who was cycling with his head down. The obstruction had been entirely inadvertent.

"Knowingly." When a statute requires knowledge of a fact, knowledge for this purpose includes not only actual knowledge of the fact in question (which may be inferred from the accused's conduct in appropriate circumstances), but also the state of mind of one who deliberately refrains from making enquiries the result of which he might not care to have. On the other hand it does not include constructive notice, *i.e.* an unintentional failure to make enquiries which a prudent person would have made and which would have revealed the fact in question (*Roper* v. *Taylor's Central Garage* (1951), D.C., per Devlin J.; note also *Grays Haulage Co. Ltd.* v. *Arnold, infra.*). A person is deemed to have knowledge of an event which occurs in his absence if he intends that event to occur. For example, if a licensee regularly manages the premises in a way which involves breaches of the conditions of his licence, and during his temporary absence from the premises those breaches continue, as he intended that they should, he is deemed to know of their occurrence (*Ross* v. *Moss* (1965), D.C.).

We have already seen that the use of the word "knowingly" generally excludes vicarious liability. (See above under *Vicarious liability* (*statutory offences*).)

"Suffers," "permits," etc. When a statute makes it an offence to "suffer" or "permit" something to be done, this term is not limited to consciously allowing the event to occur, but includes also a failure to take proper precautions to prevent the occurrence if the circumstances are such that a breach of the law is likely to occur if precautions are not taken. For example, in *Browning v. J. W. H. Watson* (1953), D.C., the owner of a motor-coach was charged with permitting the vehicle to be used as a public service vehicle without the necessary road service licence, contrary to section 72 of the Road Traffic Act 1930. The vehicle had been hired to take the supporters of a football club to a football match, and no road service licence would have been necessary if the outing had been confined to members of the club. However, two Ministry of Transport officers who were not members of the club obtained seats on the motor-coach without difficulty. The vehicle owner was held guilty of the offence, because he had failed to take precautions (*e.g.*, by instituting a ticket system) to prevent a breach of the Act in circumstances in which such a breach was likely to occur if precautions were not taken. On the other hand in *James & Son v. Smee* (1955), D.C., a vehicle owner (a company) was held not guilty of permitting the use of the vehicle on a road with defective brakes, contrary to the Motor Vehicles (Construction and Use) Regulations 1951, because the company (through its responsible servants) did not know of the defect and had not been negligent in failing to discover it. (Ironically, the company could have been convicted of using the vehicle contrary to the regulations (an offence which does not require *mens rea*), because user by the driver is regarded as user by the vehicle owner for this purpose (*Green v. Burnett* (1955), D.C.).) In *Grays Haulage Co. Ltd. v. Arnold* (1966), D.C. the court held that "permitting" requires knowledge, but knowledge includes the knowledge which arises either from shutting one's eyes to the obvious or failing to do something or doing something not caring whether contravention takes place or not, and this, perhaps, expresses the true principle.

The term "vicarious liability" is often applied to offences of suffering or permitting. But in fact the principles are different.

Chapter Four

GENERAL DEFENCES TO CRIMINAL LIABILITY

(1) Duress Per Minas

IT seems clear that the law recognizes *duress per minas* (by threats) as a possible defence to criminal liability. It is a defence even to a charge of treason, where the accused's participation was of a minor character (*R. v. McGrowther* (1746)). It is a necessary condition of the defence that the duress should have been the cause of the accused's commission of the offence, so that the defence will not apply if he had an opportunity of escaping from the threats. In *R. v. McGrowther, supra*, it was held that the threats must be of death, but it may be that that rule applies only to a charge as serious as that of treason and that lesser forms of duress would suffice for charges of a less serious character. Probably the defence does not apply on a charge of murder, although there is no conclusive authority upon the point. (The defence was not allowed in *R. v. Tyler and Price* (1838) but there were other reasons for rejecting the defence in this case.)

The ground of the defence, in general, is the impairment of the accused's willpower in consequence of the threats: it would not be just to hold him criminally responsible in the circumstances. There is, however, an alternative ground for the defence where the crime requires proof of some specific intent. In such cases the duress may negative the intent required for the crime. For example, in *R. v. Steane* (1947), C.C.A., the accused was charged with an offence against the Defence Regulations which were current during the last war, on the ground that he had done certain acts "with intent to assist the enemy," and he put forward the defence of duress. The Court of Criminal Appeal held that in such a case a jury, if properly directed, might take the view that the accused had not done the act with the required intent, but by reason of the threats.

Apart from the defence of insanity and apart from any statutory provision which places the burden of proving a given fact upon the accused, it is a general rule that if there is any evidence of a defence

21

to a charge it is for the prosecution to negative that defence, and not for the accused to establish it. This rule has been held to apply to the defence of duress *per minas* (*R.* v. *Gill* (1963), C.C.A.).

(2) Marital Subjection

At common law when a wife committed certain crimes in her husband's presence a presumption arose that she had done so under her husband's coercion. She was, therefore, entitled to be acquitted unless the prosecution could prove that in fact she had acted freely and voluntarily, and not under her husband's coercion. This presumption was abolished by the Criminal Justice Act 1925, s. 47, which, however, makes it a defence, except upon a charge of treason or murder, for a wife to prove that she committed the crime in her husband's presence and under his coercion. Today, therefore, she must prove the coercion, as well as the presence.

Presumably, the coercion required to give a wife a defence under section 47 is less than that required to establish the defence of duress *per minas*. Otherwise there would be no point in giving the wife the statutory defence.

(3) Necessity

The term "necessity" is here used in the sense that the accused by committing the offence in question has caused a lesser evil than some evil which he has averted, or has sought to avert, by its commission. It might be said, for example, that a doctor has acted under such necessity if in hurrying to a critically ill patient he has exceeded the speed limit in his car. There is no English authority for the existence of the defence. It seems clear that such a defence does not apply to a charge of the murder of an innocent person. In *R.* v. *Dudley and Stephens* (1884) shipwrecked seamen who had been at sea in an open boat for nineteen days in the tropics, fearing death by starvation, killed and ate one of their number, a cabin boy. Their defence of necessity was rejected by the Court for Crown Cases Reserved.

Although there is probably no general defence of necessity, it must be admitted that necessity is an element in some particular defences which are recognized by law, *e.g.*, the defence of self-defence on a charge of unlawful homicide, or the necessity of saving the mother's life which is a defence to a charge of abortion or of child destruction.

Except where the sentence is fixed by law, as in the case of murder, evidence of necessity can, of course, be put forward in mitigation of sentence, and it is probably by reason of the wide discretion that the courts have on matters of sentence that there is so little authority with regard to this suggested defence.

The case is sometimes posed of two climbers who are roped together when one of them slips and is dragging the other to his death, whereupon the other cuts the rope. It would seem that in such a case, if the survivor could not have saved his companion by reasonable efforts, he cannot be regarded as having caused the other's death. It would seem to be quite unnecessary to consider the supposed defence of necessity in such a case.

(4) **Obedience to Orders**

Superior orders will not in themselves be a defence (though see "military orders" in the following paragraph) but they may help an accused person to establish some other defence. For example, if a statute makes it an offence to do something "maliciously," it is a defence that the accused honestly thought that he had a right to do the act, and the fact that his master ordered him to do the act may have induced in him the belief that the act was lawful. Thus in *R.* v. *James* (1837) the accused was charged with unlawfully and maliciously obstructing the air-way of a mine. He had built a wall across the air-way under his master's instructions, and it was held that if in consequence of the master's orders he believed the act to be lawful, he could not be convicted of the offence charged.

It is possible that superior *military* orders are in themselves a defence if the act ordered to be done is not manifestly unlawful. Certainly justice requires that the soldier should have such a defence, because in most circumstances he is not in a position to test the lawfulness of the orders which he receives. There is no binding English authority in support of the defence, but Willes J. expressed himself in favour of it in *Keighley* v. *Bell* (1866), and these dicta were accepted as correct in the South African case of *R.* v. *Smith* (1900). On the other hand, the British Manual of Military Law (which is not authoritative) expresses the view that no such defence exists.

(5) **Insanity**

The legal rules governing insanity as a defence to criminal liability are known as the *M'Naghten* rules (1843). These rules are, in fact, answers given by the judges to a series of questions propounded to them by the House of Lords in consequence of the acquittal on grounds of insanity of one Daniel M'Naghten on a charge of murdering Edward Drummond, Sir Robert Peel's secretary, by shooting him as he was walking up Whitehall on January 20, 1843. The acquittal had caused some public disquiet and the House of Lords had been debating the matter. Despite the somewhat irregular manner in which the rules were laid down, they are treated by the courts as having the same authority as a decision of the House of Lords, and it is useless to argue against them in the courts; only Parliament can amend them. Although *M'Naghten's* case was one of delusional insanity and the judges' answers were given in that context, the rules are regarded as expressing the law of insanity generally. The main rules are as follows:

(i) Every man is to be presumed to be sane, and to possess a sufficient degree of reason to be responsible for his crimes, until the contrary be proved to the satisfaction of the jury.

(ii) To establish a defence on the ground of insanity, it must be clearly proved that, at the time of committing the act, the party accused was labouring under such a defect of reason, from disease of the mind, as not to know the nature and quality of the act he was doing, or, if he did know it, that he did not know he was doing what was wrong.

(iii) If the accused was under an insane delusion as to existing facts, he must be considered in the same situation as to responsibility as if the facts with respect to which the delusion existed had been real. For example, if under the influence of his delusion a person supposes another man to be in the act of attempting to take away his life, and he kills that man as he supposes in self-defence, he would be exempt from punishment. But if his delusion was that the deceased had inflicted a serious injury to his character and fortune, and he killed him in revenge for such supposed injury, he would be liable to punishment.

The following points may be noticed on the interpretation of these rules:

(*a*) The burden of proving insanity is upon the defence, but it is not necessary for the defence to establish the insanity beyond reasonable doubt: a balance of probability suffices, *i.e.*, it is sufficient if upon the evidence it appears that the accused was probably insane within the rules. (The same rule applies when a statute puts the burden of proving any fact upon the accused in a criminal case (*R.* v. *Carr-Briant* (1943), C.C.A.)).

(*b*) The expression "disease of the mind" does not imply a distinction between mental and bodily disease. In *Bratty* v. *Attorney-General for Northern Ireland* (1963), H.L., Lord Denning expressed the opinion that any mental disorder (including epilepsy or cerebral tumour) which has manifested itself in violence and is prone to recur is a disease of the mind; nor is it at all necessary that the mental disease should be permanent. (And see *R.* v. *Kemp* (1957).)

(*c*) The fact that the accused, through mental disease, was unable to resist an impulse to do the act (the defence of "irresistible impulse"), does not of itself bring him within the rules: the accused is not within the rules if he knew the nature of the act and that it was wrong (*R.* v. *Kopsch* (1925), C.C.A.). This is generally considered to be one of the most serious defects in the rules (which in any event are widely regarded as anachronistic in character in the second half of the twentieth century); the defect has been partially removed by the introduction of the statutory defence of diminished responsibility, which is considered below.

(*d*) The expression "nature and quality" of the act means no more than the nature of the act (*R.* v. *Codère* (1916), C.C.A.).

(*e*) The accused is outside the rules if he knew the nature of the act and that it was wrong. The judges' replies themselves indicate that the accused need not have known what the law was: if he was conscious that the act was one which he ought not to do, and if that act was at the same time contrary to the law of the land, he is punishable. On the other hand, if he knew that his act was contrary to law, the accused must be taken to have known that it was wrong, and again he is outside the rules: in such a case it will afford him no defence that he believed the act to be morally right (*R.* v. *Windle* (1952), **C.C.A.**).

By the Criminal Procedure (Insanity) Act 1964, when the defence of insanity succeeds the jury's verdict is to be "not guilty by reason of insanity," and the court will then order that the accused be admitted to such hospital as may be specified by the Secretary of State; he will then become subject to provisions of the Mental Health Act 1959 and will not be released, even if he recovers his sanity, until such time as the Home Secretary may decide to release him. This detention is not, of course, by way of punishment, but merely to protect the public against a repetition of such conduct by the accused. The verdict is technically an acquittal, but nevertheless the accused may now appeal against it either upon the ground that he did not do the act in question, or upon the ground that he was not insane, or upon both grounds.

These provisions of the Act of 1964 do not apply to offences dealt with summarily by magistrates' courts. But the Act of 1959 contains provisions which enable such a court to secure the admission of the accused to hospital and for special restrictions to be imposed upon his discharge therefrom.

The Act of 1964 (s. 6) provides that if, on a charge of murder, the accused puts forward the defence of insanity, the prosecution may bring evidence to rebut that defence and may adduce evidence that the accused was suffering from abnormality of mind within the provisions of section 2 of the Homicide Act 1957 (below). Conversely, if the accused puts forward the defence of diminished responsibility under the Act of 1957, the prosecution may adduce evidence to rebut that defence and to show that the accused was insane within the M'Naghten rules. If the accused does not put forward either of the defences mentioned, it is doubtful whether the prosecution can adduce evidence of insanity. The older practice, supported by some of the modern decisions, was certainly against the right of the prosecution to do this, but there are some modern decisions the other way, and in *Bratty's* case, *supra*, Lord Denning expressed the opinion that it is always open to the prosecution to adduce evidence of insanity.

(6) Diminished Responsibility

This is not strictly a general defence to criminal liability, because the defence applies only on a charge of murder. Nevertheless, this is a convenient place in which to consider it.

The Homicide Act 1957, s. 2, provides that on a charge of murder it shall be a defence for the accused to prove that at the time of the act he was suffering from such abnormality of mind (whether arising from a condition of arrested or retarded development of mind, or any inherent causes, or induced by disease or injury) as substantially impaired his mental responsibility for his acts and omissions. The defence, if successful, reduces the homicide from murder to manslaughter; it is therefore only a partial defence, and the punishment is within the discretion of the court. As has been indicated, the burden of proof is upon the defence; but proof on a balance of probability suffices (*R. v. Dunbar* (1958), C.C.A.).

It is, of course, for the jury to decide upon the evidence whether the terms of section 2 have been satisfied. The question whether the abnormality of mind, if any, "substantially" impaired the accused's mental responsibility is not a scientific question, and on this matter the jury may have regard to the whole of the evidence; they are not restricted to a consideration of the expert medical evidence. On the other hand the aetiology of the abnormality, *i.e.*, whether it arose from a condition of arrested or retarded development of mind, etc., is a scientific question which the jury should decide upon the expert evidence alone. (See *R.* v. *Byrne* (1960), C.C.A.)

(7) Automatism

A state of automatism is one in which the accused's actions are involuntary in the sense that they are not under the control of his conscious mind. Such a condition may be due to mental disease, in which case the defence must be put forward, if at all, as one of insanity within the M'Naghten rules (*Bratty* v. *Attorney-General for Northern Ireland* (1963), H.L., which see generally on this defence). On the other hand, the condition may not be due to disease of the mind, in which case the defence is known as that of sane automatism. If this defence succeeds, the verdict must be a simple verdict of acquittal, and the court has no power to order the detention of the accused for the protection of the public. It is not surprising, therefore, that the judges have viewed the defence with disquiet and have hedged it about with certain restrictive rules. The following points should be noted:

(*a*) It is not the duty of the trial judge to direct the jury with regard to the law of sane automatism unless there is evidence worthy of their consideration that the accused was in such a state: there must be a "proper foundation" for the defence (*Bratty's* case, *supra*). Thus, it was decided in *Hill* v. *Baxter* (1958), D.C., that on a charge of dangerous driving it is not sufficient that the accused states that by reason of sudden illness at the time he can remember nothing of the incident. (This case is notable for an express recognition by Lord Goddard, the then Chief Lord Justice, of the existence of the defence. He said: "suppose he had a stroke or an epileptic fit, both instances of what may properly be called 'acts of God,' he might well be in the driver's seat, even with his hands on the wheel, but in such a state of unconsciousness that he could not be said to be driving.") On the other hand, if the defence does lay "a proper foundation" for the defence, it is for the prosecution to negative that defence, not for the accused to establish it; the prosecution must satisfy the jury that the accused was *not* in a state of automatism.

(*b*) The movement of the accused's body or limbs must have been quite involuntary. Mere confusion of mind (*e.g.*, as the result of a diabetic taking too much insulin) is not sufficient (*Watmore* v. *Jenkins* (1962), D.C.).

(*c*) At any rate for the purpose of driving offences, the accused must suddenly and unexpectedly have been deprived of all thought, and this deprivation must not have been connected with any deliberate act of his. Thus, the defence was not allowed in *R.* v. *Sibbles* (1959) (in which on a charge of dangerous driving it appeared that the accused had had a blackout) because the accused had been suffering from blood pressure for years and shortly before the incident he had been drinking at a public-house. (And see *R.* v. *Spurge* (1961), C.C.A.) Similarly, on a charge of dangerous or of careless driving it is no defence that the accused had fallen asleep at the wheel, because he should have stopped the vehicle when he felt himself getting drowsy (*Kay* v. *Butterworth* (1945), D.C.).

A very remarkable case (although not strictly one of automatism) was that of *R.* v. *Kitson* (1955), C.C.A., in which it appeared that the accused, who was intoxicated, had been a passenger in a car driven by his brother-in-law; he woke up to find that his brother-in-law had left the car, which was running down a hill, whereupon he steered the car to the bottom of the hill and brought it safely to rest. It might be thought that his action in the circumstances was almost a reflex action for which he should not have been held responsible, but the Court of Criminal Appeal decided that the circumstances afforded him no defence to a charge of driving while under the influence of drink, and he was in fact sentenced to four months' imprisonment and disqualified from driving for three years.

(8) Intoxication

It is hardly necessary to state that intoxication, which may be due to drugs as well as to drink, is not of itself a defence. (It may, of course, constitute an offence, *e.g.*, being found drunk in a highway or other public place (Licensing Act 1872, s. 12) or driving whilst unfit to drive through drink or drugs (see Chap. 24).) As the House of Lords decided in the leading case of *D.P.P.* v. *Beard* (1920) the mere fact that the accused's self-control was diminished by intoxication is no defence. On the other hand, drunkenness may indirectly afford a defence in two ways. First, persistent drunkenness may cause insanity falling within the M'Naghten rules, in which case the prisoner may put forward the defence of insanity. As Lord Birkenhead L.C. said in *Beard's* case, "The law takes no note of the cause of the insanity," *i.e.*, the law does not deprive the prisoner of the defence by reason of the fact that he has brought the insanity upon himself by his own misconduct. Secondly, evidence of intoxication may show that the accused did not form the *mens rea* required for the crime charged, in which case he cannot be guilty of that crime (although he may be guilty of some other crime not requiring the same *mens rea*). Thus, in *Beard's* case the accused had caused the death of a young girl in the course of committing a rape upon her; he had placed his hand over her mouth and his thumb on her throat and thereby suffocated her. His defence was that he was too drunk to understand the dangerous nature of his acts, but the defence was rejected because, as the law then stood, intent to commit a violent felony, such as rape, was itself sufficient *mens rea* for murder, where the death had been caused, however inadvertently, by an act of violence done in the course or furtherance of that violent felony; and it was clear that Beard was not too drunk to form the intent to rape. On the other hand, in the earlier case of *R.* v. *Meade* (1909), C.C.A., (which was reviewed by the House of Lords in *Beard's* case) the accused caused the death of a woman by means of a brutal assault committed upon her; as he was not engaged in the commission of a felony (apart from the assault itself) the prosecution, in order to substantiate a charge of murder, had to prove that he had intended to kill the woman or to cause her grievous bodily harm. It was therefore held that if the evidence of his drunken condition showed that he simply did not form that intent, he would not be guilty of murder, although he would be guilty of manslaughter, for which intent to cause any bodily harm is sufficient *mens rea*. Whereas a sober man would realize the extent of the violence he was using, a drunken man might well not do so. (See also *R.* v. *Cruse* (1838).) This position would appear to be the inevitable result of the doctrine of *mens rea*: if a man, for whatever reason, does not form the *mens rea* required for the crime charged, he does not commit that crime. Unfortunately, some remarks of Lord Denning in *Attorney-General for Northern Ireland* v. *Gallagher* (1963), H.L., cast doubt upon this interpretation of *R.* v. *Meade*. Lord Denning said: "It [drunkenness] may impair a man's powers of perception, so that he may not be able to foresee or measure the consequences of his actions, as he would if he were sober. Nevertheless, he is not allowed to set up his self-induced want of perception as a defence. Even if he did not himself appreciate that what he was doing was dangerous, nevertheless, if a reasonable man in his place, who was not befuddled with drink, would have appreciated it, he is guilty."

Gallagher's case is also interesting in another connection. It would appear from Lord Denning's speech in that case that in his opinion if a psychopath (who is not legally insane) forms the intent to kill, and in order to give himself dutch courage drinks a quantity of whisky, he cannot plead the defence of insanity even if the effect of the drink was to make him insane within the M'Naghten rules at the time of the homicide. The other law lords in this case, however, appear to have taken a different view, and to have come to the conclusion that the trial judge in fact directed the jury to consider whether *at the time of the homicide* the accused's mental condition fell within the M'Naghten rules.

In an earlier period the law did not allow self-induced intoxication as a defence in any circumstances, but intoxication which was not self-induced (*e.g.*, which resulted from medical treatment) was allowed by the law as a possible defence. There would seem to be no difference today between the rules governing self-induced, and those governing involuntary, intoxication, although perhaps they might be applied more leniently in the second case.

If there is evidence of intoxication which is capable of affording a defence within the above rules (other than that of insanity), it is for the prosecution to rebut the defence, and not for the prisoner to establish it (*R.* v. *Foote* (1964), C.C.A.).

(9) Mistake

There is no particular merit in having made a mistake, any more than there is in having got drunk, and when mistake is allowed as a defence it is admitted on the same principle as that upon which intoxication is allowed, namely, that it shows that the accused has not formed the *mens rea* required for the crime charged and has not therefore committed that crime. For example, in *R.* v. *Tolson* (1889), C.C.R., Mrs. Tolson was charged with bigamy, but the evidence showed that when she re-married during the lifetime of her husband she honestly believed that he was dead. Had the facts been as she imagined them to be her act in re-marrying would have been lawful; her mistake, therefore, afforded her a defence. Mistake is also not a defence if, had the facts been as the accused supposed, he would have been committing another crime of the same kind; for example, if he entered one house with the intention of stealing property therein but under the mistaken belief that it was another house in the same road (*R.* v. *Prince* (1875), C.C.R., *per* Bramwell B.).

Some of the cases require that the mistake should be founded upon reasonable grounds, and this may be the rule for certain crimes, including bigamy. It is, however, doubtful whether there is such a *general* rule, and in *Wilson* v. *Inyang* (1951), D.C., it was stated that *honesty* of belief is all that is required, although a jury may take the view that the accused did not in fact make an alleged mistake if there were no reasonable grounds for it; in other words, reasonableness is of evidentiary value, but no more.

In any event it seems clear that where mistake, however unreasonable, negatives some specific *mens rea* required for the crime charged, it must be a defence. For example, on a charge of murder by shooting, if it appears that the accused mistakenly believed the gun to be unloaded, then however unreasonable his mistake may have been he cannot be guilty of murder; that crime requires intent to kill or cause grievous bodily harm, and that intent was clearly lacking (Foster, 265). (But the accused might in such a case be guilty of manslaughter, for which gross negligence suffices, as we shall see later (*post*, Chap. 7).)

To be a defence the mistake must generally be one of fact, and not of law (*R.* v. *Bailey* (1800) (a strong case because the statute under which the accused was charged was passed while he was at sea; the judges recommended a pardon)). *Ignorantia juris neminem excusat.* This is not by any means a rule of ideal justice, but a rule which the courts have felt bound to adopt because otherwise there would be a wide gap in the law through which too many guilty persons could pass; in most cases it would be exceedingly difficult to disprove a plea of ignorance of the law. There are, however, exceptional cases in which mistake of law may indirectly provide a defence by negativing the *mens rea* required for the crime charged. For example, as we shall see later (*post*, Chap. 12), the offence of theft requires that the appropriation of the property by the accused should not have been in the belief that he had in law the right to deprive the other of it. Thus it is a complete defence to a charge of theft that the accused honestly thought that he had a right to take the property. His mistaken belief may have stemmed from a misunderstanding of the law, but nevertheless if he had the belief that he had a right to take the property, he is clearly not guilty of theft (see *R.* v. *Clayton* (1920), C.C.A.).

As we have seen, the ground of the defence of mistake is that it shows that the accused did not form the *mens rea* required for the crime charged. It follows that so far as *mens rea* is not required for a statutory crime, mistake will not be a defence to a charge of that crime. If the reader will refer back to the cases which we considered on the question how far *mens rea* is required for a statutory offence (see Chap. 3), he will find that almost all the cases cited were cases in which the accused sought to put forward the defence of mistake.

(10) **Infants**

(i) *Under ten*
By the Children and Young Persons Act 1963, s. 16, there is an

irrebuttable presumption that a child under the age of ten is incapable of committing crime.

(ii) *Ten to fourteen*

There is a presumption that a child who has attained the age of ten, but has not yet attained the age of fourteen, is incapable of committing crime (*doli incapax*) but this presumption is rebuttable by proof that the child knew that he was doing wrong: *malitia supplet aetatem* (malice supplies age) (*R.* v. *Gorrie* (1918)). It seems that such proof is required even when the child is charged with a statutory offence for which *mens rea* is not generally necessary. Any evidence from which an inference of guilty knowledge can reasonably be drawn is admissible to rebut the presumption, *e.g.*, evidence that the child came from a good home background, or that the child took steps to conceal the commission of the act, or that he lied about it when questioned (but this is by no means conclusive, because the very fact that he was questioned may have made him realize for the first time that the act was wrong).

There is an irrebuttable presumption that a male under fourteen is incapable of committing an offence which requires sexual capacity (such as the actual commission of rape (*R.* v. *Groombridge* (1836)), or unlawful sexual intercourse with a girl under thirteen (*R.* v. *Waite* (1892), C.C.R.)), or an offence which requires intention to have sexual intercourse, such as the statutory offence of assault with intent to ravish (*R.* v. *Eldershaw* (1828)), or (presumably) attempted rape (but see *R.* v. *Williams, infra, per* Hawkins J., for a contrary view). But he can be convicted of indecent assault, an offence which does not require actual or intended sexual intercourse (*R.* v. *Williams* (1893), C.C.R.). There is some authority for the proposition that a boy under fourteen cannot be convicted as an aider and abettor to a sodomy committed against himself (*R.* v. *Tatam* (1921), C.C.A. (in which it was held that, for the purposes of the law of evidence, such a boy is not ranked as an accomplice)). But if this is so, it must presumably be because the boy is regarded as being merely the victim of the offence and requiring protection against himself, even if in fact he was a willing participant—sexual capacity in the boy is obviously not in issue in such a case. (Compare the rule that a girl under sixteen cannot be indicted for abetting or inciting a man to have unlawful sexual intercourse with her (*R.* v. *Tyrrell* (1894), *post,* Chap. 8).

Once a child attains the age of fourteen he assumes full criminal capacity, although there are special rules with regard to the trial and punishment of youthful offenders; these are dealt with later in the section on Procedure.

(11) **Corporations**

At one time the common law did not admit the possibility of the
criminal liability of a corporation. The reasons for this rule were
partly theoretical (such as the difficulty of attributing *mens rea* to
a corporation) and partly practical (*e.g.*, with some exceptions, it
was the rule that a person charged with a criminal offence had to
appear in person at the bar of the court in order to plead to the
charge). In the nineteenth century, however, the importance and
economic power of corporations increased to such an extent that
the courts began to take the view that corporations could not safely
be left beyond the reach of the criminal law. Today both the procedural (see *post*, Chap. 27) and the theoretical difficulties have been
overcome and the general rule is that a corporation has the same
criminal responsibility as a human person. Probably, however, it
will never be possible to assimilate the position of a corporation to
that of a human being completely, and the general proposition is
subject to certain qualifications.

First, the courts will not stultify themselves by holding the trial
of a corporation only to find at the end of the day that the court is
powerless to inflict any punishment upon the corporation. Hence a
corporation cannot be convicted of an offence (*e.g.*, murder) for
which the law allows only a corporal punishment, such as imprisonment. In other words, the offence must be punishable by fine.
Before 1948 a court could usually punish a misdemeanour by a fine
but the rule precluded the possibility of a corporation's being convicted of any felony other than manslaughter, because felonies, with
the exception stated, were not finable. However, the Criminal Justice
Act 1948, s. 13, rendered finable all felonies other than those, such
as murder, for which the law allowed only one fixed punishment,
and now, by the Criminal Law Act 1967, s. 7(3), all offences are
finable except those for which the sentence is fixed by law.

Secondly, a corporation cannot be convicted of a crime unless
the court is prepared to treat as the act and mind of the corporation the act and mind of the person who in fact committed the crime.
In *R.* v. *I.C.R. Haulage Ltd.* (1944), C.C.A., one of the modern
leading authorities, it was held that whether the court will make
this attribution in a particular case depends upon the extent of the
authority enjoyed by the servant or agent who in fact committed
the crime, the nature of the offence, and all the circumstances of the
particular case. (The comparative vagueness of this rule is perhaps
an indication that the law is still in a transitional state.) It is clear
from the decided cases that much depends upon the extent of the

servant's or agent's authority. In the *I.C.R. Haulage* case itself it was the acts of the company's managing director which rendered it liable for the offence charged (the common law misdemeanour of conspiracy to defraud). The principle was vividly expressed by Denning L.J. (as he then was) in the civil case of *H. L. Bolton (Engineering) Co.* v. *T. J. Graham & Sons* (1957): "A company may in many ways be likened to a human body. It has a brain and nerve centre which controls what it does. It also has hands which hold the tools and act in accordance with directions from the centre. Some of the people in the company are mere servants and agents who are nothing more than hands to do the work and cannot be said to represent the mind or will. Others are directors and managers who represent the directing mind and will of the company and control what it does. The state of mind of these managers is the state of mind of the company and is treated by the law as such . . . in the criminal law, in cases where the law requires a guilty mind as a condition of a criminal offence, the guilty mind of the directors or the managers will render the company itself guilty." By way of contrast with the *I.C.R. Haulage* case, in *John Henshall (Quarries) Ltd.* v. *Harvey* (1965), D.C., it was held that on a charge against a company of aiding and abetting the driving of an overladen lorry, a weighbridge attendant employed by the company was too subordinate a servant for his knowledge to be regarded as that of the company.

As regards the "nature of the crime" referred to above, it was said in the *I.C.R. Haulage* case that certain crimes, such as bigamy, perjury and rape, are of too personal a character to be attributed to a corporation.

The liability of a corporation under the above rules is distinct from the vicarious liability which the law sometimes imposes on a master for a crime committed by his (or its) servant. Under the above rules the corporation is regarded as itself committing the crime, not as being vicariously liable for a crime committed by another. (See *Lennard's Carrying Co. Ltd.* v. *Asiatic Petroleum Co. Ltd.* (1915) *per* Viscount Haldane L.C. for a clear statement of the distinction. Before the development of the modern rules the doctrine of vicarious liability was almost the only weapon that could be used to impose liability on a corporation, a point that has to be borne in mind when studying some of the older cases.)

Chapter Five

THE PARTIES TO A CRIME

THE law in relation to the parties to a crime has been substantially amended by the Criminal Law Act 1967. In order to understand the present position, however, it is necessary to know the law prior to the Act, and an understanding of many of the cases decided before the Act also requires a knowledge of the previous position. We must therefore consider first the law in relation to the parties as it was before the Criminal Law Act 1967, and then the present position.

A. Before the Criminal Law Act 1967

Felonies

There were four ways in which one could become implicated in the commission of a felony—one could be a principal in the first degree, a principal in the second degree, an accessory before the fact, or an accessory after the fact. The first three ways of participating were equally applicable to misdemeanours, and cases decided by the courts on participation in misdemeanours were, therefore, relevant to participation in felonies, while cases decided on the first three ways of participating in felonies were relevant to participation in misdemeanours. This, as we shall see, is important in relation to the present law.

Principal in the first degree. He was one who took part in the commission of the *actus reus* itself, or who committed it through the medium of an innocent agent. Thus, if two men went out to commit a burglary and one of them entered the dwelling-house while the other remained on watch outside, it was only the one who entered the premises who was a principal in the first degree (the other, as we shall see, was a principal in the second degree). Several persons could take part in the commission of the *actus reus*, in which case they were all principals in the first degree, as where, in the illustration just taken, several persons entered the premises.

35

As has been said, one who committed a felony through the medium of an innocent agent was a principal in the first degree, as where A supplied B with a poisoned drink to be administered to C and B administered it to C in all good faith (*R. v. Michael* (1840)), or where A instigated a child who was under the age of criminal responsibility to commit a felony and the child did so (Fost. 349; 1 Hawk, c. 31; see also *R. v. Tyler and Price* (1838) (insane person as innocent agent)). As will be seen below, where the agent was himself *guilty*, the instigator was an accessory before the fact, not a principal in the first degree.

Principal in the second degree. He was one who took no part in the commission of the *actus reus* but aided and abetted its commission *at the time that it was being committed* (these last words distinguished him from an accessory before the fact).

Aiding and abetting meant helping or encouraging. Thus, presence of itself was not sufficient, unless in the circumstances it amounted to encouragement. For example, in the case of *R. v. Allan* (1965), C.C.A., persons who were merely spectators at an affray (a fight between two or more persons) were held not to have aided and abetted that misdemeanour, even if they harboured the secret intention of joining in on one side or the other if that side looked like losing. Any encouragement of the fight, however, would have rendered them guilty. This case may be contrasted with *Wilcox v. Jeffery* (1951), D.C., in which a foreign musician had been permitted to enter this country on condition that he did not accept any employment. He broke this condition by performing at a concert, thereby committing an offence against the Aliens Order 1920. Wilcox, a journalist, who was aware of the breach of condition involved, attended the concert, applauded the performance, and reported it in his paper. He was held to have aided and abetted the offence committed by the musician.

In *National Coal Board v. Gamble* (1959), D.C., a weighbridge operator employed by the Coal Board allowed a customer's lorry to leave the premises of the Coal Board overladen to the extent of nearly four tons. The driving of the overladen vehicle constituted an offence against the Motor Vehicles (Construction and Use) Regulations 1955, and the customer was afterwards convicted of using the motor vehicle in these circumstances. The National Coal Board was held guilty of aiding and abetting the commission of the offence. It was held on the facts that the weighbridge operator could have prevented the lorry from leaving the Coal Board's premises, as the property in the coal did not pass to the customer until the weight had been agreed. The operator's intention to assist the vehicle driver to do an act which was a breach of the regulations amounted to aiding and abetting, for which the Coal Board was liable. An oft-cited dictum by Devlin J. in this case that "it would be wrong to conclude . . . that proof of encouragement is necessary to every form of aiding and abetting" must be taken to have referred to express encouragement. Assisting another to commit an offence was a form of encouragement (see *R. v. Allan, supra*). (This case may be distinguished from *John Henshall (Quarries) Ltd.* v. *Harvey* (1965), D.C. (*ante*, Chap. 4) on the basis that in that case the weighbridge attendant was too subordinate a servant for his knowledge to be as that of the company, while in the present case this was not so.)

Where there was a legal duty to intervene to prevent the commission of an offence, an omission to do so could amount to aiding and abetting. For example, in *R. v. Harris* (1964), C.C.A., the supervisor of a learner-driver was held to have aided and abetted the offence of causing death by dangerous driving on the ground that he had failed to stop the driver from going dangerously fast.

In addition to the act of encouragement, aiding and abetting the commission of an offence necessitated a mental element, *viz.*, knowledge of the facts which constituted that offence. For example, if a man committed bigamy by marrying again during the lifetime of his lawful spouse, the woman that he married was a principal in the second degree if, but only if, she knew that the man was already married. Moreover, for this purpose the knowledge of a servant could not be imputed to the master. For example, it was held in *Ferguson* v. *Weaving* (1951), D.C., that a licensee could not be convicted of counselling and procuring or of aiding and abetting the offence committed by customers of consuming intoxicating liquor on the premises outside permitted hours, unless the licensee knew that the liquor was being consumed, and that for this purpose the knowledge of waiters employed by her could not be imputed to her. (For "counselling and procuring" see below under Accessory before the fact.) On the other hand, an aider and abettor was liable for such crimes as were committed by the principal in the first degree in the execution of their common purpose. For example, if they had agreed to the commission of robbery with violence involving grievous bodily harm, and the principal in the first degree caused the death of the victim, both would be guilty of murder: as we shall see (in Chap. 6), intent to cause grievous bodily harm was (and still is) sufficient *mens rea* for murder, and both shared that *mens rea* (*R. v. Betts and Ridley* (1930), C.C.A.). On the other hand, if two men agreed to assault a third, but without causing him any serious harm, and during the assault one of them formed the intent to kill or cause grievous bodily harm and did in fact kill the

victim, he would be guilty of murder, but the other would be guilty
only of manslaughter even if, *e.g.*, he knew the other was carrying
a knife (*R.* v. *Betty* (1963), C.C.A.)—and he would not be guilty
even of manslaughter if the death was caused solely by the act of
his companion and that act (*e.g.*, the use of a knife) went beyond
the scope of their common enterprise (*R.* v. *Anderson and Morris*
(1966), C.C.A.).

It was generally stated that "presence makes principals, absence
makes accessories". This proposition, however, could not be supported without introducing a doctrine of constructive presence. We
have seen, for example, that a principal in the first degree could
commit the crime through the medium of an innocent agent, in
which case he need not have been present at the time. Again, it
was held that it was sufficient if an aider and abettor was near
enough to the scene of the crime to render any assistance that might
be required: he was then said to be constructively present (*R.* v.
Betts and Ridley, supra). But, where one man entertained another
to dinner whilst his confederate was breaking and entering the
other's dwelling-house in a different town, it seems absurd to
suggest that the first man was constructively present in the different
town, and yet it would appear that he was a principal in the second
degree (see the American case of *Breese* v. *The State* (1861)). As
this rule is still relevant today it would, perhaps, be better to
abandon the doctrine of presence altogether and, as we have suggested, to define the principal in the second degree as one who
aided and abetted the commission of the crime *at the very time that
it was being committed.*

One question which arose (and is still relevant) was whether there
could be a principal in the second degree if there was no principal
in the first degree. On general principles it would seem that there
could not: one could not aid and abet a crime which had not been
committed by any other person. This view was supported by *dicta*
in certain cases, and received support from the decision in *Thornton* v. *Mitchell* (1940), D.C. In this case a bus driver needed to
reverse his vehicle, but was unable to see to the rear; he therefore
enlisted the aid of his conductor, through whose negligence in the
directions that he gave the bus knocked down a pedestrian. It was
held that as the driver had been acquitted of careless driving
(because he had not been careless) the conductor could not be convicted of aiding and abetting that offence. (Contrast *Liddon* v.
Stringer (1967), D.C., in which it was held, on the facts, that the
driver had been careless, because he had not ensured that the
conductor was in a position to see.) But in *R.* v. *Bourne* (1952),
C.C.A., a man forced his wife by duress to commit an unnatural

sexual offence with a dog. It was held that he could be convicted of that offence as an aider and abettor, although it was admitted that, if the wife had been charged with the offence, she would have been entitled to an acquittal by reason of the duress; it was said that she had committed the offence although she would have had a defence to it if she had been charged—perhaps, a somewhat remarkable doctrine. Possibly the husband's conviction could have been justified on the ground that he was in fact the principal in the first degree, having committed the offence through the medium of an innocent agent. We will consider below what effect, if any, the Criminal Law Act 1967 has upon this question.

Accessory before the fact. He was one who, by some act done before the commission of the felony, counselled or procured its commission. The minimum that the law would accept as a sufficient counselling or procuring was active encouragement. (*Cf.* the principal in the second degree, *supra.*) Thus in *R. v. Taylor* (1875), C.C.R., in which a prize fight led to the death of one of the combatants, it was held insufficient to make a man an accessory before the fact to manslaughter that he had merely agreed to act as stakeholder. The supply of materials, such as a car, to be used in the commission of a felony would generally be a sufficient act of instigation to make the supplier an accessory before the fact. But in such a case the supplier had to know the kind of felony intended, although he need not have known the particular offence contemplated; for example, it was sufficient if he knew that the offence intended was one of breaking and entering, even if he did not know the date on which the principal intended to commit the felony, or the address of the premises which he intended to break and enter (*R. v. Bainbridge* (1960), C.C.A.).

If the principal committed a different felony from that instigated, the instigator could not generally be held responsible for that (although a mere difference in the manner of execution would not excuse him). But if the other felony was committed by the principal inadvertently, and its commission was a natural consequence of a genuine attempt by him to commit the felony instigated, the instigator would be responsible for that. For example, if A hired B to murder C, whose description A gave to B, and B murdered D believing him to be C, A would be an accessory before the fact to murder (Foster 370 (a hypothetical case)). Similarly, if A procured B to carry out an illegal abortion, and B inadvertently caused the woman's death, A would be an accessory before the fact to manslaughter (*R. v. Creamer* (1966), C.C.A.). A borderline case was that of *R. v. Saunders and Archer* (1573). A encouraged B to use a poisoned apple for the purpose of ridding himself of his wife. The wife took one bite at the apple, but finding it bitter handed the apple to their child. The child ate the apple and died. A was held not to be an accessory before the fact to the murder of the child that B was held to have committed, by reason of the improbability that a different homicide would occur in the circumstances.

Accessory after the fact. This category of offender, as we shall see later, was almost completely abolished by the Criminal Law Act 1967 and it is therefore only necessary to consider it in outline. An accessory after the fact was one who knowing that another had committed a felony, harboured or relieved him. The giving of any active assistance for the express purpose of helping the principal to escape justice was a sufficient "relieving" (*R. v. Levy* (1912), C.C.A. (removing evidence of guilt)). But inactivity, *e.g.*, failure to report the matter to the police, was insufficient. Moreover, as has been stated, the assistance had to be given for the express purpose of helping the principal to escape justice. It is for this reason that the professional receiver of stolen goods was not normally an accessory after the fact to the thefts committed by his clients: the disposal of the goods by the receiver often helped the thieves to escape justice, but that was not the purpose of the receiver's action, which was to line his own pocket (*R. v. Andrews* (1962), C.C.A.).

The law made no distinction as regards punishment between a principal in the first degree, a principal in the second degree, and an accessory before the fact, and they were all liable to whatever punishment was prescribed for the particular felony. An accessory after the fact, however, was not regarded as being as seriously implicated as the others and was generally liable only to a maximum of two years' imprisonment (Accessories and Abettors Act 1861, s. 4).

Treason

There were (and still are) the same four ways of participating in the commission of a treason as in the case of felony, but the terminology was different and all participants were called simply "**principals.**" All were liable to the same punishment (death): hence, one who harboured or relieved a traitor was liable to the death sentence.

Misdemeanours

The first three methods of participating in the commission of a felony applied equally to misdemeanours. Here again, however, the terminology was different and all participants were called principals. As in the case of felonies, all were liable to the same punishment. The fourth category had no counterpart in the law of misdemeanour, so that one could not become a party to a misdemeanour merely by harbouring or relieving a misdemeanant.

B. After the Criminal Law Act 1967

As we have seen, section 1 of the Criminal Law Act 1967 abolished all distinctions between felony and misdemeanour and provided that, subject to the provisions of the Act, on all matters on which a distinction had previously been made the law and practice in relation to all offences should be the law and practice applicable at the commencement of the Act in relation to misdemeanour. The law in relation to treason was not, however, affected (*ibid.*, s. 12(6)). The effect of these provisions in relation to the parties is that the law regarding misdemeanours and treason remains the same, but the law as regards felonies is now the same as that for misdemeanours. In addition the Act creates a new offence of assisting offenders (section 4: see below).

One result of making the law in relation to felonies the same as that for misdemeanours is that the category of accessory after the fact is abolished (except for offences committed before January 1, 1968: *R.* v. *Fisher* (1968), C.A.), although it is still one of the four ways of participating in treason (where all offenders are still called "principals"). Apart from treason there are now only three ways of participating in an offence: by taking part in the commission of the *actus reus* itself (or committing it through the medium of an innocent agent), by aiding and abetting the commission of an offence at the time it is being committed, and by counselling or procuring its commission. All participants are, however, now called "principals" and for the purpose of the indictment no distinction need be drawn between them (see Chap. 33). This was always the case as regards principals in the first and second degree and it would appear that this will now be so as regards an accessory before the fact as well. Thus in *R.* v. *Swindall and Osborne* (1846) two men drove their carriages recklessly each encouraging the other, and one of those carriages knocked down and killed a pedestrian, but the prosecution could not prove which carriage it was. It was held that both men could be convicted of manslaughter because whichever was the principal in the first degree, the other was a principal in the second degree, and there was no obligation resting on the prosecution to distinguish the one from the other. All participants are now liable to the same punishment but in practice one who has merely aided and abetted the commission of the offence (or counselled or procured it) will often be dealt with more leniently. Indeed, in practice, it is normally more convenient to speak of those who did not actually commit the *actus reus* as aiders and abettors.

One problem which remains is whether one person can be convicted of aiding and abetting a crime which has not, in fact been committed by any other person. We have seen already (under "Principal in the second degree," above) that in *Thornton* v. *Mitchell* it was held that the conductor of a bus could not be convicted of aiding and abetting the misdemeanour of careless driving because the driver had not been careless: the offence had not been committed. However, in *R.* v. *Humphreys and Turner* (1965), where one accused was charged with obtaining by false pretences (a misdemeanour) and another with aiding and abetting the commission of that offence, Judge Chapman distinguished between felonies and misdemeanours and directed the jury that the second accused could still be convicted even if the first accused was acquitted, because they were both principals. Moreover, the law formerly applicable to misdemeanours now applies to all offences. Nevertheless, it is arguable that the basis of Judge Chapman's direction was that in that case the second accused had made a confession which was admissible in evidence against him, but was not admissible in evidence against the first accused. The strange result, therefore, was that the jury might not be satisfied on the evidence which was admissible against the first accused that he had committed the offence, but, at the same time they might be satisfied on the evidence admissible against the second accused, that the first accused had committed the offence and that the second accused had aided and abetted its commission.

As we have seen (under "Principal in the second degree," above), in *R.* v. *Bourne*, it was held that the husband could be convicted as an aider and abettor even though his wife would have been entitled to an acquittal, but the offence in that case was a felony. In view of section 1 of the Criminal Law Act 1967 it would seem that the law which would apply on similar facts today is the law applicable to misdemeanours before the Act, and in view of *R.* v. *Humphreys and Turner*, *supra*, it must be considered doubtful what that law was.

On balance, the better view would seem to be that a person cannot be convicted of aiding and abetting a crime which no-one else has committed.

Assisting offenders

Section 4 of the Criminal Law Act 1967 creates a new offence of assisting offenders and as this offence is created partly to replace the former category of accessory after the fact it is convenient to consider the offence here. By section 4(1), "where a person has committed an arrestable offence, any other person who, knowing or believing him to be guilty of the offence or of some other offence, does without lawful authority or reasonable excuse any act with intent to impede his apprehension or prosecution shall be guilty of an offence." No proceedings for this offence can, however, be instituted except by or with the consent of the Director of Public Prosecutions (*ibid.*, s. 4(4)). The offence itself is punishable with a maximum term of imprisonment of from three years to ten years, depending on the gravity of the arrestable offence committed by the one whom he has assisted (*ibid.*, s. 4(3)).

The offence of assisting offenders, therefore, applies to all arrestable offences and it covers such conduct as driving an offender away after a crime, hiding him from the police or destroying fingerprints or other traces of the crime. Nevertheless, the requirement that there must be an intent to "impede" a prosecution excludes mere persuasion not to prosecute, while the exception for "lawful authority or reasonable excuse" means that, for example, a person who destroys the evidence of an offence (*e.g.*, a worthless cheque) in pursuance of a legitimate agreement to refrain from prosecuting in consideration of the making good of loss caused by that offence, does not commit the offence of assisting the offender.

As an accused, to be guilty of the offence, must "intend to impede" the apprehension or prosecution of the offender, he will not commit the offence merely by providing, or continuing to provide, the offender with accommodation in the ordinary way. However, there is no specific exemption provided for the spouse of the offender or other relatives, although the necessity for the consent of the Director of Public Prosecutions will be a safeguard in these cases.

We shall also consider in Chapter 20 the somewhat similar offences of misprision, compounding and concealing offences or giving false information.

Chapter Six

INCITEMENT AND ATTEMPT

Incitement

IT is a common law offence (m) to incite another to commit an offence, whether indictable (*R.* v. *Higgins* (1801)) or summary (*R.* v. *Curr* (1968), C.A.); however if the person incited is without criminal responsibility, it is possible that the offence is attempt, not incitement: see Attempt, *infra.* It is not necessary that the person incited should do anything to carry out the offence instigated, but it is necessary that some person should in fact be incited. For example, if the incitement is by letter which is dispatched, but not read by the person to whom it is addressed, the offence of incitement is not committed (although in those circumstances the offence of attempted incitement, itself a common law offence (m), will have been committed) (*R.* v. *Banks* (1873) (letter intercepted); *R.* v. *Ransford* (1874) (letter not read by recipient)). An incitement may be contingent in character, as where one person asks another to receive goods which he intends to steal on the morrow: he is then guilty of incitement to receive stolen goods (*R.* v. *McDonough* (1963), C.C.A.).

As we have already seen (*ante*, Chap. 5), if the offence instigated is in fact committed by the person incited, the inciter becomes a party to that crime.

Just as it is an offence to attempt to incite another to commit an indictable offence, so it is an offence to incite another to attempt to commit an indictable offence. Suppose, for example, that A supplies to B a substance which B is to administer to herself for the purpose of illegally procuring her abortion, and suppose that both A and B believe the substance to be noxious, but that it is in fact harmless. Now it is a statutory offence (see *post*, Chap. 7) for a woman to administer a noxious substance to herself for the purpose of unlawfully procuring her miscarriage, and an attempt to commit this offence is probably committed by a woman who administers to herself a substance which she mistakenly believes to be noxious. If this is so, the supplier of the powder is guilty of an

44

incitement to attempt to commit an indictable offence (*R.* v. *Brown* (1899)).

Attempt

With the exception of a few attempts which are in themselves statutory offences (*e.g.*, attempts to choke with intent to commit an offence: Offences Against the Person Act 1861, s. 21), every attempt to commit an indictable offence is a common law offence (m). A greater sentence cannot, however, be awarded for an attempt than can be given for the completed offence (see the Criminal Law Act 1967, s. 7(2)).

For reasons which will appear in a moment, it is difficult to define an attempt, but it may be described as consisting of acts done with the intention of committing an indictable offence which go beyond the stage of preparation for the commission of that offence, and are sufficiently proximate to that commission for the law to recognize them as an attempt. The *mens rea* of attempt, therefore, is clear: it is the intent to commit the indictable offence contemplated. Hence, strange as it may seem, *mens rea* which is sufficient for the commission of an offence may not be sufficient for an attempt to commit that offence. This is notably so in the case of attempted murder. As we shall see hereafter (*post*, Chap. 7), the *mens rea* of murder is intent to kill *or cause grievous bodily harm*. But to support a charge of attempted murder the prosecution must prove the full intent to murder, *i.e.*, intent to kill, and a mere intent to cause grievous bodily harm will not suffice (*R.* v. *Whybrow* (1951), C.C.A.; *R.* v. *Grimwood* (1962), C.C.A.).

As has been stated, not every act done with the intention of committing an indictable offence amounts to an attempt to commit that offence. Acts of preparation do not suffice; in the language used in the modern leading case (*R.* v. *Robinson* (1915), C.C.A., following *R.* v. *Eagleton* (1855)), the acts must have been "immediately connected" with the crime contemplated. Such expressions, however, cloak the lack of any scientific test on the question of proximity. However, it is clear that a high degree of proximity is required, *i.e.*, the accused's acts must have reached the stage at which it is possible to say that he has almost committed the crime contemplated. As with most questions of degree, it is for the jury to apply the test on a proper direction from the trial judge (*R.* v. *Cook* (1963), C.C.A.). In the leading case (*Robinson's* case, *supra*) the accused, a jeweller, had faked a robbery with the intention of making a false claim on his insurers. Upon being questioned by the police, however, he confessed his fraudulent intention and was arrested before he made a claim upon the insurers. He was convicted of an attempt to obtain money by false pretences, but his conviction was quashed by the Court of Criminal Appeal on the ground that his acts were still in the stage of preparation. Had he made a claim on the insurers, he would have been guilty of the attempt. We have already seen a case on the other side of the line in the instance of attempted incitement mentioned above (*R.* v. *Banks, R.* v. *Ransford, supra*). Again, it has been held to be attempted murder for a person to administer to another a dose of poison which he mistakenly believes to be sufficient to cause that other's death, or to administer the first of a series of doses if he intends to cause the death of another by slow poisoning (*R.* v. *White* (1910), C.C.A.). It has been strongly suggested that to incite an innocent agent (*e.g.*, a child below the age of criminal responsibility) to commit an offence amounts not to incitement but to an attempt to commit that offence (Glanville Williams, *Criminal Law: The General Part* (2nd ed.), p. 616); but there is no definite authority to that effect.

In *Davey* v. *Lee* (1968), D.C., the accused had cut the wire fencing surrounding a compound in which a copper store and other buildings were situated with the intention of breaking into the store and stealing the copper. It was held that they could properly be convicted of attempted larceny, and the Divisional Court approved two tests on the question of proximity: (1) an attempt to commit a crime is an act done with intent to commit that crime, and forming part of a series of acts which would constitute its actual commission if it were not interrupted (Stephen's *Digest of the Criminal Law,* 5th ed., 1894, art. 50); (2) the *actus reus* necessary to constitute an attempt is complete if the prisoner does an act which is a step towards the commission of the specific crime, which is immediately and not remotely connected with the commission of it, and the doing of which cannot reasonably be regarded as having any other purpose than the commission of the' specific crime (Archbold's *Criminal Pleading, Evidence and Practice,* 37th ed., 1969, para. 4104). The Court admitted, however, that Stephen's test does not help to define the point of time at which the series of acts begins. It is also to be noticed that Archbold's test retains the ambiguous requirement that the act be "immediately and not remotely connected" with the commission of the crime: the test is not simply whether the act could reasonably be regarded as having some other purpose than the commission of the specific crime, although that no doubt is an important factor. Moreover in *Jones* v. *Brooks* (1968), where the accused was charged with attempting to take and drive away a motor vehicle, the magistrates had dismissed the charge on the ground that the accused's act in trying to insert a key into a car could have been for purposes other than driving the car away, but a Divisional Court held the intention which the accused had expressed both at the time of, and after, the *actus reus* was relevant to see to what the act was directed, and the court directed the magistrates to convict.

It seems clear in principle, and there is strong persuasive authority for the view, that if the accused, with the necessary intention, has done acts which are sufficiently proximate to the crime contemplated to amount to an attempt, it is no defence to the charge that at the last moment he voluntarily desisted from committing that crime (*R*. v. *Lankford* (1959), C.C.A.—charge of attempted rape; the Court's remarks on this point were, strictly *obiter*; see also *R*. v. *Taylor* (1859)—accused guilty of attempted arson of a cornstack, although he had desisted from setting fire to it on observing that he was being watched). Once a person's conduct satisfies the definition of a crime, such as attempt, it is difficult to see how that crime can be deleted by a voluntary abstention from committing some further offence.

The fact that unknown to the accused it was impossible for him to commit the crime contemplated by the means that he was employing, or in the circumstances in question, is not of itself a defence to a charge of attempt. Thus, a person is guilty of attempted theft if he puts his hand into another's pocket intending to steal whatever he may find there, even if in fact the pocket is empty (*R*. v. *Ring* (1892), C.C.R.). On the other hand, when it was in fact impossible to commit the crime intended it may also appear that the accused's conduct was not sufficiently proximate to the crime intended to satisfy the definition of attempt, in which case he will have a defence on that ground. It was, for example, suggested by Rowlatt J. in *R*. v. *Osborn* (1919) that it would not be attempted murder for a man to shoot at a tree stump which he mistakenly believed to be his enemy, whom he intended to kill, if the intended victim were nowhere near the scene at the time: in those circumstances it could not be said that the accused was "on the thing" at all, *i.e.*, anywhere near the commission of the offence that he intended to commit. The same problem arises when a person drives a knife into the heart of another whom he intends to kill, but who in fact has died a few minutes previously, and in many other hypothetical cases more beloved of examiners than likely to arise in practice. In all such instances the question is whether it can properly be said that the accused's conduct was proximate to the actual commission of the crime that he intended to commit, and this must be a matter of opinion in each instance until, if ever, such a case arises for decision by the courts.

There has been a good deal of discussion about certain words used by Birkett J., in *R.* v. *Percy Dalton* (*London*) *Ltd.* (1949), C.C.A.: "Steps on the way to the commission of what would be a crime if the acts were completed may amount to attempts to commit that crime, to which unless interrupted they would have led; but steps on the way to the doing of something which is thereafter done and which is no crime cannot be regarded as attempts to commit a crime". In that case a company was charged with selling pears at a price in excess of that permitted by a then current price-control order. The pears were sold in boxes stated to contain 46 lbs. or more. It was probable that the weight of the pears in any box would be appreciably more than 46 lbs., and if the weight was 47 lbs. 15 ozs. or more no offence would have been committed. The prosecution could not prove that the weight was less than 47 lbs. 15 ozs., and the jury, therefore, acquitted the company of the offence charged, but convicted it of an attempt to commit that offence. The Court of Criminal Appeal quashed the conviction. The Court appears to have proceeded upon the basis that the company (through its responsible officers) believed the weight of the pears to be such that an offence was being committed against the order (otherwise there would be no point in the case). Nevertheless, the Court held that an attempt had not been committed. It is submitted that the Court's decision was perfectly correct, because, whatever the company's intention, its conduct was not proximate to the commission of an offence against the order, *i.e.*, it could not fairly be said that it had almost committed such an offence. It is suggested that, for the same reason, it would not be attempted larceny for a man to take from a restaurant an umbrella which he believed to belong to someone else, with intent to steal it, but which in fact was his own umbrella. It is sometimes suggested that Birkett J's dictum is inconsistent with the decision in *R.* v. *Hensler* (1870), C.C.R. (a decision on the old law of obtaining by false pretences; but the law in relation to obtaining by deception is still in fact the same). In that case the accused sent a letter containing false statements by means of which he endeavoured to obtain money from the prosecutor. The prosecutor, however, was not deceived and sent the money merely in order to trap the accused. The accused was convicted of attempting to obtain the money by false pretences (he was not guilty of the full offence because the obtaining was not a result of the false pretence), and this, it is submitted, was clearly right; as soon as he sent the letter his conduct amounted to an attempt, and what happened thereafter was totally irrelevant so far as a charge of attempt was concerned. This decision is not in any way inconsistent with Birkett J's dictum *supra* if the words "which is thereafter done" refer to *conduct of the accused*, as it is submitted that they do. In any event, it is a well recognized principle that a judicial pronouncement must be read in the light of the facts of the case to which it refers. In all such cases, it is submitted, the test is that of proximity, *i.e.*, whether or not the accused's conduct was proximate to an actual commission of the offence contemplated.

At common law where the offence attempted was a felony, and the attempt to commit it was a misdemeanour, it was a defence to a charge of attempt to show that the felony had in fact been committed: the attempt merged in the completed crime and ceased to exist. This strange rule was abolished, at least as regards trial on indictment, by the Criminal Procedure Act 1851, s. 12 (see *R.* v. *Males* (1962), C.C.A.). Section 12 itself was repealed by the Criminal Law Act 1967, Sched. 3, but section 6(4) of the 1967 Act expressly provides that an accused charged on indictment with attempting to commit an offence (or with any assault or other act preliminary to an offence), but not with the completed offence, may be convicted of the offence charged notwithstanding that he is shown to be guilty of the completed offence. Moreover, although the original common law rule may still have applied to summary trials before the 1967 Act (see *Rogers* v. *Arnott* (1960), D.C., in which the point seems to have been assumed), the abolition of the distinction between felonies and misdemeanours would seem to have abolished the common law rule as regards summary trials as well.

Moreover, by the Criminal Law Act 1967, s. 6, upon a trial on indictment the jury may find the accused not guilty of the full offence, but guilty of an attempt to commit it. It is not, therefore, necessary to include in an indictment a count charging an attempt, if the full offence is charged.

An offence analogous to that of attempt is the common law offence (m) of procuring something with intent to use it for a criminal purpose. Thus, it has long been established that it is a common law offence to procure indecent prints with intent to sell them (*Dugdale* v. *R.* (1853)), or to procure base coin with intent to utter it (*R.* v. *Fuller* (1816)). And in *R.* v. *Gurmit Singh* (1966) McNair J. held that the principle was quite general, and that it is a common law offence to procure anything with intent to use it for a criminal purpose.

Chapter Seven

OFFENCES OF HOMICIDE AND COGNATE OFFENCES

HOMICIDE is simply the killing of a human being and may be lawful (*e.g.*, the killing of an alien enemy in the lawful course of warfare) or unlawful. The unlawful homicides are murder, manslaughter, homicide by dangerous driving, and infanticide. But for convenience we shall also consider in this chapter suicide, child destruction, procuring abortion, and one or two other related offences.

As we have already seen (in Chap. 3), a homicide may be committed by means of an omission to act, but only where the omission constitutes a breach of a legal duty. This important principle need not detain us further.

It is an old rule of the common law, which has never been abolished, that the death must occur within a year and a day of the infliction of the injury; otherwise it is irrebuttably presumed that the death is due to some other cause (*R. v. Dyson* (1908), C.C.A.).

Homicide is restricted to the killing of one who has been born alive. Where a baby has been killed, it is therefore necessary for the prosecution to prove that the baby enjoyed an existence independent of the mother, although the umbilical cord need not have been cut (*R. v. Reeves* (1839)). There is, however, no rule that the injury must have been inflicted after birth, and the infliction of an injury before birth which causes the child's death after birth is an act of homicide (*R. v. West* (1848) (a case of induced abortion after six months' pregnancy: the child, being too weak to live, died after birth)).

Lawful Homicides

Homicides which today may be classified simply as lawful homicides were originally either justifiable homicides, considered to be legally free from blame, and sometimes even commanded by the law, or merely excusable homicides, which were not originally free from penal consequences because some element of fault was

50

considered to attach to the slayer. As no penal consequences now attach to excusable homicides, the former distinction may be disregarded. The following are the more important circumstances in which homicide is lawful.

(1) *Preventing a crime; effecting an arrest.*

A person may use reasonable force in the prevention of crime, or effecting or assisting the lawful arrest of offenders or others unlawfully at large (Criminal Law Act 1967, s. 3). If death ensues the homicide will be lawful, provided no more force has been used than is reasonable. Prior to the Criminal Law Act 1967 such force could only be employed where the offence was a felony (see Fost. 270 *et seq.* and Chap. 30 of Stephen's *Digest of the Criminal Law*, 19th ed.). Though section 3 does not itself contain restrictions on the use of force, it is likely that in practice only where the crime is a serious one will the courts consider that the use of dangerous force could be reasonable. The Criminal Law Revision Committee in their Seventh Report, Felonies and Misdemeanours (on which report the Criminal Law Act 1967 was based), said that "no doubt . . . the court, in considering what was reasonable force, [will] take into account all the circumstances, including in particular the nature and degree of force used, the seriousness of the evil to be prevented and the possibility of preventing it by other means." In the case of "very trivial offences" it will very likely be held that it is not reasonable "to use even the slightest force to prevent them." (Para. 23.)

The question is often asked whether one is entitled to shoot down a burglar whom one finds in one's house. The answer to the question, put in those terms, is probably in the negative; the offence of burglary has already been committed, so that no question of preventing the commission of that offence arises, and, unless the burglar resisted arrest, the immediate use of a lethal weapon against him would be excessive in the circumstances. But, in the particular case of burglary, a householder might readily be justified in thinking that the burglar intended to attack him and that his life was in danger. The principles expounded in the next paragraph would then apply.

(2) *Defence of self or property.*

The use of force to protect oneself or one's property may well fall within the principle, already considered, of preventing the commission of a serious crime and indeed it was for this reason that the Criminal Law Revision Committee in their Seventh Report (*supra*) considered it unnecessary for any express provision in relation to the defence of property to be incorporated in section 3 of the Criminal Law Act 1967 (para. 22). For example, if a woman kills a man who is attempting to rape her, she has done so to prevent the commission of a serious crime, and it is legally irrelevant that the offence was being attempted against herself; provided that the force which she used was reasonable in the circumstances, the homicide is lawful, as having been done for the prevention of the commission of rape, and legally the position is the same as when a third person intervenes to protect a woman from being ravished. Similarly, one can protect oneself against an unlawful attack which is likely to cause serious injury, and lawfully employ whatever force is reasonable; here again the position is legally the same as when a person intervenes to protect another against such an attack by a third person (see _R._ v. _Duffy_ (1967), C.C.A.). Similar principles apply where force is used to protect one's property against an attempt to deprive one of it, as in a case of robbery.

One is entitled to use moderate force to protect oneself against an assault that is not of a serious character; but prior to the Criminal Law Act 1967, s. 3(2), whereas when protecting oneself against an attack which was clearly felonious there was no obligation to retreat (Fost. 273), where the attack was not clearly felonious the person attacked was under an obligation to retreat, if retreat was practicable in the circumstances (_R._ v. _Smith_ (1837); _R._ v. _Knock_ (1877)). It is probable that the same principles will still be applied but according to the gravity of the attack and not according to whether the offence was previously a felony or a misdemeanour. It would also seem that similar principles apply to the defence of one's property. The use of force to _recover_ possession of land is rendered unlawful by the Statutes of Forcible Entry 1381 to 1623, but moderate force may probably be used to recover chattels of which one has been wrongfully dispossessed. A peaceful trespasser on land may not be forcibly ejected unless he has first been told to go and has refused, in which case moderate force may lawfully be used to remove him (but not a kick (_R._ v. _Wild_ (1837)). In these cases the use of dangerous force can rarely be justified. Before the Criminal Law Act 1967 there was, perhaps, an exception where the use of dangerous force was essential to defend possession of one's dwelling house (_R._ v. _Hussey_ (1924), C.C.A. (use of shotgun by tenant to resist an illegal attempt by landlady and others to oust him; the charge was of unlawful wounding)), and it may be that this exception still remains.

(3) _Homicide by misadventure._

As we shall see a little later, the least serious form of unlawful homicide known to the common law is manslaughter, and this requires either the commission of an unlawful act of a dangerous character or the commission of a lawful act done with gross negligence. It follows that if death is caused by an unlawful act which is not of a dangerous character, or by a lawful act done without gross negligence, no offence of homicide has been committed.

Murder

Murder (f), is unlawful homicide with malice aforethought. Malice aforethought is the *mens rea* required for murder, and the term must now be regarded as one of art: its meaning in law is not indicated by the ordinary sense of the words "malice" and "aforethought". It is probable that since the Homicide Act 1957 malice aforethought may be defined as an intent to kill, or cause grievous bodily harm to, anyone, whether the person killed or not. Murder is therefore committed in each of the following cases.

(1) A shoots at B with the intention of killing B, and does in fact kill B.

(2) A shoots at B with the intention of killing B, misses B and inadvertently kills C. In this type of case it is sometimes said that the malice is transferable, *i.e.*, that the malice directed against B may be regarded as transferred to C.

(3) A fires into a crowd, intending to kill someone and not caring whom; he in fact kills C. This is sometimes known as a case of universal malice.

Murder is also committed in each of the above instances if A's intention is not specifically to kill, but is merely to cause grievous bodily harm (*R.* v. *Vickers* (1957), C.C.A.; *D.P.P.* v. *Smith* (1961) H.L.); the term *implied malice* is sometimes used to denote this state of mind. Grievous bodily harm means any serious bodily injury (*Smith's* case, *supra*).

No doubt here, as generally, the accused's consciousness that his act is morally certain to cause death or grievous bodily harm satisfies the requirement of intention. But there is also some authority for the proposition that malice aforethought includes knowledge that the act done will probably cause death or grievous bodily harm (Stephen's *Digest of the Criminal Law* (9th ed.), art. 264; *R.* v. *Walters* (1841) (exposure of a child)).

In *D.P.P.* v. *Smith, supra,* the House of Lords decided in fact that, in a case of murder, an accused must be held to have intended the natural consequences of his act. Therefore, if a reasonable man would, in the position of the accused, have contemplated that grievous bodily harm to the victim was the natural and probable result of his action then the accused must be held to have contemplated that result (*i.e.* an objective test). However, section 8 of the Criminal Justice Act 1967 now provides that "a court or jury, in determining whether a person has committed an offence (*a*) shall not be bound in law to infer that he intended or foresaw a result of his actions by reason only of its being a natural and probable consequence of those actions; but (*b*) shall decide whether he did intend or foresee that result by reference to all the evidence, drawing such inferences from the evidence as appear proper in the circumstances." Moreover, in *R.* v. *Wallett* (1968) the Court of Appeal held that it would not be safe to uphold a conviction for murder because the trial judge in his summing-up to the jury had used words which suggested they could still apply an objective test. It would therefore seem clear that the test in murder cases, like the general rule in other criminal cases, is a subjective one. An accused can only be convicted if the jury are satisfied that he did foresee that his actions were likely to (or would probably) cause death or grievous bodily harm and (probably) that he intended that result.

Before the Homicide Act 1957 there were two other forms of malice aforethought, and it is necessary to bear this in mind in reading some of the older cases on the criminal law, such as *D.P.P.* v. *Beard* (1920), H.L., which, as we have seen (in Chap. 4), is the leading authority on intoxication as a defence to criminal liability. These other forms of malice aforethought were as follows:

(1) An intention to commit a violent felony, such as rape, where the death was caused by an act of violence done in the course or furtherance of that felony. This was often called the felony-murder rule, and it is exemplified by *Beard's* case (*supra*).

(2) An intention to resist by force an officer of justice, such as a police officer, acting in the execution of his duty, knowing him to be such an officer so engaged, where the death was caused by an act of violence done in the course of that resistance (*R.* v. *Appleby* (1940), C.C.A.).

In these two cases the homicide, however inadvertent, was murder: intent to kill or cause grievous bodily harm was not required. These two forms of constructive malice, as they were known, were abolished by section 1 of the Homicide Act 1957.

In *Thabo Meli* v. *The Queen* (1954) the Privy Council was confronted with the following problem. A inflicts an injury upon B with intent to kill B, and A believes that he has killed B, whereas in fact he has merely rendered him unconscious; some time later A throws the supposed corpse over a cliff, and the evidence shows that the death was caused by exposure. It was contended on behalf of the defence that in these circumstances the homicide would not be murder, on the ground that the original act, though done with malice aforethought, had not in fact caused death, and that the subsequent act, though in fact it had caused death, had been done without malice aforethought. However, this argument appeared to the Privy Council to be altogether too subtle; their lordships held that the incidents formed one transaction and that the homicide was murder. (See also the similar English case of *R. v. Church* (1966), C.C.A. (the accused was convicted of manslaughter on a lenient direction to the jury by the trial judge).)

Upon a conviction of murder the court is required by the Murder (Abolition of Death Penalty) Act 1965 to pass sentence of life imprisonment; but the court may recommend to the Home Secretary a minimum period of imprisonment that the convicted person should in fact suffer before being released under the prerogative of mercy (see Chap. 44).

Evidence
There is one more important House of Lords' decision on the law of evidence in murder cases which we must consider. In *Woolmington v. D.P.P.* (1935) the House of Lords held that the burden is upon the prosecution to prove, not only the *actus reus* of murder, but also the malice aforethought. In the words of Lord Sankey L.C.: "Throughout the web of English criminal law one golden thread is always to be seen, that it is the duty of the prosecution to prove the prisoner's guilt, subject to what I have already said as to the defence of insanity and subject also to any statutory exception. If, at the end of and on the whole of the case, there is a reasonable doubt, created by the evidence given by either the prosecution or the prisoner, as to whether the prisoner killed the deceased with a malicious intention, the prosecution has not made out the case and the prisoner is entitled to an acquittal." This means that, if there is any evidence, worthy of consideration by the jury, that the homicide was accidental or in self-defence, or that there is any other ground of defence, it is for the prosecution to rebut that defence, not for the prisoner to establish it. But it is not the duty of the judge to direct the jury with regard to the law of accident, self-defence, and so on, unless there is some evidence for the ground of defence in question.

Manslaughter

At common law manslaughter, which is an offence (f) punishable with a maximum of life imprisonment (Offences against the Person Act 1861, s. 5), may be divided into voluntary manslaughter and involuntary manslaughter, and we shall consider each separately.

(A) Voluntary Manslaughter

An unlawful homicide is said to be voluntary manslaughter when it would have been murder but for the fact that the accused was provoked to do what he did and this provocation was sufficient to reduce the homicide to manslaughter. Not all provocation is capable of having this effect: the provocation must have been such as might have deprived a reasonable man of his self-control, and it must in fact have deprived the accused of his self-control. At common law it was for the trial judge to decide if the given provocation was capable of depriving a reasonable man of his self-control, and the judges evolved a number of technical rules on the point, *e.g.*, that normally only a blow or the discovery of one's spouse in the act of adultery could be regarded as sufficiently provocative, and normally words alone could not be regarded as capable of having this effect (*Holmes* v. *Director of Public Prosecutions* (1946), H.L.). Now, however, section 3 of the Homicide Act 1957 provides that, "where on a charge of murder there is evidence on which the jury can find that the person charged was provoked (whether by things done or by things said or by both together) to lose his self-control, the question whether the provocation was enough to make a reasonable man do as he did shall be left to be determined by the jury; and in determining that question the jury shall take into account everything both done and said according to the effect which, in their opinion, it would have on a reasonable man." It is therefore open to the jury today to accept words alone as sufficient. The test is still objective (namely, that of the reasonable man), but it is now to be applied by the jury, not the judge, and the jury is not to be fettered by any technical rules on the point.

The underlying theory is well brought out by the following words used by Devlin J. (as he then was) in *R.* v. *Duffy* (1949): "Provocation is some act, or series of acts, done by the dead man to the accused, which would cause in any reasonable man, and actually causes in the accused, a sudden and temporary loss of self-control, rendering the accused so subject to passion as to make him or her for the moment not master of his mind." On the other hand, the defence is not based upon any theory that the accused's state of passion was inconsistent with the formation of malice aforethought, and therefore it is no answer to the defence to prove that the accused formed the deliberate intention to kill (*Lee Chun-Chuen* v. *The Queen* (1963), P.C.; *R.* v. *Martindale* (1966) C.-M.A.C.; remarks of Viscount Simon in *Holmes's* case (*supra*) on this question cannot now be supported, if they were intended to indicate a contrary view).

The following propositions appear to be established at common law and to be unaffected by the Act of 1957 (and, indeed, to some extent to be incorporated into the wording of section 3): (i) The provocation must have come from the person at whom the act of retaliation was aimed. This does not necessarily involve that the provoker should have been the person killed, however. Thus if A provokes B, who in striking back at A inadvertently kills C, the killing of C will be merely manslaughter if the killing of A would have been so (*R.* v. *Gross* (1913)). (ii) The provocation must have been directed against the accused or, possibly, someone near and dear to him, such as his daughter (*R.* v. *Harrington* (1866) (the point was not decided); see also *R.* v. *Porritt* (1961), C.C.A.). (iii) The killing must have been done in the heat of the moment, or, as the expression is, before the lapse of sufficient cooling time to enable a reasonable man to regain his self-control (*Mancini* v. *D.P.P.* (1942), H.L.). (iv) There must have been a reasonable proportion between the provocation and the act of retaliation (*ibid.*).

As we have seen, provocation, to reduce a homicide from murder to manslaughter, must have been sufficient to deprive a reasonable man of his self-control. The expression "reasonable man" for this purpose means a normal man in a normal condition. No allowance therefore may be made for the fact that the individual accused was sexually impotent, and that therefore a particular taunt directed at him would have a more provocative effect upon him than the same taunt would have upon a normal man (*Bedder* v. *D.P.P.* (1954), H.L.). Similarly, no special allowance may be made for the fact that the individual accused was drunk at the time and therefore more readily lost his self-control than he would have done had he been sober (*R.* v. *McCarthy* (1954), C.C.A.). Interesting questions will arise when the courts have to decide whether the notional reasonable man can be a West Indian or Nigerian immigrant or whether he must be assumed to be a native Englishman for this purpose.

It should be noticed that provocation is a possible defence only to a charge of murder, and that even so it merely reduces the homicide to manslaughter: it cannot render the homicide lawful. Hence provocation is not a possible defence to a charge of unlawful wounding, although it may mitigate the sentence (*R.* v. *Cunningham* (1959), C.C.A.) and it must be carefully distinguished from the defence of self-defence, which can render even a homicide lawful. Provocation is pleaded when a homicide was *retaliatory,* and not in genuine self-defence.

Evidence

If there is any evidence of provocation worthy of consideration by the jury, it is for the prosecution to negative the defence, and not for the prisoner to establish it. Moreover, in such circumstances it is the duty of the trial judge to direct the jury as to the law of provocation whether or not the prisoner or his counsel expressly puts forward that defence. But if there is no evidence of provocation which could satisfy the rules given above, it is no part of the duty of the trial judge to tell the jury of this defence (*Mancini* v. *D.P.P.* (1942), H.L.).

Other forms of voluntary manslaughter

We have seen already (Chap. 4) that the accused's diminished responsibility may reduce what may have been murder to manslaughter. This is a form of voluntary manslaughter. Another form occurs when, in pursuance of a suicide pact, one person is killed, but another survives (see below).

(B) Involuntary Manslaughter

Assuming that there is no sufficient evidence of malice aforethought to justify a charge of murder, involuntary manslaughter is committed when a homicide results from the performance of a lawful act done with gross (or, criminal) negligence, or an unlawful act of a dangerous character. The law was so summarized by Humphreys J. in giving the judgment of the Court of Criminal Appeal in *R.* v. *Larkin* (1943).

Criminal negligence

The nature of criminal negligence was considered by the House of Lords in *Andrews* v. *D.P.P.* (1937). In his judgment Lord Atkin said: "Simple lack of care such as will constitute civil liability is not enough: for purposes of the criminal law there are degrees of negligence; and a very high degree of negligence is required to be proved before the [criminal offence] is established. Probably of all the epithets that can be applied, 'reckless' most nearly covers the case . . . but it is probably not all-embracing, for "reckless" suggests an indifference to risk whereas the accused may have appreciated the risk and intended to avoid it and yet shown such a high degree of negligence in the means adopted to avoid the risk as would justify a conviction." Lord Atkin gave general approval to words used by Lord Hewart C.J. in the earlier case of *R*. v. *Bateman* (1925), C.C.A.: "whatever epithet be used and whether an epithet be used or not, in order to establish criminal liability the facts must be such that, in the opinion of the jury, the negligence of the accused went beyond a mere matter of compensation between subjects and showed such disregard for the life and safety of others as to amount to a crime against the State and conduct deserving punishment. . . ."

The wide variety of circumstances in which the question may arise is illustrated by these two cases of *Bateman* and *Andrews*. In *Bateman's* case the charge of manslaughter was brought against a doctor on the ground of his alleged negligence in the treatment of a woman at the birth of her child, in consequence of which the mother had died. *Andrews'* case was one of motoring manslaughter, *i.e.*, the accused was alleged to have caused the death of another through the dangerous driving of a motor car. Part of the decision in *Andrews'* case is that on a charge of motoring manslaughter it would be a misdirection to tell the jury that, if the jury were satisfied that the accused had caused the death of the deceased by driving his car dangerously (an offence under the Road Traffic Act), they would have no alternative but to convict of manslaughter. The fact that the accused was committing an offence against the Road Traffic Act does not, for this purpose, convert the essentially lawful act of driving into an unlawful act of a dangerous character. In this type of case criminal negligence must always be proved to justify a conviction of manslaughter.

Unlawful act of a dangerous character

If death results from the performance of an unlawful act of a dangerous character, the homicide is manslaughter (unless, of course, the commission of the act shows malice aforethought, in which case it is murder). At one time it was the law that manslaughter was committed by causing death as the result of *any* unlawful act, but in modern times the rule has become narrowed. An act is of a dangerous character for this purpose if any reasonable person would recognize the act as involving the risk of causing some bodily harm, albeit not serious bodily harm (*R*. v. *Church* (1966), C.C.A.). In these circumstances manslaughter is committed even if the homicide is inadvertent. Thus in *Larkin's* case (*supra*) the deceased woman had met her death as the result of her throat having been cut by a razor which belonged to the accused and which was in the accused's hand when she received the cut. The accused's evidence was that he was flourishing the open razor for the purpose of frightening another person. Oliver J. directed the jury as follows: "A man who rushes into a house flourishing a naked razor and wounds someone, even accidentally, is still guilty of manslaughter if that person dies." Flourishing an open razor in a hostile manner is an act of assault, and it is clearly dangerous. In the very similar case of *R.* v. *Hall* (1961) the prisoner followed his wife and a man with whom he believed she was associating; he had taken with him a sharp knife, and whilst searching for the couple he carried this knife unsheathed. His purpose he said was merely to frighten his wife and the man. He found the man, and the two of them walked towards one another; soon afterwards the man received a deep wound from the knife from which he died. In directing the jury Sachs J. said: "If when he went into the car park and produced that knife the intention in his mind was to use it for the unlawful purpose of terrifying his wife and this man that alone might well amount to an assault. And if in consequence of his having produced this knife he accidentally stabbed Wood with it then I direct you as a mattter of law that that is manslaughter." In both these cases convictions were upheld by the Court of Criminal Appeal.

An actual intent to commit the assault in question is, however, required. Thus in *R.* v. *Lamb* (1967), C.A., the accused in jest, with no intention of doing harm, pointed a revolver at his friend. The revolver had a five-chambered cylinder, which rotated each time the trigger was pulled, and it had two bullets in the chambers, although neither bullet was in the chamber opposite the barrel. Nevertheless, unknown to the accused, the effect of pulling the trigger was to rotate the cylinder before the striking pin operated so that when he pulled the trigger a bullet was brought opposite the barrel and this killed his friend. The Court of Appeal held that without an element of intent there can be no assault. Therefore, as, on these facts, the accused did not have an intent, his act was not unlawful and his conviction of manslaughter on this ground was quashed. Whether, on these facts, he could be guilty of manslaughter by criminal negligence was not, however, decided (although his conviction of manslaughter by criminal negligence was quashed because of a misdirection to the jury).

Homicide by Dangerous or Reckless Driving

The difficulty of persuading juries to convict of manslaughter in motoring cases led to the introduction in 1956 of a statutory offence of homicide which is now in section 1 of the Road Traffic Act 1960.

This is causing the death of another by driving a motor vehicle on a road recklessly or at a speed or in a manner which is dangerous to the public; it is an offence (m) punishable with a maximum of five years' imprisonment.

Despite the seriousness of this offence it has been held by the Court of Criminal Appeal in *R. v. Evans* (1963) and in *R. v. Ball and Loughlin* (1966) that on a charge of homicide by dangerous driving *mens rea* is unnecessary. The only questions are whether the accused was driving dangerously in fact and whether that dangerous driving caused the death of the deceased. In *R. v. Evans* it was stated that if the accused was driving dangerously in fact "it matters not whether he was deliberately reckless, careless, momentarily inattentive or even doing his incompetent best," while the decision in *R. v. Ball and Loughlin* shows that an accused may also be liable even if he was personally blameless.

Infanticide

By the Infanticide Act 1938 the offence of infanticide (f) is committed when a woman by any wilful act or omission causes the death of her child being under the age of twelve months, but at the time of the act or omission the balance of her mind was disturbed by reason of her not having fully recovered from the effect of giving birth to the child or of lactation consequent upon the birth. The offence is punishable with a maximum of life imprisonment.

This offence was introduced in 1922 (and re-enacted in an improved form in the Act of 1938); the purpose of the enactment is to remove such a homicide from the law of murder, into which it would otherwise fall. The punishment is not fixed by law, as in the case of murder, and is therefore within the discretion of the trial judge. It is not, of course, necessary that the mental disturbance should have amounted to insanity.

Suicide

At common law suicide when sane was self-murder. This principle, though of no interest to one who committed *felonia de se*, had important legal consequences. It followed that any attempt or incitement or conspiracy to commit suicide was a common law misdemeanour. Much more serious, if two persons entered into a suicide pact and one of them survived, he was guilty of murder. If he had himself killed the deceased, he was guilty as principal in the first degree; if he had aided and abetted the commission of the suicide by the deceased, and given his assistance or encouragement at the time, he was a principal in the second degree; if by some prior act he had instigated or encouraged the commission of the suicide by the deceased, he was guilty as an accessory before the fact. Similar principles applied if he had been a party to the killing of the deceased by a third person, and here again he would be guilty of murder.

The position was first modified by section 4 of the Homicide Act 1957, which provided that it should be manslaughter, and not murder, for a person acting in pursuance of a suicide pact between him and another to kill the other or be a party to the other killing himself or being killed by a third person; the burden, on a charge of murder, of proving a suicide pact was placed upon the accused, and it was provided that a suicide pact meant a common agreement between two or more persons having for its object the death of all of them, whether or not each was to take his own life. But nothing done by a person who entered into a suicide pact was to be treated as done by him in pursuance of the pact unless it was done while he had the settled intention of dying in pursuance of the pact.

The Suicide Act 1961, section 1, then provided that the rule of law whereby it was a crime for a person to commit suicide was abrogated; but the statute made it an offence punishable with a maximum of fourteen years' imprisonment for a person to aid, abet, counsel or procure the suicide of another, or an attempt by another to commit suicide. This offence imports that the other has in fact committed suicide or has attempted to do so, and incitement or attempt to commit suicide, of itself, is no longer criminal. (Conspiracy to commit suicide may, perhaps, still be criminal, because the object of a conspiracy need not be criminal: see *post*, Chap. 23.) Section 4 of the Homicide Act 1957 was amended so as to exempt from manslaughter the survivor of a suicide pact who had merely been a party to the deceased's killing himself. Today, therefore, the survivor of a suicide pact is not guilty of manslaughter unless he himself killed the deceased or was a party to the deceased's being killed by a third person.

The leave of the Director of Public Prosecutions is required before a prosecution can be brought for the offence of aiding, abetting, etc., the suicide or attempted suicide of another.

Child Destruction

By the Infant Life (Preservation) Act 1929 this offence (f) is committed when any person, with intent to destroy the life of a child capable of being born alive, by any wilful act causes a child to die before it has an existence independent of its mother; provided that the prosecution must prove that the act was not done in good faith for the purpose only of preserving the mother's life. The offence is punishable with a maximum of life imprisonment. It is provided that evidence that a woman has been pregnant for 28 weeks or more shall be prima facie proof that she was at that time pregnant of a child capable of being born alive.

The offence is not one of homicide properly speaking, because, as we have seen, homicide involves the killing of a person who has been born alive. The common law in fact had no specific offence covering the killing of a child in the womb or during the process of birth: hence the enactment in question.

It will be observed that this offence cannot be committed during the earlier stages of pregnancy, because the child must have reached the stage at which it was capable of birth alive. The offence should be contrasted with that of procuring or attempting to procure miscarriage, *infra*.

It seems clear from the statutory definition that the *mens rea* required (intent to destroy the life of a child capable of being born alive) is not transferable: the offence would not be committed if the accused's intention was to injure the woman without any thought of injuring the child in her womb, even if in fact some injury inflicted upon the woman caused the child's death before it had an existence independent of the woman.

The meaning of the expression "preserving the mother's life" was considered in *R*. v. *Bourne* (1939). In that case, a young girl had become pregnant in consequence of the commission of a rape upon her, and the accused, a medical man of the highest repute, had performed an operation upon her for the purpose of terminating the pregnancy. When he was indicted for the offence of procuring a miscarriage the defence was that there would have been a danger to the girl's health if she had had to bear the child, and it was contended that a distinction should not be drawn between danger to life and danger to health. The trial judge directed the jury that "If pregnancy is likely to make the woman a physical or mental wreck, the jury is entitled to take the view that a doctor who, in these circumstances, and led by his belief, operates, is operating for the purpose of preserving the life of the woman." The jury acquitted. Moreover, although the charge in *R*. v. *Bourne* was procuring a miscarriage and this offence is now subject to the Abortion Act 1967, the case is still relevant in connection with child destruction.

Use of Poisons and Instruments to cause Miscarriage

This offence (f) is committed when any person. with intent to procure the miscarriage of a woman, whether or not she be with child, unlawfully administers to her or causes to be taken by her any poison or other noxious thing, or unlawfully uses any instrument or other means with the like intent. A like offence is committed if a woman who is with child commits similar acts upon herself with intent to procure her own miscarriage; but the woman must in fact be pregnant. The offence is punishable with a maximum of life imprisonment (Offences against the Person Act 1861, s. 58), and is often known as attempting to procure abortion.

The expression "any poison or other noxious thing" includes a recognized poison or any substance which is harmful in the quantity in which it is in fact administered (*R.* v. *Cramp* (1880), C.C.R. (oil of juniper)); it need not be an abortifacient (*R.* v. *Marlow* (1964)). If the accused erroneously supposes the substance to be noxious it may be that he is guilty of an attempt to commit the offence in question.

The expression "any instrument or other means" is not limited to instruments that are in fact capable of procuring a miscarriage and has been held to include the fingers of the hand (*R.* v. *Spicer* (1955)).

As the statutory definition makes plain, if the acts are done upon a woman by some other person with the requisite intent, the offence is committed even if the woman is not pregnant in fact; and in such circumstances the woman, if a consenting party, is guilty of the offence as an aider and abettor (*R.* v. *Sockett* (1908), C.C.A.). If the acts are done by the woman upon herself, and she erroneously supposes herself to be pregnant, she is, it seeems, guilty of an attempt to commit the offence. (The point appears to be undecided.)

The Abortion Act 1967, s. 1(1), provides that a person shall not be guilty of an offence under section 58 "when a pregnancy is terminated by a registered medical practitioner if two registered medical practitioners are of the opinion, formed in good faith (*a*) that the continuance of the pregnancy would involve risk to the life of the pregnant woman, or of injury to the physical or mental health of the pregnant woman or any existing children of her family, greater than if the pregnancy were terminated; or (*b*) that there is a substantial risk that if the child were born it would suffer from such physical or mental abnormalities as to be seriously handicapped." Moreover, in determining whether the continuance of a pregnancy would involve such risk of injury to health as is mentioned in (*a*) above, "account may be taken of the pregnant woman's actual or reasonably forseeable environment" (s. 1(2)). (See also s. 1(4) where the termination is "immediately necessary".) Apart from these provisions, however, anything done with intent to procure the miscarriage of a woman is unlawfully done (*ibid.*, s. 5(2)). *R.* v. *Bourne, supra,* no longer applies to this offence, but is still relevant in connection with child destruction.

It is also an offence (m), punishable with a maximum of five years' imprisonment, unlawfully to supply or procure any poison or other noxious thing, or any instrument or thing, knowing that the same is intended to be unlawfully used or employed with intent to procure the miscarriage of any woman, whether or not she be with child (Offences against the Person Act 1861, s. 59). To "procure" an instrument means to obtain possession of it from another; the word does not cover taking an instrument out of a cupboard where it is already in one's possession (*R.* v. *Mills* (1963), C.C.A.). The Abortion Act 1967 applies to this offence as it applies to an offence under section 58.

Concealment of Birth

It is an offence (m), punishable with a maximum of two years' imprisonment, to endeavour to conceal the birth of a child by any secret disposition of its dead body, whether the child died before, at, or after its birth (Offences against the Person Act 1861, s. 60).

It may also be mentioned here that any disposition of a corpse with intent to obstruct or prevent a coroner's inquest when one ought to be held is a common law offence (m) (*R.* v. *Stephenson* (1884)).

Chapter Eight

SEXUAL OFFENCES

(IN this chapter all references to sections are to the Sexual Offences Act 1956 (a consolidating Act), unless otherwise indicated).

Rape

The offence (f) of rape, which is punishable with a maximum of life imprisonment (s. 1; Sched. 2), consists of having sexual intercourse with a woman or girl without her consent.

For the act of sexual intercourse itself it is not necessary to prove the completion of the intercourse by the emission of seed, but the intercourse is deemed complete upon proof of penetration only (section 44). (The same rule applies for all offences under the Act which require sexual intercourse, natural or unnatural.)

In the following cases the woman or girl is not a consenting party, although there may be some appearance of consent on her part:

(1) When her submission is obtained by threats which overbear her will.

(2) When a man induces a married woman to have sexual intercourse with him by impersonating her husband (section 1).

(3) When the consent of the woman or girl is obtained by fraud which induces in her mind a mistake of a fundamental character—it must probably be a mistake as the nature of the act (see *R.* v. *Clarence* (1888), C.C.R.), as in *R.* v. *Williams* (1923), C.C.A., in which a singing master induced a girl to have intercourse with him by pretending to her that the act was part of the normal breathing exercises.

(4) When a man has intercourse with a woman or girl while she is asleep (*R.* v. *Mayers* (1872)) or insensible through drink (*R.* v. *Camplin* (1845)).

66

(5) When a man has intercourse with a girl who is too young to give a true consent (*R.* v. *Howard* (1966), C.C.A.), or with a woman or girl who is too defective mentally to be able to do so (*R.* v. *Fletcher* (1859), C.C.R.).

It is submitted that in cases of extreme youth, drunkenness, and mental deficiency, as in cases of fraud, the test should be whether the woman or girl was able to understand the character of the act, but it cannot be said that the cases uniformly establish such a rule. (See, *e.g.*, *R.* v. *Fletcher* (1886), C.C.R. (held, a valid consent can be given by an idiot girl through mere animal instinct).)

The law of rape is supplemented by numerous other offences in the Sexual Offences Act 1956 of which we can do no more than mention a few here, and that only briefly. Examples are:

(1) It is an offence (m) for a man to have unlawful sexual intercourse with a woman or girl who is mentally defective. The woman's or girl's consent, even if a true consent, is no defence to this charge, but it is a defence that the accused did not know and had no reason to suspect that the woman was a defective. (For the meaning of "unlawful" sexual intercourse in this and the following offences see *post,* "Abduction.") The offence is punishable with a maximum of two years' imprisonment (Sexual Offences Act 1956, s. 7, as substituted by the Mental Health Act 1959, s. 127; Sched. 2 of the 1956 Act). A "defective" for this purpose is one who suffers from severe abnormality within the meaning of the Act of 1959 (Act of 1956, s. 45, as substituted by section 127 of the 1959 Act).

(2) It is an offence (m), punishable with a maximum of two years' imprisonment, to procure a woman or girl by threats or intimidation, or by false pretences or representations, to have unlawful sexual intercourse in any part of the world (ss. 2, 3). (As we have seen, *supra*, threats, etc. *can* have the effect of vitiating the woman's or girl's consent, in which case rape has been committed.)

(3) It is an offence (m), similarly punishable, to procure a girl under the age of twenty-one to have unlawful sexual intercourse in any part of the world with a third person (s. 23). The word "procure" here implies that sexual intercourse has taken place, but, if it has not, a conviction of attempt to procure is possible in appropriate circumstances (*R.* v. *Johnson* (1964), C.C.A.).

(4) The administration to a woman or girl of any drug, matter or thing with intent to stupefy or overpower her so as thereby to enable any man to have unlawful sexual intercourse with her is also an offence (m), similarly punishable (s. 4).

(5) It is an offence (f), punishable with a maximum of life imprisonment, to have unlawful sexual intercourse with a girl who is under the age of thirteen (s. 5).

(6) It is an offence (m), punishable with a maximum of two years' imprisonment, to have unlawful sexual intercourse with a girl who is under the age of sixteen (s. 6). It is not generally a defence to a charge of this offence that the accused believed that the girl had attained the age of sixteen, but if at the time the accused was under the age of twenty-four and had not previously been charged with a like offence, it is a defence that he believed the girl to be of the age of sixteen or over and had reasonable cause for the belief. (The defence has been allowed on a charge of an attempt to commit the offence (*R*. v. *Collier* (1960).) The expression "a like offence" is defined by the section to mean unlawful sexual intercourse with a girl who is under sixteen or an attempt to commit such an offence. It is also provided that where a marriage is invalid by reason of the fact that the wife was a girl under the age of sixteen at the date of the ceremony, the husband shall not be guilty of an offence because he has sexual intercourse with the girl if he believes her to be his wife and has reasonable cause for the belief. A girl under sixteen cannot be indicted for abetting a man to have unlawful sexual intercourse with her, or of incitement, even if in fact she was a consenting party (*R*. v. *Tyrrell* (1894), C.C.R.).

Indecent Assault

It is an offence (m) to commit an indecent assault on a woman (s. 14) (two years' imprisonment as a maximum) or a man (s. 15) (ten years' imprisonment as a maximum). A boy or girl under the age of sixteen cannot in law give a consent which would prevent an act being an assault for this purpose; but where a marriage is invalid because the wife was a girl under the age of sixteen at the time of the ceremony the invalidity does not make the husband guilty of an indecent assault upon her by reason of her incapacity to consent while under the age of sixteen, if he believes her to be his wife and has reasonable grounds for the belief (s. 15). In other circumstances it is not a defence that the accused believed that the girl had attained the age of sixteen; the special defence given to a man under the age of twenty-four on a charge of unlawful sexual intercourse with a girl who is under the age of sixteen (see above), has no application to a charge of indecent assault (*R*. v. *Maughan* (1934), C.C.A.).

An indecent assault is an assault accompanied by circumstances of indecency on the part of the accused towards the person alleged to have been assaulted (*Beal* v. *Kelley* (1951), D.C.). It is an indecent assault therefore if a man asks a boy to touch him in an indecent manner and upon the boy's refusing he pulls him towards himself (*ibid*), but not if he makes no movement of a hostile nature towards the boy, because there will then be no assault (*Fairclough* v. *Whipp* (1951), D.C. (the victim was a girl); see also *D.P.P.* v. *Rogers* (1953), D.C.). When it became clearly established that an indecent invitation, unaccompanied by any hostile gesture, could not amount to an indecent assault, the Indecency with Children Act 1960 was passed which makes it an offence (m), punishable with a maximum of two years' imprisonment, for a person to commit an act of gross indecency with or towards a child under the age of fourteen, or to incite a child under that age to such an act with him or another.

Abduction

There are various offences of abduction and child-stealing in the Sexual Offences Act 1956 and the Offences against the Person Act 1861. Of these, two may be mentioned here by way of example:

(1) It is an offence (m), punishable with a maximum of two years' imprisonment, to take an unmarried girl under the age of eighteen out of the possession of her parent or guardian against his will, if she is so taken with the intention that she shall have unlawful sexual intercourse, *i.e.*, intercourse outside matrimony (*R.* v. *Chapman* (1959), C.C.A.). It is a defence that the accused honestly and reasonably believed the girl to have attained the age of eighteen. (Sexual Offences Act 1956, s. 19.)

(2) It is an offence (m), similarly punishable, for a person acting without lawful authority or excuse to take an unmarried girl under the age of sixteen out of the possession of her parent or guardian against his will. (It is somewhat strange that this offence is contained in the Sexual Offences Act 1956 (s. 20), because it does not necessarily involve any sexual element.) It is a defence that the accused did not know and had no reason to know that the girl was under the lawful care or charge of a parent or guardian (*R.* v. *Hibbert* (1869), C.C.R.), but it is no defence that the accused honestly and reasonably believed that she had attained the age of sixteen (*R.* v. *Prince* (1875), C.C.R.).

Incest

It is an offence (m), punishable with a maximum of seven years' imprisonment, for a man to have sexual intercourse with a woman whom he knows to be his grand-daughter, daughter, sister (including half-sister) or mother, or for a woman of the age of sixteen or over to permit a man whom she knows to be her grandfather, father, brother (including half-brother) or son to have sexual intercourse with her by her consent. It is not necessary that the relationship should be traced through lawful wedlock. (Sexual Offences Act 1956, ss. 10, 11.) The leave of the Attorney-General is usually necessary before a prosecution can be brought for this offence unless the prosecution is initiated by or on behalf of the Director of Public Prosecutions (section 37).

Buggery

It is an offence (m), punishable with a maximum of ten years' imprisonment, for a person to commit buggery with another person or with an animal (Sexual Offences Act 1956, s. 12). The offence consists of sexual intercourse *per anum* by man with man or by man with woman or sexual intercourse by man or woman in any manner with an animal. (See Archbold, *Criminal Pleading, Evidence and Practice* (37th ed.), para. 2968, and authorities there cited.) Nevertheless, the Sexual Offences Act 1967, s. 1, provides that an act of buggery or gross indecency between two men shall not be an offence provided it is in private, the parties consent and they have both attained the age of twenty-one.

Gross Indecency

It is an offence (m), punishable with a maximum of two years' imprisonment, for a man to commit an act of gross indecency with another man, whether in public or in private, or to procure the commission by a man of an act of gross indecency with another man (s. 13), although this is also subject to section 1 of the Sexual Offences Act 1967, *supra.*

It may also be noticed here that all acts of open indecency are common law offences (m) (Archbold, para. 2997; and see *Shaw* v. *D.P.P.* (1962) in C.C.A. and H.L.), and such acts are often punishable as summary offences under the Vagrancy Act 1824 and under local enactments.

Chapter Nine

ASSAULT

(A) At Common Law

THE word "assault" is used by lawyers in a narrow sense and in a wider sense. In the narrow sense an assault is any movement, or gesture, which is intended, and does, cause another to apprehend immediate and unlawful personal violence. In the wider sense the term "assault" includes a battery, *i.e.*, the unlawful application of force to the person of another (and of course in the popular sense the word "assault" is synonymous with battery). Administering (without violence) a noxious substance to another is not an assault (*R.* v. *Walkden* (1845) ("Spanish fly" mixed with bridal party's ale)). It is often stated that unlawful imprisonment also is an assault; it is in any event a common law offence (m).

It will be observed that an assault requires some movement, or gesture. Words alone therefore cannot constitute an assault. (See *ante*, Chap. 8, "Indecent Assault." For possible qualifications to this see Smith and Hogan, *Criminal Law* (2nd ed.), p. 251.) But words which accompany a gesture may be very relevant either as showing that the gesture has a hostile character, or as depriving it of that character which otherwise it would possess (as in the well-known case of *Tuberville* v. *Savage* (1669) in which a man angrily put his hand upon the hilt of his sword, but accompanied this apparently hostile gesture with the words "If it were not assize time I would not take such language from you"). For an assault in the narrower sense it is not, it seems, necessary that the accused should have intended to inflict a battery upon the other person. Thus it appears to be an assault for A to point a firearm at another in a hostile manner with the intention, and effect, of causing him alarm, even if A knows that the firearm is unloaded (*R.* v. *St. George* (1840); *Blake* v. *Barnard* (1840), sometimes cited as being to the contrary, appears not to be inconsistent with this decision: the case (a civil one) turned on the pleadings). It would not, however, be an assault to point even a loaded firearm at another if that other were obviously out of range (see *Stephens* v. *Myers* (1830) or it was

71

pointed in jest (*R.* v. *Lamb* (1967), C.A.).

The commission of a battery may often be justified, and many of the principles have already been considered in connection with homicide. A parent or schoolmaster may also lawfully use force in the infliction of moderate chastisement upon a child. In general, the same defences apply to a criminal prosecution for assault as are applicable to civil proceedings for trespass to the person. They do, however, differ upon the question of how far the consent of the person assaulted is a defence. In both instances consent is not a defence unless it has been freely and voluntarily given. For example, as we have seen in discussing the offence of rape, a submission to intimidation is not a consent, and fraud which has induced a mistake of a fundamental character vitiates consent. But whereas a true consent is always a defence to a civil action, it is not always a defence to a criminal prosecution: it is not a defence to an assault which occasions, or is likely to occasion, actual bodily harm (*R.* v. *Donovan* (1934), C.C.A. (indecent caning of girl); consent of a boy or girl *under sixteen* is in any event not a defence to *indecent* assault: *ante* Chap. 8). Bodily harm means harm that interferes with health or comfort, at any rate if it is not merely transient and trifling (*R.* v. *Donovan, supra*), and includes the causing of an hysterical and nervous condition (*R.* v. *Miller* (1954)). It is true that the participants in manly sports or diversions, conducted with proper safeguards, may lawfully incur the risk of bodily harm, but the consent of the participants is but one of the reasons why the common law permits this: the overriding consideration is that the balance of public advantage lies in allowing such activities (see *R.* v. *Coney* (1882), C.C.R., and *R.* v. *Donovan, supra*). Similar considerations apply to surgical operations performed for legitimate reasons (see *Bravery* v. *Bravery* (1954), C.A.).

(B) Statutory Provisions

There are a number of statutory provisions with regard to assault; of these we may notice three, which are contained in the Offences against the Person Act 1861:

(1) It is an offence (f) (punishable with a maximum of life imprisonment) unlawfully and maliciously to wound or cause any grievous bodily harm to any person, with intent to do some grievous bodily harm to any person or resist or prevent the lawful apprehension or detainer of any person (s. 18). This offence is commonly known as "wounding with intent." Prior to the Criminal Law Act

1967, section 18 expressly provided that the accused should have intended "to maim, disfigure, or disable any person, or to do some other grievous bodily harm to any person . . . ," and many of the older cases are concerned with the definition of these terms. Since Schedule 3 of the 1967 Act has repealed these provisions, however, it is no longer necessary to consider these matters; nevertheless, these former provisions must be borne in mind when reading the older cases.

(2) It is an offence (m) (punishable with a maximum of five years' imprisonment) unlawfully and maliciously to wound or inflict any grievous bodily harm upon any other person (section 20). This offence is commonly known as "unlawful wounding," or as "malicious wounding."

(3) Assault occasioning actual bodily harm is an offence (m), punishable with a maximum of five years' imprisonment (s. 47).

Several of the terms used in these definitions require explanation.

Maliciously. This word always has the same meaning whenever it is used in a criminal statute. It means intention to do the particular kind of harm that is in fact done, or recklessness as to whether such harm will occur or not (*i.e.*, the accused must have foreseen that the particular kind of harm might be done and yet have gone on to take the risk of causing it). This meaning of the word was established by the Court of Criminal Appeal in *R.* v. *Cunningham* (1957), C.C.A. In that case the accused was charged with unlawfully and maliciously causing a noxious thing, namely coal-gas, to be taken by another person, so as thereby to endanger the life of that person, contrary to section 23 of the Offences against the Person Act 1861. The accused had broken open a gas meter in a house in order to steal the contents. In so doing he had inadvertently fractured a gas main, with the result that coal-gas had penetrated the house next door and been inhaled by an occupant of that house. The trial judge directed the jury that the word "malicious" meant "wicked," and the jury convicted. The conviction was quashed by the Court of Criminal Appeal on the ground that the judge had misdirected the jury in law. The offence could not be committed in such circumstances unless the accused had at least foreseen that the removal of the gas meter might cause injury to someone; the intent to steal could not of itself show the required malice. If therefore a person should throw a stone at a window and inadvertently wound a passer-by, he could not be convicted of unlawful and malicious wounding. (Compare *R.* v. *Pembliton* (1874), C.C.R. (see "malicious damage," *post* Chap. 18).) On the other hand in *R.* v. *Latimer* (1886), C.C.R., in which the accused aimed a blow at one person, but, missing his aim, wounded another, he was rightly convicted of unlawfully and maliciously wounding that other; bodily injury to one person is the same kind of harm as bodily injury to another.

To wound means to cause a breach of the whole skin; breaking the internal skin, *e.g.*, within the mouth, is sufficient. (See Archbold, *Criminal Practice, Pleading and Evidence*, 37th edition, para. 2656.)

Grievous bodily harm means any really serious bodily harm (*D.P.P.* v. *Smith* (1961), H.L.; *R.* v. *Metharam* (1961), C.C.A.).

The word *inflict* in section 20 does not include *infecting* another with disease. Thus a married man who knows, as his wife does not know, that he is suffering from venereal disease and who infects his wife by having sexual intercourse with her cannot be convicted of this offence; nor can he be convicted of an assault occasioning bodily harm under section 47, because there is no assault in such circumstances (*R.* v. *Clarence* (1888), C.C.R.). On the other hand, when a wife in order to escape from the threatened violence of her husband gets out of a window, falls, and breaks her leg, the husband can be convicted under section 20 of inflicting grievous bodily harm upon her (*R.* v. *Halliday* (1889), C.C.R.); alternatively he could be convicted under section 47 of an assault occasioning actual bodily harm (*R.* v. *Coleman* (1920)).

It will be observed that, whereas the only *mens rea* required for a charge under section 20 is statutory malice (*i.e.*, an intent to cause the *kind* of harm in question), section 18 of the Act requires, not only statutory malice, but also the specific intent to do some grievous bodily harm, or resist an arrest. Thus, if A slaps B's face without intent to do him grievous bodily harm, but he does in fact inflict grievous bodily harm, he has only committed an offence under section 20. In practice, it is only in grave cases that the prosecution presses a charge under section 18, and this factor, rather than any theoretical consideration, is likely to determine whether the accused is convicted under the one section or the other.

Chapter Ten

BIGAMY

BIGAMY, which is an offence (f) punishable with a maximum of seven years' imprisonment, is committed when any person "being married shall marry any other person during the life of the former husband or wife" (Offences against the Person Act 1861, s. 57).

It will be convenient on this occasion to consider what matters must be proved by the prosecution, and then the possible lines of defence open to the accused.

To prove a prima facie case of bigamy, the prosecution must adduce satisfactory evidence of the following:

(1) *The first marriage and its validity*

On a charge of bigamy strict proof of the first marriage is required. The prosecution must prove the solemnization of the ceremony itself, and that that ceremony to all appearances gave rise to a valid marriage. Proof that the parties cohabited and were generally known as husband and wife (which suffices to prove a marriage for most purposes) is not sufficient (*Morris* v. *Miller* (1767)). (Proof by certified copy of the marriage register and evidence of the identity of the parties is the usual method. See generally Archbold, paras. 3769 ff.) It is not, however, necessary that in each case the prosecution should expressly disprove every possible ground of invalidity of a marriage, which would be an impossible task.

A marriage contracted under polygamous law is not, it seems, sufficient (*R.* v. *Sarwan Singh* (1962), Q.S.). But a voidable marriage (*e.g.*, where one of the parties lacks sexual capacity) ranks as a valid marriage until annulled by a decree of nullity made by a court of competent jurisdiction: it is possible that such a decree affords a defence even if it had not been made at the date of the second ceremony, if it has been made before the prosecution for bigamy (see *infra* under "Defences"). A void marriage, *e.g.*, where one of the parties was already married to some other person, needs no decree of nullity to make it invalid, and it will not support a charge of bigamy.

75

(2) *The second ceremony with someone other than the lawful spouse*

This ceremony must be one which, by the law of the place of celebration, is capable of producing a valid marriage in some circumstances, but not necessarily the circumstances of the parties: it is, therefore, no defence to a charge of bigamy that the parties to the second ceremony were within the prohibited degrees of relationship (*R.* v. *Allen* (1872), C.C.R.), or that the parties had failed to fulfil some residence qualification imposed by the local law (*R.* v. *Robinson* (1938), C.C.A.). Indeed such circumstances are matters rather of aggravation than of defence; bigamy is punished primarily by reason of the abuse of the marriage ceremony, and in such circumstances the ceremony has been doubly abused.

A British subject may be tried here for bigamy committed abroad (s. 57; *Earl Russell's* case (1901), H.L.). "British subject" here will usually be limited to a citizen of the United Kingdom and Colonies (British Nationality Act 1948, s. 3). It is uncertain whether in this case a second ceremony contracted under polygamous law will suffice.

(3) *That at the date of the second ceremony the lawful spouse was still alive*

This is entirely a matter of fact for the jury, who (by reason of the so-called presumption of continuance) may be willing to infer the fact from evidence that the lawful spouse was alive shortly before the second ceremony (*R.* v. *Lumley* (1869), C.C.R.). The presumption of continuance is a presumption "of fact", *i.e.*, one on which a jury may (not must) act.

Defences

The accused may, of course, adduce evidence to rebut the prosecution evidence on any of the above matters. In addition, the following defences are open to an accused person:

(1) That the prior marriage (if voidable) has been annulled by a decree of nullity granted by a competent court, or that at the date of the second ceremony the earlier marriage had been dissolved by a decree of divorce granted by a competent court (s. 57). The section expressly requires that the accused should have been divorced *at the time of the second marriage*, but does not expressly require that a decree of nullity should have been granted before the second marriage; as a nullity decree operates retrospectively for some purposes, it is possible that it suffices that the decree was granted before the prosecution for bigamy.

(2) That at the date of the second ceremony the lawful spouse

had been continuously absent from the accused for the space of seven years then last passed, and had not been known by the accused to be living within that time (s. 57). The statute in terms gives this defence to "any person marrying a second time." But the words "second time" merely refer to the ceremony upon which the charge of bigamy is based, and it is immaterial that that ceremony is in fact a third or subsequent ceremony. Thus, if after seven years' absence, without having heard of his wife, a man marries A, and then, still not having heard of his wife, he marries B, he has a defence to a charge of bigamy founded upon the ceremony with A or upon the ceremony with B (*R.* v. *Taylor* (1950), C.C.A., in which the Court refused to follow its own decision in *R.* v. *Treanor* (1939)). (This assumes that his wife was in fact still alive at the dates of the two ceremonies.) It should be carefully noticed that, even though the man has a defence to a charge of bigamy in respect of the ceremony with A, A did not become his lawful spouse, be-cause his wife was still alive at that time. The marriage with A, therefore, cannot be alleged as a valid marriage for the purpose of supporting a charge of bigamy based upon the ceremony with B.

If the accused adduces evidence of seven years' absence, it is for the prosecution to prove that at some time during that period the accused had known his spouse to be alive (*R.* v. *Curgerwen* (1865), C.C.R.).

(3) That at the date of the second ceremony the accused honestly and reasonably believed that his lawful spouse was dead. This is the common law defence of mistake of fact: had the facts been as the accused imagined them to be, he would not have been com-mitting the crime charged. It was held in the well-known case of *R.* v. *Tolson* (1889) C.C.R., that there is nothing in the language of the statute which requires the court to hold that the common law requirement of *mens rea* is excluded in this respect, and that there-fore such an honest and reasonable belief is a defence. It will be observed that the accused must have had reasonable grounds for his belief, *e.g.,* have made proper enquiries, or have received infor-mation from a trustworthy source supporting his belief.

(4) That at the date of the second ceremony the accused honestly and reasonably believed that the prior marriage was void, *e.g.,* because the other party was already married, provided that the mistake was one of fact, and not of law. After a number of con-flicting decisions it has now been established that the common law defence of mistake of fact applies in this instance also (*R.* v. *King* (1964), C.C.A.).

(5) That at the date of the second ceremony the accused honestly and reasonably believed that the first marriage had been dissolved by a decree of divorce. Again, after conflicting decisions, it has now been held that the common law defence of mistake applies in these circumstances (*R.* v. *Gould* (1968), C.A.).

Aiding and abetting

The other party to the second ceremony is also guilty of bigamy as an aider and abettor if he or she knows that the actual offender is already married. It seems that if the party who is already married has a defence to the charge of bigamy, the other party cannot be held guilty: he (or she) cannot be said to have aided and abetted an offence that has not in fact been committed by the party already married. Thus, it would seem that, if A, honestly and reasonably believing his lawful spouse, B, to be dead, marries C, who knows B to be alive, C could not be convicted of bigamy. However, some doubt is cast on this principle by *R.* v. *Bourne* (1952), C.C.A., which we have already considered in connection with "parties to a crime" (*ante*, Chap. 5).

Chapter Eleven

OFFENCES AGAINST PROPERTY

THE law relating to offences against property has been very substantially amended by the Theft Act 1968. Nevertheless, it will help towards an understanding of the present law if we consider first an outline of the law prior to this Act. Moreover, offences committed before January 1, 1969, when the Theft Act came into force, are still subject to the old law.

1. Before the Theft Act 1968

Larceny

Larceny was a generic term for those offences which had the common element of a stealing. Thus by section 1 of the Larceny Act 1916 a person stole who, without the consent of the owner, fraudulently and without a claim of right made in good faith, took and carried away anything capable of being stolen with intent, at the time of such taking, permanently to deprive the owner. Certain minor forms of larceny were also covered by the Larceny Act 1861.

Larceny was essentially an offence against possession and a person could not, therefore, normally steal what was already in his possession. However, there were certain qualifications to this principle, for example, a servant who received his master's property only had custody, not possession, and he could therefore steal the property; while section 1 of the Larceny Act 1916 expressly provided that a bailee or part-owner could commit larceny despite his already having possession of the property. Nevertheless, it was because a person could not normally steal property of which he was already in possession that the offences of embezzlement and fraudulent conversion were created (see below).

There was also another and equally important sense in which the crime of larceny was an offence against possession: larceny was not committed if the accused obtained the ownership (and not merely the possession) of the property. Thus, if the accused by a trick induced the other person to pass ownership he was not guilty

79

of larceny, and the courts held that ownership passed if the person who parted with the property had both the power and the intention to pass the ownership to the accused. Again, it was for this reason that the offence of obtaining by false pretences was created (see below).

To commit larceny, moreover, the accused must have taken and carried away the property and this meant that the accused must not only have seized, or grasped, the property but it must have been removed from the place which it occupied or, if it was attached (*i.e.*, to something else which was not taken), it must have been completely detached. We shall see that in the new offence of theft this requirement of taking and carrying away has been replaced by a new concept of appropriating the property.

Embezzlement

Embezzlement was committed when a clerk or servant fraudulently embezzled the whole or any part of any chattel, money or valuable security delivered to, or received, or taken into possession, by him for or in the name or on the account of his master or employer (Larceny Act 1916, s. 17).

As we have seen, when a servant received property from his master and this was in the master's possession, the servant only received custody of that property and he could therefore commit larceny in relation to it. However, when a servant received property from a third person for his master, and that property was not already in his master's possession, the servant obtained possession and not mere custody and could not, therefore, be convicted of larceny if he took that property for himself. For this reason the statutory offence of embezzlement was created.

Fraudulent conversion

Fraudulent conversion was committed when a person, who had been entrusted with any property in order to retain it in safe custody or to apply, pay or deliver it for any purpose or to any person, or who had received the property for or on account of any other person, fraudulently converted it to his own use or benefit, or to the use or benefit of another (Larceny Act 1916, s. 20).

Again the accused was already in possession of the property so that he could not be convicted of larceny, and for this reason the statutory offence of fraudulent conversion was created.

Obtaining by false pretences

Obtaining by false pretences was committed by every person who, by any false pretence, with intent to defraud, obtained from any other person any chattel, money, or valuable security or caused any money to be paid, or any chattel or valuable security to be delivered to himself or to any other person (Larceny Act 1916, s. 32).

As we have seen, an accused did not commit larceny if he obtained ownership of the property and not merely possession. However, obtaining by false pretences was committed when ownership was obtained and the offence was therefore complementary to larceny in this respect. Indeed, if the accused only obtained possession and not ownership he could not be convicted of obtaining by false pretences but was instead guilty of larceny, a form of larceny known as larceny by a trick.

Other offences

Amongst other offences which existed before the Theft Act 1968 (and some of which still do exist, though in an altered form) were *robbery*, an aggravated form of larceny when force or the threat of force was used, *obtaining credit by fraud*, an offence under section 13 of the Debtors Act 1869, *demanding money with menaces*, which was commonly called blackmail, and *receiving stolen property knowing it to be stolen*. In addition, there were a number of different offences of breaking into or out of premises. Thus, for example, *burglary* was committed if an accused in the night broke and entered a dwelling-house with intent to commit an arrestable offence therein, but it was only *housebreaking* if the offence was not at night or the place was not a dwelling-house. If the building was a church or other place of divine worship, the offence which he committed was *sacrilege*. It is not, however, possible, or necessary, to consider these offences in any detail.

2. The Theft Act 1968

The Theft Act 1968, which was passed following a report by the Criminal Law Revision Committee on *Theft and Related Offences*, 1966 (Cmnd. 2977), has now repealed the whole of the Larceny Act 1916, the whole of the Larceny Act 1861 and many other statutory provisions relating to offences against property. The Act also abolished any offence at common law of larceny, robbery, burglary, receiving stolen property, obtaining property by threats, extortion by colour of office or franchise, false accounting by public officers, concealment of treasure trove and, except as regards offences relating to public revenue, cheating (Theft Act 1968, s. 32(1)).

The Theft Act 1968 came into force on January 1, 1969 and by section 35 of the Act, apart from sections 27 (evidence and procedure on a charge of theft or handling stolen goods) and 28 (restitution orders), the provisions of the Act only affect offences committed after the commencement of the Act. Therefore, an offence committed before January 1, 1969, should still be charged and dealt with under the old law. References in earlier enactments which have not been repealed by the Theft Act, have effect, as regards offences committed since the commencement of the Act, as references to the corresponding offences under the Act (*ibid.*, s. 32(2)).

The Theft Act has replaced the offences of larceny, embezzlement and fraudulent conversion by a new offence of theft, it has replaced the offences of obtaining by false pretences and obtaining credit by fraud with two new offences of obtaining property by deception and obtaining a pecuniary advantage by deception, and it has replaced burglary, housebreaking, and sacrilege with a new offence of burglary. The Act has also renamed receiving stolen property as handling stolen goods and has renamed demanding with menaces as blackmail, both offences being subjected to changes. Although the offence of robbery has been retained, it has also been subjected to changes, and the same is true of a number of other statutory and common law offences. We must, therefore, now consider the present law in greater detail.

Chapter Twelve

THEFT

As we have seen, the offence of theft has now replaced the old offences of larceny, embezzlement and fraudulent conversion. By section 1(1) of the Theft Act 1968, "A person is guilty of theft if he dishonestly appropriates property belonging to another with the intention of permanently depriving the other of it." Moreover, by section 1(1), the terms "thief" and "steal" are, within the Act, to be construed as referring to the offence of theft. The offence is punishable with a maximum of ten years' imprisonment. It is now necessary to consider the ingredients of the offence in more detail, and for this purpose we will consider first the *actus reus* and then the *mens rea*.

The Actus Reus of Theft

"Appropriates"

Probably the most important word in the definition of theft is the word "appropriates." By section 3(1) of the Theft Act 1968 "any assumption by a person of the rights of an owner amounts to an appropriation, and this includes, where he has come by the property (innocently or not) without stealing it, any later assumption of a right to it by keeping or dealing with it as owner." Thus, to appropriate property is to assume the rights of an owner and not necessarily, as was required for the offence of larceny, to take and carry the stolen goods away.

Clearly if the accused does take another's property (*e.g.*, a watch from his pocket) he will have assumed the rights of the owner by so doing and indeed this would appear to be so as soon as the accused has grasped the watch and before removing it from the pocket. This may not have amounted to larceny because there was no carrying away (see *R*. v. *Taylor* (1911), C.C.A.), but what was only attempted larceny can now constitute theft. What is more problematical is whether a rogue who, for example, points out a motor car to a potential purchaser and states that it is his motor car and that he is willing to sell it, is guilty of theft of the motor car even though he may not even have touched it. He would seem to have assumed the rights of the owner of the motor car by trying to sell it as his own, and though it might be objected that he did not intend permanently to deprive the true owner of the motor car it is sufficient, as we shall see, if the rogue's intention was to treat the thing as his own to dispose of regardless of the other's rights (Theft Act 1968, s. 6(1)).

Already in possession. The offence of theft may be committed by the accused assuming the rights of an owner over property even though he is already in possession of that property. Thus, though he has been handed the property by the owner (*e.g.*, under a contract of bailment) or has been handed the property for the owner by a third person (even though the owner does not know of the property's existence), he can be guilty of theft if he then assumes the rights of the owner, for example, by selling or attempting to sell that property (see *Rogers* v. *Arnott* (1960), D.C.). It is for this reason that the new offence of theft covers the former offences of embezzlement and fraudulent conversion. Indeed in their Report on *Theft and Related Offences* the Criminal Law Revision Committee said that "the effect will be as if fraudulent conversion were widened to include the whole of larceny and embezzlement" (para. 35).

As an accused may appropriate property after he has come by the property (innocently or not) an accused will be guilty of theft if the property is brought to him by an innocent person (*e.g.*, a child) and the accused then decides to assume over it the rights of an owner (see *Walters* v. *Lunt* (1951), C.C.A.), though whether he can be said to "assume the rights of the owner" (or to intend permanently to deprive the owner of it) if, for example, he merely leaves a tennis ball lying in his garden when he knows that it has been thrown there by the children next door, is perhaps open to doubt. By section 3(2) of the Act, where a person buys property in good faith but he later finds that the seller had no title (*e.g.*, he had stolen it) the innocent purchaser will not become guilty of theft if he then keeps the property or otherwise deals with it as the owner.

Accused's mistake. The accused may have acquired the property innocently but as a result of a mistake. Thus in *R.* v. *Riley* (1853) the accused, when rounding up his own flock of twenty-nine black-faced lambs, inadvertently included a white-faced lamb which did not belong to him. Later when he offered the flock to a farmer it was pointed out to him that there were thirty lambs but he sold the thirty. This would clearly now amount to theft of that extra lamb because, although he came by it innocently, the accused appropriated the lamb when he discovered the mistake, for he dealt with it as owner by selling it. Moreover, there may have been a mistake on the part of the owner of the goods as well as on the part of the accused. Thus in *R*. v. *Ashwell* (1885), C.C.R., the accused, in the dark, asked the prosecutor for the loan of a shilling and the prosecutor handed to him what at that time both believed to be a shilling, but what in fact was a gold sovereign. Later, when he discovered the mistake, the accused decided to appropriate the sovereign by keeping it. Such action also would now clearly amount to theft. In fact, in both *R*. v. *Riley* and *R*. v. *Ashwell* the accused were convicted of larceny but the somewhat doubtful constructions of the then current provisions which these convictions required are no longer necessary. (As to mistake, see also below.)

Intimidation and trick. Under the former law of larceny there were certain other ways in which an accused might steal property. Thus, larceny could be committed by the use of intimidation or by a trick (see the Larceny Act 1916, s. 1(2)). These forms of stealing are no longer expressly mentioned in the Theft Act 1968 and though they would appear to be covered, at least in part, by the new offence of theft they are also covered by other offences. In *R*. v. *McGrath* (1869), C.C.R., where a woman had attended a mock auction, a lot for which she had not bid was knocked down to her, and she was told that she could not leave the auction room until she paid the money. In fear, she paid the money in order to escape. It would seem that this will still amount to stealing because the accused appropriated the money which was handed to him and the property in the money had clearly not passed to him because there was no contract between them (see *The Law of Theft* by J. C. Smith, para. 51). However, although the offence of theft is not committed if the property in the money passes to the accused, it would seem that cases where goods are obtained by intimidation are covered by the offence of blackmail (see Chap. 14) and this offence in fact, carries a greater maximum term of imprisonment than does theft (but see also the offence of robbery, below).

Similarly, if the accused obtains possession of goods by a trick and the trick is such that the property in the goods does not pass then the offence will be theft. This will be so if the trick is as to the very nature of the goods (see *R*. v. *Bramley* (1861)) or as to the identity of the accused (see the civil case of *Cundy* v. *Lindsay* (1878), H.L.). However, obtaining possession by a trick is also covered by the offence of obtaining property by deception and, as this can be committed whether or not the property in the goods passes to the accused and it is punishable with the same maximum term of imprisonment, the accused, in these circumstances, should be charged with the offence of obtaining rather than with that of theft.

Mistake on the part of the owner. Another example of larceny under the Larceny Act 1916 was larceny under a mistake on the part of he owner and, as we have seen, this type of stealing is retained by the Theft Act 1968. Moreover, although the offence was formerly restricted to obtaining possession, section 5(4) now extends the offence to obtaining ownership as well, for "where a person gets property by another's mistake, and is under an obligation to make restoration (in whole or in part) of the property or its proceeds or of the value thereof, then to the extent of that obligation the property or proceeds shall be regarded (as against him) as belonging to the person entitled to restoration, and an intention not to make restoration shall be regarded accordingly as an intention to deprive that person of the property or proceeds." Thus, by reason of section 5(4) the new offence of theft covers not only cases which were examples of larceny under a mistake (*e.g.*, *R.* v. *Middleton* (1873), C.C.R.) but also cases which could not be brought within that doctrine (*e.g.*, *Moynes* v. *Coopper* (1956), D.C.).

In *R.* v. *Middleton*, the accused was a depositor in the Post Office Savings Bank and he gave notice of his wish to withdraw the sum of ten shillings. The bank sent to him a warrant for that sum encashable at a particular post office but when he presented the warrant at the post office the clerk by mistake consulted a letter of advice concerning another depositor and he pushed a larger sum across the counter. Although the accused realized that a mistake had been made he took up the money and was subsequently convicted of larceny. A majority of the judges in the Court for Crown Cases Reserved held that by reason of the clerk's mistake the property in the money had not passed. However, in *Moynes* v. *Coopper* the accused had received part payment of his week's wages in advance, but this fact had not been notified to the firm's wages clerk. In consequence, the wages clerk made up an envelope containing a full week's wages, and handed it to the accused. At the time when he received his wages packet the accused did not know that it contained more than was due to him but when later he discovered the mistake he decided to appropriate the whole sum to his own use. A Divisional Court held that the accused was not guilty of larceny, apparently because the property in the money had passed to him. Now, however, as we have seen, similar conduct would amount to theft because he would be under an obligation to restore the excess sum to his employers.

Theft by finding. Larceny by finding was yet another form of larceny which was expressly mentioned in section 2(1) of the Larceny Act 1916 but which is not so mentioned in the Theft Act. Again, however, this form of stealing still remains and, as we have seen, the finder of lost property can now commit theft not only if he believes, at the time of the actual finding, that the person to whom the property belongs can be discovered by taking reasonable steps, but if he forms this belief later yet still appropriates the property. Similarly, if an accused, having found goods, intends to return them to their owner or to hand them to the police but he then changes his mind and keeps them he commits theft, provided he believes, when he changes his mind, that the person to whom the property belongs can be discovered by taking reasonable steps.

Although it will not be theft if the finder of the goods never does believe that the person to whom they belong can be discovered by taking reasonable steps (Theft Act 1968, s. 2(1) (c)) the "person to whom they belong" does not necessarily mean the original owner. As we shall see, it may mean merely one who has possession or control of the goods and if the lost goods have already come into another's possession then the later possessor is the "person to whom they belong." Thus in *Hibbert* v. *McKiernan* (1948), D.C., a golf club took steps to exclude intruders from the course with the express intention of making a periodical collection of golf balls which had been lost by players and selling such balls for the benefit of the club. The accused, knowing that he had no right to do so, trespassed on the course for the purpose of collecting such golf balls as he could find, and on the occasion in question he took a number of them. It was held that in the circumstances the golf club had possession of the balls, and that the accused was guilty of larceny (and now of theft) from the club.

Owner's consent. One requirement of larceny which is not reproduced in the Theft Act is that the obtaining must have been without consent of the person to whom the property belonged, but, as we shall see, an appropriation will not be dishonest if done in the belief that the accused would have that person's consent if he knew of the appropriation and the circumstances of it (Theft Act 1968, s. 2(1) (b)). It is clear, therefore, that it will not be theft if the other person consents to the accused appropriating the property and the accused knows that this is so. Where difficulty has arisen in the past, however, is when the other person, unknown to the accused, has consented to the accused obtaining possession of the property but only in order to trap him. Thus, in *R.* v. *Turvey* (1946), C.C.A., the accused approached a servant of the Ministry of Works and suggested to him that he should hand certain property of his masters to the accused. The servant reported this approach to his masters and was directed by them to hand the property to the accused so that he might be caught. It was held that he was not guilty of larceny because he had obtained the property with the consent of the owner. It would seem likely, however, that an accused in such circumstances would now be guilty of theft.

Attempted theft. One further effect of the new definition of appropriating is that a number of cases which were formerly only attempted larcenies will now amount to the full offence of theft. Larceny was only committed when the property had been taken and carried away but theft is committed as soon as there has been any assumption of the rights of an owner. Therefore, as we have seen, an accused may commit theft merely by grasping another's watch with the intention of removing it or merely by attempting to sell another's property. However, it is still an attempted theft, for example, for an accused to place his hand into another person's empty pocket with the intention of stealing whatever property he might find in that pocket.

"Property"

Theft is committed when an accused "dishonestly appropriates property" and for this purpose "property" includes "money and all other property, real or personal, including things in action and other intangible property" (Theft Act 1968, s. 4(1)). The category of property which may be stolen is somewhat wider than the corresponding category under the Larceny Act 1916. It includes land, things in action and other intangible property (*e.g.*, shares in a company or a bank balance) which were not covered by the law of larceny. Thus, if the accused draws a cheque on another's bank in that other person's name it will be theft of the debt owed by the bank to the other. Nevertheless, section 4 imposes important restrictions on the theft of land, growing plants and wild creatures and these must therefore be considered in more detail.

Land. Section 4(2) of the Theft Act 1968 provides that "a person cannot steal land, or things forming part of land and severed from it by him or by his directions, except in the following cases, that is to say—(*a*) when he is a trustee or personal representative, or is authorized by power of attorney, or as liquidator of a company, or otherwise, to sell or dispose of land belonging to another, and he appropriates the land or anything forming part of it by dealing with it in breach of the confidence reposed in him; or (*b*) when he is not in possession of the land and appropriates anything forming part of the land by severing it or causing it to be severed, or after it has been severed; or (c) when, being in possession of the land under a tenancy, he appropriates the whole or part of any fixture or structure let to be used with the land." Therefore, apart from a trustee, etc., or a tenant, a person can only steal land by severing it or after it has been severed but this will include, for example, the digging up of rock, coal or peat or even the removal of soil. It is no longer necessary, moreover, that the accused should have abandoned possession of the soil, etc., between severing it and removing it.

Growing plants. By section 4(3) of the Theft Act 1968 "a person who picks mushrooms growing wild on any land, or who picks flowers, fruit or foliage from a plant growing wild on any land, does not (although not in possession of that land) steal what he picks, unless he does it for reward or for sale or other commercial purpose." Thus, as "plant" includes any shrub or tree it means, for example, that a person who picks holly from a tree growing wild for his own use will not be guilty of theft but if he picks it for the purpose of resale he will be guilty of theft. Moreover, these restrictions only apply to plants growing wild so that if the accused, for example, picks apples from a cultivated apple tree he will be guilty of theft of those apples. Further, if the accused removes the whole plant (*e.g.*, he pulls out a bluebell by the roots) he is guilty of theft because that is not the picking of a flower, fruit or foliage from a plant and the same would seem true if, for example, he saws off a Christmas tree, even though he leaves the roots.

Wild creatures. Section 4(4) of the Theft Act 1968 provides that "wild creatures, tamed or untamed, shall be regarded as property; but a person cannot steal a wild creature not tamed nor ordinarily kept in captivity, or the carcase of any such creature, unless either it has been reduced into possession by or on behalf of another person and possession of it has not since been lost or abandoned, or another person is in course of reducing it into possession." Section 4(4) has not, of course, any application to domestic animals (*e.g.*, a cat, a dog, a sheep or a cow) and these may be stolen like other objects.

The effect of section 4(4) is that a wild creature can only be stolen if it has been tamed or is ordinarily kept in captivity (*e.g.*, a lion at a zoo) or if it has been reduced into and retained in the possession of some other person or some other person is in the course of reducing it into possession. An untamed wild creature is not otherwise in the possession of the owner of the land where it is for the time being to be found, or of any other person, and, though a wild creature which has been killed (*e.g.*, by a poacher) and abandoned becomes the property of the owner of the land it cannot thereby be said to have been reduced into possession, etc., by that owner within the meaning of section 4(4). Therefore, if a poacher kills game on another's land he will not be guilty of theft even if he temporarily abandons possession of the game but if, in the mean time, the owner of the land had found the game and reduced it into his possession (*e.g.*, by placing it in his, the land owner's, bag) and then the poacher returns and retakes the game it will be theft.

Poaching is also covered by certain other enactments: the Night Poaching Act 1828, the Game Act 1831, as amended by the Game Laws (Amendment) Act 1960, and Poaching Prevention Act 1862. In addition, the poaching of deer and fish, which were originally dealt with in the Larceny Act 1861, are now covered by Schedule 1 of the Theft Act 1968.

Electricity. Electricity, it seems, unlike water (*Ferens* v. *O'Brien* (1883)) and gas (*R.* v. *Frith* (1869), C.C.R.), cannot be stolen because it is not "property" within the meaning of section 4(1), but section 13 of the Theft Act 1968 provides that "a person who dishonestly uses without due authority or dishonestly causes to be wasted or diverted, any electricity shall on conviction on indictment be liable to imprisonment for a term not exceeding five years." This offence is sometimes charged when a person dishonestly makes a telephone call.

"Belonging to another"

For the offence of theft to be committed the property must belong to another (Theft Act 1968, s. 1(1)). We will consider below the meaning of "belong" in this context but first we must note that if the property belongs to no one then that property cannot be stolen. Thus, a human corpse is not the property of any person and cannot therefore be stolen (*R.* v. *Haynes* (1614)), but this principle probably does not extend to a skeleton on which work has been done and which is used for demonstration purposes in a school of anatomy. Also water that flows naturally in a stream is not regarded as being the property of the landowner on whose land it happens to be at a given moment of time and it cannot, therefore, be stolen. But, as we have seen, water which is the property of a person (*e.g.*, water in the pipes of a water company) can be stolen (*Ferens* v. *O'Brien*, *supra*). Likewise, a wild creature while alive normally belongs to no one. We have already considered the position if it is killed.

Things abandoned by their owner are not generally the property of any person, and cannot therefore normally be stolen. But if when the property is abandoned it falls into the possession of another person, then the property belongs to that other person for the purposes of theft, and the property is capable of being stolen. Thus, in the case of *Hibbert* v. *McKiernan*, which we have already noticed in connection with theft by finding, it makes no difference whether we regard the golf balls as having been lost or having been abandoned by their owners, in either case the golf club obtained possesion of them and they remained capable of being stolen. Moreover, a householder does not abandon goods which he places in his dustbin for he intends them to be collected by, and thereby to be taken into the possession of, the local authority. If a third person (including the dustman himself) then appropriates the goods from the dustbin he may be guilty of theft (*Williams* v. *Phillips* (1957) C.C.A.).

To belong. We saw in the last chapter that the offence of larceny was an offence against possession rather than against ownership and the same is basically true of the offence of theft. Although we have sometimes, for the sake of convenience, spoken in this chapter of "the owner" this term must be interpreted in the sense which is given, by section 5 of the Theft Act 1968, to the words "belonging to another." Thus, by section 5(1) "property shall be regarded as belonging to any person having possession or control of it, or having in it any proprietary right or interest (not being an equitable interest arising only from an agreement to transfer or grant an interest)." Moreover, by section 5(2), "where property is subject to a trust, the persons to whom it belongs shall be regarded as including any person having a right to enforce the trust, and an intention to defeat the trust shall be regarded accordingly as an intention to deprive of the property any person having that right." Therefore, the same property may belong to a number of persons at the same time and one of such persons may himself steal the property by assuming the rights of the others, for example, by unilaterally selling the property.

By reason of section 5(1) theft may be committed against any person who has possession or control of property or who has in it any proprietary right or interest. Thus, if the owner of property (in the strict sense of the word) lends property to another and the accused then steals from that other he has committed theft against both the owner of the goods and against the person to whom they were lent. Moreover, it follows from this that one thief can steal property from another thief and an owner can be guilty of stealing his own property if he takes it dishonestly from one who has possession of it. For example, in *Rose* v. *Matt* (1951), D.C., the owner of a clock deposited it with a shopkeeper to secure a debt which he owed to him, and later, without the shopkeeper's knowledge or consent, took back the clock, thereby depriving the shopkeeper of his lien on it. The owner of the clock was held guilty of larceny of the clock, and would now be guilty of theft of it: he had dishonestly taken it from the possessor with the intent permanently to deprive the possessor of it. It has been doubted whether an owner can be guilty of stealing his own property from a mere bailee at will (*e.g.*, one to whom he has merely lent the property), but these doubts are probably unfounded. Nevertheless, as we have seen, section 5(1) excludes an equitable interest arising only from an agreement to transfer or grant an interest, so that, although when a seller agrees to sell property the buyer occasionally obtains an equitable interest, the seller will not, on that account, be guilty of theft if he then sells to another. He may, of course, be liable for breach of contract.

Already having possession. Although theft is an offence against possession in the sense in which we have just been considering this term, it is not an offence against possession in the sense that if the accused is already in possession of the property then he cannot be guilty of stealing it. This was basically true of the offence of larceny but, as we have seen, an accused can now be guilty of theft if he, though in possession, then appropriates property belonging to another. It is because of this extension of the law of theft that the offence now covers what was formerly embezzlement and fraudulent conversion. Moreover, section 5(3) of the Theft Act 1968 provides that "where a person receives property from or on account of another, and is under an obligation to the other to retain and deal with that property or its proceeds in a particular way, the property or proceeds shall be regarded (as against him) as belonging to the other." Therefore, a bailee or servant who has received property can be guilty of stealing that property if he subsequently appropriates it. However, the provision only applies if the recipient of the property is under an obligation to retain and deal with that property or its proceeds in a particular way. If, for example, a painter agrees to paint a house and is paid money in advance he will not be guilty of stealing that money even though he subsequently decides to keep the money paid without painting the house (see *R.* v. *Jones* (1948), C.C.A.; see also *R.* v. *Hotine* (1904)), but if he was paid the money for the express purpose of buying the paint then he may be guilty of theft. Moreover, although section 5(3) covers the proceeds of the property it does not cover money obtained by merely using the property, if that money was not received on account of the other. Thus, in *R.* v. *Cullum* (1873), C.C.R., the accused was employed as captain of a barge belonging to his master. In breach of his master's express instructions he carried a cargo of manure in the barge and kept for himself the freight money that he received for doing so. The person who paid the freight money did not know whether Cullum was owner of the barge or a mere servant. It was held that Cullum could not be convicted of embezzlement and he could not now be convicted of theft.

Obtaining ownership. We have already seen that whether an accused is guilty of theft may depend upon whether the property in the money, etc., which he appropriates passes to him. It is still basically true to say that if the accused obtains ownership and not merely possession then he cannot be guilty of theft. It is for this reason that a separate offence of obtaining property by deception is still necessary and why, if the accused obtains the property by a trick, it is safer always to charge that offence. Nevertheless, as we have also seen, section 5(4) provides an exception to this general rule when a person gets property by another's mistake and is under an obligation to make restoration, and section 5(3) also provides an exception when a person receives property from another; even though he receives ownership he may be guilty of theft if he appropriates that property when he was under an obligation to the other to retain and deal with it or its proceeds in a particular way.

Property of a spouse. Before the Theft Act 1968 special restrictions applied to the stealing by one spouse of the property of the other spouse. Now, however, section 30(1) of the Theft Act provides that the Act applies in relation to the parties to a marriage, and to property belonging to the wife or husband, whether or not by reason of an interest derived from the marriage, as it would apply if they were not married and any such interest subsisted independently of the marriage. This applies not only to theft but to all other offences under the Act. Nevertheless, proceedings cannot normally be instituted against a person for any offence in relation to his or her wife or husband except by or with the consent of the Director of Public Prosecutions (*ibid.*, s. 30(4)). There are also certain special rules relating to the accused's spouse being called as a witness in such proceedings (see s. 30(2), (3)).

The Mens Rea of Theft

Theft is committed when a person dishonestly appropriates property belonging to another with the intention of permanently depriving the other of it (Theft Act 1968, s. 1(1)). Therefore, to constitute the offence of theft the accused must have acted dishonestly and he must have intended permanently to deprive the other of the property. However, before we consider these two requirements we must notice that it is not necessary that the accused should have done so for gain. Section 1(2) of the Theft Act 1968 provides that "it is immaterial whether the appropriation is made with a view to gain, or is made for the thief's own benefit," while section 2(2) of that Act provides that a person's appropriation of property "may be dishonest notwithstanding that he is willing to pay for the property."

"Dishonestly"

The term "dishonestly" has replaced that of "fraudulently," which was the term used in the Larceny Act 1916, and though no precise definition is given of the term "dishonestly" (it is only partly defined in section 2(1) of the Theft Act 1968) it is possible that its meaning is rather narrower than that of "fraudulently." In *R*. v. *Williams* (1953) the Court of Criminal Appeal stated that the word "fraudulently" meant that the taking must have been done intentionally under no mistake, and with knowledge on the part of the taker that the thing taken is the property of another person. In practice, however, the term "fraudulently" did not seem to add any additional qualification to what would otherwise amount to the offence of larceny. Thus, in *R*. v. *Cockburn* (1968), C.A., the manager of a shop was held to be guilty of larceny when he had taken money from the till of the shop on a Saturday, intending to replace it with a cheque from his daughter on the following Monday. Although he may not have realized that what he was doing was a criminal offence the Court of Appeal held that his actions were done fraudulently within the principles laid down in *R*. v. *Williams, supra*. It would, of course, have been different if the accused had taken property with the intention of replacing that identical property because he would not then have intended permanently to deprive the owner of it (see below).

The word "dishonestly" was chosen by the Criminal Law Revision Committee and subsequently embodied in the Theft Act 1968 because, as the Committee state in their report on *Theft and Related Offences* (para. 39), it is a term which it is easier for a jury to understand than that of "fraudulently." Although it would seem that the Committee did not intend to change the law by this alteration, it is possible, and perhaps also desirable, that conduct such as that in *R*. v. *Cockburn* will no longer amount to a criminal offence. Nevertheless, as we have seen, the appropriation of property may be dishonest even though the accused is willing to pay for the property.

By section 2(1) (*a*) of the Theft Act a person's appropriation is not to be regarded as dishonest "if he appropriates the property in the belief that he has in law the right to deprive the other of it, on behalf of himself or of a third person." This replaces a provision in the Larceny Act 1916 that the taking must have been without a claim of right made in good faith but the change would not appear to have materially altered the law. If the accused honestly thinks that he has a right to take the property he is not guilty of theft, and it makes no difference why he formed the belief: his mistake may even have sprung from a misunderstanding of the law (see *R.* v. *Clayton* (1920), C.C.A.). But a belief that he has a moral claim to the money (*e.g.*, that his employer should have given him a rise) is no defence (*Harris* v. *Harrison* (1963), D.C.).

Section 2(1) of the Theft Act 1968 also contains two further qualifications on the term dishonest. As we have noticed, it is not dishonest if the person appropriating the property of another does so in the belief that he would have the other's consent if the other knew of the appropriation and the circumstances of it (s. 2(1)(*b*)). Further, it is not dishonest if the person appropriating the property (except where the property has come to him as trustee or personal representative) does so in the belief that the person to whom the property belongs cannot be discovered by taking reasonable steps (s. 2(1) (*c*)). As we have seen, however, the finder of lost property may subsequently become guilty of theft if he later discovers the person to whom the property belongs or believes that he could then discover his identity by taking reasonable steps.

Intent permanently to deprive

The condition that the accused must have had "the intention of permanently depriving the other of it" was a condition of the offence of larceny and is still retained for the offence of theft. Nevertheless, section 6 of the Theft Act 1968, by its partial definition of this provision, mitigates certain of its effects while other sections circumvent certain other effects. We will consider these sections below.

It is because of the requirement of an intent permanently to deprive that it is not normally theft to take another's property without permission, but with the intention of returning it. Moreover, if the intent required by the Theft Act is not present, no other form of *mens rea* will suffice as a substitute. For example, in *R.* v. *Holloway* (1849) the accused was employed to dress skins belonging to his master and was paid so much per skin. He took certain skins which had already been dressed from the storeroom where they were kept, with the dishonest intention of claiming payment for having dressed them. It was held that he could not be convicted of larceny, as the fraud that he intended involved the return of the skins to his master. On the other hand, it was held that there was a sufficient intent permanently to deprive where a person appropriated another's property with the intention of selling it back to him as a different thing (*R*. v. *Hall* (1848). Moreover, by reason of section 6(1) of the Theft Act 1968, it is now theft whenever the accused's intention is to treat the property as his own (e.g., by selling it back to the true owner: see below) even though he does not mean the other "permanently to lose the thing itself."

Section 6(1) of the Theft Act provides that "a person appropriating property belonging to another without meaning the other permanently to lose the thing itself is nevertheless to be regarded as having the intention of permanently depriving the other of it if his intention is to treat the thing as his own to dispose of regardless of the other's rights; and a borrowing or lending of it may amount to so treating it if, but only if, the borrowing or lending is for a period and in circumstances making it equivalent to an outright taking or disposal."

As we have just seen, one case where this provision may apply is where the accused appropriates another's property with the intention of selling it back to him. However, section 6(1) would have no application to the facts of *R*. v. *Holloway*, *supra*, because there the accused did not intend to treat the skins as his own; he intended throughout to treat them as his master's property.

Other situations apparently covered by section 6(1) are where the accused, while not retaining the property, leaves it in circumstances in which the owner is not likely to find it, or where the accused purports, or tries, to sell the property to a third person, even though he knows that the owner of the property will be able to recover the property from the third person. In addition, the borrowing of property for an inordinate time is expressly covered though only if the borrowing is equivalent to an outright taking.

Section 6(2) of the Theft Act 1968, moreover, provides that "where a person, having possession or control (lawfully or not) of property belonging to another, parts with the property under a condition as to its return which he may not be able to perform, this (if done for his own purposes and without the other's authority) amounts to treating the property as his own to dispose of regardless of the other's rights." Therefore, for example, if the accused pawns another's property hoping to redeem it eventually, he can be guilty of theft (see *R*. v. *Medland* (1851)).

One important change effected by the Theft Act 1968 in relation to the *mens rea* is the stage at which the accused must have the necessary intent. Under the Larceny Act 1916 this must have been at the time he took the goods but now, as we have seen, although the accused must have the necessary intent when he appropriates the property, this may occur after he has come by the property (innocently or not).

Although an accused cannot be guilty of theft unless he has the necessary intent permanently to deprive the other of the property, the Theft Act 1968 creates certain other analogous offences where this intent is not required. It is convenient to consider these offences here.

Removal of articles from places open to the public. Section 11(1) of the Theft Act 1968 provides that "where the public have access to a building in order to view the building or part of it, or a collection or part of a collection housed in it, any person who without lawful authority removes from the building or its grounds the whole or any part of any article displayed or kept for display to the public in the building or that part of it or in its grounds shall be guilty of an offence" which is punishable with a maximum term of five years' imprisonment. "Collection," moreover, includes a collection got together for a temporary purpose but not one made or exhibited for the purpose of effecting sales or other commercial dealings (s. 11(1)).

This offence was created following the removal from the National Gallery of Goya's portrait of the Duke of Wellington. In that case the accused did not intend permanently to deprive the gallery of the painting and it was therefore held that he was not guilty of larceny of it (although he was guilty of larceny of its frame which he had destroyed). Similar conduct would now constitute an offence under section 11(1) in relation to the painting itself.

An offence under section 11(1), however, can only be committed if the building is open to the public and, though it is immaterial that the public's access is limited to a particular period or occasion, if the thing removed does not form part of, or is on loan for exhibition with, a collection intended for permanent exhibition to the public, an offence is not committed unless the thing is removed on a day (though not necessarily at a time) when the public have access to the building (*ibid.*, s. 11(2)). If the thing removed does form part of a permanent public exhibition (*e.g.*, a painting in the National Gallery) then an offence is committed even though it is removed on a day when the building is not open to the public.

For an offence to be committed, moreover, the removal must be without lawful authority and, by section 11(3), an offence is not committed if the person concerned believes that he has lawful authority or that he would have it if the person entitled to give it knew of the removal and the circumstances of it.

Taking any conveyance without authority. Under section 12(1) of the Theft Act 1968, it is an offence, punishable with a maximum of three years' imprisonment if a person "without the consent of the owner or other lawful authority, . . . takes any conveyance for his own or another's use or, knowing that any conveyance has been taken without such authority, drives or allows himself to be carried in or on it." Moreover, "conveyance" means "any conveyance constructed or adapted for the carriage of a person or persons whether by land, water or air, except that it does not include a conveyance constructed or adapted for use only under the control of a person not carried in or on it" (*ibid.*, s. 12(7) (*a*)), and "owner," in relation to a conveyance which is the subject of hiring agreement or hire-purchase agreement, means the person in possession of the conveyance under that agreement" (*ibid.*, s. 12(7) (*b*)). This provision replaced somewhat similar provisions in the Road Traffic Act 1960, s. 217, and the Vessels Protection Act 1967, s. 1.

An accused can commit an offence under section 12 either (i) by taking the conveyance himself or (ii) by driving it or allowing himself to be carried, knowing that it has been so taken. An accused may, however, *take* a conveyance, within the meaning of section 12, without actually driving it, for example, by releasing the handbrake of a vehicle and causing it to run down a hill with no one inside it (*R.* v. *Roberts* (1964), C.C.A.) or by lifting it on to a lorry by a crane; although it is very unlikely that he would do so unless his intention were permanently to deprive the owner of it, when he would be guilty of the theft of the conveyance. It was held in *Mowe* v. *Perraton* (1952), D.C., that a servant in control of his master's van does not commit this offence by deviating from the authorized route in the course of a journey on his master's behalf, but it can amount to the offence if, after the day's work, he uses his master's vehicle for his own purposes, because he is not then driving the vehicle as his master's servant (*R.* v. *Wibberley* (1965), C.C.A.). Nevertheless, "a person does not commit an offence under this section by anything done in the belief that he has lawful authority to do it or that he would have the owner's consent if the owner knew of his doing it and the circumstances of it" (*ibid.*, s. 12(6)).

There is a similar summary offence (punishable with a maximum fine of £50) where a person takes a pedal cycle without authority or rides a pedal cycle knowing that it has been taken without authority (*ibid.*, s. 12(5)).

Robbery

Robbery, which is an aggravated form of theft, is committed when a person steals and immediately before or at the time of doing so, and in order to do so, he uses force on any person or puts or seeks to put any person in fear of being there and then subjected to force (Theft Act 1968, s. 8(1)). A person guilty of robbery, or of an assault with intent to rob, is liable to a maximum of life imprisonment (*ibid.*, s. 8(2)).

To amount to robbery, the force, or threat of force, must be used in order to steal, so that it is not sufficient if force is merely used after the stealing; for example, to get away or to prevent the victim recovering his property (*R.* v. *Harman* (1620)). Moreover, although it is no longer necessary that the person on whom the force is used should be present at the actual stealing, it is necessary that the force should have been used immediately before or at the time of the theft. Thus, if a gang are stealing property in a factory it will be robbery if one of the gang who is keeping watch in the road outside uses force on a passer-by because he believes that he may have become suspicious, but it will not be robbery merely because force was used, for example, on the factory manager at his home, some hours before the theft in order to obtain from him the combination number of the factory's safe. Nevertheless, the commission of robbery depends on the commission of theft so that if the accused has a defence to a charge of theft (*e.g.*, he appropriated the property in the belief that he had in law the right to deprive the other of it) then he cannot be guilty of robbery, even though he did not think that he was entitled to use force (*R.* v. *Skivington* (1968), C.A.) (although in that case, he was guilty of an assault and would also now be guilty of blackmail, see Chap. 14).

Chapter Thirteen

FRAUD

THE Theft Act 1968 creates a number of offences involving fraud of which the two most important are obtaining property by deception and obtaining a pecuniary advantage by deception. In addition, there are a few other offences which are still covered by the common law or by other statutes. These various offences will be considered in this chapter.

Obtaining Property by Deception

By section 15(1) of the Theft Act 1968 "a person who by any deception dishonestly obtains property belonging to another, with the intention of permanently depriving the other of it" commits an offence punishable with a maximum of imprisonment for ten years. As we have seen, this offence replaces the former offence of obtaining by false pretences.

"Obtains"

This may be regarded as the key word in the definition of obtaining property by deception, just as the word "appropriates" is the key word in the definition of theft. To "obtain" means to obtain ownership, possession or control of the property and it includes obtaining for another or enabling another to obtain or to retain (Theft Act 1968, s. 15(2)). As we have seen, theft is not committed if the accused obtains the ownership of the property in question (subject to the qualifications which we have also considered), but he may commit this offence of obtaining by deception. Nevertheless, unlike the old offence of obtaining by false pretences, obtaining property by deception is not restricted to obtaining ownership but covers obtaining possession or control as well. It is for this reason that conduct which amounts to theft by a trick may also amount to obtaining by deception. Moreover, as we have noticed, it is in practice normally prudent in such cases to charge obtaining by deception because it will not then matter whether the accused obtained the ownership of the property or not. It should also be noticed that it is sufficient if the accused obtains ownership of the property without necessarily obtaining possession.

"Property"

The meaning of "property" in relation to obtaining by deception is basically the same as for the offence of theft (section 4(1) of the Theft Act 1968 applies to obtaining by deception as it applies to theft: Theft Act 1968, s. 34(1)); but the qualifications set out in section 4(2), (3) and (4) do not apply to the offence of obtaining by deception. "Property," therefore, in relation to obtaining by deception, covers land, plants and wild creatures.

"Belonging to another"

Again, "belonging to another" has basically the same meaning as it has in relation to theft (see s. 34(1) of the Theft Act 1968). Therefore, an accused may be guilty of obtaining his own property by deception in circumstances similar to those in which he can be guilty of theft of his own property.

"By any deception"

The word "by" in this phrase requires that the deception should be the effective cause of the obtaining. Thus in *R.* v. *Clucas* (1949), C.C.A. (a case of obtaining by false pretences but the law in this respect is still the same), the accused by certain false pretences induced a bookmaker to open an account for him. Some of the bets he made were successful, and the bookmaker paid. It was held that the accused could not be convicted of obtaining the winnings by false pretences, because the false pretences that he had made were not the effective cause of the obtaining; the only factor operating on the bookmaker's mind at the time when he parted with his money was the fact that the horses in question had won. In other words the pretence was too remote a cause of the obtaining to justify a conviction. (But a conviction of conspiracy to defraud was obtained on the full facts of the case and such conduct would now amount to obtaining a pecuniary advantage by deception: see below). This case may be contrasted with *R.* v. *Button* (1900), C.C.R., in which the accused, by impersonating another athlete, obtained an undue start in a handicap race for a prize; he won the race and would have claimed the prize but for the fact that the organizers had become suspicious and began to ask awkward questions. It was held that he was guilty of attempting to obtain the prize by false pretences and that, if he had obtained the prize, he would have been guilty of the full offence, despite the fact that his winning the race would have been one of the causes of the obtaining; his false representations leading to the undue start, would also have been a substantial cause.

The term "deception" is defined in section 15(4) of the Theft Act 1968. This section provides that "deception" "means any deception (whether deliberate or reckless) by words or conduct as to fact or as to law, including a deception as to the present intentions of the person using the deception or any other person." We will now consider the ingredients of this definition in turn.

"Deliberate or reckless." It is sufficient if the accused makes an untrue representation without caring whether it is true or false (see *Derry* v. *Peek* (1889), H.L.).

"Words or conduct." Like the old offence of obtaining by false pretences, obtaining property by deception can be committed by conduct as well as by express words. Thus in *R.* v. *Barnard* (1837), where the accused had entered a shop in Oxford wearing a fellow-commoner's cap and gown, Bolland B. said that he would still have been guilty of falsely representing that he were a fellow-commoner even if he had said nothing. Moreover, the giving of a cheque in payment for goods impliedly represents that the drawer has an account at the bank on which the cheque is drawn and that the cheque is a good and valid order for the amount for which it is given, so that if the drawer has only a colourable account at the bank, has no authority to overdraw, and knows that the cheque will be dishonoured on presentation, he can be convicted (*R.* v. *Hazleton* (1874), C.C.R.). But it does not represent that at the time when the cheque is given there is sufficient money in the account to meet the cheque. Again, the giving of a promise to do work of a technical character may imply that one has the special knowledge or skill to do that work. Nevertheless, in many of the cases of obtaining by false pretences, where the court held that there was an implied representation of fact, the court did so because a mere promise was not sufficient for the offence. As a representation as to present intentions is now sufficient for obtaining by deception, courts are no longer concerned with whether a promise amounted to an implied representation of fact, if the accused did not intend to keep it.

It should also be noticed that it is necessary for the accused to have deceived by "words or conduct." If, therefore, the victim deceives himself, for example, as to the age of a motor car, the accused is not guilty of obtaining by deception even though he may realize that the victim is under a misapprehension provided that no words or conduct of his have induced that misapprehension.

"Fact or law." It was never decided whether a false representation as to the law could suffice for the offence of obtaining by false pretences, but section 15(4) expressly states that it can be sufficient for the offence of obtaining property by deception.

"Present intentions." As we have just seen, a representation by an accused as to his present intentions can amount to a sufficient deception. Thus, a person who obtains a meal at a restaurant knowing that the meal will not be paid for would seem to be guilty of this offence (formerly he was only guilty of obtaining credit by fraud which, like the new offence of obtaining a pecuniary advantage by deception, carried a lesser maximum sentence). Another example of deception by a representation as to present intentions is the man who obtains an advance from a householder on the false pretence that he will paint or repair the house.

One problem on which the Theft Act is silent is whether a false statement of opinion can be sufficient. It was not sufficient for the offence of obtaining by false pretences (see *R. v. Bryan* (1857), C.C.R.) but it may now be sufficient for obtaining property by deception in that it implies a fact. i.e., that it is indeed the maker's opinion.

"Dishonestly"

The partial definition of "dishonest" given in section 2(1) of the Theft Act 1968 applies only to the offence of theft and not to obtaining property by deception. Nevertheless, the term would appear to have basically the same meaning for the two offences, and if a person obtained property by deception but he believed that he was entitled to that property it seems unlikely that he would be held to be dishonest.

"Intention of permanently depriving"

This has the same meaning as for the offence of theft and section 15(3) of the Theft Act 1968 expressly provides that section 6 of the Act applies also to the offence of obtaining property by deception.

Obtaining a Pecuniary Advantage by Deception

By section 16(1) of the Theft Act 1968 "a person who by any deception dishonestly obtains for himself or another any pecuniary advantage" commits an offence punishable with a maximum of imprisonment for five years. This offence replaces the former offence of obtaining credit by fraud, although the scope of the new offence is much wider.

"Deception"

The term "deception" has the same meaning as it has in relation to the offence of obtaining property by deception (Theft Act 1968, s. 16(3)).

"Pecuniary Advantage"

Section 16(2) of the Theft Act 1968 sets out the three cases in which a pecuniary advantage is to be regarded as obtained for the purpose of this offence. These three cases must now be considered in turn.

(a) By section 16(2) (a) a "pecuniary advantage" is obtained where "any debt or charge for which [the accused] makes himself liable or is or may become liable (including one not legally enforceable) is reduced or in whole or in part evaded or deferred." Examples of when a debt or charge is *reduced* include where an accused obtains a reduction on the purchase price of goods by falsely pretending that he is a member of a professional association, or where he obtains a reduction on the entrance fee to a cinema by falsely pretending that he is an old age pensioner, or where, having hired a car on a charge which depends upon the mileage travelled, he turns back the mileometer. Examples of when a debt or charge is *evaded* or *deferred* include where an accused induces another person to perform a service for him on a promise to pay for that service on completion of it but with the intention of not paying, or having agreed to pay immediately the service is performed he induces the other to agree to a postponement of the payment by a false pretence. Another example would be if the accused had obtained a night's lodging knowing that it would not be paid for, and (as we have seen) if, in addition, he obtained food or other property he would also be guilty of obtaining property by deception.

One problem which remains is whether an offence is committed if a rogue induces another to render a service (*e.g.*, to paint the rogue's house) on the false promise by the rogue that in return he will render a service (*e.g.*, dig the other's garden). In *Fisher* v. *Raven* (1964) the House of Lords held that the term "credit," for the purposes of obtaining credit by fraud, did not cover a mere obligation to render a service and it would seem possible that neither does the word "charge" in section 16(2) (a).

As we have seen, section 16(2) (a) expressly states that "debt or charge" includes one not legally enforceable. Therefore, this offence covers, for example, a debt incurred by a contract for the sale of

an interest in land even though the contract is unenforceable because
there is no sufficient memorandum (see the Law of Property Act
1925, s. 40). But it is arguable that the offence does not cover a
debt which is void (*e.g.*, a gaming debt or one incurred by an infant
other than for necessaries) because it can be said that in this case
the civil law does not recognize a debt at all, and does not merely
hold that it is legally unenforceable. Nevertheless, it seems probable
that the courts will hold that a void debt is covered by section
16(2)(*a*) because even the civil law does recognize a void debt for
certain purposes (see Anson's *Law of Contract*, 22nd ed., p. 336).

(*b*) By section 16(2) (*b*) a "pecuniary advantage" is obtained where
an accused "is allowed to borrow by way of overdraft, or to take out
any policy of insurance or annuity contract, or obtains an improve-
ment of the terms on which he is allowed to do so."

(*c*) By section 16(2) (*c*) a "pecuniary advantage" is obtained where
an accused "is given the opportunity to earn remuneration or greater
remuneration in an office or employment, or to win money by
betting." Thus, as we have seen, the offence of obtaining property
by deception would not seem to cover the facts of a case such as
R. v. *Clucas* (1949), C.C.A., because the winnings were not obtained
by the deception but because the horses won. However, the facts of
that case would now amount to an offence of obtaining a pecuniary
advantage by deception. The same is also true when the accused,
by a deception (*e.g.*, as to his qualifications) obtains an appointment
(see *R*. v. *Lewis* (1922)).

"Dishonestly"

The term "dishonestly" has basically the same meaning as it
has in the offence of obtaining property by deception and if a claim
of right is a defence to that offence it should also be a defence to
a charge of obtaining a pecuniary advantage by deception. We
have just seen, however, that the offence of obtaining a pecuniary
advantage by deception may be committed by an accused who
obtains an appointment by deception and it would seem, therefore,
that it will not be a defence that he intended to work diligently if
appointed and would in fact earn every penny which he was paid.
Similarly, it seems unlikely that it will be a defence that an accused,
who obtains a loan by deception, intended to repay the loan as
agreed.

As we have also seen, section 16(1) provides that this offence may
be committed by a person who obtains a pecuniary advantage for
himself or another. Therefore, the offence will be committed, for
example, if the accused gives a false reference so that a third person
may obtain an appointment. The fact that the accused obtains no

personal pecuniary benefit from the appointment will be no defence.

False Accounting

By section 17(1) of the Theft Act 1968, it is an offence "where a person dishonestly, with a view to gain for himself or another or with intent to cause loss to another, (*a*) destroys, defaces, conceals or falsifies any account or any record or document made or required for any accounting purpose; or (*b*) in furnishing information for any purpose produces or makes use of any account, or any such record or document as aforesaid, which to his knowledge is or may be misleading, false or deceptive in a material particular." This offence, which replaces an offence under the Falsification of Accounts Act 1875, is punishable with a maximum term of imprisonment for seven years.

The offence covers "any account" and would therefore cover a mechanical account (*e.g.*, a taxi-meter or a gas-meter), but it would seem that it would not normally cover, for example, the mileometer of a car because that is not normally a record "made or required for any accounting purpose." The term "to falsify," moreover, is partly defined in section 17(2), which provides that "a person who makes or concurs in making in an account or other document an entry which is or may be misleading, false or deceptive in a material particular, or who omits or concurs in omitting a material particular from an account or other document, is to be treated as falsifying the account or document" We will consider the term "with a view to gain" in relation to the offence of blackmail where it would appear to have the same meaning.

Other Offences Involving Fraud

The Theft Act 1968 also contains two further offences involving fraud. Thus, by section 19 it is an offence (punishable with a maximum of seven years' imprisonment) for an officer of a body corporate or incorporated society (*e.g.*, a company director) to publish or concur in publishing a written statement or account, which he knows is misleading, false or deceptive in a material particular, with intent to deceive members or creditors of the body corporate or association about its affairs. Also, by section 20, it is an offence (punishable with a maximum of seven years' imprisonment) for a person dishonestly, and with a view to gain or with intent to cause loss, either to destroy, deface or conceal any valuable security, any will or other testamentary document or any document of any court of justice or government department, or to procure by any deception the execution of a valuable security.

Cheating

Section 32(1) of the Theft Act 1968 abolished the common law offence of cheating (m) except as regards offences relating to the public revenue. This is conduct which tends to the perpetration of a fraud in relation to public revenue and which is intended to have that effect. For example, the supplying to an Inspector of Taxes of false trading accounts for the purpose of avoiding the payment of income tax (even if the Inspector is not in fact deceived (*R. v. Hudson* (1956), C.C.A.).

Fraudulent gaming

By the Gaming Act 1845, s. 17, as amended, it is an offence (m) punishable with a maximum term of imprisonment for, on conviction on indictment, two years or, on summary conviction, six months, for a person to win from another any sum of money or valuable thing by fraudulent gaming or wagering, *e.g.*, by cheating at cards, or by making bets with a bookmaker with the intention (at the time of placing the bets) of accepting the money if the bets are successful and of not paying if they are unsuccessful (*R. v. Leon* (1945), C.C.A.). (As we have just seen, this conduct may also constitute the offence of obtaining a pecuniary advantage by deception.) If no money or valuable thing is in fact obtained, the full offence under section 17 is not committed, but in appropriate circumstances the accused can be convicted of an attempt to commit that offence, for example, where the accused has made false representations to a bookmaker to induce him to open an account with him, but the bookmaker has discovered the fraud before making any payment to the accused (*R. v. Harris* (1963), C.C.A.).

Other offences: bribery

There are a number of other offences involving fraud, *e.g.*, under the Fraudulent Mediums Act 1951, which it is difficult to classify under any general heading. It may also be convenient to mention here briefly the offence of bribery. It is a common law offence (m) to bribe, or attempt to bribe, a privy councillor, or other public official, or for such an official to take a bribe (see Archbold, *op. cit.* para. 3483), and this common law offence is supplemented by statutory provisions, including the Public Bodies Corrupt Practices Act 1889, s. 1. The bribing of, or attempting to bribe, an agent in relation to the affairs of his principal, and an agent's taking or soliciting such a bribe, are offences under provisions of the Prevention of Corruption Act 1906, s. 1.

Chapter Fourteen

BLACKMAIL

By section 21(1) of the Theft Act 1968 "a person is guilty of black-mail if, with a view to gain for himself or another or with intent to cause loss to another, he makes any unwarranted demand with menaces." The offence is punishable with a maximum of fourteen years' imprisonment.

Although they come at the end of the definition set out above, the two most important terms in relation to the offence of blackmail are "unwarranted demand" and "menaces," and we will therefore consider these first.

"Unwarranted demand"

Section 21(1) provides that "a demand with menaces is un-warranted unless the person making it does so in the belief (*a*) that he has reasonable grounds for making the demand; and (*b*) that the use of the menaces is a proper means of reinforcing the demand." The test is therefore a subjective one, depending on the accused's state of mind, but it is necessary that he should believe not only that he has reasonable grounds for making the demand but that the use of menaces is a proper means of doing so. For example, if an accused is owed money by another man and he therefore has reason-able grounds for demanding payment of that debt, it will still be blackmail if he couples with the demand a threat (*e.g.,* to publicly disclose the man's homosexual activities), which he knows is not a "proper" means of obtaining payment. "Proper," moreover, means that the test under section 21(1) (*b*) is not whether the accused believes that he has a legal right to make the demand with menaces but whether he believes that he has a moral right to do so (*i.e.,* whether he believes that the means used are morally and socially acceptable: Criminal Law Revision Committee, *Theft and Related Offences,* para. 123). Accordingly, it would seem that an accused may believe that he has a moral right to make the threat even though he knows that he has no legal right to do so. In addition, it would seem that an accused who makes a demand with menaces may technically be guilty of blackmail even though he has a legal right to make the demand in the way he makes it if he believes that he has no reasonable grounds or that it is not a proper means of doing so.

Provided the demand is unwarranted, and it is made with a view to gain or intent to cause loss (see below), the nature of the demand is not important. Indeed, section 21(2) of the Theft Act 1968 provides that "the nature of the act or omission demanded is immaterial, and it is also immaterial whether the menaces relate to action to be taken by the person making the demand." Therefore, it will be sufficient if the accused demands that his victim should pay to him money on the threat that if he does not do so he will be assaulted by a third person.

"Menaces"

The word "menaces" was also used in the corresponding sections of the Larceny Act 1916 and it would seem that the term bears the same meaning. In *Thorne* v. *Motor Trade Association* (1937), H.L., Lord Wright said that "the word 'menaces' is to be liberally construed and not as limited to threats of violence but as including threats of any action detrimental to or unpleasant to the person addressed." It therefore includes a threat to damage property and, as we have seen, a threat to make public details of the other person's homosexual activities, and the menaces, like the demand, can be implied. In the language of Pilcher J. in *R.* v. *Collister* (1955), which was approved by the Court of Criminal Appeal in that case, "You need not be satisfied that there was an express demand for money in words. You need not be satisfied that any express threat was made, but if the evidence satisfies you that, although there was no such express demand or threat, the demeanour of the accused and the circumstances of the case were such that an ordinary reasonable man would understand that a demand for money was being made upon him and that that demand was accompanied by menaces—not perhaps direct, but veiled menaces—so that his ordinary balance of mind was upset, then you would be justified in coming to the conclusion that a demand with menaces had been made. . . ."

One important limitation, however, is that a threat does not amount to a menace unless "it is of such a nature and extent that the mind of an ordinary person of normal stability and courage might be influenced or made apprehensive so as to accede unwillingly to the demand" (*per* Sellers L.J. in *R.* v. *Clear* (1968), C.A.). Therefore, it is not sufficient if the threat is of such a trivial nature that an ordinary person would not be affected by it (unless, possibly, the accused knows that this particular victim will indeed be influenced by it), but it may be sufficient if, on the facts as the accused believes them to be, an ordinary person would be influenced, even though in fact the person threatened is unaffected. Thus, in *R.* v. *Clear, supra,* the accused, who was to be a defence witness in a civil case arising out of the theft of certain goods from a lorry, threatened the defendant that unless he paid the accused money he would alter his evidence. It was held that the accused was guilty of blackmail even though in fact the defendant was unmoved by the threat because the defendant knew that if he lost the action it was his insurers and not himself who would have to pay the value of the stolen goods.

A view to gain or intent to cause loss. As we have seen, for the offence of blackmail, the accused must make the demand "with a view to gain for himself or another or with intent to cause loss to another" (s. 21(1)). Moreover by section 34(2) (*a*) of the Theft Act 1968, although "gain" and "loss" are to be construed as extending only to gain or loss in money or other property, they do extend "to any such gain or loss, whether temporary or permanent; and (i) 'gain' includes a gain by keeping what one has, as well as gain by getting what one has not; and (ii) 'loss' includes a loss by not getting what one might get, as well as a loss by parting with what one has." Therefore, it may be blackmail, for example, if the accused by threats forces the victim to lend him his car but it will not be blackmail if the intent is to have sexual intercourse with the victim because that is not a gain or loss in money or other property. Moreover, as it is sufficient if the demand is with a view to causing gain or loss to another, an accused can commit blackmail if he demands that his victim should release a third person from a debt which the third person owes to that victim.

Chapter Fifteen

HANDLING STOLEN GOODS

By the Theft Act 1968, s. 22(2), a person who is guilty of the offence of handling stolen goods is liable to a maximum term of imprisonment for fourteen years. Moreover, by section 22(1), "a person handles stolen goods if (otherwise than in the course of the stealing) knowing or believing them to be stolen goods he dishonestly receives the goods, or dishonestly undertakes or assists in their retention, removal, disposal or realization by or for the benefit of another person, or if he arranges to do so." The offence of handling stolen goods has replaced the former offence (under s. 33 of the Larceny Act 1916) of receiving stolen goods, but section 33 of the Larceny Act 1916 had already been substantially amended before the Theft Act 1968 came into force (*e.g.*, by s. 4(7) of the Criminal Law Act 1967), and the Theft Act, in fact, makes few changes of a substantial nature. We must now consider the various ingredients of this offence.

"Handles"

As we have just seen, a person may handle stolen goods by (i) receiving them, or (ii) undertaking their retention, removal, disposal or realization by or for the benefit of another person, or (iii) assisting in their retention, removal, disposal or realization by or for the benefit of another, or (iv) arranging to do any of those methods of handling listed under (i), (ii) and (iii). An accused receives goods if he takes them into his possession or control, although this may be for only a temporary purpose (*e.g.*, concealment from the police : *R. v. Richardson* (1834)) and it is unnecessary that the accused should himself obtain any benefit from the transaction. An accused, moreover, may retain, remove, dispose or realize goods by merely, for example, storing them in his garage or carrying them from one place to another or helping to load them on to a lorry, but he must do so by or for the benefit of another person. An accused has not *received* goods if they are still in the exclusive possession of the thief, even if the thief and the accused are in the course of negotiating a price which the accused is to pay for them (*R. v. Wiley* (1850)), but the accused has *removed* them if, with the necessary knowledge,

111

he has carried the thief, who is still in possession of the goods, in the accused's car, though not if this formed part of the theft itself.

"Stolen goods"

The term "stolen goods" includes goods stolen in England or Wales or elsewhere, provided the stealing amounted to an offence where the goods were stolen (Theft Act 1968, s. 24(1)) and it also includes goods obtained by blackmail and goods obtained by an offence of obtaining property by deception (*ibid.*, s. 24(4)), while "goods" includes money and every other description of property except land (see Chap. 13), and includes things severed from the land by stealing (*ibid.*, s. 34(2) (*b*)). Moreover, by section 24(2) of the Theft Act 1968, the term "stolen goods" includes, "in addition to the goods originally stolen and parts of them (whether in their original state or not), (*a*) any other goods which directly or indirectly represent or have at any time represented the stolen goods in the hands of the thief as being the proceeds of any disposal or realization of the whole or part of the goods stolen or of goods so representing the stolen goods; and (*b*) any other goods which directly or indirectly represent or have at any time represented the stolen goods in the hands of a handler of the stolen goods or any part of them as being the proceeds of any disposal or realization of the whole or part of the stolen goods handled by him or of goods so representing them." Thus, in *D'Andrea* v. *Woods* (1953), D.C., some girls had stolen savings stamps which they had then sold, and the accused had received some of the bank notes which the girls had obtained on the sale, with full knowledge of the circumstances. It was held that he was guilty of receiving (and would now be guilty of handling stolen goods) because, although the notes themselves were not stolen, they represented the proceeds of the disposal of the stolen savings stamps. The same would also be true if the girls had passed the stamps on to one handler of stolen goods and he, after selling the stamps, had passed on to the accused the notes which were the proceeds of that sale.

For an offence to be committed under section 24, however, the goods must have been, and at the time of the handling still remained "stolen goods" within the meaning which we have seen this term carries. Therefore, if the alleged thief was not guilty of the offence because, for example, he had not attained the age of criminal responsibility, then a person who has received the goods from him cannot be guilty of handling stolen goods, whatever his belief may have been (*Walters* v. *Lunt* (1951), D.C.), although, as we have seen (Chap. 13), he may be guilty of theft of those goods. Likewise, if the goods ceased to be "stolen goods" before they were handled by the accused then he cannot be guilty of handling stolen goods. Moreover, section 24(3) of the Theft Act 1968 provides that "no goods shall be regarded as having continued to be stolen goods after they have been restored to the person from whom they were stolen or to other lawful possession or custody, or after that person and any other person claiming through him have otherwise ceased as regards those goods to have any right to restitution in respect of the theft." Accordingly, the goods will cease to be "stolen goods" if the owner or his agent (including a police officer) discovers the stolen goods and exercises acts of dominion over them (*R. v. Schmidt* (1866), C.C.R.; *R. v. Villensky* (1892), C.C.R.), but not if he merely discovers the goods and does not perform any such acts in relation to them (*R. v. King* (1938), C.C.A.).

"Otherwise than in the course of the stealing"

The thief himself cannot be guilty of handling those same goods merely by stealing them, and the same is true if the theft is by two or more persons. Where a thief, having stolen goods, immediately hands them to another person the answer to the question whether that other person is guilty of handling rather than stealing (handling, of course, carries a higher maximum sentence) would seem to depend on whether the other person can be convicted as an aider and abetter of the thief. If he can, he is guilty of theft and cannot be convicted of handling. Were it not for this express qualification in section 22(1) of the Theft Act 1968 it would seem that a thief would often also be guilty of handling the same stolen goods. Moreover, where a person is guilty of handling stolen goods it would seem that he is normally also guilty of theft of those goods because by handling the goods he has assumed the rights of the owner. It is clear, however, that the words "otherwise than in the course of *the* stealing" in section 22(1) refer to the same act of stealing which the handler must know or believe has already occurred and not to any further act of stealing which occurs when he handles the goods. Nevertheless, it would seem doubtful whether a handler of stolen goods who has, for example, merely conveyed the goods in his lorry from one place to another can be said to have assumed the rights of the owner by so doing.

"Dishonestly"

To be guilty of this offence the handler of the stolen goods must do so dishonestly. Therefore, if at the time he received the goods he intended to hand them to the true owner or to the police he is not guilty of handling (*R. v. Matthews* (1950), C.C.A.). Nevertheless, if he afterwards decides to keep the goods for himself he will be guilty of theft, because by so doing he assumes the rights of the owner (see Chap. 12).

"Knowing or believing them to be stolen goods"

It is sufficient if the accused knows or believes that the goods are "stolen goods" in the sense which we have seen this term carries. It does not matter that the accused did not know whether the goods were obtained by theft or by blackmail or by deception. Formerly the accused had to know that the goods were stolen goods, and it was not sufficient if he merely had "a pretty good idea" (*R.* v. *Woods* (1968), C.A.). But now that *belief* is enough it would seem that "a pretty good idea" would be sufficient.

Evidence of guilty knowledge or belief

The following special rules of evidence apply to proof of guilty knowledge or belief.

(1) *The common law doctrine of recent possession.* If a person is found in possession of recently stolen goods, a presumption of fact arises that he either stole the goods or received them with guilty knowledge. A presumption of fact is one upon which a jury may act, but is not obliged to act. Thus, it would be a misdirection for the trial judge to tell the jury that in such circumstances the burden of proof is upon the accused to establish that he came by the goods innocently. Moreover, if the accused offers a reasonable explanation of his possession, the presumption loses its effect entirely, and the jury may not then convict him of handling unless they are fully satisfied, by other evidence, of his guilty knowledge (*R.* v. *Schama and Abramovitch* (1914), C.C.A.). The length of time for which goods remain recently stolen depends upon the nature of the goods and, in particular, upon how readily goods of that kind pass from hand to hand; as typical illustrations, a roll of cloth may remain recently stolen for as long as two months (*R.* v. *Partridge* (1836)), but three months is too long for an axe, saw and mattock (*R.* v. *Adams* (1829)).

It was stated in *D.P.P.* v. *Nieser* (1959), D.C., however, that the doctrine of recent possession does not apply to property which has been obtained otherwise than by stealing (*e.g.*, by blackmail), and though this decision was before the Theft Act 1968, the Act would not appear to have changed the position.

(2) *By section 27(3) of the Theft Act 1968,* where an accused is charged with handling stolen goods, and that offence alone, then, if evidence has been given that he handled the goods, the prosecution

may adduce as evidence to prove guilty knowledge (*a*) that he has had in his possession stolen goods (or has assisted in their retention, removal, disposal or realization) from any theft taking place not earlier than twelve months before the offence now charged; and (*b*) that he has within the five years preceding the date of the offence now charged been convicted of theft or of handling stolen goods (provided that seven days' notice in writing has been given to him of the intention to prove the conviction).

Other offences

In addition to the offence of handling stolen goods, there are a number of other offences in relation to stolen goods. Thus, by section 23 of the Theft Act 1968 it is a summary offence (punishable with a maximum fine of £100) to use, in any public advertisement of a reward for the return of goods stolen or lost, words to the effect that no questions will be asked, or that the person producing the goods will be safe from apprehension or inquiry, or that any money paid for the purchase of the goods or advanced by way of loan on them will be repaid. Moreover, by the Metropolitan Police Courts Act 1839, s. 24, any person having in his possession or conveying any thing which may be reasonably suspected of being stolen or unlawfully obtained may be brought before a magistrate, and commits an offence (m), punishable with a fine not exceeding £5 or imprisonment for not more than two months, if he does not give an account to the satisfaction of the magistrate how he came by the same.

Chapter Sixteen

RESTITUTION ORDERS

SECTION 28(1) of the Theft Act 1968 provides that where goods have been stolen, and a person is convicted of any offence with reference to the theft (whether or not the stealing is the gist of his offence), the convicting court may order anyone having possession or control of the goods to restore them to any person entitled to recover them from him. "Stealing," moreover, in this context includes blackmail and obtaining property by deception (*ibid.*, s. 28(6)), and, as the section covers a person "convicted of any offence with reference to the theft," an order may be made following a conviction for handling the stolen goods, robbery, burglary or aggravated burglary (provided that in these last two offences a theft of the goods had occurred, or even an offence not covered by the Theft Act 1968, for example, impeding the apprehension of a thief: see the Criminal Law Act, 1967, s. 4(1)). Nevertheless, a court should not make a restitution order unless the relevant facts have been sufficiently established by the evidence at the trial or by documents which were available as evidence or by admissions (Theft Act 1968, s. 28(4)).

Alternatively, the court may order the convicted person to deliver to the applicant any other goods which directly or indirectly represent the stolen goods, because they are the proceeds of any disposal or realization of the whole or part of the stolen goods (*ibid.*, s. 28(1) (*b*)). Moreover, in addition to, or in substitution for, such an order, the court may order that there should be paid to the applicant a sum not exceeding the value of the stolen goods out of any money which was in the possession of the convicted person at the time of his apprehension (*ibid.*, s. 28(1) (*c*)). But the total value of any goods or money delivered or paid to the applicant must not exceed the value of the stolen goods (*ibid.*, s. 28(2)).

When an order for the actual restoration of stolen goods has been made, but the goods had been sold to a bona fide purchaser, or the convicted person had borrowed money on the security of them from a bona fide lender, then on the application of that purchaser or lender the court may order that there should be paid to him, out of money found in the possession of the convicted person at the time of his apprehension, a sum not exceeding the amount paid for the goods or the amount owed in respect of the loan (*ibid.*, s. 28(3)).

It must be appreciated that section 28 of the Theft Act 1968 merely provides a summary procedure for restoring stolen property to the true owner of that property, and thereby saves him the trouble and expense of taking civil proceedings for the recovery of that property. It is the civil law which decides who is the true owner and this is not affected by the conviction itself (*ibid.*, s. 31(2)). Moreover, as we have seen, the court should only make an order under these provisions if the relevant facts have been sufficiently established. Normally, when goods are stolen, the property in the goods will not pass, even if the goods are sold by the thief to a bona fide purchaser for value, but, for example, under the Factors Act 1889, a purchaser may acquire a good title even to stolen goods and it would seem, therefore, that in such a case a restitution order cannot be made. The same is also true in any other case where the title in the goods passed to the thief.

It may also be mentioned here that the Police (Property) Act 1897 empowers a magistrates' court to make orders for the disposal of property coming into the possession of the police in connection with any criminal charge.

Chapter Seventeen

BURGLARY

Burglary

By section 9(1) of the Theft Act 1968, burglary, which is an offence punishable with a maximum of fourteen years' imprisonment, is committed if a person (*a*) enters any building or part of a building as a trespasser and with intent to commit certain listed offences (see below), or (*b*) having entered any building or part of a building as a trespasser, steals or attempts to steal anything in the building or that part of it or inflicts or attempts to inflict on any person any grievous bodily harm. As we have seen (Chap. 11) this new offence of burglary covers the old offences of burglary, housebreaking and sacrilege. Moreover, for the new offence the time of entry to the building is not relevant, nor is it necessary to prove that the accused broke into the building, as entry without a breaking is sufficient.

An offence under section 9(1) (*a*) can, therefore, be committed only if the accused actually has an intent to commit one of the listed offences at the time he enters the building or a part of the building, but section 9(1) (*b*) covers the situation when an accused enters without the necessary intent but then steals, etc. An example would be if a tramp enters an empty house with the sole intention of spending the night there but, having entered the house, he steals an overcoat which he finds in the house. Nevertheless, even the tramp in this example may commit an offence under section 9(1) (*a*) if he goes from one part of the building to another with the necessary intent, and this may be relevant because section 9(1) (*b*) requires that the accused must actually commit the offence (including an attempt), while a mere intention to commit is sufficient for section 9(1) (*a*). Therefore, if the tramp is caught before he can commit the crime it can only be an offence under section 9(1) (*a*). Moreover, section 9(1) (*a*) covers a greater number of offences than does section 9(1) (*b*). Thus the offences covered by section 9(1) (*a*) are stealing anything in the building or part of a building in question, inflicting on any person therein any grievous bodily harm or raping any woman therein, and doing unlawful damage to the building or anything therein (*ibid.*, s. 9(2)), whereas, as we have seen, section 9(1) (*b*) is restricted to theft, inflicting grievous bodily harm and attempts to commit these offences. An accused who, having entered a building, then commits rape is not thereby guilty of burglary, but rape itself is punishable with a heavier maximum punishment (*i.e.*, life imprisonment) than is burglary. However, this is not true of an attempt to rape (maximum of seven years' imprisonment) nor of most forms of unlawful damage (see the Malicious Damage Act 1861, ss. 1-51, and *post*, Chap. 18). It would also seem clear that the term "stealing" in section 9 is confined to the offence of theft and does not cover, for example, obtaining property by deception or blackmail. We must now consider the other ingredients of this offence in more detail.

"Building"

The term "building" would seem to cover any form of building, whether made of brick, wood, iron or other material and it covers not only dwelling-houses but shops, factories, offices, churches and all other types of building. It therefore covers, for example, the outbuildings of a house, or a row of detached garages, or farm buildings but it would seem that the building must have some degree of permanence and a tent is not therefore covered, even though it might be some person's home. In addition, section 9(3) of the Theft Act 1968 provides that the term "building" includes an inhabited vehicle or vessel, even when the person having an habitation in it is not there, so that it also covers caravans and houseboats. Nevertheless, this only covers *inhabited* vehicles and vessels so that if it is one which is only inhabited during part of the year (*e.g.*, during holiday periods) it is possible that it is only a "building" during the time that it is inhabited, though it is not necessary that there should be anyone in the vehicle or vessel at the moment when the accused enters it. If, however, the vehicle or vessel is a permanent home then it would appear to remain a "building" even though its inhabitants are away, for example, on holiday.

The Act does not define the term a "part of a building," but it clearly covers two separate flats so that if the inhabitant of one flat enters the other flat he can be guilty of burglary. The same is also true if a lodger within a house enters another part of the house or a customer in a shop goes behind the counter. However, as we have seen, for an offence of burglary to be committed the accused must enter the building or the part of the building as a trespasser and the lodger or the customer can, therefore, only be guilty of burglary if they have entered a part of the building where they have no right to be, at least at the time when they have done

so (see below). Whether, in the case which we have already considered, where a tramp enters a house merely to spend the night
there and he then goes into another room in the same house, it can
be said that he has thereby entered another part of the house, is
perhaps not so clear, but it would seem likely that even the other
room is another part of the house for the purposes of burglary.

"Enters . . . as a trespasser"

The word "enters" would seem to bear the same meaning as it
bore both at common law and for the purposes of burglary under
section 25 of the Larceny Act 1916. If this is so there is a sufficient
entry when any part of the body, if only a hand or finger, goes over
the threshold (*R*. v. *Davis* (1823)). There is also a sufficient entry
if any instrument held in the hand is pushed over the threshold for
the purpose of effecting the ulterior offence, for example, if the
accused thrusts a long handled fishing net in at a window with
intent to scoop up jewels within the room (see *R*. v. *Hughes* (1785)).
The insertion of an instrument merely for the purpose of gaining
entry to the building, and not for the purpose of effecting the
ulterior offence, would not, however, be a sufficient (*R*. v. *Hughes,
supra*).

For the offence of burglary, the accused must have entered the
building as a trespasser, which is a civil law concept, and an
understanding of this offence therefore requires some knowledge of
this branch of the law of torts (see, *e.g., Salmond on Torts*, 15th ed.,
pp. 67-82). Any intentional, reckless or negligent entry into a building can amount to a trespass if made without the consent of the
person who is in possession of that building (*e.g.,* a tenant, though
not a mere guest) and mistake is not a defence. However, an involuntary entry is not a trespass so that if the accused is dragged
against his will into the building or is carried there while unconscious this does not amount to a trespass. If, as we have just seen,
the accused enters with the consent of the occupier of the building
then it will not be a trespass, but it would seem that an apparent
consent may be vitiated by fraud. If, for example, the accused
obtains entry by impersonating another particular person his entry
will be a trespass, but it is somewhat more uncertain if the entry
is obtained merely by a trick. Thus, in *R*. v. *Boyle* (1954), C.C.A.,
the accused obtained entry to a house by falsely pretending to be
an official of the B.B.C. and to be endeavouring to locate radio
interference. His offence was held to be burglary under the Larceny
Act 1916 but it is possible that as the householder consented to that
particular accused entering, even though as a result of the false
pretence, it will not now amount to burglary. Nevertheless, it is

probable that the courts will still hold that on facts like those in
R. v. *Boyle* the crime of burglary has been committed.

Even though a building may be open to certain members of the
public it may not be open to persons only entering because they
have ulterior motives. Thus a bank may be open to its customers
but it may be a trespass if it is entered by bank robbers, and the
same may also be true of a shop. Moreover, although a bank or
shop may be open to the public for certain hours of the day it will
be a trespass if the accused enters at some other time. Thus, an
accused who enters a shop with the intention of stealing goods
within that shop, and not of buying goods may be guilty of burglary
whether he enters while the shop is open to the public or is shut.
Nevertheless, these suggested possibilities in relation to trespass are
tentative only, and the courts may interpret "trespass" in relation
to burglary as having a narrower (or possibly wider) meaning than
we have considered.

For the offence of burglary the accused must *enter* the building
as a trespasser (for this reason it seems unlikely that the civil law
doctrine of trespass *ab initio* applies to burglary) and it is not,
therefore, sufficient if he enters as an invitee or licensee and later
becomes a trespasser. For example, if a customer enters a shop
while it is still open to the public with the intention of buying
goods within the shop and he then decides to hide in the shop until
it has been closed, he does become a trespasser when the shop has
been closed but he is not necessarily guilty of burglary because he
did not enter as a trespasser. Nevertheless, if, as is likely, he then
enters another part of the shop (*e.g.*, goes behind the counter or
into a storeroom) he will have entered a part of the building as a
trespasser and so can be guilty of burglary.

Aggravated Burglary

By section 10 of the Theft Act 1968, a person is guilty of aggravated
burglary (which is punishable with a maximum of life imprisonment) if he "commits any burglary and at the time has with him
any firearm or imitation firearm, any weapon of offence, or any
explosive." "Firearm" includes an airgun or air pistol and "imitation firearm" means anything which has the appearance of being
a firearm, whether capable of being discharged or not" (*ibid.*, s.
10(1) (*a*)). Moreover, "weapon of offence" means any article made
or adapted for use for causing injury to or incapacitating a person,
or intended by the person having it with him for such use" (*ibid.*,
s. 10(1) (*b*)) and " 'explosive' means any article manufactured for

the purpose of producing a practical effect by explosion, or intended by the person having it with him for that purpose" (*ibid.*, s. 10(1) (*c*)). Therefore, "weapon of offence" includes, for example, a knuckleduster, cosh or a broken bottle and even a bicycle chain or stone if the accused intends to use it to cause injury. Moreover, it is sufficient if the article was made or adapted or intended for incapacitating a person, so this includes, for example, handcuffs, gags, sleeping pills or even rope if the intention was to tie up the occupier of the building.

It is necessary for this offence of aggravated burglary that the accused had the offensive weapon, etc., with him at the time that he committed burglary. Therefore, if the accused commits burglary by entering a building with the necessary intent, he must have the weapon of offence, etc., with him when he actually enters, but, if he commits burglary by committing the specified offence after he had entered, he must have had the weapon of offence, etc., with him when he commits the specified offence. One matter, however, which is uncertain is whether the accused must know at the time he commits the burglary that he has with him the weapon of offence, etc., and also whether he must intend at that time if necessary to use it. However, where similar words have been used in other statutes (*e.g.*, Prevention of Crime Act 1953, s. 1) it has been held that the accused must know that he has the relevant object and it would seem likely that this will be held to be so under section 10 of the Theft Act 1968. Moreover, it has been held under section 1 of the Prevention of Crime Act 1953 that if an accused does make use of a potential weapon of offence then he must be held to have had it with this intention, even though this may not be true (*Woodward* v. *Koessler* (1958), D.C.). Again, it may be that this principle also applies to aggravated burglary.

Going Equipped for Stealing

By section 25(1) of the Theft Act 1968 a person commits the offence of going equipped for stealing (which is punishable with a maximum of three years' imprisonment) if, when not at his place of abode, he has with him any article for use in the course of or in connection with any burglary, theft or cheat. "Theft," moreover, includes taking a conveyance without authority (contrary to s. 12(1) of the Theft Act 1968) and "cheat" means an offence of obtaining property by deception (*ibid.*, s. 25(5)). Although this offence of going equipped for stealing is not a form of burglary it is perhaps convenient to consider it here.

The essence of this offence is not that the article was necessarily one normally used in stealing, etc., but that the accused intended to use it in committing one of the offences mentioned. Thus, it could include, for example, not only firearms or a jemmy but a key, rubber gloves, a mask or even sticky paper which the accused intended to use in removing a glass window. Moreover, proof that the accused had an article with him made or adapted for use in committing a burglary, theft or cheat is evidence that he had it with him for such use (*ibid.*, s. 25(3)).

Chapter Eighteen

MALICIOUS DAMAGE AND ARSON

Malicious Damage

THE Malicious Damage Act 1861 contains numerous offences of unlawfully and maliciously damaging particular kinds of property specified in the Act, and these offences are of widely varying gravity. For example, maliciously damaging a dwelling-house, any person being therein, by means of an explosion is an offence (f) punishable with a maximum of life imprisonment (section 9), whereas maliciously damaging a plant in a garden is a mere summary offence (section 23). These provisions are too detailed to concern us here, but we must notice the residuary provision of section 51 of the Act, which provides that unlawfully and maliciously damaging any property, real or personal, for which no punishment is otherwise provided in the Act shall be an offence (m) punishable with a maximum of two years' imprisonment (five years' imprisonment if the offence is committed between the hours of 9 p.m. and 6 a.m.). By the Criminal Justice Administration Act 1914, section 14, as amended by the Malicious Damage Act 1964, section 1, the offence may be tried summarily if the amount of the damage does not exceed £100, and must be tried summarily if it does not exceed £5; lower maximum punishments are provided when the offence is tried summarily.

As we have seen in considering the statutory assaults (*ante*, Chap. 9), the word "maliciously" always has the same meaning when it appears in a criminal statute. Its primary meaning is intention to cause the kind of harm forbidden by the statute or recklessness as to whether that kind of harm will be caused or not. It follows that if A throws a stone at B, and the stone misses B and breaks a window, A cannot be convicted of maliciously damaging property, unless he foresaw the risk to the window (*R. v. Pembliton* (1874), C.C.R.).

The use of the word "maliciously" also implies that a bona fide claim of right will be a defence. For example, in *R. v. Twose* (1879) the accused was charged with unlawfully and maliciously setting

124

fire to furze growing on a common contrary to section 16 of the Act of 1861. There was evidence that other persons living near the common had sometimes set fire to the furze in order to improve the growth of the grass, although there was no proof that they had the right to do this. The learned judge directed the jury that if the accused set fire to the furze thinking that she had a right to do so she would not be guilty of the offence. In this and some other cases it has not been held to be a condition of this defence that the accused's mistaken belief should have been reasonable. But in *R. v. Clemens* (1898) C.C.R., in which local inhabitants demolished a wooden structure on private land which they supposed to infringe their right of access to the land, it was held that they would be guilty of malicious damage if they had done more damage than they could reasonably have believed to be necessary for the assertion or protection of their supposed right. Again, it is clearly established that on a charge of unlawfully and maliciously killing a dog, contrary to section 41 of the Act of 1861, if the accused pleads that he did the act in defence of property, such as poultry or sheep, it must appear that there was imminent danger to the property from the dog and that either there was in fact no practicable means other than shooting of stopping the attack, or that the accused, having regard to all the circumstances, acted reasonably in regarding the shooting as necessary for the protection of the property (*Cresswell v. Sirl* (1948), C.A.; *Goodway v. Becker* (1951), D.C.). Moreover it was held in *Gott v. Measures* (1948), D.C., that sporting rights over land are not a form of property which can justify the killing of a dog whose activities are interfering with the game, and that it would be no defence that the accused honestly thought that he had a right to shoot the dog in the circumstances. Lord Goddard C.J. said "Just as you cannot have a bona fide claim of right if the right is one which the law does not recognize, so it seems to me you cannot honestly believe that it is necessary to shoot a dog to protect your property when you have no property to protect." This dictum has been very much criticized and would seem very difficult, if not impossible, to square with such cases as *R. v. Twose, supra.*

Arson

Arson (f) consists of unlawfully and maliciously setting fire to certain types of property specified in the Malicious Damage Act 1861 and certain other enactments. Here again the offences are too numerous and detailed for it to be possible to set them all out here, but some examples will be given. In each case it may be assumed that the setting fire must be unlawful and malicious and that the punishment stated is the maximum. The sections indicated are those of the Malicious Damage Act 1861.

Buildings
(1) Any place of divine worship (s. 1; life imprisonment).

(2) Any dwelling-house, any person being therein (s. 2; life imprisonment). It was held in *R*. v. *Arthur* (1968) that it is not sufficient for this offence if the only person in the dwelling-house was the accused himself. Howard J., in this case, refused to follow the decision of Lord Coleridge C.J. in *R*. v. *Pardoe* (1894), where it was held that the accused's presence was sufficient.

(3) Any building specified in section 3, with intent to injure or defraud (s. 3; life imprisonment). The specified buildings range from houses, warehouses and shops to hovels, sheds and folds.

(4) Any building not specified in the Act (s. 6; fourteen years' imprisonment).

Other property
(5) Anything in, against, or under a building, under such circumstances that if the building were thereby set on fire the accused would be guilty of an offence under any of the preceding sections (s. 7, as amended by the Criminal Law Act 1967, Sched. 2; fourteen years' imprisonment).

(6) Any ship or vessel, whether complete or unfinished (s. 42; life imprisonment). This offence is also committed by destroying or casting away any ship or vessel.

(7) Any crops or plantation or any heath, gorse, furze or fern (s. 16; fourteen years' imprisonment).

(8) Any stack of corn, grain, coal, wood [or other matter specified in the section] (s. 17; life imprisonment).

Arson of royal ships of war, arsenals, dockyards and certain other premises and materials is a capital offence under the Dockyards Protection Act 1772.

When the definition of an offence under the Act of 1861 does not expressly require intent to injure or defraud, the offence is committed even though the accused is in possession of the property in question if he does the act with intent to injure or defraud (s. 59). An intent to injure or defraud will be presumed when the accused has set fire to someone else's property, but not where he has set fire to his own (*R.* v. *Farrington* (1811)).

We have already considered the meaning of the term *maliciously* in a criminal statute (see above under *Malicious Damage* and *ante*, Chap. 9, under *Statutory Assaults*), but it may be useful to give one or two further illustrations connected with the offence of arson. In *R.* v. *Faulkner* (1877), the accused, a sailor, broached a cask of rum in the hold of his ship, intending to steal some of the rum; to assist him, he lit a match, the rum caught fire, and the ship was burnt out. The Irish Court for Crown Cases Reserved held that he could not be convicted of arson of the ship, as he obviously had not foreseen the danger to the ship, and his larcenous intention did not show the *mens rea* required for arson. Similarly, it was held in *R.* v. *Child* (1871), C.C.R., that, on a charge under section 7 of the Act of 1861 (*supra*), it must be proved that the accused intended to set fire to the building or foresaw that the building would probably catch fire and deliberately took the risk; it is not sufficient that he intentionally set fire to something in, against or under the building (see also *R.* v. *Nattrass* (1882)).

There is a sufficient *setting fire* if any part of the property in question is consumed by fire. Thus there is a sufficient setting fire to a building if part of a floor has been charred (*R.* v. *Parker* (1839)), but not if it has been merely scorched (*R.* v. *Russell* (1842)).

Chapter Nineteen

FORGERY AND COINAGE OFFENCES

Forgery

THE forgery of a writing, with intent to defraud, is an offence at common law, but in fact forgery should be charged under some statutory provision, and almost always under some section of the Forgery Act 1913. For the purposes of that Act "forgery is the making of a false document in order that it may be used as genuine, and in the case of the seals and dies mentioned in this Act the counterfeiting of a seal or die" (section 1). The seals mentioned include various State seals and the seal of any court of record, the forgery (f) of which is punishable with a maximum of life imprisonment, and certain other seals, where the maximum punishment is less severe. The dies mentioned include those used by the Commissioners of Inland Revenue and the Commissioners of Customs and Excise; the forgery (f) of these is punishable with imprisonment for not more than fourteen years. All these provisions are in section 5, and in each case intent to defraud or deceive must be proved. The provisions relating to the forgery of documents are of much greater importance and must be considered in some detail.

The forgery of many specified documents is specially punishable by the Act. For example, the forgery, with intent to defraud, of a will, deed, or bank note, is an offence (f) punishable with a maximum of life imprisonment, and the forgery, with the like intent, of a valuable security or insurance policy, is an offence (f) punishable with a maximum of fourteen years' imprisonment (section 2); and the forgery, with intent to defraud *or deceive*, of certain public documents, such as registers of births, marriages and deaths and certified copies of entries therein, court records, and marriage licences, is an offence (f) punishable as provided by section 3 of the Act (the prescribed maximum punishments varying from life imprisonment to seven years' imprisonment). Section 4 of the Act then creates a residuary offence (m), punishable with a maximum of two years' imprisonment, covering the forgery of any

128

document, if committed with intent to defraud, and the forging of any public document, if committed with intent to defraud *or deceive*.

Forgery and uttering

Forgery is the *making* of a false document, with the requisite intent. Using, or publishing, a forged document, knowing it to be forged, is the separate offence of uttering, which is punishable in the same way as the forgery of that particular kind of document; the same intent (to defraud, or to defraud or deceive) is required as is necessary for the forgery (Forgery Act 1913, s. 6). It has been held that publishing a photostat copy of a forged document amounts to uttering the document (*R.* v. *Harris* (1966), C.C.A.).

"Document"

This word has not been judicially defined, nor is it defined by the statute. Moreover, there appear to be few cases in which the point has arisen. However, in *R.* v. *Closs* (1858), C.C.R., it was held that a painting is not a document. In that case a dealer had painted the name John Linnell on a painting which was not by that artist, and he was held not to be guilty of forgery. It was held (rather oddly, perhaps) that the signature could not be regarded as being itself a writing, being "merely in the nature of a mark put upon the painting with a view to identifying it" (*per* Cockburn C.J.). (The terms *document, instrument*, and *writing* appear to have been used synonymously in relation to forgery at common law.) Again, in *R.* v. *Smith* (1858), C.C.R., the accused had sold baking powder in packets wrapped in printed papers designed to resemble those used by the well-known manufacturer Borwick, and it was held that he could not be convicted of forgery, because, even if the wrappers could be regarded as documents (which was improbable), they were not false documents: the fraud lay in the improper use of them (a somewhat thin argument?).

Section 1 of the Act provides that it is immaterial that a forged document is incomplete or not binding in law.

"False"

At common law a document was false, for the purposes of forgery, only if in some way it purported to be what it was not: the falsity had to relate to the *document*. A deed, for example, was false, if it purported to have been signed by a person who did not sign it, or if it purported to have been executed on a day different from that on which it was executed (if the date was material), but not if it contained a false statement (*e.g.*, that the property was free from incumbrances) which did not relate to the deed (see *R.*

v. *Ritson* (1869), C.C.R.). This principle has been broadly followed
by section 1 of the Forgery Act 1913, which declares a document
to be false in many instances in which the courts had so held at
common law, *e.g.*, when the document purports to be made by or
on behalf or on account of a person who did not make it nor
authorize its making, or if the time or place of making the document (if material) is falsely stated therein (as in *R. v. Riley* (1896),
C.C.R. (false time of despatch inserted by telegraph clerk in telegrams backing horses that had already won)); and the section (again
following the common law) makes it clear that a document is false
if it purports to have been made by or on behalf of a person who
did not make or authorize its making, even if that person is ficti-
tious or deceased, or if the document is made in the name of an
existing person, but with the intention that it should pass as having
been made by some other person (as when a bill of exchange made
payable to one Henry Davis got into the hands of another person
of the same name, who fraudulently endorsed the bill with his own
signature (*Mead* v. *Young* (1790)).

It is further enacted by the Criminal Justice Act 1925, s. 35, that
a document may be false for the purposes of forgery even if it is
not false in such a manner as is described in section 1 of the Act
of 1913. This provision would seem to indicate an intention to
rely upon the common law principle of falsity for the purposes of
forgery. But in *R.* v. *Hopkins and Collins* (1957), the Court of
Criminal Appeal took a different view and held that making false
entries, by entering false amounts, in a cash book could amount
to forgery. Lord Goddard, C.J. stated ". . . we are only concerned
now with the Forgery Act 1913. . . . The Act starts in sect. 1 by
saying: '(1) For the purposes of this Act, forgery is the making of
a false document in order that it may be used as genuine.' I think
the prevalent opinion of the court is that if a man has a cash book
and proceeds to make false entries in it so that it does not represent the truth and does not represent what he received and what
he paid out, that book is a false document, and it is made false
by the person who keeps it."

This decision perhaps casts some doubt on the decision in *R.* v.
Martin (1879), C.C.R., in which it was held that to sign a cheque in
a false name does not make it a false document if one gives the
cheque as one's own and one is not pretending to be someone other
than the person that one is. In that case the accused bought a pony
and carriage from a dealer to whom he was well-known; in the
dealer's presence he made out a cheque and signed it in a false
name, in which he had no account at the bank. The dealer did not
notice the discrepancy and gave delivery of the pony and carriage.

It was held that the accused could not be convicted of forgery.

It is clear that a document is false if a person is given authority to complete a partly made document and he completes it in breach of that authority, *e.g.*, if a master signs a cheque, but leaves the amount blank and instructs his clerk to fill it in for a certain amount, and the clerk fills it in for a larger amount, which he obtains from the bank and appropriates to his own use (*R.* v. *Wilson* (1847)).

The mens rea of forgery

As has been stated, where the document is a private document proof of intent to defraud is required, whereas for the forgery of a public document proof of intent to defraud or deceive is sufficient. In the civil case of *Re London and Globe Finance Corporation* (1903) these terms were defined by Buckley J. as follows: "To deceive is to induce a man to believe that a thing is true which is false and which the person practising the deceit knows or believes to be false. To defraud is to deprive by deceit; it is by deceit to induce a man to act to his injury. More tersely it may be put, that to deceive is by falsehood to induce a state of mind; to defraud is by deceit to induce a course of action." This definition has been adopted by the criminal courts and has been liberally interpreted by them. Thus, it has been held that an intent to induce a man to act to his injury is an intent to defraud, even if there is no intention to deprive him of anything of economic value, and that a man is induced to act to his injury if he is by deceit induced to do (or refrain from doing) something which, had he known the truth, it would have been his right and duty to refuse to do (or to do, as the case may be). For example, in *R.* v. *Bassey* (1931) the accused, in order to secure admission to the Inner Temple as a student, put forward certain forged documents relating to his educational qualifications, and it was held by the Court of Criminal Appeal that his intent to induce the Benchers of the Inn to admit him was an intent to defraud. This decision was cited with approval in *Welham* v. *D.P.P.* (1961), in which the House of Lords held that an intent to deceive a possible Board of Trade investigator into believing, contrary to the fact, that there had been no breach of credit restriction regulations in connection with certain hire-purchase transactions, and so to induce him to refrain from taking action that, had he known the facts, it would have been his duty to take, was an intent to defraud.

Demanding, etc., by virtue of a forged instrument

By section 7 of the Act of 1913 it is an offence (f), punishable with a maximum of fourteen years' imprisonment, with intent to defraud, to (*inter alia*) demand, receive or obtain any money, security for money or other property under, upon, or by virtue of any forged instrument, knowing the same to be forged. It is not necessary to prove that the obtaining of the property was *caused* by the forged instrument with the same strictness as it is necessary on a charge of obtaining property by deception, contrary to section 15 of the Theft Act 1968, to prove that deception was truly the cause of the obtaining. It suffices that the forged instrument was the indirect cause of the obtaining, *e.g.*, that in consequence of having entered into a hire-purchase agreement with a finance company in a false name (that of a credit-worthy person) a lorry has been obtained from a firm of dealers (*R.* v. *Hurford* (1963), C.C.A.).

Other offences

The mere possession, without lawful authority or excuse, of a forged bank note, knowing it to be forged, is an offence (f), punishable with a maximum of fourteen years' imprisonment, under section 8 of the Act of 1913. There are other kindred offences too numerous to mention here.

Coinage offences

The law relating to coinage offences was consolidated by the Coinage Offences Act 1936. We shall limit our attention to the offences of counterfeiting and uttering, but the Act contains a number of kindred offences, such as those of defacing coinage and of making or possessing coining implements.

By section 1 of the Act a person who falsely makes or counterfeits any coin resembling any current coin shall be guilty of an offence (f) and on conviction shall be liable (a) where the coin resembles a current gold or silver coin, to imprisonment for life; and (b) where the coin resembles a current copper coin, to imprisonment for a term not exceeding seven years. The section declares that the offence of counterfeiting shall be deemed to be complete although the coin counterfeited was not in a fit state to be uttered or the making or counterfeiting thereof had not been finished or perfected.

By section 5 of the Act the uttering of any false or counterfeit coin resembling any current coin, knowing it to be false or counterfeit, is an offence (m). The maximum punishment varies according to the circumstances; whereas it is normally one year's imprisonment, it is two years' imprisonment in certain circumstances, *e.g.*, where the accused at the time had other false or counterfeit coin in his possession. By the same section the mere possession of three or more false or counterfeit coins resembling any current gold or silver coin, knowing them to be counterfeit and with intent to utter them, is an offence (m), punishable with imprisonment for a term not exceeding one year. As with the offence of counterfeiting itself, it is not necessary for the offence of uttering that the coin should be in a fit state to be uttered or that the counterfeiting should have been finished or perfected.

Chapter Twenty

PERJURY AND OTHER OFFENCES
AGAINST PUBLIC JUSTICE

Perjury

BY section 1 of the Perjury Act 1911 perjury, which is an offence (m) punishable with imprisonment for not more than seven years, is committed when any person lawfully sworn as a witness or as an interpreter in a judicial proceeding wilfully makes a statement material in that proceeding which he knows to be false or does not believe to be true. The Act contains a number of other offences concerned with the making of false statements, but only the offence so defined is called perjury. In addition, by section 89 of the Criminal Justice Act 1967, it is a like offence (punishable with imprisonment for not more than two years) for a person to wilfully make a statement, which he knows to be false or does not believe to be true, in a written statement which is admissible in evidence in committal proceedings or in a trial on indictment, under sections 2 or 9 of that Act (see Chaps. 32, 37).

If a witness makes several false statements in a judicial proceeding he commits only one offence of perjury; the several false statements are known as assignments of the perjury.

An interpreter commits the offence when he gives a deliberately false translation. For simplicity's sake in the rest of the discussion we shall consider the commoner case where a witness is alleged to have committed perjury.

"Lawfully sworn"

In general the effect of this term in the definition of perjury is that a form of oath must have been tendered to the witness which was appropriate to his religious belief. However, by section 15 of the Act, a witness is deemed to be lawfully sworn if he has taken the form of oath tendered without objection, or has declared it to be binding on him. Moreover, by the same section, the expression "oath", in the case of persons for the time being allowed by law to affirm or declare instead of swearing, includes affirmation and declaration. A solemn affirmation may be made, instead of taking an oath, in the following cases: (*a*) where a witness objects to be sworn on the ground that he has no religious belief or that the taking of an oath is contrary to his religious belief; (*b*) when it is not reasonably practicable to administer to the witness an oath in a form which is appropriate to his religious belief (Oaths Acts 1888 and 1961).

"Judicial proceeding"

By section 1 of the Act of 1911, the expression "judicial proceeding" includes a proceeding before any court, tribunal or person having by law power to hear, receive and examine evidence on oath. Proceedings that take place after the judge has left the room are not, therefore, within the ambit of the expression (*R.* v. *Lloyd* (1887), C.C.R.). On the other hand, the view has been expressed that if a tribunal has authority by law to receive evidence on oath, a proceeding before it would be a judicial proceeding even if in the particular circumstances the court lacked complete jurisdiction. And in *R.* v. *Castiglione* (1912), C.C.A., it was held (*obiter*) that an action brought against a non-existent person could be a judicial proceeding.

Affidavit evidence prepared for use in a judicial proceeding and properly sworn, is deemed to have been given in the proceeding. Further, a statement made by a person lawfully sworn in England for the purpose of a judicial proceeding abroad is to be treated as a statement made in a judicial proceeding in England. Conversely, where for the purposes of a judicial proceeding in England a person is lawfully sworn under the authority of an Act of Parliament in another part of Her Majesty's dominions, or before a British tribunal or a British officer abroad, the statement is to be treated as having been made in the judicial proceeding in England, unless the particular Act of Parliament under which it was made otherwise specifically provides.

"Material in that proceeding"

The question whether the statement on which a charge of perjury is based was material is a question of law to be determined by the court of trial. In any judicial proceeding much evidence will be given that is not material to the issue before the court. For example, in *R.* v. *Holden* (1872) A saw B maltreating a horse, in consequence of which words passed between them and A referred to B as "a squinting, lying devil". B then took out a summons against A before the magistrates for using language calculated to provoke a breach of the peace. During the hearing of this summons several witnesses gave evidence that they had seen B ill-treating the horse. In his evidence, however, B denied doing so, and by reason of this denial he was afterwards charged with perjury. The trial judge held that a charge of perjury could not be sustained, as the matter of the treatment of the horse was merely collateral to the issue before the magistrates.

On the other hand, evidence which is not directly relevant to the issues in a case can be material. Thus the credit of a witness is always material. When a witness is being cross-examined it is permissible for counsel to ask him questions which are designed to show that he is not a person upon whose word reliance can be placed. Should the witness give a deliberately false answer to such a question he will commit perjury (*R*. v. *Baker* (1895), D.C.). Moreover, evidence which ought not legally to have been admitted may be material. Thus the general rule is that when a witness gives an answer to a question that relates solely to the witness's credit, evidence cannot be called in that proceeding to contradict the witness's answer (because otherwise the proceeding might be indefinitely protracted). Yet, if a witness *is* called to contradict the answer given by the first witness, and the second witness gives deliberately false evidence upon the question, his evidence will be material: it affects the credit of the first witness, which, as we have seen, is material (*R*. v. *Gibbons* (1862), C.C.R.). Lastly, it may be noticed that evidence may be material although it does not relate to the principal issue in the case. For example, in a criminal case evidence given by a prisoner on oath after conviction in mitigation of sentence is material (*R*. v. *Wheeler* (1917), C.C.A.).

"Which he knows to be false or does not believe to be true"

The words "or does not believe to be true" make it plain (thereby following the common law rule upon the point) that a witness may commit perjury by making a statement which is true in fact, if he believes that he is lying, or by swearing positively upon a matter as to which he has no knowledge one way or the other.

Corroboration

In general there is no rule in English law that a person cannot be convicted of a criminal offence upon the evidence of only one witness. But there are some cases in which corroboration is required, and perjury is amongst these. It is provided by section 13 of the Act of 1911 that a person shall not be liable to be convicted of any offence against the Act, or of any offence declared by any other Act to be perjury or subornation of perjury, solely upon the evidence of one witness as to the falsity of any statement alleged to be false. The requirement of corroboration is clearly satisfied if two witnesses can be found to swear directly to the falsity of the statement. But the rule is equally satisfied if one witness gives evidence as to the falsity of the statement and his evidence is corroborated in some other way, *e.g.*, by proof that the accused on some other occasion made a statement which is inconsistent with the statement that forms the subject of the charge of perjury (*R.* v. *Hook* (1858)).

A person cannot be convicted of perjury merely upon proof that upon two different occasions he gave sworn evidence which is mutually inconsistent. The prosecution must prove which statement was false, and cannot seek simply to impale the witness upon the horns of a dilemma (*R.* v. *Jackson* (1823); *R* v. *Wheatland* (1838)).

Subornation

Procuring the commission of perjury, which is called subornation, is punishable in the same way as perjury (Perjury Act 1911, s. 7).

Offences akin to Perjury

Apart from perjury, the making of false statements in certain circumstances is made punishable by the Perjury Act 1911 and by certain other Acts. Three examples may be taken from the Act of 1911. By section 3, the making of false statements for the purpose of procuring a marriage or a marriage licence is an offence (m) punishable with a maximum of seven years' imprisonment. By section 4, the making of false statements in registering a birth or death is similarly punishable. By section 6, the making of false statements in order to procure registration on a register kept under any public general Act of Parliament of persons qualified by law to practise any vocation or calling is an offence (m) punishable with imprisonment for not more than twelve months.

Misprision and Compounding

The former offences of misprision of felony and compounding a felony were abolished by the Criminal Law Act 1967. Misprision of felony was abolished as a result of the abolition of the distinction between felonies and misdemeanours (see Chap. 1), while compounding a felony was expressly abolished by section 5(5). Nevertheless, misprision of treason and compounding treason are retained. Section 5, moreover, creates the new offences of conceal-ing offences and of giving false information and these also will now be considered.

(1) *Misprision of treason*

Misprision (m) consists of concealing a treason known to have been committed. A curious relic of an older period, which has sur-vived the general abolition of forfeiture by the Forfeiture Act 1870, attaches to a conviction of misprision of treason: the offender's goods are forfeited, as also are the profits of his lands for the rest of his life.

Failure to report to a magistrate or to the police a treason which one knows to have been committed is a sufficient concealment to render one guilty of misprision. The leading case on misprision is now *Sykes* v. *D.P.P.* (1962) in the House of Lords (a case on mis-prision of felony but the same principles apply to misprision of treason); this case finally decided that it is not a necessary ingredient of misprision that the accused should have converted the conceal-ment into a source of emolument to himself. Lord Denning also considered some of the possible defences to a charge of misprision, but as much of what he said was only relevant to misprision of felony it need not concern us here. Nevertheless, Lord Denning thought that non-disclosure might sometimes be justified or excused on grounds of privilege, *e.g.*, where a lawyer is told by his client or a doctor by his patient or a clergyman by a parishioner that he has committed treason, although close family or personal ties would not be sufficient where the offence was of so serious a character that it ought to be reported (and this would surely apply to treason).

Where the duty to disclose exists the offence is not committed unless the accused has had a reasonable opportunity of making a report and has failed to do so within a reasonable time. This is a question for the jury, as also is the question whether the accused's knowledge was so definite that it ought to have been disclosed: there is no duty to report mere rumours or gossip.

It was decided by the Court of Criminal Appeal in *R.* v. *King* (1965) that the accused's silence after he has been warned by a police officer that he need not say anything cannot amount to mis-prision, and that it is also a defence that the accused remained silent for fear of incriminating himself of the offence in question or of any other offence.

(2) *Compounding treason*

The offence (m) of compounding is committed by entering into an agreement not to prosecute in return for some advantage.

(3) *Concealing offences or giving false information*

"Where a person has committed an arrestable offence, any other person who, knowing or believing that the offence or some other arrestable offence has been committed, and that he has information which might be of material assistance in securing the prosecution or conviction of an offender for it, accepts or agrees to accept for not disclosing that information any consideration, other than the making good of loss or injury caused by the offence, or the making of reasonable compensation for that loss or injury," commits the new offence of concealing offences, which is punishable with a maximum of two years' imprisonment (Criminal Law Act 1967, s. 5(1)). The offence is only committed, however, if the accused accepted or agreed to accept some consideration for not disclosing the information so that it does not cover a person who refrains from giving information because he does not think it right that the offender should be prosecuted.

"Where a person causes any wasteful employment of the police by knowingly making to any person a false report tending to show that an offence has been committed, or to give rise to apprehension for the safety of any persons or property, or tending to show that he has information material to any police inquiry," he commits the new summary offence of giving false information, which is punishable with a maximum of six months' imprisonment or a fine of not more than two hundred pounds or both (Criminal Law Act 1967, s. 5(2)).

Proceedings cannot be instituted, however, for either of these offences except by or with the consent of the Director of Public Prosecutions (*ibid.*, s. 5(3)).

See also Chapter 5 for the offence of assisting offenders.

Other Offences Against Public Justice

Although the offence of compounding a felony has been abolished, we have seen (Chap. 15) that it is a summary offence, under section 23 of the Theft Act 1968, to state in any public advertisement of a reward for the return of goods stolen or lost that no questions will be asked, or that the person producing the goods will be safe from apprehension, or that money paid for the goods will be repaid. In addition there are a number of common law offences (m) which should also be noted.

(1) *Embracery*

Embracery consists of an attempt to influence jurors by bribes or by any other corrupt means.

(2) *Contempt of court*

Contempt of court may be either civil contempt, *i.e.*, refusing to carry out an order of the court, or criminal contempt. Criminal contempt, which is a common law offence (m) includes the following:

(a) Contempt in face (*ex facie*) of the court, *e.g.*, by insulting the judge or refusing to be sworn or refusing to answer questions.

(b) Scandalizing the court, *e.g.*, by suggesting, whether in words or in writing, bias or corruption in the court. Honest discussion, within the bounds of moderation, of the merits of a jury's verdict or the decision of a judge does not amount to contempt (see *McLeod* v. *St. Aubyn* (1899), P.C.).

(c) Conduct which is calculated (*i.e.*, likely, whether or not intended) to obstruct or interfere with the due process of the court, *e.g.*, interference with jurors, or the publication of matter which is likely to prejudice the fair trial of any pending proceeding (see *ante*, Chap. 3).

Criminal contempt is generally punished in a summary way by committal, but an indictment for the offence will lie.

The common law offence of contempt has been supplemented by statutory provisions, *e.g.*, the wilful insulting of a county court judge is a specific offence under the County Courts Act 1959, s. 157.

(3) *Barratry, Maintenance, Champerty*

These ancient and obsolete offences were abolished by the Criminal Law Act 1967.

Chapter Twenty-One

TREASON AND KINDRED OFFENCES

Treason

PROSECUTIONS for treason, which is still a capital offence, are extremely rare in times of peace and the offence will be dealt with very briefly here. As we have seen (Chap. 1), the Criminal Law Act 1967, s. 12(6), retains treason as a separate category of offence, but the procedure on trials for treason is the same as on trials for murder (*ibid.*). Treason is an offence at common law, but the main heads are now set out in the Treason Act 1351 as follows:

(i) When a man doth compass or imagine the death of our lord the King, or of our lady his Queen, or of their eldest son and heir.

(ii) If a man do violate the King's companion, or the King's eldest daughter unmarried, or the wife of the King's eldest son and heir.

(iii) If a man do levy war against our lord the King in his realm, or be adherent to the King's enemies in his realm, giving to them aid and comfort in the realm, or elsewhere.

(iv) If a man slea (slay) the chancellor, treasurer, or the King's justices of the one bench, or the other, justices in eyre, or justices of assize, and all other justices assigned to hear and determine, being in their places doing their offices.

It is provided by the Treason Act 1495 that service in war under the King *de facto* for the time being shall not be deemed to be treason against the King *de jure*.

The last, and one hopes the second, head of treason may be regarded as picturesque survivals, and we will concentrate our attention upon the others.

(1) *Compassing or imagining (i.e., intending) the death of the sovereign, etc.*

In theory the mere formation of the guilty intention constitutes treason under this head, but practically this is not so, because the statute itself requires that the accused be attainted of the offence "of open deed"; *i.e.*, proof of one or more overt acts is required. A conspiracy to kill the sovereign is a sufficient overt act. Spoken words which manifest a similar intention are also sufficient, but not "loose words, spoken without relation to any act or project" (*R. v. Charnock* (1694), *per* Holt C.J.). The publication of a writing inciting persons to assassinate the sovereign is clearly sufficient, but it seems now to be settled that an unpublished writing is not of itself sufficient, although such a writing may be admissible in evidence as tending to prove some other overt act. A conspiracy to depose the sovereign from any part of his or her realm is probably sufficient (*R. v. Maclane* (1797)).

(2(a)) *Levying war against the sovereign in his realm*

The word "war" has received a liberal interpretation from the judges, and a rising or tumult of even three or four persons may be sufficient; but the purpose of the insurrection must be of a public or general nature, and not merely private or local. It is the generality of the purpose which distinguishes this form of treason from the offence of riot which we shall consider in Chapter 22: for riot a local or private purpose is sufficient. The point is well illustrated by the case of *R. v. Damaree* (1709), in which a mob proceeded to demolish the meeting houses of protestant dissenters with the object of frustrating the Toleration Act, which had recently been passed with the object of extending religious toleration to such dissenters. Had the mob taken exception to the remarks of a particular dissenting minister, and had their purpose been to demolish only his meeting house, their conduct would not have been treasonable.

(2(b)) *Being adherent to the King's enemies in his realm, giving to them aid and comfort in the realm, or elsewhere*

We have repeated these words in full because they have given rise to a particular difficulty of construction. At first sight they might seem to require an act of adherence to the sovereign's enemies within the realm, but in fact the words have been construed to mean "adhering to the King's enemies in his realm or elsewhere by giving to them aid and comfort in the realm or elsewhere", *i.e.*, the words "or elsewhere" must be read after the word "realm" on both occasions on which that word appears: or, looking at it another way, the words "giving . . . aid and comfort" [to the King's enemies] are words in apposition, explaining what is meant by being adherent (*R.* v. *Casement* (1917), C.C.A.). Thus, in *Casement's* case itself, it was held to be treason to endeavour in an enemy country to persuade British prisoners of war in that country to join the armed forces of the enemy. For a British subject to become naturalized as the subject of a hostile state in time of war is an act of treason under this head (*R.* v. *Lynch* (1903)). The word "enemies" requires that the Crown should be in a state of war. A rebellion against the Crown by British subjects is insufficient: such subjects cannot be enemies of the Crown within the statute.

In *R.* v. *Ahlers* (1915), C.C.A., it was held that a British subject acting as German consul at Sunderland who after the outbreak of the first World War assisted German subjects of military age to return to Germany could not be convicted of treason under this head if he had acted in the genuine belief that it was his duty to assist such German subjects to return to Germany, and he had not acted with the intention of assisting the King's enemies—a decision which perhaps shows some confusion between intention and motive.

Treason as the breach of a duty of allegiance

Treason is essentially the breach of a duty of allegiance to the British Crown. A British subject is said to owe a natural duty of allegiance to the Crown which he takes with him wherever he goes. So far as the particular head of treason allows, he may therefore commit treason by acts done without the realm as readily as by acts done within it. Nor can a British subject naturalize himself in a foreign state at war with this country so as to put off his duty of allegiance; indeed, as we have seen, such an act is itself treasonable (*R.* v. *Lynch* (1903)). For the purposes of the English law of treason section 3 of the British Nationality Act 1948 has the broad effect of confining the term "British subject" to one who is a citizen of the United Kingdom and colonies.

An enemy alien who is not under the protection of the British Crown owes no duty of allegiance to it, so that, for example, members of a foreign invading army would not be guilty of treason. But a friendly alien who is under the protection of the Crown may owe a duty of allegiance to it: his duty is sometimes said to be "local", although this is a somewhat misleading term, as we shall see. It is clear that a friendly alien owes a duty of allegiance to the Crown so long as he is present within the realm, but if he can properly be regarded as *resident* within the realm he continues to owe that duty during periods of absence abroad, during which therefore he may commit acts which will make him guilty of treason. Moreover, an alien who is resident within any of the dominions of the Crown is

guilty of treason if he joins an invading force of his own country-
men: in English law his duty of allegiance is not dissolved by
reason of the fact that the forces of the Crown have temporarily
retired (*De Jager* v. *Att.-Gen. for Natal* (1907), P.C.). In the much
discussed case of *Joyce* v. *D.P.P.* (1946) it was even held by the
House of Lords that an American citizen who assisted the enemy
by broadcasting over the German wireless during the second World
War was guilty of treason because he held a current British passport, which he had obtained by representing himself to be a British
subject; his continued holding of the passport was held to be a claim
to the protection of the Crown sufficient to impose upon him a continued duty of allegiance. In this case it was held that the Crown's
duty of protection and the duty of allegiance are correlative, and
this despite the fact that the duty of protection is not legally enforceable and that the power of the Crown to afford effective protection may be very slight in the particular circumstances.

Treason Felony

By reason of the reluctance of juries in many cases to convict of
the capital offence of treason, particularly where the conduct alleged
did not fall within the natural meaning of the language of the
Statute of Treasons, the Treason Felony Act 1848 was passed which
allows the principal forms of treason to be charged instead as ordinary offences (f), punishable not with death, but with a maximum
term of life imprisonment. The Act includes the conduct of any
person who shall, within the United Kingdom or without, compass,
imagine, or intend to depose the sovereign from any part of his or
her realm, or to levy war against the Crown in any part of the
United Kingdom in order by force of constraint to compel the
Crown to change its measures, or to intimidate either House of
Parliament, or to incite any foreigner or stranger with force to
invade any part of the Crown's Dominions. Proof of an overt act
or deed is required, as in the case of treason.

Sedition

Sedition, which is a common law offence (m), may be defined briefly
as conduct, falling short of treason, which threatens, or excites
disaffection against, the constitutional order or government of the
United Kingdom or any organ thereof (including the judicature),
or the exciting of feelings of illwill between different classes of

the sovereign's subjects. Thus it clearly includes any incitement to the use of unlawful force in any public matter connected with the State. On the other hand, candid and reasoned discussion of any public matter, including discussion of social injustices, with a view to their removal but without inciting to unconstitutional measures, does not amount to sedition. Prosecutions for sedition are rarely successful in modern times and the common law has been supplemented by more specific statutory enactments. For example, by the Incitement to Disaffection Act 1934 it is an offence maliciously and advisedly to endeavour to seduce any member of the armed forces from his duty or allegiance to the Crown; and there are similar provisions with regard to the police. More recently the Race Relations Act 1965 has made it a criminal offence to do certain acts which are intended and are likely to stir up hatred against any section of the public in Great Britain distinguished by colour, race, or ethnic or national origins. The acts in question are publishing or distributing written matter which is threatening, abusive, or insulting, or using language of a similar character in any public place or at any public meeting. But a prosecution can be brought only by, or with the consent of, the Attorney-General.

Official Secrets

The Official Secrets Acts 1911-1939 contain sweeping provisions for the protection of government secrets. These provisions are far too detailed for it to be possible to set them out here. A typical provision is that of section 1(1) of the Act of 1911, which provides that if any person for any purpose prejudicial to the safety or interests of the State—(a) approaches, inspects, passes over, or is in the neighbourhood of, or enters any prohibited place within the meaning of the Act, or (b) makes any sketch, plan, model or note which is calculated to be or might be or is intended to be directly or indirectly useful to an enemy, or (c) obtains, collects, records or publishes or communicates to any other person any secret official code word or password or any sketch, plan, model, article or note or other document or information which is calculated to be or might be or is intended to be directly or indirectly useful to an enemy, he shall be guilty of an offence (f). The maximum punishment for this offence is fourteen years' imprisonment. Although the side note to this section refers to penalties for "spying" no such motive is in fact necessary (*Chandler* v. *D.P.P.* (1964), H.L.).

Chapter Twenty-Two

OFFENCES AGAINST PUBLIC ORDER AND INTERNATIONAL LAW

Affray

WHEN two or more persons fight together "to the terror of the Queen's subjects" they constitute an affray, which is a common law offence (m). Despite the traditional words which speak of the terror of the Queen's subjects, it is sufficient if there is proof that the fight was of such a nature as might well intimidate or frighten reasonable people, and there need not be proof that anyone was in fact put in fear (*R. v. Sharp and Johnson* (1957), C.C.A.). As was said by Lord Goddard C.J. in the case cited "if two lads indulge in a fight with fists, no one would dignify that as an affray, whereas if they used broken bottles or knuckle dusters and drew blood, a jury might well find it was, as a passer-by might be upset and frightened by such conduct". It was also held in this case that it is a defence to a charge of affray that the accused was acting in genuine self-defence.

For many years it was thought that an affray could be committed only in a public place, but it has now been held that this is not so (*Button and Swain* v. *D.P.P.* (1966), H.L.).

An affray (or an analogous common law offence (m)) is also committed when persons go about (or even, it seems, if one person goes about) armed with unusual and dangerous weapons in a manner which is calculated to cause alarm to others. There is no modern authority with regard to this offence, and none is likely to be forthcoming because there is a number of statutory provisions under which prosecutions can more conveniently be brought. For example, it is an offence under the Prevention of Crime Act 1953 (sometimes known as the Cosh Act), s. 1, for a person without lawful authority or reasonable excuse to have an offensive weapon with him in any public place; and "offensive weapon" is defined to mean any article made or adapted for use for causing injury to the person, or intended by the accused for such use by him. A momentary possession suffices, as when a person picks up a stone in the street

146

for the purpose of throwing it at another (*Harrison* v. *Thornton* (1966), D.C.). Reference may also be made to the extensive provisions of the Firearms Act 1968.

Unlawful Assembly

The common law offence (m) of unlawful assembly is constituted by a meeting of three or more persons "assembled under such circumstances as, according to the opinion of rational and firm men, are likely to produce danger to the tranquillity and peace of the neighbourhood" (*R.* v. *Vincent* (1839), *per* Alderson B.). Thus, the definition includes a meeting of persons who have assembled for the purpose of committing a crime by open force, but the offence may also be committed even though the purpose of the meeting is lawful in itself if the circumstances of the meeting are such as to cause alarm, *e.g.*, by reason of the number of those assembled and the hour of the meeting (see *R.* v. *Williams* (1848)). On the other hand, if even large numbers of persons assemble in a peaceful manner for a lawful purpose (*e.g.*, members of the Salvation Army parade for the purpose of forming a religious procession), the fact that it is known that other persons will offer them violent, but *unprovoked* and unlawful, opposition will not render them an unlawful assembly at common law even if local magistrates and the police have purported to forbid the meeting (*Beatty* v. *Gillbanks* (1882), D.C.). It seems, however, from *Duncan* v. *Jones* (1936), D.C., the principles of which are not very clear, that if a police officer reasonably apprehends that if a meeting (even though perfectly lawful) is held a breach of the peace will ensue, he may order those assembled to disperse, and any who disobey will then commit the statutory offence (*infra*) of obstructing the police in the execution of their duty.

The common law of unlawful assembly has been supplemented by a number of statutory enactments, *e.g.*, the Seditious Meetings Act 1817, s. 23, which renders unlawful a meeting of more than fifty persons within a mile of Westminster Hall, during sittings of Parliament or of the Superior Courts, for the purpose of petitioning the Crown or either House of Parliament for the alteration of any matter in Church or State. There are also extensive provisions in the Unlawful Drilling Act 1819 and the Public Order Act 1936 which are directed against the formation of private military or quasi-military forces. On the other hand, the Public Meeting Act 1908 penalizes endeavours to break up lawful public meetings, and it may be noticed that it is an offence under section 5 of the Public

Order Act 1936 for a person in a public place or at a public meeting to use threatening, abusive or insulting words or behaviour intended or calculated to provoke a breach of the peace.

Rout

Rout, which is a common law offence (m), may be described as an incipient riot: it is an assembly of persons which would have constituted a riot except for the fact that those persons have not begun the execution of their common purpose, but have only made some move towards that execution, *e.g.*, have begun to march towards the place where the common purpose is to be executed.

Riot

At common law a riot (m) occurs when the following elements are present: (i) three or more persons assembled together; (ii) a common purpose, which may be lawful or unlawful in itself; (iii) execution or inception of the common purpose; (iv) an intent to help one another, by force if necessary, against anyone who may oppose them in the execution of the common purpose; (v) force or violence displayed in such a manner as to alarm at least one person of reasonable firmness and courage (*Field* v. *Receiver of Metropolitan Police* (1907), D.C.). However, in *R.* v. *Sharp and Johnson* (1957), C.C.A., a case on affray which we noticed *supra*, it was doubted whether proof that some person was in fact alarmed is required, and it is probable that it is sufficient that the circumstances of the assembly are calculated to cause alarm to a person of ordinary courage.

Under the Riot (Damages) Act 1886 a claim often lies against local police funds for compensation in respect of damage to premises or property therein caused by rioters, and most of the modern cases in the law reports (such as *Field's* case, *supra*) relate to such claims. In *Field's* case a gang of youths congregated in a low neighbourhood and engaged in horseplay, in the course of which they pushed down part of a wall which enclosed a yard, but dispersed when the caretaker of the premises came out into the street. The action failed, because there was no evidence of elements (iv) and (v) mentioned above; element (v) is not supplied by the use of force in carrying out the common object unless it is calculated to alarm a person of reasonable courage.

In law, riot is by no means limited to the kind of tumult exempli-

fied by the Gordon riots, so vividly described by Dickens in
Barnaby Rudge. Thus, damage caused by rioters was established
in *Ford* v. *Receiver of Metropolitan Police District* (1921), D.C., in
which a crowd on Peace night, 1919, broke into an empty house and
stripped it of its woodwork in order to feed a bonfire, and again
in *Munday* v. *Metropolitan Police District Receiver* (1949), D.C., in
which a number of persons who had been unable to obtain entry to
a football match invaded private premises and climbed on to a
garage roof in order to obtain a view of the pitch, causing con-
siderable damage in the process; in both cases there was evidence
that persons of reasonable courage were put in fear. Again, as Lord
Goddard C.J. pointed out in *R.* v. *Sharp and Johnson, supra*, three
persons who enter a shop and forcibly or by threats steal goods
therein constitute a riot. (But for a claim to succeed under the Riot
(Damages) Act 1886, in addition to a technical riot, there must be
an element of public tumult (*Dwyer* v. *Metropolitan Police District
Receiver* (1967)).)

Statutory Riot

The former felony of statutory riot (which was created by the Riot
Act 1714) need no longer concern us. The Act of 1714 was repealed
by the Criminal Law Act 1967, Sched. 3.

Dispersing Unlawful Assemblies

It is a common law offence (m) for a magistrate to neglect to take
proper steps to disperse rioters or other unlawful assemblies which
a magistrate of reasonable courage would have taken, and such
force as is reasonable and necessary for the purpose may lawfully
be employed to disperse those who are unlawfully assembled (*R.*
v. *Neale* (1839)). In an extreme case even the infliction of death
may be justified. Finally it may be noticed that it is a common
law offence (m) for the ordinary citizen to refuse, without justification, to assist a peace officer, such as a police constable, in the
execution of his duty in preserving the peace, when called upon to
do so (*R.* v. *Brown* (1841); *R.* v. *Sherlock* (1866)).

Obstructing the Police

It is an offence to assault, resist or wilfully obstruct a constable in the execution of his duty or a person assisting a constable so acting (Police Act 1964, s. 51). To warn an offender of the presence of the police will often amount to an obstruction, as where motorists who were exceeding the speed limit were warned by the accused of the existence of a police speed trap ahead (*Betts* v. *Stevens* (1910), D.C.; contrast *Bastable* v. *Little* (1907), D.C., where the facts were similar except that there was no evidence that the motorists were exceeding the limit, and it was held that the offence of obstruction was not committed, as at most the accused had merely warned the motorists not to commit an offence).

The words "in the execution of his duty" have given rise to some difficulty. Probably it is necessary that the constable should have been acting within the ambit of his powers *and* in pursuance of some duty imposed upon him by common law or by statute (*e.g.*, his duty to preserve the peace, as in *Duncan* v. *Jones* (1936), which we have noticed under "Unlawful Assembly", *supra*). In *R*. v. *Roxburgh* (1871) it was held that if a constable assists a private person in the enforcement of his rights, *e.g.*, to eject an intruder from his premises, and is assaulted in the process, a conviction of ordinary assault may be obtained; but the offence of assaulting a constable in the execution of his duty is not committed (*R*. v. *Prebble* (1858)). *A fortiori* a constable who is acting in excess of his powers is not acting in the execution of his duty, as when, in order to investigate a supposed offence, he enters private premises without a warrant or other lawful authority, thereby committing a trespass, and he refuses to leave when told to do so (*Davis* v. *Lisle* (1936), D.C.), or where he believes that a car has been involved in an offence and, having no legal power to do so, he attempts to prevent the owner from driving it away (*R*. v. *Waterfield* (1964), C.C.A.). In such cases the use of reasonable force against the constable will not amount to any offence at all.

A citizen is not, in general, bound to answer questions put to him by a constable, even if the constable reasonably suspects him of having committed a crime, and his refusal to answer such questions cannot then be treated as obstruction (*Rice* v. *Connolly* (1966), D.C.).

It was held in *R*. v. *Forbes* (1865), Q.S., that on a charge of assaulting a constable in the execution of his duty knowledge that the person assaulted is such a constable is not necessary, and in *McBride* v. *Turnock* (1964), D.C., it was held that the offence is committed where A unlawfully strikes at B, who is not a constable, and inadvertently hits C, who is a constable on duty.

Piracy

At common law the offence (f) of piracy (also termed piracy *jure gentium*) consists, broadly, of the seizure or attempted seizure by violence (actual or threatened) of a ship on the high seas or within the Admiralty jurisdiction. It can be committed by those on board the ship, as well as by persons outside, but not by persons acting under the commission of any State. The purpose may be to take the ship itself or any goods on board her.

The common law has been supplemented by several statutes and the term piracy extended to trading in slaves by the Slave Trade Act 1824.

If the offence is committed with violence it is a capital offence (Piracy Act 1837, s. 2).

Foreign Enlistment

The Foreign Enlistment Act 1870 contains a number of provisions designed to prevent private persons from embroiling the Crown in foreign wars. For example, it is an offence for a British subject, without the licence of the Crown, to enlist in the forces of a foreign state which is at war with a foreign state that is at peace with the Crown (section 4). Fitting out naval or military expeditions against friendly states is also penalized (section 11).

Chapter Twenty-Three

LIBEL

THE term "libel" indicates that offending matter is in writing or in some other permanent form (*e.g.*, that of an effigy or statue). In the criminal law the word is chiefly applied to defamatory libel, seditious libel, blasphemous libel and obscene libel. We have already considered sedition (*ante*, Chap. 21), and in this chapter we shall be concerned with the other forms of libel.

Defamatory Libel

Defamatory libel (commonly called "libel" *simpliciter*) is a common law offence (m), but the maximum punishment is prescribed by the Libel Act 1843, *i.e.*, two years' imprisonment if the accused knew the matter to be false (section 4), and otherwise one year (section 5). There are a number of special statutory provisions with regard to libels in newspapers, *e.g.*, by section 8 of the Law of Libel Amendment Act 1888 the leave of a judge in chambers is necessary before a criminal prosecution can be brought in respect of such a libel.

In modern times criminal prosecutions for libel are comparatively rare, and libels are generally sued upon in civil proceedings for damages. Indeed, the judges tend to discourage criminal prosecutions unless there is some good reason for not bringing a civil action, *e.g.*, where the defendant would not be worth suing. Libel is dealt with at length in textbooks on the law of torts and we shall deal with it but briefly here.

A defamatory statement has been variously defined, and probably no one test will cover every case. A statement is defamatory of a person if it exposes him to public hatred, contempt or ridicule, or renders him liable to be generally shunned by society, or tends to lower him in the estimation of right-thinking members of the community. Merely spoken words which are defamatory may often form the subject of a civil action, but not generally of a criminal prosecution (*R.* v. *Langley* (1704)).

In general, the rules governing the tort of libel are equally applicable to a criminal prosecution. For example, the defences of absolute privilege (*e.g.*, that the matter was contained in a report published by order of either House of Parliament) and qualified privilege (*e.g.*, that the matter was contained in a reference given by a master in respect of his servant) are applicable to the crime as well as the tort; and, as in the law of torts, the defence of qualified privilege is rebutted by proof of express malice, *i.e.*, that the defendant was actuated by an indirect or improper motive in making the defamatory statement. Nevertheless, there are some differences in the rules, most of which spring from the fact that the object of a civil action is to obtain damages for loss of deserved reputation, whereas libel is punishable as a crime by reason of its tendency to provoke a breach of the peace. The following differences may be noticed.

(1) *Publication*

For the purposes of the tort of libel the defamatory matter must have been published to someone other than the plaintiff or the defendant's spouse. But for the purposes of the crime publication to the person defamed suffices (*Barrow* v. *Lewellin* (1615)). In *R.* v. *Adams* (1888), C.C.R., it was held that an indictment would lie for writing a letter to a young woman suggesting that she should have sexual intercourse with the writer: the proposal was by implication defamatory.

(2) *Truth*

The substantial truth of the defamatory matter (technically known as the plea of justification) is a complete defence to a civil action: damages cannot be obtained for loss of an undeserved reputation. But at common law the truth of the defamatory matter is no answer to a criminal prosecution. Indeed, the common law had a maxim "the greater the truth the greater the libel", because the greater the tendency to provoke a breach of the peace. Now, however, by the Libel Act 1843, s. 6, it is a defence to a criminal prosecution for the defendant to prove the truth of the defamatory matter and that the publication was for the public benefit. It will be observed that truth alone is still not a defence.

(3) *Libel on the dead*

There is some authority for the proposition that a libel upon a deceased person is indictable (the case *De Libellis Famosis*; and see *R.* v. *Labouchere* (1884), D.C.). A civil action will not lie in such circumstances.

(4) *Classes of persons*

A civil action will not lie in respect of the defamation of a class of persons, unless the class is so small that what is said of the class reflects directly and substantially upon each individual member of it; but in some circumstances, at any rate, a criminal prosecution will lie, *e.g.*, where there is a distinct tendency to provoke a breach of the peace and the persons defamed are in a public or semi-public position (*R.* v. *Williams* (1822) (clergy of the Diocese of Durham)).

Blasphemy

The publication of a blasphemous libel is a common law offence (m), as also is the utterance of blasphemous words. At common law any vilification of the Christian religion was blasphemous. Today, however, if the decencies of controversy are observed even the fundamentals of religion may lawfully be attacked (*R.* v. *Ramsey and Foote* (1883); and see *Bowman* v. *Secular Society, Ltd.* (1917), H.L.). Prosecutions for blasphemy are virtually unknown today.

Obscene Libel

The publication of an obscene libel is a common law offence (m). At common law the test of obscenity is whether the tendency of the matter is to deprave and corrupt those whose minds are open to such immoral influences and into whose hands a publication of the sort in question may fall (*R.* v. *Hicklin* (1868)). The common law has, however, been substantially superseded by the Obscene Publications Act 1959, as amended by the Obscene Publications Act 1964. The publication of an obscene libel must now be prosecuted under the Act, and not at common law; a charge under the Act may be tried summarily or on indictment, and if tried on indictment is punishable with a maximum of three years' imprisonment or a fine or both (section 2). Under the Act an article is deemed to be obscene if its effect or (where the article comprises two or more distinct items) the effect of any one of its items is, if taken as a whole, such as to tend to deprave and corrupt persons who are likely, having regard to all the relevant circumstances, to read, see or hear the matter contained or embodied in it. The term "article" is widely defined and includes photographic negatives. The statutory offence includes not only the publication of an obscene article (whether for gain or not), but also the possession of such an article for publication for gain (whether gain to the accused himself or to another).

It is a defence to the accused to prove that he had not examined the article in question and had no reasonable cause to suspect that it was such that his publication of it (or his possession of it, as the case may be) would make him liable to be convicted of the offence. It is also provided that, where the charge relates to publication, the question whether an article is obscene shall be determined without regard to any publication by another person, unless it could reasonably have been expected that the publication by the other person would follow from the publication by the person charged; and that, on a charge of possession, the question of whether the article is obscene shall be determined by reference to such publication for gain of the article as in the circumstances it may reasonably be inferred that he had in contemplation, and to any further publication that could reasonably be expected to follow from it, but not to any other publication. Hence the sale by a shopkeeper of indecent photographs to experienced police officers whose minds would not be affected by the photographs and who had made the purchase for the purposes of bringing a prosecution, would not amount to the offence of publication under the Act (*R.* v. *Clayton and Halsey* (1963), C.C.A.); but the shopkeeper's possession of the photographs for general sale would make him guilty of the offence of possession.

For the sake of brevity the term "possession" has been used above, but in fact the Act speaks of "ownership, possession or control".

Section 4 of the Act introduces a defence of "public good" which was quite unknown to the common law. It is a defence for the accused to prove that publication of the article in question was justified as being for the public good on the ground that it was in the interests of science, literature, art or learning, or of other objects of general concern. The opinion of experts as to the literary, artistic, scientific or other merits of an article is rendered admissible either to establish or to negative the said ground.

It was held in *John Calder* (*Publications*) *Ltd.* v. *Powell* (1965), D.C., that matter is obscene if it tends to deprave and corrupt in any way, *e.g.*, by inducing drug addiction, and not only when it tends to do so sexually.

Chapter Twenty-Four

CONSPIRACY

THE offence of conspiracy is constituted by the forming of an agreement between two or more persons to carry out an unlawful purpose or a lawful purpose by unlawful means. In a few instances conspiracy has been rendered a statutory offence, as in the case of conspiracy to murder (m), under section 4 of the Offences against the Person Act 1861. In other cases it is a common law offence (m).

The mere formation of the agreement constitutes the offence and it is not necessary that the parties to the agreement should have done anything to carry out their common purpose. It was however held in *R.* v. *Thomson* (1965), C.C.A., that a person cannot be convicted of conspiracy unless he did genuinely *intend* to carry out the purpose in question; in this respect *mens rea* is a necessary ingredient of the offence. An agreement requires overt acts and a plurality of persons. It requires overt acts because an agreement is something different from the formation of similar intentions by different persons, albeit at the same time. There need not, however, be express evidence of an agreement between the accused persons, and the existence of an agreement between them may be inferred from the fact that they appeared to be acting in pursuance of a common purpose (see *R.* v. *Meyrick and Ribuffi* (1929), C.C.A.).

A plurality of persons is required because a person cannot be said to have formed an agreement with himself. It follows that if two persons are charged with conspiring together and one is acquitted but the other convicted, the conviction of the other will be quashed on appeal (*R.* v. *Plummer* (1902), C.C.R.). Moreover, whether by reason of a doctrine of conjugal unity or not, husband and wife cannot be convicted of conspiring together (*R.* v. *Whitehouse* (1852)). It is not, however, necessary that on a charge of conspiracy there should be two persons before the court; a single person can be convicted of conspiracy if there is evidence which establishes that he conspired with some other person or persons, whether known or unknown. In *R.* v. *McDonnell* (1966) it was held that conspiracy requires not only a plurality of persons but also a plurality of minds, and that therefore a man cannot be convicted of

156

conspiring with a corporation if he alone controls the corporation's activities, even though in law a corporation is a person distinct from the members who comprise it at any given time.

A conspiracy may have an element of contingency, *e.g.*, where persons agree to carry out an illegal abortion if further investigation should show that the operation can safely be performed; but there must be a distinct agreement, and it is not sufficient that the parties have entered into negotiations with a view to forming an agreement (*R.* v. *Mills* (1963), C.C.A.).

The Object of the Agreement

The following objects are sufficiently unlawful for the purposes of the crime of conspiracy.

(1) *Criminal acts*

An agreement to commit a crime is an indictable conspiracy, and this is so even if the crime intended is a mere summary offence (*R.* v. *Blamires Transport Services* (1964), C.C.A.). Provided that what the parties agreed to do was, on the facts known to them, an unlawful act, they are guilty of conspiracy even though they did not realize that it was unlawful (*R.* v. *Clayton* (1943), C.C.A.). Nevertheless, if on the facts known to them what they agree to do is lawful they do not become guilty of conspiracy by the existence of other facts, not known to them, which render what they do a criminal offence, and this is so even though the crime is one which does not itself require *mens rea* (*Churchill* v. *Walton* (1967), H.L.). Thus in *Churchill* v. *Walton* the House of Lords held that persons could not be convicted of conspiracy to use in road vehicles gas oil in respect of which the appropriate duty had not been paid to the Commissioners of Customs and Excise, contrary to section 200(2) of the Customs and Excise Act 1952, because those persons did not know that the duty had not been paid.

It is at first sight strange to observe that an agreement to commit a mere summary offence is an *indictable* offence. The rule reflects the view of the common law that concerted action represents a greater threat to the security of the community than the action of one person on his own. This outlook will become even more evident when we consider the remaining heads of unlawfulness.

A person may be convicted of conspiracy to commit a crime even if he could not himself be convicted of that crime. For example, we have seen (*ante*, Chap. 7) that a woman who is not in fact pregnant cannot be convicted of the offence of using an instrument, etc., upon herself with intent to procure her miscarriage; nevertheless, a woman who is not in fact pregnant can be convicted of conspiring with another person to procure her own abortion (*R*. v. *Whitchurch* (1890), C.C.R.). (See also *R*. v. *Duguid* (1906), C.C.R., in which it was held that a person could be convicted of conspiring with a woman to abduct her child, contrary to section 56 of the Offences against the Person Act 1861, although the Act does not allow the woman herself to be convicted of that offence.)

In general, a conspiracy formed in this country to commit a crime abroad is not triable here (*R*. v. *Cox* (1968), C.A.), but it is so triable if the crime is one of those exceptional offences which can be tried here even though committed abroad, *e.g.*, murder or manslaughter committed by a British subject on land abroad (*Board of Trade* v. *Owen* (1957), H.L., in which it was admitted that there might be some other cases in which the conspiracy would be triable here, *e.g.*, if the commission of the crime abroad would injure a person in England by causing him damage abroad).

(2) *Civil wrongs*

An agreement to commit a legal wrong that is not also a crime if committed by one person will often amount to a criminal conspiracy. The scope of this head of unlawfulness is uncertain. It probably does not include every tort. In particular, an agreement to commit a mere civil trespass has been held not to be a criminal conspiracy (*R*. v. *Turner* (1811)). (This decision was criticized in *R*. v. *Rowlands* (1851), C.C.R., but apparently only upon the ground that the trespass in *Turner's* case was itself criminal in the circumstances.) On the other hand, a conspiracy to cheat and defraud is certainly criminal (*R*. v. *Warburton* (1870), C.C.R.). In most cases the deception intended will itself be criminal, but there may be circumstances in which this is not so. For example, as we have seen (*ante*, Chap. 13), it was held in *R*. v. *Clucas* (1949), C.C.A., that where a person by false pretences induced a bookmaker to open an account with him, and later collected the winnings upon certain successful bets, he could not be convicted of obtaining the money by false pretences (and could not now be convicted of obtaining property by deception), because the false pretences were not sufficiently direct cause of the obtaining; but where two or more persons conspire to impose upon a bookmaker in this way, they can be convicted of a criminal conspiracy as *Clucas's* case itself shows. In *R*. v. *Willetts* (1906) it was held at the Old Bailey that a conspiracy to pirate copyright music was a criminal conspiracy.

It is often stated that a conspiracy to commit a tort involving malice (in the popular sense of that word) is criminal, and certainly an agreement having as its object the tort of malicious prosecution is criminal (*Poulterer's case* (1610)); but the proposition as stated may well be too wide. In many cases the borderline (if it exists at all) between the head of unlawfulness which we are now considering and the third and last head is difficult to discern.

(3) *Other acts*

An act may be sufficiently unlawful for the purposes of the law of conspiracy although it would not be even a civil wrong if committed by one person. Agreements in this category are often alleged as conspiracies to commit a public mischief, and it is the present policy of the courts to leave uncertain the scope of public mischief for this purpose (*Shaw* v. *D.P.P.* (1962), H.L., which we considered in Chapter 2). The following are some examples of agreements that have been held to be criminal conspiracies under this head: (a) An agreement to raise the price of Government stock by false rumours (*R.* v. *De Berenger* (1814)); (b) an agreement to effect a woman's seduction (a term that implies that the woman is a consenting party) (*R.* v. *Howell* (1864)); (c) a conspiracy to obtain decorated domestic pottery for sale on the home market in breach of a statutory regulation which was designed to protect the currency by promoting the export of such pottery, but which did not make the infringement of the order in this way a criminal offence in itself (*R.* v. *Newland* (1954), C.C.A.); (d) a conspiracy to corrupt public morals by publishing a directory of prostitutes, whether or not conduct calculated or intended to corrupt public morals is in itself a criminal offence (*Shaw* v. *D.P.P.* (1962), H.L.).

There is some authority for the proposition that an agreement to commit a mere breach of contract can be a criminal conspiracy (*Vertue* v. *Lord Clive* (1769)), but only, it is submitted, where the object of the agreement can be brought under this third head of unlawfulness, or where the breach of contract is itself a criminal offence. This brings us to the question of industrial disputes as to which a few words must be said.

Industrial disputes

By section 3 of the Conspiracy and Protection of Property Act 1875, an agreement to do an act in contemplation or furtherance of a trade dispute between employers and workmen is not to be indicted as a conspiracy unless the act would be punishable as a crime if committed by one person. Inasmuch as a breach of contract is not generally criminal in itself it follows that a strike in breach of contract cannot generally be indicted as a criminal conspiracy (whatever the position might otherwise be). In a few instances, however, a breach of contract is itself a criminal offence, *e.g.*, the wilful and malicious breaking of a contract of service by a person employed by suppliers of gas or water, if that person knows or has reasonable cause to believe that the probable consequence of his so doing, either alone or in combination with others, will be to deprive the inhabitants of any place wholly or partly of their supply of gas or water (Act of 1875, s. 4). This provision was extended to electricity undertakings by the Electricity Supply Act 1919, s. 31.

There is a number of other statutory provisions with regard to industrial disputes (*e.g.*, provisions which legalize peaceful picketing, but make it unlawful in circumstances of intimidation), but these do not relate specifically to conspiracy.

Chapter Twenty-Five

TRAFFIC OFFENCES

THE following are the traffic offences of more general interest to the lawyer, apart from those of homicide by dangerous driving and the taking of a conveyance without authority, which we have already considered (*ante,* Chaps. 7 and 12). In each case, unless otherwise stated, the statutory reference is to the Road Traffic Act 1960 (a consolidating enactment), and it may be assumed that the offence is triable summarily or on indictment.

(1) *Reckless or dangerous driving (section 2)*

This offence is committed by driving a motor vehicle on a road recklessly, or at a speed or in a manner which is dangerous to the public, having regard to all the circumstances of the case, including the nature, condition and use of the road, and the amount of traffic which is actually at the time, or which might reasonably be expected to be, on the road.

To support a charge of dangerous driving it is sufficient to show that the driving was potentially dangerous, and no actual danger to any member of the public need be proved (*Bracegirdle* v. *Oxley* (1947), D.C.). Moreover, driving is dangerous for this purpose if it was dangerous in fact, and no question arises as to the state of the accused's mind in this connection: *mens rea* is not required (*Hill* v. *Baxter* (1958), D.C.; and see *R.* v. *Evans* (1963), C.C.A., and *R.* v. *Ball and Loughlin* (1966), C.C.A., (causing death by dangerous driving)). On the other hand the offence is not committed where the accused cannot properly be said to have been driving, as where he was in a state of automatism. This defence has already been considered (*ante,* Chap. 4). Again the offence is not committed if the danger arose from a mechanical defect in the vehicle, and the accused neither knew nor ought to have known of that defect (*R.* v. *Spurge* (1961), C.C.A.).

(2) *Careless driving (section 3)*

This offence, which is a mere summary offence, is committed by driving a motor vehicle on a road without due care and attention,

161

or without reasonable consideration for other persons using the road.

In practice the distinction between this offence and that under section 2 is normally one of degree, although dangerous driving is not necessarily careless driving because it is necessary to prove a lack of due care for the lesser offence (see *R.* v. *Scammell* (1967), C.A.). As with the offence of dangerous driving, however, the question whether the driving falls within the terms of the section is an objective one, and *mens rea* is not required (*Simpson* v. *Peat* (1952), D.C.). In *Kay* v. *Butterworth* (1945), D.C., it was held no defence to the charge that the accused had fallen asleep at the time of the offence, because he should have stopped when he felt himself getting drowsy.

The words "other persons using the road" in section 3 are wide enough to cover passengers in the vehicle that the accused was driving. Thus, a bus driver who drove his vehicle without reasonable consideration for the passengers has been held guilty of the offence (*Pawley* v. *Wharldall* (1966), D.C.).

(3) *Driving, or being in charge, when under the influence of drink or drugs* (*section 6 as amended by the Road Safety Act 1967, s. 1*).

(a) It is an offence to drive or attempt to drive a motor vehicle on a road or other public place while unfit to drive through drink or drugs. (b) It is also an offence (but less severely punishable) to be in charge of a motor vehicle which is on a road or other public place while unfit to drive through drink or drugs. It is a defence to this second charge for the accused to prove that at the material time the circumstances were such that there was no likelihood of his driving the vehicle so long as he remained unfit to drive through drink or drugs.

A "public place" is one to which the public has access in fact, whether or not as of right. Thus it will generally include a public house car park (*R.* v. *Waters* (1963), C.C.A.).

The Road Traffic Act 1962, section 1, provides that for the purposes of both the offences under section 6 of the Act of 1960 a person shall be taken to be unfit to drive if his ability to drive properly is for the time being impaired. This is a stricter test than that which was originally laid down by the Act of 1960, under which it had to be proved that the accused was incapable of having proper control of a motor vehicle. Section 2 of the Act of 1962 renders admissible, on a charge of either offence under section 6 of the Act of 1960, evidence of the proportion or quantity of alcohol or of any drug which was contained in the blood or present in the body of the accused, and the section contains elaborate provisions with regard to proof of these matters.

See also (4), *infra*.

(4) *Driving, or being in charge, with an undue proportion of alcohol in the blood* (*Road Safety Act 1967, s. 1*)

By this section it is an offence to drive or attempt to drive, or to be in charge of a motor vehicle on a road or other public place, having consumed alcohol in such a quantity that the proportion thereof in the blood exceeds the prescribed limit (80 milligrammes of alcohol in 100 millilitres of blood or such other proportion as may be prescribed by statutory instrument: *ibid.*, s. 7(1)). It is, however, a defence, to a charge of being in charge, if the accused proves that at the material time the circumstances were such that there was no likelihood of his driving the motor vehicle so long as there was any probability of his having alcohol in his blood in a proportion exceeding the prescribed limit.

Section 2 of the Act makes provision for a constable in uniform to require any person driving or attempting to drive a motor vehicle on a road or other public place to provide a specimen of breath for a breath test if the constable has reasonable cause to suspect him of having alcohol in his body, or of having committed a traffic offence while the vehicle was in motion. Moreover, a constable has the same powers when an accident has occurred and he has reasonable cause for believing that the person to be tested was driving or attempting to drive the vehicle at the time of the accident. Where the breath test is positive, the constable may arrest that person and section 3 provides that he may then be required to provide a specimen of blood or urine for a laboratory test. If a person refuses to take a breath test he commits a summary offence, and if he refuses to provide a specimen for a laboratory test (which he may be required to do even though he refused to take a blood test) he is guilty of an offence under section 1 (*ibid.*, s. 3).

Notice of intended prosecution

By section 241 of the Road Traffic Act 1960, where a person is prosecuted for certain offences mentioned in the section (including dangerous driving, careless driving and certain speeding offences), he shall not be convicted unless either:

(a) he was warned at the time the offence was committed that the question of prosecuting him for some one or other of the specified offences would be taken into consideration; or

(b) within fourteen days of the commission of the offence a summons for the offence was served on him; or

(c) within the said fourteen days a notice of the intended prosecution, specifying the nature of the offence and the time and place where it is alleged to have been committed, was served on or sent by registered post or recorded delivery to him or the person, if any, registered as the owner of the vehicle at the time of the commission of the offence.

This requirement is in every case to be deemed to have been complied with unless and until the contrary is proved. Further, failure to comply with the requirement is not to be a bar to conviction if the court is satisfied:

(a) that neither the name and address of the accused, nor the name and address of the registered owner, if any, could with reasonable diligence have been ascertained in time for a summons to be served, or for a notice to be served or sent in compliance with the said requirement; or

(b) that the accused by his own conduct contributed to the failure.

There are a few other cases in which compliance with the requirement is not necessary; for example, on a charge of manslaughter or of causing death by dangerous driving the jury is to be at liberty to convict the accused, instead, of dangerous driving notwithstanding that the requirement of section 241 has not been complied with as respects that offence.

Chapter Twenty-Six

VAGRANCY

OFFENDERS against the Vagrancy Act 1824, as amended by the Vagrancy Act 1935 and other statutes, fall into three categories: (1) Idle and Disorderly Persons. (2) Rogues and Vagabonds. (3) Incorrigible Rogues.

(1) *Idle and Disorderly Persons*

A person is so characterized if he is convicted of one of three offences, *i.e.*, briefly, (a) trading as a pedlar without a licence; (b) being a prostitute and behaving in a riotous or indecent manner in a public place; (c) begging in a public place or causing a child to do so. The offence is a summary one, and the maximum punishment is one month's imprisonment or a fine of £5.

(2) *Rogues and Vagabonds*

These comprise the following: (a) Every person committing one of the offences mentioned above, having previously been convicted as an idle and disorderly person. (b) A person convicted of one of a number of other offences specified in the Act, *e.g.* (briefly), (i) fortune-telling, (ii) wandering abroad and failing to give a good account of oneself, (iii) being found in or upon enclosed premises for a criminal purpose, (iv) being a suspected person or reputed thief loitering with intent to commit an arrestable offence. (c) Every person apprehended as an idle and disorderly person, and violently resisting arrest, and being subsequently convicted of the offence for which he was arrested. The offence is a summary one, punishable with a maximum of three months' imprisonment or a fine of £25.

(3) *Incorrigible rogues*

These comprise: (a) Every person who breaks out of confinement after being ordered to be confined under the Vagrancy Act. (b) Every person committing, and being convicted of, an offence for which he is liable to be dealt with as a rogue and vagabond, after a previous conviction as a rogue and vagabond. (c) Every person apprehended as a rogue and vagabond, and violently resisting arrest, and being subsequently convicted of the offence for which he was arrested. The charge is triable summarily, but, upon conviction, the magistrates' court cannot sentence the accused: they may commit him to the next quarter sessions, and that court may order the convicted person to be imprisoned for not more than one year.

PART 2

CRIMINAL PROCEDURE

Chapter Twenty-Seven

INTRODUCTION TO CRIMINAL PROCEDURE

Classification of Crimes

Indictable, summary and hybrid offences

For procedural purposes the fundamental classification of criminal offences is into indictable offences, summary offences and hybrid offences.

Indictable offences. All common law offences are indictable offences and so also are all statutory offences unless a statute provides that they are summary or hybrid offences. All of the more serious offences are indictable offences and they include treason, murder, rape, **robbery, theft, arson and forgery.**

Summary offences. Summary offences, or petty offences as they are sometimes called, are statutory offences which are expressly made triable summarily (see below). Most minor statutory offences are summary offences and there is a great number of such offences. They include many offences under the Road Traffic Acts (*e.g.*, careless driving and speeding), many offences in relation to food and drugs (*e.g.*, selling food unfit for human consumption), cruelty to animals, obstructing a police officer in the execution of his duty and breaches of local authority byelaws.

Hybrid offences. Hybrid offences are statutory offences which by the creating statute may be tried either as summary offences or as indictable offences (see Chap. 40). In practice a hybrid offence is created by a statute providing two maximum punishments, one on summary trial, the other on trial on indictment. The number of hybrid offences, though still comparatively small, has been increasing in recent years, as they provide more flexibility in the manner of trial and possible punishments. Examples are drunken driving, dangerous driving, being in possession of an offensive weapon in a public place, assaulting a police officer in the execution of his duty, cruelty to children and offences under the Race Relations Act 1965.

Felonies and misdemeanours

Before the Criminal Law Act 1967 there were a number of procedural differences between the trials of felonies and misdemeanours (see Chap. 1). However, section 1 of that Act abolishes the distinction between felonies and misdemeanours and subject to the provisions of the Act, on all matters on which a distinction has previously been made, the law and practice in relation to misdemeanours now prevails.

Outline of Procedure

Although these matters will be dealt with in detail later, it is convenient at this stage to mention the courts which deal with criminal cases.

Trial on indictment

If an offence is to be tried on indictment committal proceedings will first be held in a magistrates' court to see whether there is a prima facie case against the accused. Subject to the magistrates' power to commit for trial without consideration of the evidence (see Chap. 32), only if the prosecution makes out a prima facie case can the accused be committed for trial; otherwise he must be discharged. If the accused is committed for trial he will be tried at assizes or quarter sessions and the offence(s) with which he is charged will be set out in a formal written document, called an indictment. Moreover, an accused tried on indictment who pleads not guilty will be tried by a jury, and in practice it is common to speak of trial on indictment as trial by jury.

Where an accused has been convicted at a trial on indictment, he may appeal to the Criminal Division of the Court of Appeal, and from the Criminal Division a further appeal lies, at the instance of either the accused or the prosecutor, to the House of Lords.

Summary trial

If an offence is tried summarily the accused is tried in a magistrates' court and without a jury. If he is then convicted the accused may appeal to quarter sessions and if he does so either the accused or the prosecutor may appeal from quarter sessions to a Divisional Court of the Queen's Bench Division and from there to the House of Lords. Alternatively either side may appeal direct from a magistrates' court to a Divisional Court of the Queen's Bench Division and from there to the House of Lords.

Mode of trial

If the offence with which the accused is charged is an indictable offence it will normally be tried on indictment, while a summary offence will normally be tried summarily. It is possible, however, in certain circumstances, for an indictable offence to be tried summarily, or a summary offence to be tried on indictment, and these will be considered in Chapter 40. A hybrid offence, by definition, is an offence which may be tried either as a summary offence or as an indictable offence and the manner in which this is decided will also be considered in Chapter 40. Moreover, whether an offence is tried on indictment or summarily the procedure to be followed depends on the method of trial and not on the type of offence. Thus, if an offence is tried on indictment the procedure is basically the same whether the offence is an indictable offence, a summary offence or a hybrid offence, and the same rule applies to summary trials.

Parties

The parties to a criminal trial are the prosecutor and accused, although there may be more than one accused.

Prosecutor

Every prosecution is in theory conducted on behalf of the Crown, but the prosecutor himself (*i.e.*, the one who lays the information, see Chap. 31) may be a police officer, a private person, the Director of Public Prosecutions (see Chap. 29) or, in appropriate cases, the representative of a government department or local authority. Moreover, the prosecutor need not normally have any personal knowledge of the facts, although in a few cases he must be the party aggrieved (see, *e.g.*, Offences Against the Person Act 1861, s. 42). As a general rule a private person may institute any criminal proceedings (although leave to prosecute is sometimes required, see Chap. 30), but the Director of Public Prosecutions may take over a prosecution after it has started (Prosecution of Offences Act 1908, s. 2(3)). In practice the prosecutor is most commonly a police officer but, in so far as he prosecutes as an individual, even a police prosecution may be said to be a private prosecution. In a magistrates' court a prosecutor may either conduct the prosecution in person or be represented by counsel or a solicitor, but in a court of assize or quarter sessions he must be represented by counsel or, in certain quarter sessions, by a solicitor. Moreover, under certain Acts it is possible in a magistrates' court for someone other than the one who laid the information or counsel or a solicitor to conduct the prosecution.

Examples are an inspector appointed under the Factories Act 1961 (who may prosecute or defend proceedings under that Act: s. 149) and a member or officer of a local government authority (who may institute or defend proceedings by or against the local authority: Local Government Act 1933, s. 277).

Accused

The accused (or defendant or prisoner, as he is sometimes called) is normally an individual, but a corporation may sometimes be charged with a criminal offence (see Chap. 4) and in this case there are certain procedural differences. Thus a corporation may appear at a trial on indictment by a representative (Criminal Justice Act 1925, s. 33) and a representative may also make a statement before the magistrates at committal proceedings (see Chap. 32) or consent or object to summary trial or claim trial by jury (see Chap. 40) (Magistrates' Courts Act 1952, Sched. 2). Moreover, under section 29 of the Criminal Justice Act 1967, a representative may plead for a corporation at a summary trial or even plead guilty by post (see Chap. 39). Although an ordinary accused may always defend himself, a corporation should, at a trial on indictment, be represented by counsel or a solicitor. (See also "Committal for trial," Chap. 32.)

Chapter Twenty-Eight

COURTS WITH A CRIMINAL JURISDICTION

Magistrates' Courts

As we have just seen, almost every criminal case is dealt with, at least in part, in a court of summary jurisdiction (or a magistrates' court, as it is normally called). The procedure in a magistrates' court is, to a large extent, now governed by the Magistrates' Courts Act 1952 and the Magistrates' Courts Rules 1968, but these do not cover every aspect, and recourse must also be had both to other statutes and to the common law procedure. Thus, where no statutory provision is relevant, the basic rule is that the magistrates must act in accordance with the rules of natural justice (see "Certiorari," Chap. 42).

Magistrates

The terms magistrate and justice of the peace are synonymous, but for the sake of consistency "magistrate" is used throughout this book except where the magistrates are conducting committal proceedings where the usual term of "examining justices" is used.

Magistrates may either be appointed for life (though their names are placed on a supplemental list at the age of seventy) or hold office *ex officio*. However, under s. 1 of the Justices of the Peace Act 1968 the number of *ex officio* magistrates is in fact now severely limited.

Magistrates for counties are appointed by the Crown, usually on the recommendation of a local advisory committee appointed by the Lord Chancellor to inform and advise him through the *custos rotulorum* (normally the Lord Lieutenant of the county), while borough magistrates are appointed by the Crown on the advice of the Lord Chancellor (though there is often a local advisory committee to advise him).

Ex officio magistrates formerly included the mayor of a borough, the chairman of a county council and the chairman of a district council but now only the Lord Mayor and aldermen of the City of

London are magistrates *ex officio* (Justices of the Peace Act 1968, s. 1). Judges of the High Court are magistrates by virtue of office, as also are the Attorney-General and the Solicitor-General, while the recorder of a borough is also a magistrate of that borough.

Stipendiary magistrates

The majority of magistrates are unpaid laymen (though they may be entitled to a travelling or subsistence allowance), but in certain boroughs stipendiary magistrates have been appointed. These are appointed by the Crown on the advice of the Lord Chancellor and they must be barristers or solicitors of not less than seven years' standing (Justices of the Peace Act 1949, s. 29). They normally hold office until the age of seventy.

Stipendiary magistrates in London are called *Metropolitan stipendiary magistrates*. They must also be barristers or solicitors of not less than seven years' standing (Administration of Justice Act 1964, s. 10).

Magistrates' clerks

For each county and county borough there must normally be a magistrates' courts committee, and it is the duty of this committee to appoint one or more magistrates' clerks for their area. The clerk, who may be either full-time or part-time, is paid a commensurate salary and he must normally be a barrister or solicitor of not less than five years' standing (Justices of the Peace Act 1949, s. 20(1)).

The magistrates' clerk must advise the magistrates on the questions of law and procedure and their powers of sentence and he will also advise them on the practices, in relation to sentence, of neighbouring courts (see the Justices of the Peace Act 1968, s. 5(2)). Particularly in courts presided over by lay magistrates, the clerk, therefore, performs a most vital function and the magistrates tend to rely heavily upon his advice. Nevertheless, the magistrates themselves must decide on the facts and their clerk must not attempt to influence their decision (*R. v. Stafford JJ., ex p. Ross* (1962), D.C.). Indeed, the former practice of the clerk going with the magistrates when they retire to consider their verdict has been disapproved (*R. v. Welshpool JJ., ex p. Holley* (1953), D.C.; *Practice Note (Justices' Clerks)* (1953)): instead, should the magistrates require advice on the law after they have retired, they may send for their clerk, but the clerk should normally return to the open court as soon as his advice has been given. Nevertheless, when questions of law and fact are intimately interwoven it may not be wrong for the clerk to retire with the magistrates so that they have his advice throughout (*R. v. Consett JJ., ex p. Postal Bingo Ltd.* (1967), D.C.).

The functions of magistrates' courts

In relation to the trial of criminal offences a magistrates' court has a two-fold jurisdiction: it may try offences summarily and it may conduct committal proceedings where an offence is to be tried on indictment. In addition a magistrates' court has a purely preventive jurisdiction to bind over a person to keep the peace and be of good behaviour, without convicting him of an offence.

Summary trial. For the trial of offences summarily there should normally be a minimum of two and a maximum of seven magistrates (though only in exceptional circumstances will there be more than five) sitting in open court in a petty sessional court-house (*i.e.*, a court-house at which magistrates are accustomed to assemble or a place which is for the time being appointed as a substitute therefor: Interpretation Act 1889, s. 13). However, a few summary offences may be tried before a single magistrate (*e.g.*, drunkenness in a public place: Criminal Justice Administration Act 1914, s. 38), although in this case, or if the court is sitting in an occasional court-house (*i.e.*, a court-house other than a petty sessional court-house), which is not possible if the court is trying an indictable offence summarily, the court cannot impose imprisonment for a period exceeding fourteen days or order (whether by fine, costs, compensation or otherwise) a person to pay more than twenty shillings (Magistrates' Courts Act 1952, s. 98(5)). Nevertheless, a stipendiary magistrate sitting alone has all the powers of a court of two or more lay magistrates (*ibid.*, s. 121(1)), and a single lay magistrate may issue a summons or warrant (*ibid.*, s. 1).

Committal proceedings. Committal proceedings may be held before one lay magistrate (Magistrates' Courts Act 1952, s. 4(1)), although in practice it is normal for there to be two or more magistrates or one stipendiary.

The examining justices must sit in open court except where any enactment (*e.g.*, Official Secrets Act 1920, s. 8(4)) contains an express provision to the contrary or where it appears to the justices, as respects the whole or any part of the proceedings, that the ends of justice would not be served by them sitting in open court (Criminal Justice Act 1967, s. 6). Nevertheless, section 3 of the Criminal Justice Act 1967 places restrictions on the reporting of committal proceedings. Thus, as a general rule, it is not lawful to publish or broadcast in Great Britain a report containing any other matter than (*a*) the identity of the court and the names of the examining justices; (*b*) the names, addresses and occupations of the parties and witnesses and the ages of the accused and witnesses; (*c*) the offence(s) charged; (*d*) the names of counsel and solicitors engaged in the proceedings; (*e*) any decision of the court to commit the accused for trial, or any decision not to commit one or some of the accused; (*f*) the charge(s) on which the accused was committed for trial and the court to which he was committed; (*g*) the date of any adjournment and the place to which the proceedings were adjourned; (*h*) any arrangements made as to bail; and (*i*) whether legal aid was granted to the accused (s. 3(4)).

These restrictions on the reporting of committal proceedings no longer apply, however, if the accused, or one of the accused, applies for their removal (Criminal Justice Act 1967, s. 3(2)) and an application by one co-accused means that the restriction must be lifted in respect of all the accused (*R.* v. *Russell, ex p. Beaverbrook Newspapers, Ltd.* (1969), D.C.). A full report may always be published if the court determines not to commit the accused, or all the accused for trial, or once the trial on indictment of the accused, or all of the accused, has been concluded (*ibid.*, s. 3(3)). In addition, where committal proceedings against two or more accused are started but the justices proceed to try the indictable offences charged against one, or some, of the accused summarily (see Chap. 40), while they commit the other accused for trial on indictment, the report of the summary trial may include particulars of that part of the committal proceedings which occurred before the justices proceeded to the summary trial (*ibid.*, s. 3(3)). Further, section 4 of the Criminal Justice Act 1967 provides that the clerk to the examining justices must display in a part of the court-house to which the public have access, on the day when the committal proceedings are concluded or the next day, a notice stating the accused's name, address and age (if known) and, if the accused was committed for trial, the charge(s) on which he was committed and the court to which he was committed, or, otherwise, the offence charged and that the court dismissed the charge.

Binding over to keep the peace, etc. The magistrates have power to bind over a person to keep the peace whenever some other person has shown by evidence on oath that he has just cause to fear some bodily harm (*R.* v. *Dunn* (1840)), for example, being killed or beaten (1 Hawkins P.C., c. 28, s. 6); and they have power to bind over to be of good behaviour on more comprehensive grounds, which include threatened disturbances of the peace, even though it is not alleged that anyone has been put in bodily fear or apprehension of violence (*Lansbury* v. *Riley* (1914), D.C.). In neither case need the person bound over have been convicted of an offence (*R.* v. *County of London Quarter Sessions Appeals Committee, ex p. Metropolitan*

Police Commissioner (1948), D.C.,) although some actual or threatened breach of the peace (*e.g.*, a fight or eavesdropping) must be shown, and in practice, notwithstanding the theoretical difference between the two forms of binding over, it is normal for the magistrates to bind over to keep the peace and be of good behaviour. (For consideration of whether a person may be bound over although no criminal offence has been committed, see Glanville Williams, "Preventive Justice and the Rule of Law" (1953) 16 M.L.R. 417.)

An application for a person to be bound over is made before a magistrates' court by a complaint (Magistrates' Courts Act 1952, s. 91), which may be made in writing or orally, but a formal complaint is not necessary if the person is already before the court (*ex p. Davies* (1871)). Thus where, for example, there has been a fight between the complainant and the person complained of, and possibly other persons as well, the court may in addition to, or instead of, binding over the person complained of, bind over the complainant and/or a witness in the proceedings, provided that they have been shown to be guilty of a breach of the peace, etc. Nevertheless, a person cannot be bound over unless he has first been warned of the possibility and been given an opportunity of making representations with regard to the matter (*Sheldon* v. *Bromfield JJ.* (1964), D.C.: but see *R.* v. *Aubrey-Fletcher, ex p. Kepper* (1967), D.C.).

When a person is bound over to keep the peace or to be of good behaviour it means that he must enter into a recognizance, with or without sureties, to keep the peace or to be of good behaviour towards the complainant (Magistrates' Courts Act 1952, s. 91(1), and this will be for a specified period, not normally exceeding twelve months. A recognizance is a written undertaking by the person bound over (the principal) whereby if he does not keep the peace or be of good behaviour throughout the time specified he will be liable to have to pay to the Crown the amount of money fixed in the recognizance. Sureties are other persons who enter into similar recognizances in relation to the principal whereby they will also be liable to have to pay to the Crown the amount fixed if the principal does not keep the peace or be of good behaviour (see the similar provisions which apply to bail, Chap. 43). If the person ordered to enter into a recognizance fails to enter into the necessary undertaking, or he defaults in finding the necessary sureties, the magistrates may commit him in custody for a period not exceeding six months or until he sooner complies with the order (*ibid.*, s. 91(3)). A surety, moreover, who has reason to believe that the principal has been, or is about to be, guilty of conduct constituting a breach of the conditions of the recognizance, may apply by complaint to the magistrates for the discharge of the recognizance, and the magistrates may, unless they adjudge the recognizance to be forfeited, order the principal to enter into a new recognizance, with or without sureties (*ibid.*, s. 92).

Even though the power to bind over to keep the peace or to be of good behaviour is not in the nature of a punishment, but is to prevent the threatened breach of the peace, and the person bound over has not necessarily been convicted of an offence, he does have a right of appeal to quarter sessions against the order (Magistrates' Courts (Appeals from Binding Over Orders) Act 1956, s. 1) (see Chap. 41).

Although the power to bind over, which was, at least in part, originally derived from the Justices of the Peace Act 1361, is normally exercised by the magistrates in a magistrates' court, it is possible for the power to be exercised by the magistrates at quarter sessions (*R. v. Dunn, supra*) or even by a High Court judge (*e.g.*, in the Criminal Division of the Court of Appeal) in his capacity as a magistrate (*R. v. Biffen* (1966), C.C.A.: where the accused's conviction was quashed on appeal but he was bound over to keep the peace for twelve months) (see also s. 1(7) of the Justices of the Peace Act 1968).

For the power to bind over after conviction of an offence, see Chapter 44.

Bias

The jurisdiction of a particular magistrate over a particular case is sometimes ousted by some special factor and similarly a magistrates' clerk may be unable to officiate in a particular case by reason of his own special circumstances. Thus, a magistrate must not sit if he has a pecuniary interest in the case (*per* Blackburn, J. in *R. v. Rand* (1866), D.C.), nor if he has any other interest provided that a real likelihood of bias can be shown (*R. v. Barnsley JJ., ex p. Barnsley Victuallers' Association* (1960), C.A.); and the same rules apply to a magistrates' clerk (*R. v. Sussex JJ., ex p. McCarthy* (1924), D.C.). Likewise, a magistrate who is a member of a local authority must not sit in any case in which the authority is a party (Justices of the Peace Act 1949, s. 3), but in this case the rule does not apply to a magistrates' clerk (*R. v. Camborne JJ., ex p. Pearce* (1955), D.C.).

Juvenile courts

These are special magistrates' courts which were established under the Children and Young Persons Act 1933, s. 45, to deal with criminal offences committed by children and young persons. A child is one who is under the age of fourteen years (Children and Young

Persons Act 1933, s. 107(1)), although, as we have seen (Chap. 4), a child under ten cannot be guilty of a criminal offence; while a young person is one who has attained fourteen but is under the age of seventeen years (*ibid.*, s. 107(1)). If an accused was under seventeen when the proceedings commenced, a juvenile court may continue to deal with the offence even though he becomes seventeen, but if he is then charged with a further offence, even one arising out of the same circumstances, this cannot be dealt with in the juvenile court (*R. v. Chelsea JJ., ex p. Director of Public Prosecutions* (1963), D.C.).

Juvenile courts deal with the summary trials of children and young persons, and also with the committal proceedings when any child or young person is to be tried on indictment. Nevertheless, in practice, it is rare for a child to be tried on indictment and most young persons are also dealt with summarily (see Chap. 40). If a child or young person is charged jointly with an adult (*i.e.*, one who has attained the age of seventeen), the charge cannot be dealt with in a juvenile court (Children and Young Persons Act 1933, s. 46(1)). But where a child or young person is convicted by a court other than a juvenile court of any offence except homicide, the court must, unless satisfied that it would be undesirable to do so, remit him to a juvenile court to be dealt with by that court (*ibid.*, s. 56, as amended).

A juvenile court must normally be composed of not more than three magistrates (including a man and a woman) and these magistrates must be members of the juvenile court panel. This is a special panel (which is normally appointed every three years by the magistrates themselves) composed of those magistrates (who must normally be under sixty-five years of age) who are considered to be most suitable to deal with juveniles. If, however, a stipendiary magistrate is the only member of the panel present and it is inexpedient in the interests of justice to adjourn the proceedings, he may sit alone (Juvenile Courts (Constitution) Rules 1954; though for London see the Children and Young Persons Act 1963, Sched. 2, Pt. II).

A juvenile court must not sit in the same room in which any other court has sat or will sit within one hour, and the public, though not the press, are excluded (Children and Young Persons Act 1933, s. 47, as amended by the Children and Young Persons Act 1963, s. 17(2)). Moreover, no newspaper report of any proceedings in a juvenile court should reveal the name, address, school or other identifying detail of any child or young person concerned in the proceedings, whether as the accused or as a witness, nor should any picture of any such child or young person be published in a newspaper; except that the court or the Home Secretary may, in any case, if satisfied that it is in the interests of justice, by order dispense with any of these restrictions to such extent as may be specified (Children and Young Persons Act 1933, s. 49).

Where a child or young person is charged before a juvenile court, the magistrates must, except where he is legally represented, allow his parent or guardian to assist him in the conduct of his defence (Summary Jurisdiction (Children and Young Persons) Rules 1933, r. 5) and the court may require the attendance of a child's or young person's parent or guardian in any proceedings in which the child or young person is charged with an offence or otherwise brought before the court (Children and Young Persons Act 1963, s. 25). Moreover, the court must explain to the child or young person the substance of the charge in simple language suitable to his age and understanding (Summary Jurisdiction (Children and Young Persons) Rules 1933, r. 6) and the terms "finding of guilt" and "order made upon a finding of guilt" must be used instead of "conviction" and "sentence" (Children and Young Persons Act 1933, s. 59). In practice, in juvenile courts, certain other variations from the practice normal in ordinary magistrates' courts usually occur; the proceedings on the whole being far less formal. (For the position when children and young persons are concerned in other proceedings, see "Children and young persons," Chap. 37.)

In addition to their criminal jurisdiction, juvenile courts also deal with children and young persons in need of care, protection or control (see the Children and Young Persons Act 1933, ss. 60-63, as amended).

Quarter Sessions

As we saw in Chapter 27, courts of quarter sessions have a two-fold jurisdiction. The majority of offences tried on indictment are tried at quarter sessions (see Chap. 32), while the court also hears appeals from magistrates' courts and, sometimes, sentences an accused who has been convicted summarily. When the court is hearing an appeal or merely sentencing an accused it does not sit with a jury.

When trying offences on indictment the court sits under the commission of the peace, and the clerk to quarter sessions is called the clerk of the peace. He must have the same legal qualification as a clerk of a magistrates' court but because a court of quarter sessions usually sits with a qualified chairman he will not normally be called upon to advise the court on points of law and procedure.

As the name denotes, quarter sessions basically meets four times a year, but today many courts in fact sit more often by means of adjourned sessions.

The composition of a court of quarter sessions depends on whether it is a borough quarter sessions or a county quarter sessions. Certain towns and cities have their own quarter sessions but otherwise a court of quarter sessions has jurisdiction over a particular county or a part of a county.

In a borough quarter sessions the sole judge is a recorder (*i.e.,* a barrister of at least five years' standing, who is usually an eminent practising lawyer), except that when the court is hearing an appeal from a juvenile court the recorder will, where practicable, be assisted by two members (a man and a woman) of the local juvenile court panel, who act as assessors (Children and Young Persons Act 1963, s. 19). The term "recorder" in this paragraph also includes an assistant recorder, who must have the same legal qualification.

In county quarter sessions the court is normally composed of a bench of two to nine magistrates presided over by a chairman. Moreover, although the magistrates are normally laymen, the chairman is usually an eminent lawyer. Thus, since the Administration of Justice (Miscellaneous Provisions) Act 1938, s. 1, a county quarter sessions has been able to apply to the Lord Chancellor for the appointment of a legally qualified chairman (*i.e.,* a barrister or solicitor of not less than ten years' standing or a holder of certain other legal offices) and now, by the Criminal Justice Administration Act 1962, s. 5, no chairman can be elected by them unless he is "legally qualified." Where the legally qualified chairman is the only magistrate present and it appears to him to be undesirable to postpone the trial, he may himself try the case, although this does not allow him on his own to hear an appeal or impose sentence after summary conviction (Criminal Justice Administration Act 1962, s. 4(5)). (For the wider jurisdiction as to trial of a court presided over by a "legally qualified chairman," see Chap. 32).

In practice one or more deputy chairmen are also appointed for each county quarter sessions and provided they have the same necessary legal qualifications they may preside over the court in the same manner as a legally qualified chairman.

Although the composition of a county quarter sessions is usually the same whether it is trying an accused on indictment or hearing an appeal, etc., when the court hears an appeal from a juvenile court not less than half the magistrates sitting must be magistrates whose names appear on the juvenile court panel, and of these one must be a man and one a woman (Criminal Justice Administration Act 1962, s. 4). Moreover, a magistrate should not hear an appeal from his own decision.

Greater London is, however, governed by special provisions. Thus, it is divided into five areas (Inner London, North-East London, South-East London, South-West London and Middlesex), each of which has its own quarter sessions (Administration of Justice Act 1964, s. 2). Each quarter sessions, moreover, has a whole-time chairman and deputy chairman (*i.e.*, a barrister or solicitor of not less than ten years' standing) and the courts sit almost continuously throughout the year.

Assizes

England and Wales (outside London) is divided into seven assize circuits (South-Eastern, Midland, Oxford, Western, Wales and Chester, North-Eastern and Northern) and in each of the assize towns in the circuit assizes are normally held three times a year. Traditionally the judges travelled around the circuit from one assize town to the next, but the present position is somewhat more complicated and assizes are now held simultaneously in more than one assize town on the same circuit (see the Assize Order 1964).

The judges at assizes sit by virtue of the commission of assize (which includes the ancient commissions of oyer and terminer and gaol delivery). Moreover, although the commissioners are normally Queen's Bench Division judges the commission may be granted to other judges or to Queen's Counsel, who may then sit at the assizes with basically the same powers as commissioners who are also High Court judges (Supreme Court of Judicature (Consolidation) Act 1925, s. 70(3)).

As we shall see in Chapter 32, the more serious indictable offences are tried at assizes.

Central Criminal Court

The Central Criminal Court (or "Old Bailey" as it is colloquially called) was established in 1834 by the Central Criminal Court Act, and it is now the assize court of Greater London (Administration of Justice Act 1964, s. 1(1)). The court also has jurisdiction to try offences committed within the jurisdiction of the Admiralty of England (see Chap. 30) (Administration of Justice Act 1964, Sched. 1, para. 5), and by the Administration of Justice (Miscellaneous Provisions) Act 1938, s. 11(2), the High Court has power, instead of directing trial at bar (see Queen's Bench Division, *post*), to direct trial at the Central Criminal Court before three judges of the Queen's

Bench Division. Nevertheless, this last power has never been exercised. The Central Criminal Court, like all courts of assize, is a branch of the High Court (Supreme Court of Judicature (Consolidation) Act 1925, s. 70).

The Central Criminal Court must hold at least four sessions in every year (Administration of Justice Act 1964, s. 1(2)). The length of the sessions is not fixed; however, it is decided in the October of each year, and in practice the court is sitting almost continuously throughout the year.

The judges of the Central Criminal Court are certain *ex officio* judges (the Lord Chancellor, the Lord Chief Justice, all Queen's Bench Division judges, the Lord Mayor and Aldermen of the City of London, the Recorder of London and the Common Serjeant), not more than six full-time additional judges, and any other persons to whom the commission (of oyer and terminer and gaol delivery) is granted (Administration of Justice Act 1964, Sched. 1). The full-time additional judges are appointed by the Queen on the recommendation of the Lord Chancellor and they must be barristers of not less than ten years' standing (City of London (Courts) Act 1964, s. 5). In practice, moreover, the Lord Chancellor rarely, if ever, sits and the Lord Mayor and Aldermen of the City of London sit only on ceremonial occasions.

Crown Courts at Liverpool and Manchester

These were established as permanent criminal courts for their respective areas by the Criminal Justice Administration Act 1956, s. 1. Nevertheless, unlike the Central Criminal Court, they are not only criminal assize courts but quarter sessions as well (*ibid.*, s. 2(3)). The Crown Courts must hold at least eleven sessions each year (*ibid.*, s. 1(5)).

The judges of the Crown Courts include all High Court judges (although in practice, only Q.B.D. judges sit) and the Recorders of Liverpool and Manchester respectively. The Recorderships of Liverpool and Manchester, like the Recordership of London, are, therefor, full-time judicial appointments.

Queen's Bench Division

In addition to the appellate jurisdiction of its Divisional Court, the Queen's Bench Division also has an original criminal jurisdiction and the Divisional Court has a supervisory jurisdiction. These will now be considered.

Original jurisdiction

The High Court still has power to direct the trial of an indictment or inquisition at bar (Administration of Justice (Miscellaneous Provisions) Act 1938, s. 11). Originally trial at bar was widely used for grave offences (particularly political offences) and it meant that the accused appeared before the bar of the Court of King's Bench and was tried by all the judges (*i.e.*, four) of the King's Bench and a jury. In modern times the practice has become virtually obsolete, the last case being the trial of Sir Roger Casement for high treason in 1916, when the court was comprised of three judges of the Q.B.D. and a jury. We have already noticed the alternative power of the High Court to direct trial at the Central Criminal Court.

Appellate jurisdiction

We have seen in Chapter 27 that appeals lie to a Divisional Court of the Q.B.D. from a magistrates' court and from quarter sessions. These appeals are by way of case stated and will be considered further in Chapter 41. A minimum of two, but normally three, judges of the Q.B.D. sit for the Divisional Court's appellate jurisdiction.

Supervisory jurisdiction

The Divisional Court of the Q.B.D. has a very important supervisory jurisdiction over inferior courts by reason of the orders of certiorari, mandamus and prohibition. Thus, by an order of certiorari, the Divisional Court may order the record of the proceedings before an inferior court to be transmitted to the High Court to be quashed; by an order of mandamus the Divisional Court may require an act to be performed by an inferior court; and by an order of prohibition the Divisional Court may restrain an inferior court from exceeding its jurisdiction. For the meaning of an "inferior court" and further consideration of these orders, see Chapter 42.

The Divisional Court also issues writs of habeas corpus but it is not possible within the scope of this work to consider this jurisdiction in detail.

The composition of the Divisional Court for its supervisory jurisdiction is the same as for its appellate jurisdiction.

The Criminal Division of the Court of Appeal

As we have seen in Chapter 27, appeals from trials on indictment, at assizes or quarter sessions, lie to the Criminal Division of the Court of Appeal. This court was established by the Criminal Appeal

Act 1966 (following a recommendation of an Interdepartmental Committee on the Court of Criminal Appeal (Chairman: Lord Donovan), 1965), and it took over the jurisdiction of the former Court of Criminal Appeal, which is now extinct. The powers of the Criminal Division are, however, basically the same as were those of the Court of Criminal Appeal. These will be considered further in Chapter 41.

The Lord Chief Justice and the Lords Justices of Appeal are members of the Criminal Division of the Court of Appeal and, in addition, the Lord Chief Justice may, after consultation with the Master of the Rolls, request any judge of the Queen's Bench Division to sit as a member of the court (Criminal Appeal Act 1966, s. 1(3)), although a judge cannot sit on an appeal from his own judgment or order (*ibid.*, s. 2(3)). Administrative functions in relation to the court are exercised by the registrar of criminal appeals (who must have been a practising barrister or solicitor of not less than ten years' standing) or by an assistant or deputy assistant registrar of criminal appeals (*ibid.*, s. 3).

An appeal to the Criminal Division of the Court of Appeal must be heard by not less than three judges (*ibid.*, s. 2(2)), although a single judge may hear applications for leave to appeal or for an extension of time in which to appeal (see Chap. 41). When the Criminal Division has to sit in two or more courts, one is normally presided over by the Lord Chief Justice, sitting with a Lord Justice of Appeal and one puisne judge of the Q.B.D., while each of the others is presided over by a Lord Justice of Appeal, sitting with two puisne judges of the Q.B.D. If, in any appeal, there is a division of opinion, the dissenting judge may, in practice, ask that the appeal be re-heard before a court of five judges (usually the Lord Chief Justice, two Lords Justices of Appeal and two puisne judges of the Q.B.D.).

A single judgment is normally pronounced in the Criminal Division of the Court of Appeal, but separate judgments may be pronounced when the presiding judge states that in his opinion the question is one of law on which it is convenient that there should be separate judgments (*ibid.*, s. 2(4)) (see, *e.g.*, *R.* v. *Harz* (1966), C.C.A.).

The House of Lords

The House of Lords is the final court of appeal in criminal cases, and appeals to the House will be considered further in Chapter 41. In theory the House of Lords may also try cases of impeachment, the last being the trial of Lord Melville in 1805.

Coroners' Courts

A coroner's court is not strictly a criminal court and it is not concerned with the guilt or innocence of an accused. Nevertheless, it is normally concerned with the cause of death of a dead body and when that cause of death is found to be homicide by a known person that person will have to be committed to assizes for trial for that homicide.

A coroner must be a barrister, solicitor or medical practitioner of not less than five years' standing (Coroners (Amendment) Act 1926, s. 1(1)) and he will normally be appointed for a particular area. It is the coroner's duty to hold inquests on treasure found within his area to decide whether it is treasure trove (the Crown has a right to treasure trove, *i.e.*, gold or silver (whether in bullion coin or not) hidden in or on the land deliberately, and not merely lost, when the true owner is unknown) and also to decide on the cause of death of dead bodies found within that area.

A coroner must hold an inquest on a dead body when the death appears to have been violent, or unnatural, or sudden and the cause unknown, or in prison, or otherwise in such circumstances as to require an inquest. (See *Jervis on Coroners* (9th ed.), p. 77.) However, where the cause of death is unknown the coroner would normally order a post-mortem examination to be held and if this showed that the death was from natural causes an inquest would not be held.

In certain cases an inquest must be held with a jury (which consists of a minimum of seven and a maximum of eleven persons) and the coroner may then accept the verdict of a majority of the jury provided the minority consists of not more than two. Otherwise the coroner must discharge the jury and summon another (Coroners (Amendment) Act 1926, s. 15). The cases when the coroner must sit with a jury are set out in the Coroners (Amendment) Act 1926, s. 13(2), *i.e.*, when there is reason to suspect (*a*) that the deceased came to his death by murder, manslaughter or infanticide; or (*b*) that the death occurred in prison; or (*c*) that the death was caused by an accident, poisoning or disease, notice of which death is required to be given to a government department (*i.e.*, an industrial accident, poisoning or disease); or (*d*) that the death was caused by an accident arising out of the use of a vehicle in a public highway; or (*e*) that the death occurred in circumstances the continuance or possible recurrence of which would be prejudicial to the health or safety of the public.

The coroner himself must always view the body before the inquest and if he so directs, or a majority of the jury so desires, the body will be viewed by the jury (Coroners (Amendment) Act 1926, s.

14(1)). The coroner may also summon the deceased's medical practitioner, or any medical practitioner who is in practice near where
the death occurred, to conduct a post-mortem and to give evidence
thereof (Coroners Act 1887, s. 21).

As we have seen, a coroner's court is not concerned with the
guilt or innocence of an accused, but with the cause of death of the
deceased. The procedure is therefore inquisitorial, not accusatorial,
and the coroner himself will call the witnesses and normally examine
them first (Coroners Rules 1953, r. 17). The inquest, however, must
be held in public (*ibid.*, r. 14) and any person who, in the coroner's
opinion, is an interested person is entitled to examine any witness
at the inquest, either in person or by counsel or solicitor (*ibid.*,
r. 16). Moreover, any person whose conduct is likely to be, or is in
fact, called in question must, if not called as a witness, be notified
of the time and place of the inquest, or the inquest must be
adjourned so that he may be notified (*ibid.*, rr. 19, 20). Further,
although the strict laws of evidence do not necessarily apply, a
witness is not obliged to answer any question tending to incriminate
him (*ibid.*, r. 18) and an inquest is subject to the rules of natural
justice so that the coroner's findings must be based upon evidence
(*R.* v. *Huntbach, ex p. Lockley* (1944), D.C.) (see also Chap. 42).

If the coroner's jury return a verdict that the cause of death was
murder, manslaughter or infanticide by a named person, that person
must be committed in custody by the coroner to assizes to stand
trial for that homicide (see the Coroners (Amendment) Act 1926,
s. 25). Unless the named person is already in custody, the coroner
must also issue his warrant for arresting that person, but if the
offence charged is manslaughter or infanticide the coroner may
allow him bail (see Chap. 43) (Coroners Act 1887, s. 5; Infanticide
Act 1938, s. 1(1)).

Nevertheless, in practice, an accused is rarely committed for trial
on a coroner's inquisition because, if a homicide by a known person
is suspected, an inquest will normally be adjourned until after the
ordinary criminal proceedings have taken place and if, before the
coroner's jury's verdict the accused has already been charged with
murder, manslaughter, infanticide or causing death by dangerous
driving the inquest must be adjourned (Coroners (Amendment) Act
1926, s. 20; Road Traffic Act 1960, s. 1(3)). The coroner then has a
discretion whether to resume the inquest (*e.g.*, to ascertain the cause
of death if the accused was acquitted on indictment) but if the
accused has been charged on indictment, the coroner's verdict must
be consistent with that of the trial court (Coroners (Amendment)
Act 1926, s. 20(2)). Even if an accused is committed for trial on
a coroner's inquisition, committal proceedings will normally also be

held and the accused may then be committed both on inquisition and on indictment. He must still appear at assizes charged on the inquisition even though the examining justices refuse to commit on indictment, although in such cases the prosecution normally offer no evidence at the trial.

If an accused is committed for trial on the coroner's inquisition, the coroner must make witness orders in respect of the witnesses at the inquest to ensure their attendance at the trial (Criminal Procedure (Attendance of Witnesses) Act 1965, s. 7; Coroners (Indictable Offences) Rules 1965, r. 5). Moreover, in a case of murder or manslaughter (and probably also infanticide) the coroner must put into writing the statements on oath of the witnesses, and any such deposition must be signed by the witness and also by the coroner (Coroners Act 1887, s. 4(2)) (for the admissibility of such depositions at the trial, see Chap. 37).

In addition to the power of the High Court to control the proceedings of a coroner's inquest by means of orders of certiorari, mandamus and prohibition (see Chap. 42), application may be made to the High Court, by or under the authority of the Attorney-General, for an order that another inquest should be held on the ground that it is necessary or desirable in the interests of justice (Coroners Act 1887, s. 6; Coroners (Amendment) Act 1926, s. 19).

Chapter Twenty-Nine

MINISTERS AND LAW OFFICERS OF THE CROWN

ENGLAND, unlike many countries, has no Minister of Justice. The conduct and supervision of criminal proceedings are not concentrated in the hands of one Minister or Ministry, but are divided amongst a number of Ministers and Law Officers of the Crown. It is not possible, within the scope of this work, to consider these various Ministers and Officers and their duties in detail, but an outline of certain of their powers and functions will be given.

The Lord Chancellor

The Lord Chancellor, in his judicial capacity, may preside in the House of Lords when the House is hearing an appeal regarding a criminal case. In his executive capacity, however, he does not play an important part in the direct control of criminal proceedings, although he does exercise a wide range of judicial appointments. Thus, as we have seen, not only are High Court judges appointed on the recommendation of the Lord Chancellor, but so also are magistrates, recorders and most other persons exercising a judicial function.

The Home Secretary

The Home Secretary does play an important part in the control and supervision of at least certain aspects of the criminal process. Thus the Home Secretary has control over penal institutions (see Chap. 44) and he advises the Crown on the exercise of the prerogative of mercy (see also the Criminal Appeal Act 1968, s. 17: Chap. 41).

The Home Secretary also appoints the Director of Public Prosecutions (see below) (Prosecution of Offences Act 1879, s. 1) and he exercises an important measure of supervision over the police.

In addition, the Home Secretary has certain more particular powers. Thus he may grant an accused bail in cases of treason (Magistrates' Courts Act 1952, s. 8), and he may grant leave to prosecute aliens for offences committed within British territorial waters (Territorial Waters Jurisdiction Act 1878, s. 3). These powers and duties will be considered again in the appropriate part of this book.

The Attorney-General

The Attorney-General also plays an important part in the control and supervision of the criminal process (in addition to those cases where he is actually the prosecutor or appears as counsel for the prosecution). Thus, the consent of the Attorney-General is required for the institution of prosecutions for a number of criminal offences (see Chap. 30) and he exercises a power of supervision over the Director of Public Prosecutions (see below).

One of the most important powers of the Attorney-General is his right to enter a *nolle prosequi* in respect of proceedings on indictment or inquisition. This has the effect of putting an end to the proceedings but the accused is not thereby acquitted and he may, at least in theory, subsequently be re-indicted for the same offence (*R.* v. *Ridpath* (1712)). A *nolle prosequi* may be entered at any time after the signing of the bill of indictment or inquisition and before judgment. Whether a *nolle prosequi* is in fact entered is in the complete discretion of the Attorney-General and is not subject to any control by the courts (*per* A. L. Smith L.J. in *R.* v. *Comptroller-General of Patents* (1899), C.A.), although the Attorney-General does tend to enter a *nolle prosequi* in certain settled circumstances. Thus, for example, it may be entered when the accused is unfit to stand his trial and the unfitness is likely to be permanent. It is not possible, however, to consider the many other cases where a *nolle prosequi* has been entered.

The Solicitor-General

The Solicitor-General has no independent special powers or duties in respect of criminal proceedings but any function authorized or required to be discharged by the Attorney-General may be discharged by the Solicitor-General if (*a*) the office of Attorney-General is vacant; or (*b*) the Attorney-General is unable to act owing to absence or illness; or (*c*) the Attorney-General authorizes the Solicitor-General to act in any particular case (Law Officers Act 1944, s. 1).

The Director of Public Prosecutions

The office of Director of Public Prosecutions is an office which was created by the Prosecution of Offences Act 1879. The purpose of the office is, "under the superintendence of the Attorney-General, to institute, undertake, or carry on such criminal proceedings . . . and to give such advice and assistance to chief officers of police, clerks to justices, and other persons . . . as may be for the time being prescribed by regulations under this Act, or may be directed in a special case by the Attorney-General" (s. 2).

The Director of Public Prosecutions must be a barrister or solicitor of at least ten years' standing and he is appointed by the Home Secretary. The Home Secretary may also appoint a number of assistant directors who must be barristers or solicitors of not less than seven years' standing (Prosecution of Offences Act 1908, s. 1). The Director also has a substantial department to assist him in his duties.

It is the duty of the Director of Public Prosecutions to institute, undertake or carry on criminal proceedings when (*a*) the offence is punishable with death; (*b*) the case has been referred to him by a government department and he considers that criminal proceedings should be instituted; and (*c*) the case appears to him to be of importance or difficulty or for any other reason it requires his intervention (Prosecution of Offences Regulations 1946, reg. 1). Moreover, by section 98(2) of the Criminal Justice Act 1967, on any appeal to the Criminal Division of the Court of Appeal or on any appeal to the House of Lords from the Criminal Division or from a Divisional Court of the Queen's Bench Division, it is the duty of the Director to appear for the Crown or the prosecutor if he is directed to do so by the court (*i.e.*, the Criminal Division or the Divisional Court). In all these cases the Director will not, of course, himself actually conduct the proceedings but his department, at least in the higher courts, will nominate counsel to appear for the Director.

The chief officer of every police district also has the duty to report to the Director of Public Prosecutions (*a*) offences which are punishable with death; (*b*) offences for which the Director must prosecute or for which the prosecution requires his consent (see Chap. 30); (*c*) prosecutions for indictable offences which have been wholly withdrawn or not proceeded with in a reasonable time; (*d*) where the Director himself makes a request for information; (*e*) offences in respect of which the advice or assistance of the Director is desirable; and (*f*) certain other specific offences, for example, incest, offences under the Official Secrets Acts 1911-1939, sedition, manslaughter, rape, abortion and prosecutions for obscene or indecent libels (Prosecution of Offences Regulations 1946, reg. 6). The Director will then tender such advice as he considers desirable and, where necessary, he will institute or take over the proceedings.

Chapter Thirty

CONSIDERATIONS PRELIMINARY TO PROCEEDINGS

BEFORE criminal proceedings can be commenced certain matters must be considered. Amongst these are whether or not the English courts will have jurisdiction over the offence and the accused, whether the proceedings will be outside a statutory time limit and whether leave is necessary to commence the proceedings.

(1) Jurisdiction

The term *jurisdiction* has a variety of meanings. It is used to denote whether any magistrates' court or court of quarter sessions may try a particular offence, or whether the court for one particular locality may try an offence (*i.e.*, venue) (these meanings of the term will be considered later), but in the context of this chapter the question is whether the English courts may try an offence which has been committed abroad, or on the high seas, or in the air (*i.e.*, territorial jurisdiction), and whether the accused may claim sovereign, diplomatic or other immunity.

Jurisdiction over the offence

(See also "Venue and the Ambit of Criminal Law" by Glanville Williams (1965) 81 L.Q.R. 276, 395 and 518.)

The basic common law rule is that English courts exercise jurisdiction only over offences committed in England (*i.e.*, including Wales, and English and Welsh rivers and inlets and bays of the sea, provided that a man on one shore can see what is being done on the other (2 East P.C. 804), and also the air space above). Thus, subject to statutory exceptions, the English courts claim no jurisdiction over offences committed abroad, whether by British subjects or foreigners, although certain jurisdiction has always been exercised over the high seas.

Since the Offences at Sea Act 1536 the common law courts have exercised the criminal jurisdiction of the Court of Admiralty

193

(although this is still referred to as the jurisdiction of the Admiralty) and this extends to indictable offences committed on British ships (*i.e.*, those owned by British subjects) on the high seas. The high seas, moreover, in this context, include foreign coastal waters and rivers, below the bridges, where the tide ebbs and flows and where great ships go (*R*. v. *Anderson* (1868), C.C.R.). Further, the English courts have always exercised jurisdiction over piracy committed by any ship upon the high seas.

Where an offence is committed partly within and partly outside the jurisdiction, whether the English courts exercise jurisdiction would appear to depend on whether the gist of the offence is committed within the jurisdiction, and this depends on the particular offence (*R*. v. *Harden* (1963), C.C.A.). Thus if a man outside the jurisdiction fires a shot which kills another man within the jurisdiction the English courts will exercise jurisdiction (*R*. v. *Coombs* (1786)).

The basic common law rule as to jurisdiction is subject, moreover, to many statutory exceptions and a number of the more important statutory exceptions will be mentioned.

Treason. By the Treason Act 1351 treason may be committed abroad provided the accused owes allegiance to the Crown (see Chap. 21).

Murder. By the Offences Against the Person Act 1861, s. 9, the English courts have jurisdiction over murder and manslaughter committed in any foreign country by a British subject. "British subject" in this section, and in other provisions relating to territorial jurisdiction, means a citizen of the United Kingdom and Colonies (British Nationality Act 1948, s. 3).

Bigamy. By the Offences Against the Person Act 1861, s. 57, a British subject may be tried for bigamy committed abroad.

In addition to the specific offences mentioned above, the English courts have jurisdiction over offences committed abroad by colonial governors (Offences by Officials Abroad Act 1699, as amended), over indictable offences committed in foreign countries by Crown servants when acting or purporting to act in the course of their employment (Criminal Justice Act 1948, s. 31) and over offences committed by members of the armed forces when abroad (Army Act 1955, s. 70; Air Force Act 1955, s. 70; Naval Discipline Act 1957, s. 42).

Apart from the criminal jurisdiction of the Admiralty over British ships the English common law courts did not exercise jurisdiction over British territorial waters until the Territorial Waters Jurisdiction Act 1878. Now by s. 2 of that Act an indictable offence committed by a person, whether a British subject or a foreigner, within British territorial waters is an offence within the jurisdiction of the Admiral even when committed on board a foreign ship. Nevertheless, leave to prosecute is required (see below). Certain summary offences committed in territorial waters are also covered by particular statutory provisions (see *e.g.*, Oil in Navigable Waters Act 1955, s. 7). The Continental Shelf Act 1964, s. 3, also extends the jurisdiction of the English courts to offences committed on or near installations (oil or otherwise) within the English part of the continental shelf.

Merchant ships. By the Merchant Shipping Act 1894, s. 686(1), the English courts have jurisdiction over any offence committed by a British subject on board a British ship on the high seas or in any foreign port or harbour or on board any foreign ship (provided he is not a member of the crew) and over any offence committed by a foreigner on board a British ship on the high seas. This, therefore, extends the jurisdiction of the English courts to summary offences committed in these circumstances (*Robey* v. *Vladinier* (1935), D.C.) and also to indictable offences committed by British subjects on board foreign ships. Section 687 of the same Act provides that offences committed out of Her Majesty's dominions (whether ashore or afloat) by any master, seaman or apprentice who is, or within three months previously has been, employed in any British ship may be dealt with in the same manner as if committed within the jurisdiction of the Admiralty (see *R.* v. *Dudley and Stephens* (1884)). The section would appear to apply to alien members of the crew as well as to British members, although the marginal note refers to "offences committed by British seamen at foreign ports."

Civil aircraft. By the Tokyo Convention Act 1967, s. 1(1), "any act or omission taking place on board a British controlled aircraft while in flight elsewhere than in or over the United Kingdom which, if taking place in, or in a part of, the United Kingdom, would constitute an offence under the law in force in, or in that part of, the United Kingdom shall constitute that offence." It must also be remembered that under the common law English courts have jurisdiction over offences committed in aircraft flying over England.

Jurisdiction over the accused

No child under the age of ten can be guilty of a criminal offence (Children and Young Persons Act 1933, s. 50, as amended), but apart from this exception, the courts have jurisdiction over every accused, apart from those who can claim sovereign, diplomatic or other immunity. It is not possible within the scope of this *Outline* to deal in detail with these various immunities but both the Queen and foreign reigning sovereigns are exempt from all criminal jurisdiction. Foreign ambassadors, High Commissioners and diplomatic staff (including members of their families who form part of their households) also enjoy immunity from the criminal process, but the privilege is that of the sovereign whom they represent and it may be waived by that sovereign (see *R.* v. *A.B.* (1941), C.C.A.), not by the diplomat himself. (See now the Diplomatic Privileges Act 1964.) Certain other persons also have immunities, for example, members of certain visiting forces (Visiting Forces Act 1952, s. 3) and members of certain international organizations (International Organizations Act 1968).

(2) Time Limits

Under the common law there are no time limits to a prosecution (*nullum tempus occurrit regi*) so that, for example, an accused may be charged with a murder which he is alleged to have committed many years before. Nevertheless, this common law rule is subject to a number of statutory exceptions and some of these exceptions will be mentioned. Moreover, for this purpose, a prosecution normally commences when the information is laid (see Chap. 31) or the accused is arrested (*Beardsley* v. *Giddings* (1904); though see *R.* v. *Austin* (1845)).

Indictable offences

Treason. Indictments for treason must normally be signed within three years (Treason Act 1695, s. 5), but this limit does not apply if the offence was designing, endeavouring or attempting to assassinate the Queen (*ibid*, s. 6), nor if it was committed on the high seas or in a foreign country.

Unlawful sexual intercourse with a girl under sixteen. A prosecution for this offence, or for an attempt to commit the offence, may not be commenced after twelve months (Sexual Offences Act 1956, s. 37 and Sched. II, 10(*a*)).

Trade descriptions. No prosecution for an offence against the Trade Descriptions Act 1968 can commence after three years from the commission of the offence or one year from its discovery by the prosecutor, whichever is the earlier (section 19).

Summary offences

In the case of summary offences, the general rule is that the information must have been laid within six months from the time when the offence was committed (Magistrates' Courts Act 1952, s. 104). This limit does not apply, however, to indictable offences which are tried summarily (*ibid*, s. 104) and though a hybrid offence cannot, by reason of section 104, be tried summarily unless the information was laid within the six months, it may still be tried on indictment. Moreover, the six months limit does not apply to those summary offences for which a statute provides some other limit, for example, wilfully applying a wrong warranty to food: twelve months (Food and Drugs Act 1955, s. 108); offences under the Obscene Publications Act 1959: twelve months (section 2); failure to notify alteration in rules of registered club: twelve months (Licensing Act 1964, s. 48); summary offences under the Companies Act 1948: maximum of three years (section 442).

Notice of intended prosecution. These statutory time limits must not be confused with the notices of intended prosecution which are required in the case of certain traffic offences (see Chap. 25).

(3) Leave to Prosecute

Under the common law it is not necessary to obtain leave to commence criminal proceedings, but this rule is subject to a number of statutory exceptions. Some of these exceptions have already been mentioned, but they, together with a few further exceptions, will be listed here.

Leave of a secretary of state

Proceedings for offences against the Territorial Waters Jurisdiction Act 1878 cannot be instituted against an accused who is not a British subject except with the consent of a secretary of state (*ibid.*, s. 3) (see also above).

Leave of a judge in chambers

See criminal libel in a newspaper, *ante*, Chap. 23.

Leave of the Attorney-General

See offences under the Official Secrets Act 1911 (*ibid.*, s. 8); and

incest (unless the prosecution is by the Director of Public Prosecutions), *ante*, Chap. 8.

Leave of the Director of Public Prosecutions

See aiding and abetting suicide, *ante*, Chap. 7; assisting offenders,
ante, Chap. 5; concealing offences or giving false information, *ante*,
Chap. 20; and the stealing of, or doing unlawful damage to, the
property of the accused's spouse, *ante*, Chap. 12.

Chapter Thirty-One

COMMENCEMENT OF PROCEEDINGS

(1) Process for Procuring Appearance of Accused

As we have seen, criminal proceedings almost always commence by the accused appearing before the magistrates, whether for summary trial or for committal proceedings. The appearance of the accused before the magistrates may be procured by the issue of a summons or warrant or, in some cases, arrest without a warrant, and these will now be considered.

A summons or warrant

A summons. A summons is addressed to the accused and it directs him to appear before a magistrates' court at a stated time and place. It must state shortly the substance of the information which has been laid against the accused (see below) and it must either be signed by the magistrate who issued it or must state his name and be authenticated by the signature of the clerk of the magistrates' court (Magistrates' Courts Rules 1968, r. 81; Magistrates' Courts (Forms) Rules 1968, form 2). The form of a summons is as follows:

In the county of   . Petty Sessional Division of   .
To A.B., of   .
Information has this day been laid before me, the undersigned [or state name] Justice of the Peace, by   that you on the   day of   , 19   , at   in the county afforesaid (*state shortly particulars of offence*):
You are therefore hereby summoned to appear on   the day of   , 19   , at the hour of   in the noon, before the Magistrates' Court sitting at   , to answer to the said information.
Dated the   day of   , 19   .
                                  J.P.,
Justice of the Peace for the county first above mentioned.
[*or* This summons was issued by the above named justice of the peace
                                  J.C.
Clerk of the Magistrates' Court sitting at   .]

199

A warrant. A warrant is in practice addressed to the police (*i.e.*, to each and every police officer of a particular police force), although in theory it could be addressed to a private person. It calls upon the police (or other person to whom it is addressed) to arrest the accused and to bring him before a particular magistrates' court. It must name or otherwise describe the person for whose arrest it is issued, and it must describe the offence charged in the information which has been laid against the accused (see below) (Magistrates' Courts Rules 1968, r. 80). A warrant which is not directed against a particular person (*i.e.*, a general warrant) is normally invalid. Nevertheless, a warrant authorizing a police officer to enter premises and to arrest any person found therein committing or having committed an offence under the Betting, Gaming and Lotteries Act 1963, may be issued by a magistrate (s. 51(1)).

The form of a warrant is as follows:

In the county of   . Petty Sessional Division of   .
To each and all of the constables of   .
Information on oath has this day been laid before me, the undersigned Justice of the Peace, by   that A.B. (hereinafter called the defendant) on the   day of   , 19   , at   in the county aforesaid, (*state shortly particulars of offence*) being an offence punishable with imprisonment [*or* being an indictable offence] [*or* and that the address of the defendant is not sufficiently established for a summons to be served on him]:
    You are hereby commanded to bring the defendant before the Magistrates' Court sitting at   , or a justice of the peace of the petty sessional division in which the court is situate, forthwith.
        Dated the   day of   , 19   .
                                J.P.,
            Justice of the Peace for the county first above
                                mentioned.

A warrant for arrest may also be endorsed with the direction that the accused, on arrest, shall be released on bail (see Chap. 43).

Laying an information. To obtain either a summons or a warrant (which are collectively called "process") the prosecutor (either in person or by his counsel or solicitor: Magistrates' Courts Rules 1968, r. 1(1)) must lay an information before a magistrate (Magistrates' Courts Act 1952, s. 1(1)). In practice an application for a summons or warrant is normally made not in open court but when the court is not sitting as such (see *Stone's Justices' Manual*, notes to the Magistrates' Courts Act 1952, s. 1), and, if necessary, an information can even be laid at a magistrate's home. If a warrant is applied for, the information must be written and sworn (*ibid.*, s. 1(1)) and in practice this is often done when a summons is required. Moreover, every information, summons or warrant must describe the offence charged in ordinary language, and if it is a statutory offence the relevant section and statute must be cited (Magistrates' Courts Rules 1968, r. 83). In fact, an information must charge only one offence (see Chap. 39), but a single summons may be issued in respect of several informations (*ibid.*, r. 81(3)).

Jurisdiction to issue process. Jurisdiction, in this sense, means the jurisdiction of the magistrates' court for a particular locality, and, as a general rule, process should be issued by a magistrate within whose district the offence was committed or is suspected of having been committed (Magistrates' Courts Act 1952, s. 1(2) (*a*)). Nevertheless, an offence committed on the boundary between two or more districts, or within five hundred yards of such a boundary, or in any harbour, river, arm of the sea or other water lying between two or more districts, may be treated as having been committed in any of these districts (*ibid.*, s. 3(1)). An offence begun in one district and completed in another may be treated as having been wholly committed in either (*ibid.*, s. 3(2)), while an offence committed on any person, or on or in respect of any property, in or on a vehicle or vessel engaged on any journey or voyage through two or more districts may be treated as having been committed in any of those jurisdictions (*ibid.*, s. 3(3)). The jurisdiction of a court whose district is situated on the coast or other navigable water also extends to ships which are on, or lying or passing off, the coast or are in that navigable water (Merchant Shipping Act 1894, s. 685).

Process may be issued by a magistrate in whose district the accused resides or is present, or is believed to reside or to be present (Magistrates' Courts Act 1952, s. 1(2) (*c*)). Nevertheless, where the offence charged is not an indictable offence a summons cannot be issued under this provision and, though a warrant may be issued, it must require the accused to be brought before a magistrates' court which will have jurisdiction to try the offence (and this must normally be the court of the district where the offence was committed: see "Jurisdiction to Try," below, Chap. 39) (proviso to s. 1(2) of the Magistrates' Courts Act 1952).

In addition, process may be issued when it appears to the magistrates necessary or expedient that some other person should be tried jointly with, or in the same place as, an accused who is within their jurisdiction (Magistrates' Courts Act 1952, s. 1(2) (*b*)). Thus, process could be issued against a handler of stolen goods in order that he might be tried with the thief, or with another handler, who was within the jurisdiction (*R.* v. *Blandford* (1955), C.C.A.).

Whether process will be issued. A magistrate has a judicial discretion whether to issue process, but if he refuses it must appear that he did so in the exercise of his discretion, otherwise he may be compelled to do so by an order of mandamus (*R.* v. *Adamson* (1875), D.C.: this case was decided under s. 9 of the Indictable Offences Act 1848, but though this section was repealed by the Magistrates' Courts Act 1952, it would seem that the principle remains the same). Thus a magistrate was justified in refusing to issue process against a Jewish baker in respect of an alleged offence against a local Bread Act (in that he had sold bread on a Sunday) on the ground that if the process had been sought under the Sunday Observance Acts the magistrate would have been entitled under the Acts to have refused to issue it (*R.* v. *Bros* (1901), D.C.). But a magistrate was not justified in refusing to issue process for an offence of criminal libel on the ground that the applicant had a civil remedy, for this was taking into consideration matters which could not be properly considered (*R.* v. *Bennett* (1908), D.C.). Nor can a magistrate refuse on the ground that, though the offence alleged in the information has been committed, he considers that a more serious offence ought to have been alleged (*R.* v. *Nuneaton JJ., ex p. Parker* (1954), D.C.).

Whether summons or warrant. By section 24(1) of the Criminal Justice Act 1967, a warrant must not be issued in respect of an accused who has attained seventeen years unless (*a*) the offence is an indictable offence or is punishable with imprisonment, or (*b*) the address of the accused is not sufficiently established for a summons to be served on him. Subject to these provisions, however, the basic rule is that it is at the discretion of the magistrates whether a warrant, rather than a summons, is issued, although it is most unlikely that a warrant would be issued unless a warrant, and not a summons, had been requested by the applicant who laid the information. Moreover, even where a warrant is requested, it will not be issued unless there is a reason why it is required (*O'Brien* v. *Brabner* (1885), D.C.; *R.* v. *Thompson* (1909), D.C.). In addition, although section 24(1) (*b*) of the 1967 Act would seem to imply that a warrant ought to be issued in the circumstances mentioned, the same is not true of section 24(1) (*a*).

Execution of a warrant. A warrant for arrest remains in force until executed or withdrawn and it may be executed anywhere in England

and Wales by any person to whom it is directed or by any police officer acting within his own police area (Magistrates' Courts Act 1952, s. 102). Thus, for example, if a warrant is addressed to each and every police officer of the Essex police, an Essex police officer may arrest the accused on that warrant in Sussex or in any other part of England and Wales, but a Sussex police officer can only arrest on that warrant in Sussex.

A warrant issued in England or Wales may also be executed in Scotland by a Scottish police officer acting within his police area (Criminal Justice (Scotland) Act 1963, s. 39) but before a warrant can be executed in other parts of the British Isles it must be backed (*i.e.*, indorsed by a local magistrate) (Indictable Offences Act 1848, s. 13, as extended by the Magistrates' Courts Act 1952, s. 103). There are special provisions for the English and Scottish border counties (Police (Scotland) Act 1967, s. 18).

It is not necessary that a police officer should have the warrant for arrest in his possession when he executes it, but, if the person arrested so demands, it must be shown to him as soon as practicable (Magistrates' Courts Act 1952, s. 102). (For a warrant endorsed for bail, see Chap. 43.)

Arrest without a warrant

Arrestable offences. Any person may arrest without a warrant anyone who is, or whom he with reasonable cause suspects to be, in the act of committing an arrestable offence (Criminal Law Act 1967, s. 2(2)). Also, where an arrestable offence has been committed, any person may arrest without a warrant anyone who is, or whom he with reasonable cause suspects to be, guilty of the offence (*ibid.*, s. 2(3)). "Arrestable offence" means an offence for which the sentence is fixed by law or for which a person (not previously convicted) may under or by virtue of any enactment be sentenced to imprisonment for a term of five years, and an attempt to commit any such offence (*ibid.*, s. 2(1)) or any other offence which is expressly made an "arrestable offence" (*e.g.*, taking a conveyance without authority: Theft Act 1968, s. 12(3)). Nevertheless, under section 2(3), the offence for which the accused was arrested must in fact have been committed by someone, though not necessarily by the one arrested, so long as, with reasonable cause, the person effecting the arrest suspected him of being guilty. If, therefore, the particular offence had not been committed by anyone, the arrest will be unlawful whether or not there was reasonable cause (*Walters* v. *W. H. Smith* (1914)).

In addition to the cases already noted when "any person" may arrest, a police officer who, with reasonable cause, suspects that an arrestable offence has been committed, may arrest without a warrant anyone whom he, with reasonable cause, suspects to be guilty of the offence (Criminal Law Act 1967, s. 2(4)). In this case the arrest will be lawful provided the police officer, with reasonable cause, suspects that the offence has been committed, and it will not be unlawful merely because the offence was not committed by anyone. Further, a police officer may arrest without a warrant any person who is, or whom he with reasonable cause suspects to be, about to commit an arrestable offence (*ibid.*, s. 2(5)).

There are also certain other powers of arrest under the common law. Thus, a police officer may arrest any person obstructing him in the execution of his duty, if the obstruction is such as to cause or to be likely to cause a breach of the peace (*Levy* v. *Edwards* (1823); *Gelberg* v. *Miller* (1961), D.C.).

Arrests under particular statutes. In additon to the powers of arrest under the common law and for "arrestable offences," many statutes give further powers of arrest in specified circumstances. Thus, to give a few examples:

Any person may arrest anyone found committing an indictable offence in the night (Prevention of Offences Act 1851, s. 11).

Any person may arrest anyone who is, or whom he with reasonable cause suspects to be, committing an offence under section 25 of the Theft Act 1968 (going equipped for stealing) (s. 25(4)).

Any police officer, or the owner of the property (or his servant) may arrest anyone found committing any offence against the Malicious Damage Act 1861 (s. 61).

A police officer may arrest any person reasonably suspected by him to be committing an offence under section 1 (wearing a uniform in connection with political objects), section 4 (possessing an offensive weapon at a public meeting or procession) and section 5 (using threatening, abusive or insulting words or behaviour in a public place or at a public meeting) of the Public Order Act 1936 (s. 7(3)).

Whether a statute allows the arrest of a person who is reasonably suspected of being an offender but who is in fact innocent depends on the wording of the particular statute (*Barnard* v. *Gorman* (1941), H.L.; *Wiltshire* v. *Barrett* (1966), C.A.).

Effecting an arrest. On arrest without a warrant by either a police officer or a private person, the one arrested must be told the correct reason for his arrest, unless he is caught in the act or he makes it impossible to tell him (for example) by counter-attack or running away (*Christie* v. *Leachinsky* (1947), H.L.). Nevertheless, the one arrested need not be told the reason in legal terminology; it is sufficient if he is merely made aware of the reason for the arrest (*Gelberg* v. *Miller* (1961), D.C.).

On arrest by a private person the one arrested must be brought before a magistrate or be handed over to a police officer as soon as is reasonably practicable (*John Lewis & Co. Ltd.* v. *Tims* (1952), H.L.). But a police officer, unlike a private person (*Hall* v. *Booth* (1834)), may, before bringing the arrested person before a magistrate, take such steps as are reasonable to investigate the offence (*Dallison* v. *Caffery* (1965), C.A.) and the arrest will not necessarily be rendered unlawful if the one arrested is then released without a charge having been preferred against him (*Wiltshire* v. *Barrett* (1966), C.A.: see above). It is in fact normal practice for an arrested person to be taken to a police station and be formally charged and then be brought before a magistrate. Moreover, if a child or young person is arrested without a warrant and he is not released on bail, he must be brought before a magistrates' court within seventy-two hours unless a police officer, not below the rank of inspector, certifies that this is not possible by reason of illness or accident (Children and Young Persons Act 1963, s. 22).

Any person, whether a police officer or not, may use reasonable force in effecting or assisting in an arrest (Criminal Law Act 1967, s. 3). For the power to release on bail after arrest without a warrant, see Chapter 43.

(2) Search Warrants and Powers of Search

Search warrants
Common law. A common law search warrant is a warrant authorizing the police officers to whom it is addressed to enter and search the place mentioned in the warrant and to seize relevant goods found therein. Reasonable force may be used if necessary.

Under the common law a search warrant may be issued by a magistrate on an information being laid alleging theft, or even a suspicion that theft has been committed (*Wyatt* v. *White* (1860)); the search itself may then disclose whether theft has in fact been committed. The search warrant need not, moreover, necessarily specify the particular goods for which the search is being made (*Jones* v. *German* (1897), C.A.), and, whether goods are specified or not, if a police officer has entered premises by reason of a search warrant, he may seize not only the goods which he reasonably believes to be covered by the warrant, but also any other goods

which he believes on reasonable grounds to have been stolen, at least
if he believes that they were stolen or "handled" by the occupier
(*Chic Fashions (West Wales) Ltd.* v. *Jones* (1968), C.A.).

A search warrant may be executed in the same way as a warrant
for arrest (Magistrates' Courts Act 1952, s. 102(2)), except that the
police officer executing the search warrant must have the warrant
in his possession at the time, and he must produce it if required
(*Codd* v. *Cabe* (1876), C.A.). It has been said, moreover, that where
there is merely a suspicion of theft the warrant must be executed
in the daytime, but that it may be executed at night if there is
positive proof (2 Hale P.C. 150).

By statute. In addition to the common law, many statutes also
provide power to issue a search warrant in particular cases. A few
of these will be considered.

Theft Act 1968, 26(1). This provides that where it appears by information on oath that there is reasonable cause to believe that
any person has in his custody or possession or on his premises any
stolen goods, a magistrate may grant a warrant to search for and
seize those goods.

Children and Young Persons Act 1933, s. 40 (as amended by the
Children and Young Persons Act 1963). This provides that where
it appears to a magistrate on information on oath that there is
reasonable cause to suspect, *inter alia*, that a child or young person
has been, or is being, assaulted, ill-treated or neglected, the magistrate may issue a warrant authorizing any police officer named
therein to search for the child or young person (if necessary by
force).

Sexual Offences Act 1956, s. 43. This allows a magistrate to issue
a warrant authorizing a named police officer to search for a named
woman (if need be by force) and to take her to a place of safety. The
magistrate may do so where it appears by information on oath that
there is reason to suspect that the woman is detained in any place
in order that she may have unlawful sexual intercourse and that she
is detained against her will, or that she is under the age of sixteen
or is a defective, or that she is under the age of eighteen and is
detained against the will of her parent or guardian The information
itself may be laid by the woman's parent, relative or guardian, or
by any other person who, in the magistrate's opinion, is acting in
the woman's interest.

Obscene Publications Act 1959, s. 3. This provides that if a magistrate is satisfied by information on oath that there is reasonable ground for suspecting that in any specified premises, or stall or vehicle, obscene articles are kept for gain, he may issue a warrant empowering any police officer within fourteen days to enter (if need be by force) and to search the premises, or to search the stall or vehicle. The police officer may also seize and remove any articles found therein or thereon which he has reason to believe to be obscene articles and to be kept for publication for gain. An information can only be laid under this section, however, by or on behalf of the Director of Public Prosecutions or by a police officer (Criminal Justice Act 1967, s. 25).

Powers of search
Premises. By the Theft Act 1968, s. 26(2), a police officer not below the rank of superintendent may in writing authorize a police officer to search any premises for stolen goods if the occupier of the premises has been convicted within the preceding five years of handling stolen goods or of any offence involving dishonesty and punishable with imprisonment, or if the premises within the preceding twelve months have been in the occupation of a person who has been convicted within the preceding five years of handling stolen goods. The police officer may then search for and seize any property he believes to have been stolen (s. 26(3)). It is not necessary for the authorising police officer to specify particular property, and he may give such authority if he has reason to believe generally that such premises are being made a receptacle for stolen goods

Apart from section 26(2), however, and the powers of a police officer to enter premises for the purpose of making an arrest (which will be considered below), neither a police officer nor any other person has a right to search premises without a search warrant. Nevertheless, in practice, householders, etc, sometimes voluntarily allow police officers to enter and search their premises in connection with offences (see *Dallison* v. *Caffery* (1965), C.A.).

Persons. A police officer has a right under the common law to search an arrested person who has so conducted himself, by reason of violence of language or conduct, that the police officer reasonably believes it right and prudent to do so (*Leigh* v. *Cole* (1853)), and it is probable that a police officer has the right to search any arrested person (*per* Horridge J. in *Elias* v. *Pasmore* (1934)). Articles or documents found on the person, or in the possession or control of the one arrested, and which will form material evidence on his prosecution for the crime charged, may then be seized (*Dillon* v.

O'Brien (1887)) and it has been held that interests of state will excuse the seizure, even if otherwise unlawful, if the documents or articles subsequently form material evidence of any crime committed by anyone (*Elias* v. *Pasmore, supra*). (See, however, "The Law of Search and Seizure" by D. A. Thomas [1967] Crim. L.R. 3.) Moreover, the police may then retain the documents or articles until the trial is concluded, but no longer (*Elias* v. *Pasmore, supra*).

A number of statutes also give a police officer power to search a person (normally in conjunction with searching premises), for example, the Incitement to Disaffection Act 1934, s. 2(2) (whereby a judge of the High Court may grant a search warrant authorizing the search both of premises and of persons found therein, in connection with offences under that Act) and the Official Secrets Act 1911, s. 9 (whereby a magistrate may grant a search warrant authorizing the search both of premises and of persons found therein, in connection with offences under that Act). Section 6 of the Dangerous Drugs Act 1967 also allows a police officer to search any person whom he has reasonable grounds for suspecting is in possession of an unauthorized drug. It is common, in modern statutes, to provide that a woman shall not be searched except by a woman (see the Incitement to Disaffection Act 1934, s. 2(3)).

Rights of entry

Under the common law a police officer with either a warrant for arrest or a search warrant may, if necessary, break open the doors to gain admittance, but before doing so he must inform those on the premises of the cause of his coming and he must request them to give him admittance (*Launock* v. *Brown* (1819)). It was once considered that if the police officer broke into the house of someone other than the one to be arrested he did so at his peril and that if the one to be arrested was not after all within the house the police officer became a trespasser (2 Hale P.C. 177). Now, however, it is probable that the police officer will be protected in every case provided he acted on a fair and reasonable ground of suspicion, having previously been refused admittance. (See *Stone's Justices Manual* (1969 ed.), p. 403.)

Even without a warrant a police officer may break into premises to suppress an affray and, under the Criminal Law Act 1967, s. 2(6), a police officer, in order to effect an arrest for an "arrestable offence," may enter (if need be, by force) and search any place where the person to be arrested is or where the police officer, with reasonable cause, suspects him to be. Moreover, a private person may break into premises to prevent murder (*Handcock* v. *Baker* (1800)). In addition, a police officer may break into premises in pursuit of persons who have made an affray in his presence, or who have escaped from lawful arrest, but the pursuit of persons who have made an affray must be a fresh pursuit (*R.* v. *Marsden* (1868), C.C.R.: where an interval of one hour was too long).

Certain statutes give police officers special rights of entry (*e.g.,* Firearms Act 1968, s. 47(5)), but apart from these statutory provisions a police officer has no general right (*i.e.,* without express or implied permission) to enter private premises without a warrant (*Great Central Rail Co.* v. *Bates* (1921), D.C.), even for the purpose of investigating past or suspected offences (*Davis* v. *Lisle* (1936), D.C.; *McArdle* v. *Wallace* (1964), D.C.).

(3) Examining Suspects

Apart from the powers of search outlined above, a police officer, or other person, has no general right to search a person suspected of having committed an offence, nor to take his finger-prints, nor even to question him. Thus a suspect who refused to give his name and address to a police officer or to accompany him to a police box, unless he was first arrested, could not be convicted of wilfully obstructing the police officer in the execution of his duty (*Rice* v. *Connolly* (1966), D.C.; and see *Kenlin* v. *Gardiner* (1967), D.C.). Nevertheless, police officers in certain localities have special statutory powers (*e.g.,* under the Metropolitan Police Acts), and if the finger-prints of a suspect or of an arrested person have been obtained evidence of them will normally be admissible in evidence against that person (see *Callis* v. *Gunn* (1964), D.C.). Indeed, as a general rule, relevant evidence will still be admissible although it was obtained unfairly or even illegally (*Elias* v. *Pasmore* (1934); *Kuruma* v. *R.* (1955), P.C.). Nevertheless, in criminal proceedings there is always a judicial discretion to exclude evidence which has been unfairly obtained (*per* Lord Goddard C.J. in *Kuruma* v. *R., supra; R.* v. *Payne* (1963), C.C.A.).

Confessions

A confession by an accused is in a special category in that to be admissible in evidence it must have been made voluntarily (*i.e.,* not induced by any promise or threat of a temporal nature held out by some person having authority over the prosecution). Moreover, if a confession is made to a police officer (or other person charged with the duty of investigating offences or charging offenders) it must not only be voluntary but it should normally comply with the Judges' Rules (1964). These provide, *inter alia,* that a police officer may question a person whether suspected or not and whether in custody or not so long as he has not been charged or informed that he may be prosecuted (Rule 1), but that as soon as a police officer has evidence which would afford reasonable grounds for suspecting that a person has committed an offence, that person must be cautioned before further questioning (*i.e,.* he must be told that he is not obliged to say anything unless he wishes to do so but what he says may be put into writing and given in evidence) (Rule 2). It is not possible to consider in detail the law in relation to confessions and the Judges' Rules within the scope of this work but recourse should be had to a textbook on evidence (*e.g., Cross on Evidence, Nokes on Evidence*). However, provided a confession was made voluntarily, it may still be admissible although obtained unfairly (*R.* v. *Spilsbury* (1835); *R.* v. *Derrington* (1826)), and the Judges' Rules are only rules of practice so that, though they should normally be complied with, a confession made in breach of them, provided it was voluntary, may still be admitted in evidence (*R.* v. *Voisin* (1918), C.C.A.).

Finger-prints

As we have seen, if the finger-prints of an accused have been obtained evidence of them will normally be admissible (*Callis* v. *Gunn* (1964), D.C.). Moreover, a magistrates' court, on the application of a police officer not below the rank of inspector, may order the finger-prints (including palm-prints) of an accused aged not less than fourteen to be taken by a police officer, when the accused has been taken into custody and been charged with an offence before that court (Magistrates' Courts Act 1952, s. 40(1)) or he has appeared before that court in answer to a summons for any offence punishable with imprisonment (Criminal Justice Act 1967, s. 33). The police officer in taking the finger-prints may then use such reasonable force as may be necessary (Magistrates' Courts Act 1952, s. 40(2)). Nevertheless, if the accused is acquitted or the examining justices refuse to commit him for trial, the finger-prints, and all copies thereof, taken under these provisions must be destroyed (*ibid.,* s. 40(4)).

Chapter Thirty-Two

COMMITTAL PROCEEDINGS

Appearance before the Magistrates

WE have already considered the methods by which the accused's presence before the magistrates may be secured. After the accused has appeared, however, the procedure will differ according to whether the offence is to be tried summarily or on indictment. The procedure for summary trial will be considered in Chapter 39.

Adjournment

Before an offence can be tried on indictment the magistrates must normally inquire into the offence as examining justices. Nevertheless, before they begin to do so it is often necessary that further enquiries should be made as to the facts of the offence, and the magistrates may therefore adjourn the committal proceedings and remand the accused in custody or on bail. The examining justices may also adjourn the proceedings and remand the accused at any time during the hearing itself (Magistrates' Courts Act 1952, s. 6(1)). After an adjournment the examining justices may adjourn again but on each occasion the accused must be remanded in custody or on bail and he cannot be released on an informal undertaking to attend the adjourned hearing (*ibid.*, s. 105). Moreover, an accused cannot be remanded for a period exceeding eight clear days (*i.e.*, eight days *between* the day of the remand and the day of the adjourned hearing) except that if the court remands him on bail it may remand him for a longer period if he and the prosecutor consent (*ibid.*, s. 105(4)). If an accused who has been remanded is unable by reason of illness or accident to appear before the court at the expiration of the period for which he was remanded, the court may, in his absence, remand him for a further time (*ibid.*, s. 106(1)).

Jurisdiction

A magistrates' court has jurisdiction as examining justices over any offence committed by any person who appears or is brought before the court, whether or not the offence was committed within the court's area (Magistrates' Courts Act 1952, s. 2(3)). Nevertheless, as we have seen (Chap. 31), process will normally be issued by the magistrates of the area where the offence was committed and in practice the accused will normally be brought before those magistrates and they will conduct the committal proceedings.

The hearing

After all necessary enquiries have been made the examining justices must decide whether the accused should be committed for trial. For this the justices may hold a preliminary investigation to see whether the prosecution can make out a prima facie case against the accused, but sometimes they may commit the accused for trial without consideration of the evidence.

Committal without consideration of the evidence

Where all the evidence before the court (whether for the prosecution or the defence) consists of written statements (with or without exhibits) which are admissible in evidence under section 2 of the Criminal Justice Act 1967 (see below), the examining justices may commit the accused for trial without consideration of the contents of those statements (Criminal Justice Act 1967, s. 1). Nevertheless, the examining justices cannot do so if the accused, or one of the accused, is not represented by counsel or a solicitor or the accused's counsel or solicitor has submitted that the statements disclose insufficient evidence to put the accused on trial by jury for the offence (*ibid.*, s. 1).

Where, at committal proceedings, the accused is represented by counsel or a solicitor and all the evidence is in the form of written statements the court must first cause the charge to be written down, if this has not already been done (which is unusual, unless the accused has claimed trial by jury under s. 25 of the Magistrates' Courts Act 1952, see Chap. 40), and be read to the accused and the court must then ascertain whether he wishes to object to any of the prosecution's statements being tendered in evidence, or to give evidence himself or to call witnesses, or to submit that the prosecution's statements disclose insufficient evidence to put him on trial by jury for the offence with which he is charged (Magistrates' Courts Rules 1968, r. 3(2)). Only if the court is satisfied that the accused, or each of the accused, does not wish to take any of these steps can it then decide to commit the accused for trial without consideration of the evidence (*ibid.*, r. 3(3)). Nevertheless, in practice, this procedure is very widely used.

Preliminary Investigation

Prosecution speeches and evidence

If a preliminary investigation is held it will begin by the prosecutor making an opening speech outlining the case against the accused and the prosecution's evidence will then be called. Witnesses called by the prosecution will give sworn evidence; they will normally be examined in chief by the prosecution, they may be cross-examined by the defence, and they may then be re-examined by the prosecution. Subject to the power of a party to put in written statements (see below) the rules of evidence which apply at a preliminary hearing are basically the same as those which apply at a trial but it is not possible within the scope of this work to state these rules in detail. Moreover, there is a tendency in practice to admit evidence at a preliminary investigation which may be excluded at the trial and a committal for trial will not be vitiated merely because the magistrates heard evidence which was really inadmissible (*R.* v. *Norfolk Quarter Sessions, ex p. Brunsden* (1953), D.C.).

Written statements

In committal proceedings a written statement by any person is admissible in evidence (either for the prosecution or the defence) to the same extent as if it were oral evidence, provided: (*a*) the statement purports to be signed by the person who made it; and (*b*) the statement contains a declaration by the maker that it is true to the best of his knowledge and belief, and that he made the statement knowing that, if it were tendered in evidence, he would be liable to prosecution if he wilfully stated in it anything which he knew to be false or did not believe to be true (Criminal Justice Act 1967, s. 2). Where the statement is made by a person under twenty-one it must also state his age (*ibid.*, s. 2(3)).

Before such a statement is tendered in evidence a copy of the statement (together with a copy of any other document referred to as an exhibit therein, or information where such a document may be inspected) must have been given to each of the other parties (or to their legal representatives: *R.* v. *Bott* (1968)) and the statement will not be admissible if any other party objects (*ibid.*, s. 2(2)). Moreover, the court may, of its own motion or on the application of any party, require the maker of the statement to attend before the court and to give evidence (*ibid.*, s. 2(4)).

Where such a written statement is admitted in evidence at a preliminary investigation it must, unless the court otherwise directs, be read aloud and, if not read aloud, an account must be given orally of the statement (*ibid*, s. 2(5)).

Further, at a preliminary investigation into a sexual offence (*i.e.*, any offence, or attempt to commit an offence, under the Sexual Offences Act 1956 or the Indecency with Children Act 1960) a child must not normally be called as a witness but any written statement of the child is admissible in evidence of any matter of which his oral testimony would be admissible (Children and Young Persons Act 1963, s. 27(1)). Nevertheless, the child must be called as a witness if the defence objects to the admissibility of his written statement or the prosecution requires the attendance of the child for the purpose of establishing the identity of any person (*ibid.*, s. 27(2)).

Depositions

Subject to the power to admit written statements, the evidence of each prosecution witness must be given in the presence of the accused (Magistrates' Courts Act 1952, s. 4(3)). The evidence must be put into writing (*i.e.*, a deposition), and as soon as may be after the examination of such a witness the court must cause the deposition to be read to him in the presence and hearing of the accused and it must then be signed by that witness (Magistrates' Courts Rules 1968, r. 4(2)). In addition, one of the examining justices must sign a certificate authenticating the depositions (*ibid.*, r. 4(3)). The rules as to the taking of depositions must, moreover, be complied with strictly and the committal for trial will be invalid if witnesses are examined from written statements, other than as outlined above, (*R. v. Gee* (1936), C.C.A.) or if the depositions already taken in relation to another accused are read out to the witnesses without those witnesses repeating that evidence orally (*R. v. Phillips* (1939), C.C.A.).

If the accused is committed for trial, copies of the depositions and of the information (if in writing) must be supplied to him on request (Magistrates' Courts Rules 1968, r. 11). We will consider in Chapter 37 when the depositions are admissible in evidence at the trial.

No case to answer

At the close of the prosecution's case the court may, on its own initiative or on the application of the defence, dismiss the case on the ground that there is no case to answer in law, *i.e.*, that the prosecution have failed to make out a prima facie case against the accused. If the case is dismissed, moreover, the accused must be discharged. Nevertheless, discharge is not an acquittal. The purpose of a preliminary investigation is not to decide whether the accused is innocent or guilty of the offence but whether the prosecution can show a prima facie case against him. Although, therefore, the examining justices have dismissed a case and the accused has been discharged, he may in theory (subject to any time limit or the requirement of leave) be charged again at a later date with the same offence.

The charge

Unless the case is dismissed as outlined above, the court must then cause the charge against the accused to be written down, provided that this has not already been done (which is unusual, see above). Magistrates' Courts Rules 1968, r. 3(2)). The charge will be based upon the prosecution's evidence, and though it will normally be substantially the same charge as that laid in the information, or upon which the accused was arrested, and upon which the accused appeared before the examining justices, it need not necessarily be the same. Thus, the accused may have been arrested and brought before the examining justices on a charge of murder, but the justices may consider that the prosecution's evidence has only disclosed a prima facie case of manslaughter. A charge of manslaughter and not murder will then be written down.

The fact that the charge is normally written down at this stage and not at the commencement of the proceedings again illustrates that this is not a trial. If it were a trial it would begin with the accused pleading guilty or not guilty and for this purpose the charge must already have been formulated. A preliminary investigation does not begin, however, with the accused pleading and no plea is taken at any time.

When the charge has been written down it must be read to the accused and its nature should be explained to him in ordinary language (Magistrates' Courts Rules 1968, r. 4(6)).

The statutory caution

The court (normally through the clerk) must then ask the accused whether he wishes to say anything in answer to the charge but, if he is not represented by counsel or a solicitor, the court, before doing so, must caution him (this caution is commonly called the statutory caution in order to distinguish it from the caution under the Judges' Rules: see Chap. 31) (Magistrates' Courts Rules 1968, r. 4(7)). If the court does so caution the accused it must say to him (or words to the same effect):

"You will have an opportunity to give evidence on oath before us and to call witnesses. But first I am going to ask you whether you wish to say anything in answer to the charge. You need not say anything unless you wish to do so. Anything you say will be taken down and may be given in evidence at your trial. You should take no notice of any promise or threat which any person may have made to persuade you to say anything."

Statement by accused

The accused (including a corporation if it appears by a representative: Magistrates' Courts Act 1952, Sched. 2, para. 3), if he wishes, may then make an unsworn statement, and this must be put into writing, be read over to him and be signed by one of the examining justices and also, if he wishes, by the accused (Magistrates' Courts Rules 1968, r. 4(8)). Such a statement by an accused will then be admissible in evidence at his trial (Criminal Justice Act 1925, s. 12(4)). Moreover, it has been held that though the court has a duty to record the whole of any statement made by the accused, the statement as signed by the justice (at least if also signed by the accused) is final as to what was said (*R.* v. *Morry* (1946), C.C.A.).

As we shall see (Chap. 37) an accused cannot normally adduce evidence at a trial on indictment in support of an alibi unless he has given prior notice of the alibi, and this notice may be given in court during, or at the end of, the proceedings before the examining justices (Criminal Justice Act 1967, s. 11(6)). Indeed, the accused should normally be warned of this requirement at the committal proceedings (including committal proceedings where he is being committed for trial without consideration of the evidence: see above) (*ibid.*, s. 11(3)). Nevertheless, it is otherwise unusual for an accused to make a statement (or to give evidence himself or to call other defence evidence) for if he does so this will affect the defence which he can put forward at his trial. In practice it is common for an accused to say merely that he pleads not guilty and reserves his defence. However, as we have seen, no plea is taken at a preliminary investigation so that in fact the accused is merely alleging his innocence and indicating that he intends to plead not guilty at the trial. Therefore, though he does say that he will be pleading not guilty at the trial, he may plead guilty, or, though he says that he will be pleading guilty, he may plead not guilty, although in this latter case his statement at the preliminary investigation will be evidence against him at the trial.

Defence evidence and speeches

Whether or not the accused has made a statement in answer to the charge he may give sworn evidence himself and/or call other defence witnesses (Magistrates' Courts Rules 1968, r. 4(10)). Nevertheless, as we have just seen it is unusual in practice for the accused to give or call evidence for the defence.

When evidence for the defence is given and the accused is represented by counsel or a solicitor, his counsel or solicitor may address the court on the accused's behalf before or after the evidence for the defence is given, at his discretion. Nevertheless, where the accused himself gives sworn evidence and other defence witnesses (*i.e.*, two or more) are also called, the accused's counsel or solicitor may, with leave of the court, address the court both before and after the defence evidence. Where the court does allow the accused's counsel or solicitor two speeches, however, though only in this case, the prosecution are entitled to two speeches, and the prosecution's second speech (the first is at the very beginning of the proceedings) will come immediately before the accused's counsel's or solicitor's second speech (Magistrates' Courts Rules 1968, r. 4(11)).

The Magistrates' Courts Rules make no provision for those cases where the accused is not represented by counsel or a solicitor (which is in fact quite common), and the examining justices in such a case may therefore follow whatever procedure is normal in that court, provided it is in accordance with the rules of natural justice. Nevertheless, in practice, the justices would probably follow the same order as applies when the accused is represented.

Committal for trial

After all the evidence and speeches, the examining justices must decide whether there is sufficient evidence to put the accused upon trial by jury for any indictable offence (Magistrates' Courts Act 1952, s. 7(1)). If the magistrates do commit for trial they will normally commit him on all or some of the charges which were written down at the end of the prosecution's case, although section 7 seems to visualize the possibility of the magistrates committing him on some other charge. If the examining justices do not consider that there is sufficient evidence to commit him for trial, the accused must be discharged, but like discharge after a finding of no case to answer, this is not an acquittal and the accused is liable, in theory, to be charged again with the same offence. If the accused is a corporation, moreover, the magistrates will commit for trial by an order in writing empowering the prosecutor to prefer a bill of indictment in respect of the offence named in the order, (but this does not prohibit the inclusion in the bill of other offences in accordance with section 2 of the Administration of Justice (Miscellaneous Provisions) Act 1933: see Chap. 33) (Magistrates' Courts Act 1952, Sched. 2, paras. 1, 2).

The decision of the examining justices may be by a majority, but while the chairman will vote with the other magistrates, in cases of equality he has no casting vote. The case must be reheard by the magistrates, or by a reconstituted court, or the accused must, after all, be discharged (*R.* v. *Hertfordshire JJ., ex p. Larsen* (1926), D.C.).

If the examining justices do commit the accused for trial by jury (whether after a preliminary investigation or without consideration of the evidence) they must commit him in custody or on bail (Magistrates' Courts Act 1952, s. 7(2)). For committal on bail see Chap. 43.

Witness Orders

If the accused is committed for trial the examining justices must make a witness order in respect of each witness who gave evidence at the preliminary investigation (or whose written statement was tendered in evidence at the preliminary investigation or other committal proceedings: Criminal Justice Act 1967, s. 2(10)), other than the accused himself and any witness of his merely as to his character, and this will require the witness to attend and give evidence before the trial court (Criminal Procedure (Attendance of Witnesses) Act 1965, s. 1(1)). Where, however, it appears to the magistrates that a witness's attendance at the trial will be unnecessary because his evidence is unlikely to be required or disputed, the order will be a *conditional witness order, i.e.,* an order which only requires him to attend if notice to that effect is given to him (*ibid.,* s. 1(2)). If a conditional witness order is made the magistrates must inform the accused of his right to require the attendance of the witness at the trial and of the steps he must take to enforce the attendance (*ibid.,* s. 1(3)).

If a High Court judge is satisfied by evidence on oath that a witness is unlikely to comply with a witness order which has been made, the judge may issue a warrant to arrest the witness and to bring him before the trial court. However, a warrant cannot be issued in respect of a witness subject to a conditional witness order unless notice has been given to that witness requiring him to attend the court (*ibid.,* s. 4(1)).

Non-attendance

Where a witness fails to attend the trial court in compliance with a witness order, that court may:

(1) in any case, cause to be served on him a notice requiring him to attend the court forthwith or at such time as may be specified in the notice;

(2) if the court is satisfied that there are reasonable grounds for

believing that he has failed to attend without just excuse, or if he has failed to comply with a notice under paragraph (1) above, issue a warrant to arrest him and bring him before the court (Criminal Procedure (Attendance of Witnesses) Act 1965, s. 4(2)).

In addition, any witness who without just excuse disobeys a witness order is guilty of contempt of court and may be punished summarily by the trial court. The maximum period of imprisonment for such contempt is three months (*ibid.*, s. 3).

A court issuing a warrant for arrest under section 4 may endorse the warrant for bail and the witness, on arrest, should then be released on bail in accordance with the terms stipulated in the warrant (*ibid.*, s. 5(2)). Otherwise, if a witness is arrested under section 4 at a time when the trial court is not sitting he should be brought before a magistrates' court for the place where he is arrested and that court should commit him to custody or release him on bail until he can be brought or appear before the trial court (*ibid.*, s. 5(1)). The trial court itself may also remand in custody or on bail a witness brought before it in pursuance of a warrant for arrest issued under section 4 until such time as the court may appoint for receiving his evidence or otherwise dealing with him (*ibid.*, s. 4(3)).

Witness summons

The attendance of witnesses, other than those in respect of whom a witness order has been made, may be secured by a witness summons. These will be dealt with in Chap. 37.

The Trial Court

If the examining justices commit the accused for trial they must commit him to a particular court. This entails three factors: committing him to assizes or quarter sessions, committing him to a particular court of assize or quarter sessions and committing him to a particular session of the trial court. Moreover, the trial court or the High Court then has power to vary the place of trial.

Assizes or quarter sessions

Provided the offence charged is triable at quarter sessions the examining justices must normally commit an accused for trial at quarter sessions and not at assizes (Magistrates' Courts Act 1952, s. 9(1)). Nevertheless, assizes do have jurisdiction to try any indictable offence.

Jurisdiction of quarter sessions. Quarter sessions has jurisdiction to try all indictable offences other than those for which a person may be sentenced to death, and those for which he may be sentenced to imprisonment for life, and certain other offences set out in List B of Schedule 1 of the Criminal Law Act 1967 (s. 8). List B of Schedule 1 (which is printed in Appendix I) includes blasphemy, some perjury and forgery offences, bribery, offences under the Official Secrets Acts 1911 to 1939, attempted murder and causing death by reckless or dangerous driving.

Moreover, certain offences which are set out in Division I of Schedule 1, List A of the Criminal Law Act 1967 are triable by all courts of quarter sessions even though most of them are punishable with life imprisonment. This list (which is printed in Appendix I) includes arson of stacks of corn, etc., and certain forgery offences.

"Legally qualified chairman." Further, we have already seen (Chap. 28) that if a court of quarter sessions is presided over by a "legally qualified chairman" it has a somewhat wider jurisdiction than if it is not. The additional offences which are only triable by a court of quarter sessions which has a "legally qualified chairman" are set out in Division II of Schedule 1, List A of the Criminal Law Act 1967 (which is printed in Appendix I) and this includes certain offences against the Perjury Act 1911 and the Forgery Act 1913, bigamy and conspiracies to commit offences punishable on summary conviction.

It should be remembered that a court of quarter sessions for a borough, presided over by a recorder or assistant recorder, does have the wider jurisdiction, and the same applies to courts of quarter sessions for the Greater London area (Criminal Law Act 1967, s. 8(3)).

Assizes instead of quarter sessions. Although the examining justices must normally commit to quarter sessions if the offence is triable by quarter sessions, the court may instead commit an accused charged with such an offence to assizes if the court is of opinion that there are circumstances that make the case unusually grave or difficult, or that serious delay or inconvenience would otherwise be caused, or that the trial is likely to be a long one (Magistrates' Courts Act 1952, s. 11, as amended by the Criminal Justice Administration Act 1962, s. 14(2)). It is not normally convenient to try long cases at quarter sessions where time is usually limited.

Venue

Internal offences

As well as deciding whether to commit to assizes or quarter sessions, the examining justices must also decide to which particular court of assize or quarter sessions to commit, and as a general rule the venue of a trial, like the issue of process, will be local. The trial will normally be held before the court of the area where the offence was committed, even though the accused, and perhaps the witnesses, come from another locality. Thus it is true to say that as a general rule process will be issued and both the committal proceedings and the trial will take place in the area where the offence was committed.

We have already seen (Chap. 31) that there are certain exceptions to the general rule as regards the issue of process, and similar exceptions apply to venue. Thus, where an offence is committed on the boundary between two or more counties, or within five hundred yards of such a boundary, or is begun in one county and completed in another, the venue may be laid in either county (Criminal Law Act 1826, s. 12). Moreover, if the offence was committed in or upon any vehicle or vessel in the course of any journey or voyage, the venue may be laid in any county through which the vehicle or vessel passed (*ibid.*, s. 13). Where an offence is committed in a city or town, which is also a county (except London, Westminster and Southwark), the venue may also be laid in the next adjoining county (Counties of Cities Act 1798, ss. 2, 10). As to certain exceptions which apply to particular offences, see, *e.g.*, Customs and Excise Act 1952, s. 284.

By the Criminal Justice Act 1925, s. 11(1), an accused may be tried for an indictable offence in any county or place in which he was apprehended, or is in custody on a charge for the offence, or has appeared in answer to a summons lawfully issued charging the offence. Thus, as we have seen, process may be issued by a magistrate merely because the accused resides or is present within the district and section 11(1) then allows that magistrate to commit the accused for trial to the local court of assize or quarter sessions. Nevertheless, the accused must not be committed under this section if he would suffer hardship thereby and if the examining justices still commit in spite of the accused's application to the contrary, the accused may appeal against the committal to the High Court (Magistrates' Courts Act 1952, s. 9(2)). An example when the accused might suffer hardship would be where all the defence witnesses resided in the area where the offence was committed.

By the Criminal Justice Act 1925, s. 11(2), where an accused is charged with two or more indictable offences he may be tried in respect of all those offences in any county or place in which he could be tried for any one of them.

By the Magistrates' Courts Act 1952, s. 10(1), the examining justices may, instead of committing the accused for trial to the normal court of assize or quarter sessions, commit him for trial at some other assizes or quarter sessions, if it appears to them to be more convenient with a view either to expediting his trial or saving expense, provided the normal court would be unlikely to be held within one month. Further, if the accused is otherwise unlikely to be tried within eight weeks of the committal the magistrates must exercise their power under section 10(1) unless they are satisfied that there are circumstances which would make the exercise of the power undesirable (Criminal Justice Administration Act 1962, s. 15(2)). The court's power under section 10(1) must not be exercised, however, if the accused would suffer hardship thereby (Magistrates' Courts Act 1952, s. 10(1) (*b*)).

Change of venue

So far we have considered to which trial court the examining justices must commit the accused. Nevertheless, the Queen's Bench Division of the High Court of Justice may then change the place of trial whenever it appears to be expedient in the interests of justice (Administration of Justice (Miscellaneous Provisions) Act 1938, s. 11(3)). It may be expedient for a variety of reasons, including the length of the trial, the time when the trial court will sit or an undue local prejudice against the accused (see the trial of Dr. John Bodkin Adams (1957)) or even in his favour (see *R.* v. *Lewis* (1936): where the accused was a Welsh nationalist). The trial may even be switched from quarter sessions to assizes (see *R.* v. *Sandfield* (1965), D.C.) or, provided the case is within the jurisdiction of quarter sessions, vice versa.

Where for any reason whatsoever the trial of an accused, who has been committed for trial for an indictable offence before any court of assize or quarter sessions, is either not proceeded with or not brought to a final conclusion before that court, the court may, if it thinks it convenient to do so with a view either to expediting the trial or re-trial (*e.g.*, after a disagreement of the jury, see Chap. 38) or to the saving of expense or otherwise, and it is satisfied that the accused will not suffer hardship thereby, direct that the trial or re-trial be before a court for some other place (Criminal Justice Act 1925, s. 14(2)). A court of quarter sessions also has an inherent power to transfer a case to the assizes for the same area (see *R*. v. *Wilson* (1967), C.A.). It is common in practice for a trial court to use these powers, particularly when the defence or prosecution would not be ready to proceed with the case if it were not delayed.

Extra-territorial offences

Where the English courts have jurisdiction over an offence committed outside England and Wales (see Chap. 30) the ordinary rule that venue is local obviously cannot apply. However, we have seen that by the Criminal Justice Act 1925, s. 11(1), an accused may be tried for an indictable offence in any county or place in which he was apprehended, or is in custody or has appeared in answer to a summons, and this section therefore allows any court of assize or quarter sessions in England and Wales to try any indictable offence committed abroad if the accused has been apprehended, etc., in that court's area. In addition, a number of statutes expressly provide that particular offences committed outside England and Wales may be tried in any county or place where the accused has been apprehended or is in custody (see, *e.g.*, Offences Against the Person Act 1861, s. 9; Criminal Justice Act 1948, s. 31(2); Perjury Act 1911, s. 8; Explosive Substances Act 1883, s. 7).

The Central Criminal Court has jurisdiction to try offences committed within the jurisdiction of the Admiralty of England (see Chaps. 28 and 30), and offences against the Merchant Shipping Act 1894 are to be dealt with as if committed within Admiralty jurisdiction (see s. 687). Nevertheless, a number of statutes expressly give jurisdiction over offences against that statute, committed within the jurisdiction of the Admiralty of England, to any county or place in which the offender is apprehended or is in custody (*e.g.*, Malicious Damage Act 1861, s. 72; Forgery Act 1861, s. 50; Offences Against the Person Act 1861, s. 68). Also, for the purpose of venue offences committed on British aircraft are deemed to have been committed in the place where the offender may for the time being be (Tokyo Convention Act 1967, s. 1(3)).

The Session

If the examining justices commit an accused for trial they must normally commit him to the *next* quarter sessions or *next* assizes for the place where he is to be tried (Magistrates' Courts Act 1952, s. 9(1)). The next court means the next sitting of that court to begin and this may be in one or two days or it may be in several months. We have already seen the power, and sometimes duty, of the examining justices to commit to some other court with a view to expediting the trial.

The examining justices normally have no power to commit to a court other than the next court, but where an accused is committed on bail (or the accused is a corporation: Magistrates' Courts Act 1952, Sched. 2, para. 6) for trial at quarter sessions and the next quarter sessions for that county or borough are due to be held within five days, the magistrates may commit him to the next quarter sessions but one (Magistrates' Courts Act 1952, s. 10(2)). This, however, is the only provision allowing the magistrates to commit to a court later than the next court so that if the accused is to be tried at assizes, or the magistrates are not prepared to commit him on bail, they must commit him to the next court even though it is to commence within the next day or two. Nevertheless, if the defence or prosecution cannot be ready in time we have already seen that application can be made to the trial court to have the trial switched to some other, and later, court.

Moreover, although the examining justices must normally commit the accused to the next sitting of the trial court to start, by the Criminal Justice Administration Act 1962, s. 14, where the court of assize or quarter sessions is being held at the time of the committal, the magistrates may commit to that court provided the accused, the prosecutor and the judge, chairman or recorder of the trial court consent. The magistrates must therefore adjourn the committal proceedings before committing the accused, in order to obtain the consent of the judge, etc.

Chapter Thirty-Three

THE INDICTMENT

(1) Drafting the Bill of Indictment

A BILL of indictment is a written or printed accusation of the crime charged made at the suit of the Crown. An indictment is a bill which has been signed by the proper officer of the court (see *Preferment*, below). (See also Archbold, *Criminal Pleading, Evidence and Practice* (37th ed.), para 1.)

The clerk of the trial court normally drafts (or draws, as it is technically called) the bill of indictment and after the committal for trial the clerk of the examining justices must, as soon as possible, send to the clerk of the trial court all relevant documents: for example, the information, depositions, any statement made by the accused before the examining justices, the names, addresses and occupations of the witnesses who are subject to a witness order and the recognizances of the accused and his sureties (if the accused was committed on bail) (Magistrates' Courts Rules 1968, r. 10(2)). The clerk of the trial court may, however, request prosecuting counsel to draft the bill, and the prosecution can insist that the bill be drafted by counsel (*Practice Note (Indictments)* (1956)). The Indictment should always be drafted by counsel if there are points of difficulty involved (*per* Lord Parker C.J. in *R.* v. *Martin* (1962), C.C.A.).

Form of indictment

The form of an indictment is laid down in the Indictments Act 1915 (as amended) and the Indictment Rules made thereunder. Examples of indictments are set out in the Appendices to these Rules, and Rule 4(5) of the Indictments Act 1915, Sched. 1, provides that the forms in the Appendices shall be used where applicable and in other cases forms to the like effect shall be used.

Commencement. An indictment contains three parts, the first of which is the "commencement." This states the name of the case (*e.g.*, THE QUEEN v. JOHN SMITH), the court of trial (*e.g.*, DURHAM

COUNTY ASSIZES held at Durham) and the presentment (*e.g.*, JOHN SMITH is charged with the following offence).

Statement of offence. The second part of the indictment is the "statement of offence." This must describe the offence shortly and in ordinary language, avoiding as far as possible the use of technical terms, and without necessarily stating all the elements of the offence (see below). If it is a statutory offence a reference to the section of the relevant statute must be made (Indictments Act 1915, Sched. 1, r. 4(3).) Where the offence is both a common law and a statutory offence (*e.g.*, rape) it should normally be indicted under the statute (*R.* v. *Pollock* (1967), C.C.A.).

Particulars of offence. The third part of an indictment is the "particulars of offence." This contains (in order) the name of the accused, the date of the offence, the county where the offence was committed and details of the offence, set out in ordinary language (see below). Where the date of the offence is not known it is common practice to say, for example, ". . . on a day unknown between the 15th day of January, 196- and the 21st day of January, 196- . . . ." (In this example the first possible date of the offence is January 16 and the last possible date is January 20, these being the dates *between* the 15th and the 21st.)

The common law basis of stating the county is to show that the trial court has jurisdiction over the offence charged. If, therefore, the trial court is a court for a county borough, it should be stated (if it is so) that the offence was committed within that county borough: for example, ". . . in the county borough of Leicester in the county of Leicester . . . ." In *R.* v. *Wallwork* (1958), however, the prosecution were uncertain as to the county in which the offence was committed, and the indictment read ". . . in the county of Sussex or elsewhere . . ."; the Court of Criminal Appeal held that this was a good indictment.

Examples of indictments

(1) *A common law offence:*

THE QUEEN v. JOHN SMITH

ESSEX ASSIZES

held at Chelmsford

John Smith is charged with the following offence:

STATEMENT OF OFFENCE

Murder.

PARTICULARS OF OFFENCE

John Smith, on the 1st day of April 196-, in the county of Essex, murdered *Bill Brown*.

(2) *A statutory offence:*

THE QUEEN v. MARY SMITH
NORFOLK ASSIZES
held at Norwich

Mary Smith is charged with the following offence:

STATEMENT OF OFFENCE

Arson, contrary to section 2 of the Malicious Damage Act 1861.

PARTICULARS OF OFFENCE

Mary Smith, on the 1st day of April 196-, in the county of Norfolk, maliciously set fire to a dwelling-house, one *Bill Brown* being therein.

(See also Appendix IV.)

Offences which may be charged

If the examining justices have committed an accused (including a corporation: Magistrates' Courts Act 1952, Sched. 2) for trial, the indictment may include, either in substitution for, or in addition to, the offences for which he was committed, any other offences founded on facts or evidence disclosed at the committal proceedings or in the depositions or written statements admitted under section 2 of the Criminal Justice Act 1967 (Administration of Justice (Miscellaneous Provisions) Act 1933, s. 2(2), as amended). It has been held that under this section the accused may be charged with a further offence for which the examining justices refused to commit him for trial, provided the offence is disclosed in the depositions, etc. (*R.* v. *Morry* (1946), C.C.A.; *R.* v. *Dawson* (1960), C.C.A.); nevertheless, to do so "is an undesirable practice . . . which ought to be very carefully regarded" (*per* Finnemore J. in *R.* v. *Dawson*, above). Moreover, the accused (and also the prosecution unless the bill was drafted by prosecuting counsel) must be notified if counts which differ materially from, or are additional to, the offences on which he was committed for trial are charged in the indictment (*Practice Note (Indictments)* (1956)) and if the accused contends that the additional offences were not disclosed in the depositions, etc., he may move the court at the trial to quash the indictment (see Chap. 35).

Joinder of accused

The rules as to whether two or more accused can be jointly

indicted are basically rules of practice and not of law. Moreover, only if accused are jointly indicted can they be tried together (see Chap. 34).

Two or more participants in the same crime (including those who aided, abetted, counselled or procured the offence: Accessories and Abettors Act 1861, s. 8, as amended) may be jointly indicted, and this also applies to conspirators. Nevertheless, counts charging conspiracy ought not normally to be added to counts charging the substantive offences (*R.* v. *Griffiths* (1966), C.C.A.).

As a general rule two or more accused cannot be jointly indicted when they have committed individual and unconnected offences, but they may be jointly indicted for individual offences when those offences are, upon the available evidence (the depositions, etc.), so related, whether in time or by other factors, that the interests of justice are best served by them being tried together (*R.* v. *Assim* (1966), C.C.A.). Thus, in *R.* v. *Assim*, there were two accused, each of whom was employed in a club, and one was charged with maliciously wounding one customer and the other with maliciously wounding another customer, both offences being committed at the same time and really part of the same incident. It was held that they could be jointly indicted and tried together. Another example when joinder is possible is when one accused is charged with theft and another with handling the same goods (see *R.* v. *Tizard* (1962), C.C.A.).

By the Theft Act 1968, s. 27(1), any number of accused may be charged in one indictment with having at different times or at the same time handled all or any of the same stolen goods. This includes not only successive handlers of the same goods but where two accused handled different goods at different times but the goods had been stolen together in the one consignment (*R.* v. *Tizard*, above).

Example

THE QUEEN V. JOHN SMITH and PAUL JONES
BEDFORD BOROUGH QUARTER SESSIONS
held at Bedford

John Smith and *Paul Jones* are charged with the following offence:

STATEMENT OF OFFENCE

Burglary, contrary to section 9(1) (*a*) of the Theft Act 1968.

PARTICULARS OF OFFENCE

John Smith and *Paul Jones*, on the 1st day of April, 196-, in the borough of Bedford in the county of Bedford, entered as a trespasser a building known as ——— and with intent to steal therein.

Joinder of offences

An accused cannot be tried on two or more indictments, so that if he is to be tried concurrently for two or more offences they must all be charged in the one indictment (see Chap. 34).

Different offences may be charged in the same indictment if these offences are founded on the same facts, or form or are a part of a series of offences of the same or a similar character (Indictments Act 1915, Sched. 1, r. 3). Thus an accused can be jointly indicted for forging a cheque, uttering that forged cheque and obtaining property by the deception that the cheque is genuine (the three offences being founded on the same facts). Similarly an accused can be charged in the same indictment with various offences of burglary, aggravated burglary, theft and attempted theft, because they are a series of offences of a similar character.

It was formerly the practice not to charge other offences in an indictment charging murder (*R.* v. *Jones* (1918), C.C.A.) or manslaughter (*R.* v. *Large* (1939), C.C.A.), but this practice was criticized in *Connelly* v. *D.P.P.* (1964), H.L., and the practice was changed by *Practice Direction* (*Homicide: Indictment*) (1964). Indeed in *Connelly's* case Lord Devlin said that as a general rule it is oppressive to an accused for the prosecution to charge him separately in two or more indictments when they could have charged him jointly with all the offences; and following this case it has been held that if the offences (whether murder or other offences) are separately indicted the judge in his discretion ought normally to prevent a subsequent trial of the later indictments (*R.* v. *Williams* (1965), C.C.A., N.I.; *R.* v. *Riebold* (1967)) (see also Chap. 34).

Separate counts

If two or more offences are charged in an indictment each must normally be charged in a separate count (Indictments Act 1915, Sched. 1, r. 4(1)). Each count then has its own "statement of offence" and "particulars of offence."

Examples
(1)

THE QUEEN v. JOHN SMITH
CAMBRIDGESHIRE ASSIZES
held at Cambridge

John Smith is charged with the following offences:

FIRST COUNT
STATEMENT OF OFFENCE
Aggravated burglary, contrary to section 10(1) of the Theft Act 1968.

PARTICULARS OF OFFENCE
John Smith, on the 5th day of March, 196-, in the county of Cambridge entered as a trespasser a building known as ———— and with intent to steal therein, and at the time of the said entry had with him a firearm, namely a shot gun.

SECOND COUNT
STATEMENT OF OFFENCE
Burglary, contrary to section 9(1) (*b*) of the Theft Act 1968.

PARTICULARS OF OFFENCE
John Smith, on the 12th day of March, 196-, in the county of Cambridge, having entered as a trespasser a building known as ————, stole therein a watch, the property of *William White*.

(2)
THE QUEEN v. JOHN SMITH, PAUL JONES and MARY BROWN
BEDFORD COUNTY QUARTER SESSIONS
held at Bedford

John Smith, *Paul Jones* and *Mary Brown* are charged with the following offences:

FIRST COUNT
STATEMENT OF OFFENCE
Theft, contrary to section 1 of the Theft Act 1968.

PARTICULARS OF OFFENCE
John Smith and *Paul Jones*, on the 28th day of April, 196-, in the county of Bedford, stole a book the property of *Simple Simon*.

SECOND COUNT
STATEMENT OF OFFENCE
Handling stolen goods, contrary to section 22(1) of the Theft Act 1968.

PARTICULARS OF OFFENCE
Mary Brown, on the 29th day of April, 196-, in the county of Bed-

ford, did handle a book, the property of *Simple Simon*, knowing or believing the same to have been stolen.

Duplicity. It is a basic rule of pleading that one count must charge only one offence, and a count which charges more than one offence is void for duplicity (*R.* v. *Molloy* (1921), C.C.A.).

It was held, however, that there was an exception to this rule in the old offence of burglary (as under s. 25 of the Larceny Act 1916). One count could charge the accused both with burglary and with having committed the arrestable offence (*e.g.* that the accused broke and entered the dwelling-house with intent to steal *and* did steal therein) (*R.* v. *Hungerford* (1790)). Nevertheless, this exception did not apply to housebreaking and the other kindred offences (*R.* v. *Nicholls* (1960), C.C.A.) and it seems doubtful whether the courts will hold that it applies to the new offence of burglary (under s. 9 of the Theft Act 1968) which covers both the previous offence of burglary and that of housebreaking, etc. In recent years the courts have shown a consistent determination to prevent further exceptions to the rule against duplicity and it would seem likely that they will take the opportunity to bring the new offence of burglary into line with all other offences.

Alternative methods of committing an offence. Where a statute provides alternative ways in which an offence may be committed, one count may charge the alternative methods of committing that offence (Indictments Act 1915, Sched. 1, r. 5(1)). One example is driving while unfit to drive through drink or drugs: Road Traffic Act 1960, s. 6(1) (see *Thomson* v. *Knights* (1947), D.C.). Nevertheless, in *R.* v. *Holmes* (1958), a case under section 13(1) of the Debtors Act 1869 (which is now repealed, but the comment would seem applicable to all such offences), Salmon J. said that it was the view of all the judges then at Leeds Assizes that the alternative methods ought to be pleaded in separate courts.

Instead of creating alternative methods of committing one offence a statute may create alternative offences, and in this case they must be charged in separate counts. There would, moreover, appear to be no infallible test for deciding whether a statute has created alternative offences or merely alternative methods of committing one offence. Thus, causing death by driving recklessly, or at a speed or in a manner which is dangerous to the public (Road Traffic Act 1960, s. 1) is three offences (see *R.* v. *Clow* (1965), C.C.A.; *Hargreaves* v. *Alderson* (1964), D.C.) and these must therefore be charged in separate counts. In fact in *R.* v. *Clow* the one count actually charged the accused with causing death by driving a car recklessly *and* in a manner dangerous to the public and it was held that as they were charged conjunctively there was only one offence. This was so even though "it is not necessary to prove the offence charged in the indictment to the whole extent laid, provided that the parts proved constitute an offence" (*per* Lord Parker C.J. in *R.* v. *Kelly* (1964), C.C.A.), so that the accused in *R.* v. *Clow* could be convicted either of causing death by reckless driving or of causing death by dangerous driving. Nevertheless, *R.* v. *Clow* can be explained on the basis that though the offences were separate offences they related to a single incident, and if there are two incidents involved they cannot be pleaded conjunctively (see *Mallon* v. *Allon* (1964), D.C.; *Fox* v. *Dingley* (1967), D.C.).

Certainly the wiser course would seem to be always to charge the alternative offences, or the alternative ways of committing one offence, in separate counts.

Attempts

With a few statutory exceptions every attempt is a common law offence and must be indicted as such. The "Particulars of Offence" may be framed on the precedents for the full offence, by inserting the words "attempted to" before the words charging the full offence. (Archbold, *Criminal Pleading, Evidence and Practice* (37th ed.), para. 4110.)

The statutory exceptions include attempts to choke with intent to commit an offence (Offences Against the Person Act 1861, s. 21).

Example

THE QUEEN v. JOHN SMITH

CENTRAL CRIMINAL COURT

John Smith is charged with the following offence:

STATEMENT OF OFFENCE

Attempted theft.

PARTICULARS OF OFFENCE

John Smith, on the 5th day of February, 196-, in the county of *London*, attempted to steal a bag, the property of *Bill Brown*.

Conviction for attempt. Where an accused is charged on indictment with the full offence, but the jury find him not guilty of that offence, they may instead convict him of an attempt (provided the facts found so warrant) (Criminal Law Act 1967, s. 6). (For other "alternative verdict offences," see Chap. 38.)

Where an accused is charged on indictment with an attempt, but the evidence discloses the full offence, the accused cannot be convicted of the full offence but (subject to the discretion of the court to discharge the jury with a view to the preferment of an indictment for the full offence) he may still be convicted of the attempt (Criminal Law Act 1967, s. 6(4)).

Previous convictions

Necessary ingredient of offence. Normally, the fact that the accused has previously been convicted of an offence must not be disclosed in the indictment. If, however, the previous conviction is a necessary ingredient of the offence charged the fact of the conviction must be stated in the "Particulars of Offence." Nevertheless, the only example of this would seem to be an offence under s. 21 of the Firearms Act 1968 (whereby it is an offence for certain convicted persons to possess firearms).

Affecting maximum sentence. The existence of a previous conviction, though not an essential ingredient of the offence charged, may increase the maximum sentence which may be imposed if the accused is convicted. Thus, by the Coinage Offences Act, 1936, s. 5(5), an accused who commits certain coinage offences, after having been previously convicted of any such offence, is liable to imprisonment for life (instead of, *e.g.*, one year). Other examples include the Malicious Damage Act 1861, s. 22 (damaging trees after two previous convictions) and the Night Poaching Act 1828, s. 1. In these cases the previous conviction must not be mentioned in the "Particulars of Offence" but must instead be charged at the end of the indictment (Indictments Act 1915, Sched. 1, r. 11).

In all such cases the accused will only be arraigned at the trial on the offence with which he is now charged and details of the previous conviction will not be read out unless and until the accused is convicted of the offence charged (Prevention of Crimes Act 1871, s. 9; and see *Faulkner* v. *R.* (1905)). An example of such an indictment is:

THE QUEEN v. JOHN SMITH
DERBY BOROUGH QUARTER SESSIONS
held at Derby

John Smith is charged with the following offence:

STATEMENT OF OFFENCE

Possessing counterfeit coin, contrary to section 5(3) of the Coinage Offences Act 1936.

PARTICULARS OF OFFENCE

John Smith, on the 16th day of February, 196-, in the borough of Derby in the county of Derby, had in his custody or possession three or more false or counterfeit coins resembling or apparently intended to resemble half-crowns, knowing them to be false or counterfeit and with intent to utter them or any of them.

John Smith has been previously convicted of possessing counterfeit coins with intent to utter them, on the 6th day of November, 196-, at the Assizes held at Nottingham.

(For extended terms of imprisonment, see Chap. 44.)

Habitual drunkard. The Inebriates Act 1898, s. 1(1), provides that where an accused is convicted on indictment for an offence to which drunkenness was a contributing cause, and the accused admits he is, or is found by the jury to be, an habitual drunkard the court may, in addition to or in substitution for any other sentence, order that he be detained for a term not exceeding three years in an inebriate reformatory. "Habitual drunkard" means a person who, while not being a mentally disordered person within the meaning of the Mental Health Act 1959, is, by reason of habitual intemperate drinking of intoxicating liquor, at times dangerous to himself or to others, or incapable of managing himself and his affairs (Habitual Drunkards Act 1879, s. 3, as amended).

The fact that the accused is an habitual drunkard should be stated at the end of the indictment in the same manner as a previous conviction (which increases the maximum sentence) (Indictments Act 1915, Sched. 1, r. 11), and the procedure at the trial for proving this fact is similar to proving the previous conviction (see Chap. 38) (Inebriates Act 1898, s. 1(2)).

Nevertheless, although these provisions in relation to habitual drunkards are still the law, there are apparently no longer inebriate reformatories to which an accused can be sent, so the power is no longer exercised.

(2) Preferring the Bill of Indictment

Administration of Justice (Miscellaneous Provisions) Act 1933, s. 2

By section 2 the bill of indictment, when it has been drafted, is preferred before the trial court, and the clerk of the trial court will then sign it if satisfied that:

(a) the accused has been committed for trial by the examining justices; or

(b) the bill is preferred by the direction of the Criminal Division of the Court of Appeal (see Chap. 41); or

(c) the bill is preferred by the direction, or with the consent, of a judge of the High Court (see below); or

(d) the bill is preferred pursuant to an order made under section 9 of the Perjury Act 1911 (see below).

Once the bill has been signed it becomes an indictment.

Bill preferred on direction, etc., of High Court judge
When application may be made. The prosecution may apply to a judge for the preferment of a bill of indictment:

(1) When no committal proceedings at all have been held or, though started, were never completed. Such an application is very rare but it may occur, for example, when the prosecution wish to charge the accused jointly with another accused who has already been committed for trial (*R.* v. *Roberts* (1966)), or when the examining justice becomes ill after the commencement of the committal proceedings (*R* v. *Rothfield* (1937), C.C.A.), or where the accused at the committal proceedings is so violent that the proceedings cannot be completed (*R.* v. *Dawson* (1954)).

(2) When committal proceedings have been held and completed, but the examining justices refused to commit the accused for trial. The prosecution may apply in these circumstances when, for example, they consider that the examining justices were wrong, on the evidence before them, in refusing to commit for trial (*Re Roberts* (1967)) (the prosecution can alternatively apply for the issue of fresh process: see Chap. 32). Although this is not an appeal from the examining justices' decision (there is in fact no right of appeal), it does allow the prosecution to circumvent the justices' refusal.

(3) When the accused has already been committed for trial by the examining justices but it is necessary or desirable to have a fresh indictment. This may occur, for example, when the original indictment was void for duplicity or when there are two separate indictments and it is desirable that they should both be incorporated in one fresh indictment (*R.* v. *Smith* (1958)).

A bill of indictment preferred on the direction, etc., of a High Court judge is known as a "voluntary bill of indictment," and the exercise by the judge of his discretion to allow or refuse such an application is not normally open to review (*R. v. Rothfield,* above).

To whom application should be made. An application to a judge for the preferment of a bill of indictment should be made by the prosecution to a Queen's Bench Division judge in chambers, or, if the bill is to be preferred at assizes, to a judge who is acting, or is to act, at those assizes or who has acted at any previous assizes for the same county or place, or, if the bill is to be preferred at quarter sessions, to a judge who is acting, or is to act, as judge at any assizes for the area which includes the area for which the quarter sessions are to be held (Indictments Procedure Rules 1933, r. 3(1)). Where at any assizes no judge of the High Court is present, then application may be made to a Commissioner of Assize who is acting, or is to act, as judge at those assizes (Administration of Justice (Miscellaneous Provisions) Act, 1933, s. 2(4)).

Procedure for applying. Every application should be made in writing, should be supported (unless the application is by or on behalf of the Director of Public Prosecutions) by an affidavit verifying that the statements contained in the application are true, to the best of the deponent's knowledge, information and belief, and be accompanied by the proposed bill of indictment (Indictments Procedure Rules 1933, rr. 4 and 5). Nevertheless, it was held in *R. v. Rothfield* (1937), C.C.A., that it is sufficient compliance with the requirement that the bill of indictment must accompany the application, if the bill is actually before the judge when he deals with the application.

When no committal proceedings have been held, the application should state the reason why, it should be accompanied by proofs of the evidence of the witnesses whom it is proposed to call in support of the charges and the application should state that this evidence will be available at the trial (*ibid.,* r. 6(1)). Where committal proceedings have been held but the examining justices refused to commit for trial, the application should be accompanied by a copy of the depositions and proofs of any additional evidence which it is proposed to call, and the application should state that this evidence will be available at the trial (*ibid.,* r. 6(2)). Where the accused has already been committed for trial by the examining justices, the application should state why it is made, it should be accompanied by a copy of the depositions (unless the judge already has them) and by proofs of any additional evidence which it is proposed to call, and the application should state that this evidence will be available at the trial (*ibid.*, r. 6(3)).

The application will normally be decided without the attendance of the applicant, although the judge may require the applicant's attendance and/or his witnesses', though not in open court (*ibid.*, r. 7). There is no provision for representation by the accused.

Perjury Act 1911, s. 9

Where a judge of, or other person presiding in, a court of record, or a magistrates' court, is of opinion that any person has, in the course of proceedings before that court, been guilty of perjury, the judge etc. may order the prosecution of that person for such perjury. The judge, etc., may then commit that person in custody, or admit him to bail, to take his trial at the proper court and may require any person to enter into a recognizance to prosecute or give evidence against the person whose prosecution is so ordered (section 9). (The legislature in abolishing the binding over of witnesses and the prosecutor after committal proceedings, by the Criminal Procedure (Attendance of Witnesses) Act 1965, would appear to have overlooked this provision.) Nevertheless, in practice, these provisions are seldom used (for an example of their use, see *R.* v. *Bruce* (1967)) and it is normal for the ordinary criminal procedure to be followed in the case of such offences.

Chapter Thirty-Four

TRIAL ON INDICTMENT –
PRELIMINARY MATTERS

(1) Presence of Accused

AN accused, unless a corporation, must always be present in order to plead, but the trial may then proceed in his absence (*R.* v. *Browne* (1906)); and he may therefore be sentenced in his absence. Nevertheless, in practice an accused is almost always present throughout the trial. Where the accused is a corporation it may appear by a representative but if it does not do so a plea of not guilty will be entered and the trial will proceed (see Chap. 35).

Procuring accused's presence

As we have seen (Chap. 32) an accused committed for trial by the examining justices is committed either in custody or on bail. If he is committed in custody the governor of the prison or remand home will ensure his presence at the trial (Criminal Law Amendment Act 1867, s. 10), but if he is committed on bail and he fails to surrender to his bail his presence may be procured either by a certificate of the signing of the indictment or by a bench warrant.

Certificate of the signing of the indictment. This is the normal method. The certificate is issued by the clerk of the trial court on the prosecutor's application and it certifies that an indictment has been signed (Magistrates' Courts Act 1952, s. 12(1)). A magistrate in whose district the offence was committed or in which the accused is believed to reside or be, will then, on production of such a certificate, issue a warrant to arrest the accused and to bring him before a magistrates' court for that area (*ibid.*, s. 12(2)) and on the accused's being brought before the court it will commit him for trial (normally to the original trial court) without further inquiry (*ibid.*, s. 12(3)).

Bench warrant. This should be applied for only where immediate arrest is necessary or it is shown that the accused is about to leave the country (*R.* v. *Whittaker* (1859)). A bench warrant is issued by a judge (at assizes) or by two magistrates or a recorder (at quarter sessions) and it directs that the accused should be arrested immediately and be brought before the trial court or, if the court is no longer sitting, before the judge who has signed the warrant or before the magistrates of the area. A bench warrant may also be used to procure the presence of an accused in respect of whom the judge has ordered the preferment of a bill of indictment under section 2 of the Administration of Justice (Miscellaneous Provisions) Act 1933 (see *R.* v. *Chandler* (1963)), but it cannot be used to procure the attendance of a witness.

(2) Judge's Discretion to Prevent Trial

We have seen that a number of prosecutions can only be commenced with leave, and that a magistrate has a discretion whether or not to issue process, but in *R.* v. *County of London Quarter Sessions, ex p. Downes* (1954), D.C., Lord Goddard C.J. did not consider that the trial judge himself has a discretion to prevent the trial. Lord Goddard said that "once an indictment is before the court the accused must be arraigned and tried thereon unless (a) on motion to quash or demurrer pleaded it is held defective in substance or form and not amended (see Chap. 35); (b) matter in bar is pleaded and the plea is tried or confirmed in favour of the accused (see Chap. 35); (c) a *nolle prosequi* is entered by the Attorney-General which cannot be done before the indictment is found (see Chap. 29); or (d) if the indictment disclosed an offence which a particular court has no jurisdiction to try, for example, an indictment at sessions for an offence punishable with imprisonment for life in the first instance."

In *Connelly* v. *D.P.P.* (1964), H.L., however, a majority of their Lordships considered that the circumstances stated by Lord Goddard were not exclusive, and it would appear that the trial judge does sometimes have a discretion to prevent a trial on indictment, although the extent of this discretion is uncertain (*R.* v. *Williams* (1965), C.C.A., N.I.). One case where the judge does have a discretion is where the prosecution is based on substantially the same facts as some earlier prosecution on which the accused was convicted or acquitted (*Connelly* v. *D.P.P.*, above; *R.* v. *Williams*, above), particularly if the judge at the first trial followed the comparatively common practice of ordering that certain other counts in the indictment (on which no verdict had been taken) were to remain on the file and were not to be proceeded on without the leave of the court, and the prosecution now desire to do so (*R.* v. *Riebold* (1967): although there has been no other decision on the legal effect of such an order, and it is uncertain whether leave is then necessarily required; see also *R.* v. *Thatcher* (1967), C.A.).

The whole question of whether the judge does (or should) have a discretion to prevent a criminal trial involves grave constitutional problems which are outside the scope of this book. With the exception of the cases outlined above it cannot be said with any degree of certainty whether such a discretion exists (see Edmund Davies J. in *R.* v. *Connelly* (1964), C.C.A.).

(3) Joint and Separate Trials

Joint trials

If two or more accused are to be tried together they must be jointly indicted, for a trial of two accused who are separately indicted is a nullity (*Crane* v. *D.P.P.* (1921), H.L.), even if the accused consent to the trial (*R.* v. *Dennis* (1924), C.C.A.). We considered in the last chapter those cases where two or more accused may be jointly indicted, but if they are separately indicted when they could be jointly indicted a High Court judge may exercise his powers under section 2 of the Administration of Justice (Miscellaneous Provisions) Act 1933, and order the preferment of a fresh indictment combining the other indictments (*R.* v. *Smith* (1958)).

Equally, one accused cannot be tried on two or more indictments, for such a trial would be a nullity (*R.* v. *Olivo* (1942), C.C.A.). Again, therefore, if the accused is to be tried concurrently for more than one offence, these offences must all be charged in the same indictment or the preferment of a fresh indictment must be ordered.

Separate trials

Even if two or more accused are charged in the same indictment, or an accused is charged in the same indictment with two or more offences, separate trials of these accused or offences may sometimes be ordered. An application by the accused for separate trials should normally be made to the judge at the trial court.

Accused. Separate trials of accused who have been jointly indicted may be ordered when the interests of justice so require (*R.* v. *Gibbins* (1918), C.C.A.). Moreover, the interests of justice may require separate trials when it appears that an essential part of one accused's defence is an attack upon a co-accused (*per* Lord Hewart C.J. in *R.* v. *Barnes* (1940), C.C.A.). However, although separate trials may be ordered in these circumstances, in practice the judge's discretion to do so is rarely exercised (see *R.* v. *Bywaters* (1922), C.C.A.; *R.* v. *Grondkowski* (1946), C.C.A.). Other occasions when the interests of justice may require separate trials are when evidence would be admissible against one accused but not against another (see *R.* v. *Griffiths* (1966), C.C.A.; *R.* v. *Smith* (1967), C.A.), and when the accused insist on their separate rights peremptorily to challenge the potential jurors (see Chap. 36).

Offences. Where, before trial, or at any stage of a trial, the court is of opinion that an accused may be prejudiced or embarrassed in his defence by reason of being charged in the indictment with more than one offence, or that for any other reason it is desirable to direct that he should be tried separately for any one or more offences, the court may order a separate trial of any count or counts of such indictment (Indictments Act 1915, s. 5(3)). Thus, where evidence would be admissible against an accused in relation to one offence but not in relation to another offence separate trials may be ordered (see Hawkins J. in *R.* v. *King* (1897), C.C.R.). This occurs, for example, when there are separate counts charging substantive offences and a conspiracy, and in *R.* v. *Griffiths* (1966) Paull J. in delivering the judgment of the Court of Criminal Appeal said: "In our judgment, except in simple cases, a conspiracy count (if one is needed at all) should be tried separately to substantive counts." Nevertheless, it is a matter of judicial discretion whether separate trials are ordered and in *R.* v. *Sims* (1946), C.C.A., Lord Goddard C.J. said that "we do not think that the mere fact that evidence is admissible on one count and inadmissible on another is by itself a ground for separate trials: because often the matter can be made clear in the summing-up without prejudice to the accused."

(4) Amendment of Indictments

Where, before trial or at any stage of a trial, it appears to the court (normally the trial court) that the indictment is defective, the court may make such order for the amendment of the indictment as it thinks necessary to meet the circumstances of the case (Indictments Act 1915, s. 5(1)). Nevertheless, the court cannot order an amendment if it would cause injustice to the accused (*ibid.*, s. 5(1)) and the court must order postponement of the trial if, in consequence of an amendment, it considers that it is expedient to do so (*ibid.*, s. 5(4)). If the court does order an amendment it may make such order, as to the payment of any costs incurred by the amendment, as it thinks fit (*ibid.*, s. 5(1)).

The judge should consider whether an amendment is required, if necessary on his own initiative (*R. v. West* (1948), C.C.A.), but normally the prosecution will apply for the amendment (see *R. v. Pople* (1951), C.C.A.), and prosecuting counsel has a duty to the court to ensure that the indictment is correct in form (*per* Lord Parker C.J. in *R. v. Martin* (1962), C.C.A.). Moreover, the judge should always invite the parties, and in particular the defence, to express their views on the matter before deciding to order an amendment (*per* Humphreys J. in *R. v. West*, above).

The court's power to order an amendment may be exercised whether the defect in the amendment is a mere formal defect or a substantial defect. Thus in *R. v. Martin* (1962) the indictment alleged that the accused had obtained property by the deception that two cheques were good, while the depositions showed that there was only one cheque. The Court of Criminal Appeal held that the indictment could be amended by adding an additional count charging the obtaining in relation to the one cheque. Moreover, *R. v. Martin* illustrates that it is not necessary that the indictment should be bad on its face before an amendment can be ordered (see also *R. v. Pople* (1951), C.C.A.; *R. v. Hall* (1968), C.A.).

Although section 5(1) of the Indictments Act 1915 allows an indictment to be amended at any stage of the trial, an amendment adding an additional count or substituting a new offence for that originally charged cannot be allowed after the arraignment, because the accused will not have pleaded to the new count or offence and will not have been put in charge of the jury on it (*R. v. Martin*, above; *R. v. Harden* (1963), C.C.A.). Nevertheless, an amendment which merely corrects a misdescription of the original offence (*e.g.*, substituting "a valuable security" for "money" in an indictment for obtaining by deception) may be made after the arraignment (*R. v. Harden, supra*).

(5) Trial on Inquisition

As we have seen (Chap. 28) if the coroner's jury at an inquest returns a verdict that the cause of death was murder, manslaughter or infanticide by a named person, that person must be committed to assizes by the coroner to stand trial for that homicide. In this case the accused will be tried on inquisition and *not* on indictment, although, as we saw, committal proceedings will normally also be held and the accused may be committed for trial on indictment as well. If the accused is committed on both indictment and inquisition he will normally be tried on indictment (though see Roscoe,

Criminal Evidence (16th ed.), p. 233), and if convicted the trial on inquisition will not be proceeded with, or if acquitted the prosecution will offer no evidence at the trial on inquisition. Nevertheless, if the accused is tried on inquisition, the procedure will basically be the same as at a trial on indictment.

Chapter Thirty-Five

TRIAL ON INDICTMENT — THE ARRAIGNMENT

THE arraignment of an accused consists of three parts: (1) the accused is called to the bar of the court by name; (2) the indictment is read to him and explained if necessary; (3) he is asked whether he pleads guilty or not guilty. If the indictment contains more than one count the accused must be asked to plead separately to each count (*R. v. Boyle* (1954), C.C.A.).

Standing Mute

If the accused is silent when asked to plead, or he refuses to plead, the question arises as to whether he is *mute of malice* or *mute by the visitation of God*. In cases of doubt a jury must be sworn in forthwith to decide the issue (*R. v. Israel* (1847)). The verdict of this jury, like the verdict of any other jury in criminal proceedings, may then be by a majority in accordance with section 13 of the Criminal Justice Act 1967 (see Chap. 38).

If the accused is mute of malice (*i.e.*, he could plead but deliberately refuses to do so), or he will not answer directly to the indictment, the court will order a plea of not guilty to be entered on his behalf and the trial will proceed (Criminal Law Act 1967, s. 6(1)(c)).

The accused may be mute by the visitation of God not only if he is mentally unable to comprehend the nature of the proceedings but if he, for any other reason, is not able to plead to the charge. Thus, he may be mute by the visitation of God if he is deaf and dumb (*R. v. Governor of Stafford Prison, ex p. Emery* (1909), D.C.; *R. v. Roberts* (1954)), or if he is merely deaf but cannot hear the indictment when read (*R. v. Halton* (1824)), or he is a foreigner and unable to understand English. The fact that the accused is mute by the visitation of God does not necessarily mean, therefore, that he cannot be tried, for the question then arises as to whether he can be made to understand the proceedings. This may simply

244

entail the provision of an interpreter or a deaf and dumb person may be communicated with by sign language (*R.* v. *MacCarthy* (1967), C.C.A.). Nevertheless, if there is doubt as to whether or not the accused can be made to understand the proceedings (*i.e.,* whether he is fit to plead) this must be decided by a jury.

Fitness to Plead

An accused is unfit to plead if he, by reason of some physical or mental condition, cannot follow the proceedings and so cannot make a proper defence (*R.* v. *Pritchard* (1836); *R.* v. *Podola* (1960), C.C.A.). Normally such a person will be unfit by reason of his mental condition, but the test is whether he can follow the proceedings at the trial, not whether he was insane (within the meaning of the McNaghten Rules, or otherwise) at the time of the offence. Thus, an accused may have been perfectly sane at the time of the offence but be suffering from mental illness and be unable to follow the proceedings at the trial (he will therefore be unfit to plead). Similarly, an accused may have been insane at the time of the offence but have recovered his sanity by the trial (he may therefore be tried, although he may be found not guilty by reason of insanity). Nevertheless, the accused, to be unfit to plead, must be unable to follow the proceedings themselves, and it is not sufficient that, though now sane, he can remember nothing of the events in question (*R.* v. *Podola, supra*). Moreover, although insanity is the normal ground of unfitness, an accused who is, for example, deaf and dumb may be unable to follow the proceedings because he is unable to communicate with his legal advisers (*R.* v. *Roberts* (1954)).

Where it is alleged (whether by the accused or otherwise) that the accused is unfit to plead a jury must be sworn in to decide the issue (Criminal Procedure (Insanity) Act 1964, s. 4). Moreover, the party which alleges unfitness must prove it, although if, as is usual, it is the accused he need prove it only on a balance of probabilities (*R.* v. *Podola*, above). If the prosecution do allege unfitness they must prove it beyond reasonable doubt (*R.* v. *Robertson* (1968), C.A.).

The question of fitness to plead will normally be determined before the trial of the general issue begins and if the accused is then found fit to plead he will be tried by a different jury (*ibid.,* s. 4(4)). Nevertheless, the court may postpone consideration of the question until any time up to the opening of the case for the defence, and if postponed the question will be whether the accused is *fit to be tried* (*ibid.,* s. 4(2)). This power to postpone gives the trial jury an opportunity to find the accused not guilty of the offence charged, even though he is unfit to be tried. Otherwise an accused who is unfit to plead is liable to be detained in a hospital, for what may be a substantial period, even though the prosecution at the trial could not have made out a prima facie case against him (see *R. v. Roberts* (1954)).

If the question of fitness is postponed a plea of not guilty will be entered on behalf of the accused (see *R. v. Roberts*, above), and if, before the question is determined, the jury return a verdict of acquittal the question will never be decided (*ibid.*, s. 4(2)). If a postponed question of fitness does have to be determined, however, it will be determined by a separate jury or by the trial jury, whichever the court directs (*ibid.*, s. 4(4)).

Should the accused be found fit to plead, or to be tried, (*i.e.*, he can be made to understand the proceedings) all necessary arrangements will be made for the trial to proceed (see *R. v. Harris* (1897): where the accused, who could neither read nor write, was unable to speak because of an unhealed wound in his throat, but the trial was adjourned so that the wound might heal). Should the accused be found unfit to plead, or to be tried, the trial cannot continue (*ibid.*, s. 4(5)). Instead the court must order that the accused be admitted to such hospital as may be specified by the Secretary of State (*ibid.*, s. 5(1)). Nevertheless, if an accused is committed to a hospital under section 5(1) and the Secretary of State is later satisfied, after consultation with the responsible medical officer, that the accused can properly be tried (*i.e.*, he has recovered and will be able to follow the proceedings), he may remit the accused to a prison or remand home for trial at the next assizes or quarter sessions for the place where, but for the finding of unfitness, he would have been tried (*ibid.*, s. 5(4)).

Motion to Quash the Indictment

An accused may move the trial court to quash the indictment on the ground that the indictment is defective on its face (*e.g.*, duplicity) (though see "Amendment of Indictment," Chap. 34), or that it has been preferred and signed without jurisdiction (the indictment must in fact be available before the trial for inspection by the accused: *Practice Note* (*Indictments*) (1956), and see the Indictments Act 1915, Sched. 1, r. 13). Thus, if a bill of indictment, which is preferred otherwise than in accordance with the provisions of section 2 of the Administration of Justice (Miscellaneous Provisions) Act 1933, is signed by the clerk of the trial court, it is liable to be quashed (section 2(3)), and this includes indictments which charge offences on which the accused was not committed for trial and which are not disclosed in the depositions (*R.* v. *County of London Quarter Sessions, ex p. Downes* (1954), D.C.). But if the accused was committed for trial for the offence, the indictment cannot be quashed even though the offence is not disclosed in the depositions (*ibid.*). Moreover, on an appeal to the Criminal Division of the Court of Appeal, an indictment cannot be quashed under section 2(3) unless an application for it to be quashed was made at the trial (section 2(3)).

Although an accused should normally move to quash the indictment before he pleads to the charge (*R.* v. *Maywhort* (1955)) it may be possible to make an application later, even after verdict (see *R.* v. *Thompson* (1914), C.C.A.). Nevertheless, even if a motion to quash is successful this is not an acquittal and a new bill of indictment can be preferred.

Plea to the Jurisdiction

Where an accused is charged on indictment before a court which has no jurisdiction over the offence (*e.g.*, charged at quarter sessions with an offence which is triable only at assizes) he may plead to the jurisdiction. Nevertheless, such pleas are extremely rare as alternatively the accused may move to quash the indictment or move in arrest of judgment (see Chap. 38) or, if convicted, raise the the matter on appeal. If the accused does plead to the jurisdiction, however, and the plea fails he may then plead not guilty (Criminal Law Act 1967, s. 6(1)(*a*)).

Demurrer

By a demurrer an accused contends that even if the facts alleged in the indictment are true they do not, in point of law, constitute him guilty of the offence charged. Demurrers are, however, in practice virtually obsolete for an accused may raise the same issue on a plea of not guilty. Nevertheless, if a demurrer is pleaded and fails, the accused may then plead not guilty (Criminal Law Act 1967, s. 6(1)(*a*)).

Special Pleas in Bar

Autrefois acquit

The plea of *autrefois acquit* is based upon "the fundamental principle . . . that a man is not to be prosecuted twice for the same crime" (*per* Lord Morris in *Connelly* v. *D.P.P.* (1964), H.L.), and it may be pleaded whenever an accused is charged on indictment with an offence of which he has already been tried and acquitted, even though the acquittal was by a foreign court (*R.* v. *Aughet* (1918), C.C.A.). The accused, however, must have been actually acquitted, so that the plea does not lie if at the first trial the jury disagreed (*R.* v. *Randall* (1960), C.C.A.), or the Attorney-General entered a *nolle prosequi*, or the examining justices refused to commit for trial, but it does lie if the accused was convicted on the first trial, and this conviction was quashed on appeal (*R.* v. *Barron* (1914), C.C.A.). Moreover, for the plea to lie the accused must have been "in peril" at the first trial, so that if the first court had no jurisdiction over the offence, or the trial was for some other reason a nullity, the plea will not lie (*Vaux's Case* (1590); *R.* v. *West* (1964), C.C.A.); although, it is not necessary that the previous acquittal should have been on the merits of the case so long as the accused was "in peril" (*Haynes* v. *Davis* (1914), D.C.).

The previous acquittal must have been for the "same offence" but this term includes not only a previous offence which was identical to the offence now charged but also a previous offence of which acquittal necessarily involved acquittal of the present offence. This will be so if all the essential ingredients of the first offence are also essential ingredients of the second offence, for then, although "acquittal of the whole offence is not an acquittal of every part of it" (*per* Pollock C.J. in *R.* v. *Salvi* (1857)), at least one of the essential ingredients could not have been proved and that same ingredient is also essential for the second offence (see Coltman J. in *R.* v. *Walker* (1843)). Nevertheless, it will not be so if merely one of the ingredients essential for the first offence is not essential for the second, for then the previous acquittal may possibly have been because that one ingredient was not satisfied. Thus, on a charge of murder, *autrefois acquit* lies in respect of a previous acquittal of manslaughter where the victim is the same (*R.* v. *Holcroft* (1579)), but not in respect of a previous acquittal of wounding with intent to murder, because one of the essential ingredients of wounding with intent to murder (*i.e.*, an actual intention to kill) is not necessary for murder, where a mere intent to cause grievous bodily harm may suffice (*R.* v. *Salvi,* above). It is not, moreover, sufficient merely that the evidence to be presented at the second trial is the same (*Connelly* v. *D.P.P.* (1964), H.L.).

Acquittal of the first offence will also involve acquittal of the second offence when the accused, at the first trial, could have been convicted of the second offence by way of alternative verdict (see

Chap. 38). "Thus an acquittal on a charge of murder is a bar to a subsequent indictment for manslaughter, as the jury could have convicted of manslaughter" (*per* Lord Reading C.J. in *R*. v. *Barron* (1914), C.C.A.). As the accused was not convicted of the second offence by way of alternative verdict he was impliedly acquitted of it. In addition a statute occasionally provides that an accused acquitted of one offence shall not be liable to be tried again for some other offence, for example, Unlawful Oaths Act 1797, s. 7. (See Archbold, *Criminal Pleading, Evidence and Practice* (37th ed.), para. 437.)

It has been suggested that the plea of *autrefois acquit* lies if the offence charged "is in effect the same, or is substantially the same" as the offence of which the accused was previously acquitted (*per* Lord Morris in *Connelly* v. *D.P.P.* (1964), H.L.), but, while this test applies to *autrefois convict* (see below), there is otherwise little judicial support for Lord Morris' contention (see Lord Devlin in *Connelly* v. *D.P.P.*, above).

Procedure. The plea of *autrefois acquit* is a formal plea which must be made in writing and a written replication may then be pleaded by the prosecution. Nevertheless, the plea is merely the machinery for giving effect to the principle that a man is not to be tried twice for the same offence and, as Lord Goddard C.J. said in *Flatman* v. *Light* (1946), D.C., "in common justice and fairness, if during the course of a case it turned out that a man had been previously . . . acquitted of the same offence . . . the court would, of course, allow him to plead it and would give effect to that plea". This would not technically be a plea of *autrefois acquit* but it would have the same effect.

A plea of *autrefois acquit* must be tried by a jury, although in practice the only issues which normally arise are points of law (*e.g.*, whether the previous acquittal was for the same offence), and on these the judge will direct the jury and they will find accordingly. If the accused does plead *autrefois acquit* the burden of proof will rest upon him and he will have the right to begin. If a plea of *autrefois acquit* fails, the accused may then plead not guilty (Criminal Law Act 1967, s. 6(1)(*a*)).

Autrefois convict

The plea of *autrefois convict*, which is closely related to *autrefois acquit*, may be pleaded whenever an accused is charged on indictment with an offence of which he has already been tried and convicted. Again, however, the accused must have been convicted by a court of competent jurisdiction, so that the plea will not lie if the former trial was a nullity (see *R.* v. *Marsham, ex p. Pethick Lawrence* (1912), D.C.). Nor did it lie when an accused, who was charged with the criminal offence of prison breaking, contended that he could not be tried because he had already been punished by a visiting committee of justices. The justices had punished him merely for breach of internal prison discipline in escaping and they had no jurisdiction over the criminal offence. Nevertheless, the fact that he had already been punished was relevant in relation to sentence. (*R.* v. *Hogan* (1960), C.C.A.; see also *Lewis* v. *Morgan* (1943), D.C.)

The accused, moreover, must actually have been convicted at the previous trial and it is not sufficient if the offence was merely taken into consideration (*R.* v. *Neal* (1949), C.C.A.) (see Chap. 38). Nevertheless, it is not necessary that the accused should have been punished, for "it is the conviction and not the sentence which constitutes the bar" (*per* Charles J. in *R.* v. *Miles* (1890), C.C.R.).

Autrefois convict lies not only when the offence charged is identical to the offence of which the accused has previously been convicted, but when the offences are "practically the same" (*R.* v. *Kendrick* (1931), C.C.A.) or "substantially the same" (*R.* v. *Thomas* (1950), C.C.A.). Nevertheless, although *autrefois convict* will normally lie when the accused is charged again with the same offence in a more aggravated form (*per* Cockburn C.J. in *R.* v. *Elrington* (1861), D.C.) this does not apply when the consequences have changed, for example the victim has died (*per* Lord Parker C.J. in *R.* v. *Hogan* (1960), C.C.A.). An accused charged with murder cannot, therefore, plead *autrefois convict* by reason of a previous conviction of wounding with intent to murder (*R.* v. *Thomas,* above). We have seen that the same result applies to *autrefois acquit,* but the reasons are quite different. An accused cannot plead *autrefois acquit* in relation to a previous acquittal of wounding with intent to murder because acquittal of that offence does not necessarily involve acquittal of murder (see above: though for a contrary view see Lord Hodson in *Connelly* v. *D.P.P.* (1964), H.L.). It has already been suggested that the test of "practically the same offence" or "substantially the same offence" does not apply to *autrefois acquit.*

Procedure. The procedure for pleading *autrefois convict* is the same as for pleading *autrefois acquit.* Moreover, Lord Goddard C.J. in *Flatman* v. *Light* (1946), D.C., extended his remarks, that a former acquittal might be raised during a trial, to a former conviction. Further, should a plea of *autrefois convict* fail the accused is then able to plead not guilty (Criminal Law Act 1967, s. 6(1)(*a*)).

A pardon

A pardon, whether granted by statute or the Crown, may be pleaded in bar to an indictment. Moreover, although an accused will not lose the benefit of a pardon under statute even if it is not pleaded, a Royal pardon must be pleaded at the first reasonable opportunity, for if the accused pleads to the general issue instead (*i.e.*, guilty or not guilty) he waives the benefit of the pardon (2 Hawk. P.C., c. 37, s. 67). Nevertheless, if the accused unsuccessfully pleads a pardon he may then plead not guilty (Criminal Law Act 1967, s. 6(1)(*a*)). A plea of pardon is now virtually obsolete.

Plea of Justification

On the trial of a charge of criminal libel the accused may, in addition to pleading not guilty, make a written plea of justification (Libel Act 1843, s. 6). The prosecution may then plead a written replication. For a plea of justification to succeed, however, the accused must prove not only the truth of the matters stated but that publication was for the public benefit (see Chap. 23).

Plea of Guilty

An accused may plead guilty to any offence, including an offence of murder (*R.* v. *Vent* (1935), C.C.A.). Nevertheless, the accused must plead guilty personally, not merely his counsel on his behalf (*R.* v. *Heyes* (1951), C.C.A.), and it should be clear that the accused understands the charge and that he does in fact intend to plead guilty. If the court wrongly holds an imperfect or ambiguous plea to be a plea of guilty the conviction will be quashed on appeal and the accused may (*R.* v. *Hussey* (1924), C.C.A.), or may not (*R.* v. *Field* (1943), C.C.A.), be sent back for trial. (For the position when the accused is a corporation, see below.)

A court is normally reluctant to accept a plea of guilty to a serious crime and it may advise the accused to reconsider his plea. If the accused insists on a plea of guilty, however, the court must generally accept the plea, although this does not apply where the accused is charged in the same indictment with two alternative offences and he tries to plead guilty to the lesser offence. Thus in *R.* v. *Cole* (1965) the accused was charged with armed robbery and with receiving and the Court of Criminal Appeal held that the trial judge was justified in refusing to accept the accused's plea of guilty to the receiving charge. Moreover, a plea of guilty does not rank as a conviction until judgment is pronounced (*R.* v. *Cole* (1965), C.C.A.). and the court may allow the accused to change his plea before this time. But if the accused has made an unequivocal plea of guilty, the court is not bound to allow him to change his plea (*R.* v. *McNally* (1954), C.C.A.).

If the accused does plead guilty a jury will not be sworn in to try his guilt and he will normally be sentenced forthwith (see Chap. 38), although if he is jointly charged with a co-accused and the co-accused pleads not guilty he will only be sentenced forthwith if he is to give evidence against the co-accused; otherwise, if the co-accused is convicted, he will be brought up for sentence with him, so that the trial judge might by then have a clearer understanding of the respective parts played by the two accused.

Plea of Guilty to Alternative Verdict Offence

An accused charged in an indictment with one offence may sometimes be convicted instead of an alternative offence (see Chap. 38). Moreover, by the Criminal Law Act 1967, s. 6(1)(*b*), where an accused is liable to be convicted of an alternative offence he may plead not guilty of the offence charged but guilty of the alternative offence. The prosecution must then be consulted, but even if they would agree, the judge always has a discretion to refuse such a plea (*R.* v. *Soanes* (1948), C.C.A.). If the plea of guilty to the alternative offence is accepted, the accused must be acquitted of the offence charged (*ibid.*, s. 6(5)).

Plea of Not Guilty

If the accused pleads not guilty at a trial on indictment a jury must, unless the prosecution proposes to offer no evidence against him, be sworn in to try the issue of his guilt (see below). Moreover, any ambiguous plea must be entered as a plea of not guilty and, as we have seen, if the accused is mute of malice a plea of not guilty will be entered on his behalf.

The trial court may, however, allow the accused to change his plea to one of guilty (or guilty of an alternative verdict offence) at any stage of the trial before verdict, but once a jury has been sworn in to try his guilt that jury must return the verdict. If, therefore, a jury has been sworn in before the court allows the accused to change his plea to one of guilty, the judge must direct the jury to return the verdict of guilty, and if the verdict is not returned by the jury the trial is a nullity (*R.* v. *Heyes* (1951), C.C.A.).

Corporations

If the accused is a corporation it may enter in writing by its representative a plea of guilty or not guilty, but if either the corporation does not appear by a representative or, though it does so appear, he fails to enter a plea, the court must order a plea of not guilty to be entered (Criminal Justice Act 1925, s. 33(3)).

Chapter Thirty-Six

TRIAL ON INDICTMENT—THE JURY

Qualifications of Jurors

To be qualified to sit as a juror a person must be included on the register of electors (Juries Act 1922, s. 8(2) (*b*)). Not every person whose name is included is qualified to sit, and generally speaking a juror must be between the ages of twenty-one and sixty, and either be a householder residing in premises of a sufficient rateable value (£30 p.a. in London, £20 elsewhere) or be possessed of, for example, certain leaseholds (see the Juries Act 1825, s. 1, as amended). Moreover, any person who, during the previous ten years, has served (in the United Kingdom, the Channel Islands or the Isle of Man) any part of a sentence of imprisonment or detention, being a sentence for a term of three months or more (or a sentence of Borstal training), is disqualified from serving on a jury. So also is any person who has been sentenced at any time (in the United Kingdom, etc.) to imprisonment or detention for life (including a sentence to be detained during Her Majesty's pleasure) for a term of five years or more or to penal servitude for such a term (Criminal Justice Act 1967, s. 14). Nevertheless, should a person who is disqualified in fact sit on a jury the verdict of that jury would not thereby be void (*ibid.*, s. 15). (For details, see the Report of the Departmental Committee on Jury Service (Chairman: Lord Morris) (1965: Cmnd. 2627).)

In addition to those persons who are disqualified from jury service, certain other persons are exempt, for example, peers, clergymen, judges and practising barristers and solicitors, and the last three are exempt until ten years after they have ceased to hold office or to practise their profession (Criminal Justice Act 1967, s. 16).

Women are as eligible as men to serve on juries (Sex Disqualification (Removal) Act 1919, s. 1). Indeed, the proportion of women on the jury panel (see below) should be the same as in the county, etc., as a whole and in any case their number should not normally be less than fourteen (Women Jurors (Criminal Cases) Rules 1920, r. 3). Nevertheless, because fewer women have the necessary property qualification in practice juries are composed predominantly of men. The trial judge, moreover, in his discretion, on the application of the prosecution or accused or at his own instance, may order that the jury be composed of men only or of women only, as the case may require (Sex Disqualification (Removal) Act 1919, s. 1). (For criticism of a judge's decision to order an all-female jury, see *R.* v. *Sutton* (1968), C.A.)

Jury panel

Certain jurors are summoned for each sitting of the trial court and the names of those summoned, and not thereafter excused, are set out in the jury panel. The panel is, in fact, chosen by the under-sheriff, on behalf of the sheriff, or by the borough clerk of the peace (in the case of a borough quarter sessions). It must then be available for inspection by the parties at least seven days before the sitting of the court (Common Law Procedure Act 1852, s. 106).

The Trial Jury

As we saw in the last chapter, if, at a trial on indictment, the accused pleads not guilty then, unless the prosecution proposes to offer no evidence against him, a jury must be sworn in to try the issue of whether he is guilty or not. If the prosecution does propose to offer no evidence against the accused, the judge may order that a verdict of not guilty be recorded without the accused being given in charge to a jury (Criminal Justice Act 1967, s. 17). Similarly, if, at the arraignment, the accused pleads guilty, judgment against him will be entered and a jury will not be sworn in .

If a jury is sworn in, its members are drawn from the names of the potential jurors on the jury panel. The clerk of the court himself selects the jury, subject to any challenges and to any requests that a juror should stand by (see below). The jury, moreover, at the commencement of the proceedings, must number twelve, for while there are provisions for a reduction in the number during the trial (see below) there are no provisions which allow proceedings to commence with any other number than twelve. If, therefore, some of the original twelve are successfully challenged these must be replaced (for the power to pray a *tales de circumstantibus*, see below). A husband and wife must not serve on the same jury (Women Jurors (Criminal Cases) Rules 1920, r. 2).

One of the jury will be appointed foreman of the jury, although the method of choosing the foreman varies from court to court (*e.g.*, he may be appointed by the court or by the other jurors). The foreman's function is to act as the spokesman of the jury when they return their verdict, but he will also normally act as chairman when the jury have retired to decide upon their verdict. Nevertheless, the foreman does not have any kind of superior status to his fellow jurors and his views ought to carry no greater weight than theirs.

Challenges

The potential members are called to the jury box and take the oath in turn. Before they are called, however, the accused should be informed of his rights of challenge.

Peremptory challenges

An accused indicted for any offence may challenge not more than seven jurors peremptorily (*i.e.*, without disclosing, or necessarily having, a cause) (Criminal Justice Act 1948, s. 35 (1)). Peremptory challenges are occasionally made for various reasons, but the right of peremptory challenge only applies if the accused is arraigned on indictment. Therefore, where it is necessary after conviction for a jury to try whether the accused has a previous conviction (see Chap. 38), the accused has no right of peremptory challenge in relation to such a jury (*R.* v. *Batchelor* (1952), C.C.A.). Nevertheless, if an accused who has a right of peremptory challenge is deprived of that right, the trial will be a nullity (*R.* v. *Page* (1965), C.C.A.).

Even though two or more accused are charged jointly in an indictment, the indictment will normally be tried by the one jury. If, therefore, one accused exercises his right to challenge peremptorily one or more jurors, those jurors cannot sit on the jury which is trying the other accused as well, and if two accused jointly indicted exercise their right to challenge seven potential jurors, fourteen jurors will be challenged in all. As we have seen (Chap. 34), the fact that joint accused insist on exercising their rights of peremptory challenge separately may result in the trial judge ordering separate trials: then the jurors challenged by the one accused will be eligible to sit on the jury trying the other.

The prosecution have no right of peremptory challenge (Juries Act 1825, s. 29), but they are entitled to demand that a potential juror "stand by," *i.e.*, that the juror should be replaced by another juror on the jury panel if one is available (*e.g.*, *R.* v. *Casement* (1917)). Nevertheless, unlike the position after a peremptory challenge, if the juror cannot be replaced from the jury panel the prosecution will have to accept him unless they can challenge for cause. As the accused now has the right of peremptory challenge in all trials, he has no similar right to demand that a juror "stand by" (*R.* v. *Chandler* (1964), C.C.A.).

Challenges for cause

Challenges for cause, which may be made by the prosecution or by the accused, may be made either to the array or to the polls.

Challenges to the array. These are challenges to the whole jury panel and should be made in writing, but "the only ground upon which the challenge to the array is allowed by the English law is the unindifferency or default of the sheriff" (*per* Lord Tindal C.J. in *O'Connell* v. *R.* (1844), H.L.) (because he is the officer who ultimately chooses the jury panel).

A challenge to the array may be either a principal challenge or for favour. *A principal challenge* may, for example, be because the sheriff is the actual prosecutor or party aggrieved (*R.* v. *Sheppard* (1773)) or because he has a pecuniary interest in the event. *A challenge for favour* may be made on the ground of the sheriff's less apparent partiality, for example, where one of the parties is tenant to the sheriff or the sheriff and one of the parties are indirectly connected by marriage.

Challenges to the polls. These are challenges to individual jurors as they are about to be sworn and they are normally made orally. Like challenges to the array, a challenge to the polls may be either a principal challenge or for favour.

A principal challenge may be:

(1) *Propter honoris respectum, i.e.,* where a potential juror is a peer.

(2) *Propter defectum, i.e.,* on account of some personal objection such as infancy (*R.* v. *Tremearne* (1826)), or want of the requisite property qualification. Nevertheless, where a disqualified juror is on the panel and no challenge is made, the presence of the juror does not invalidate the trial (*R.* v. *Kelly* (1950), C.C.A.; Criminal Justice Act 1967, s. 15).

(3) *Propter affectum, i.e.,* on the ground of some presumed or actual partiality in the juror such as an affinity to either party, or any circumstance similar to those which would support a principal challenge to the array because of the sheriff's lack of impartiality. In *R.* v. *O'Coigley* (1798) one of the jurors was successfully challenged because he was heard to exclaim about the accused, "damned rascalls."

(4) *Propter delictum.* At common law a juror could be challenged on the ground that he had been convicted of an infamous crime. This ground would now appear to have been superseded by section 14 of the Criminal Justice Act 1967 (see Qualifications of jurors, above), at least if the conviction was in the United Kingdom, the Channel Islands or the Isle of Man, but if a person who is disqualified from jury service under that section should attempt to serve on a jury he could be successfully challenged at this stage (*i.e., propter defectum*).

A challenge to the polls *for favour* may be made on the ground that there are reasonable grounds for suspicion that the juror will act under some prejudice or undue influence, but where the juror's partiality is not enough for a principal challenge.

A challenge for cause must be tried by the judge, chairman of quarter sessions or recorder (Criminal Justice Act 1948, s. 35(2)). Moreover, although the party challenging is not entitled to question a juror before challenging him, once the challenge has been made the juror may be examined as to his qualifications or his general opinons (*R.* v. *Dowling* (1848)) and other witnesses may be called to support or oppose the challenge. It should also be remembered that the parties may obtain a copy of the jury panel at least seven days before the sitting of the trial court (see Jury panel, above).

Insufficient Jurors

As we have seen, a jury at the commencement of a trial must number twelve, and if jurors are successfully challenged they must be replaced by other jurors to bring the number up to twelve. If there are not sufficient jurors, either initially or to replace those who have been successfully challenged, the number may, on the request of either side, be made up to twelve by the court praying a *tales de circumstantibus*. The law in relation to praying a *tales* is somewhat uncertain: it has been suggested that in a criminal court a *tales* cannot be prayed without a warrant from the Attorney-General (2 Hawk., c. 43, s. 18), but even if this was true it would appear to be true no longer. However, at assizes the talesmen must be so many of such other able men of the county then present and who are duly qualified (Juries Act 1825, s. 37), although the exact meaning of this provision, for example, whether they must have the normal property qualifications, has never been decided. At quarter sessions, where the common law prevails, it is even more uncertain what the necessary qualifications of the talesmen are, but in *R.* v. *Solomon* (1958), C.C.A. (a quarter sessions case, although the law is almost certainly the same in this respect at assizes), where there were no qualesmen (*i.e.*, jurors on the jury panel) present, and the accused was tried by a complete jury of talesmen, it was held that the trial was a nullity.

Where the jury panel is exhausted and no *tales* has been prayed, the trial judge may order the sheriff to return a panel *instanter*, i.e., to summon a new panel of jurors immediately (see Archbold, *Criminal Pleading, Evidence and Practice* (37th ed.), para. 522).

Discharge of Juror or Jury

Subject to the circumstances discussed below, a judge has a general power to discharge a jury or individual jurors (though at common law this necessitated discharge of the whole jury) if he considers it necessary to do so. Thus, if a jury cannot agree by the necessary majority as to their verdict, the judge will discharge them (*R.* v. *Newton* (1849)) (and see Chap. 38). Discharge of the jury is not, however, an acquittal and the accused may then be remanded for a fresh trial (*R.* v. *Davison* (1860)).

Criminal Justice Act 1965, s. 1

By section 1(1), "where in the course of a criminal trial any member of the jury dies or is discharged by the court whether as being through illness incapable of continuing to act or for any other reason, but the number of its members is not reduced below nine, . . . the trial shall proceed. . . ." Nevertheless, on the death or discharge of a member of the jury the judge may discharge the whole jury if he sees fit to do so (*ibid.*, s. 1(3)), and on a trial for murder or for any offence punishable with death the trial cannot continue after the death or discharge of a juror unless assent to its continuance is given in writing by or on behalf of both the prosecution and the accused, or each of the accused (*ibid.*, s. 1(2)).

There is no recorded authority on the scope of section 1(1) and in particular on the meaning of "for any other reason." In *R.* v. *Browne* (1962), C.C.A., it was held that the judge could allow the trial to continue after a juror had been discharged because, after an adjournment overnight, he was unable to reach the court due to snow. It would seem arguable that, on the principle *noscitur a sociis*, "for any other reason" is confined to reasons, such as death, illness or snow, which are outside the juror's control. In practice section 1(1) has been applied when jurors have been discharged for misconduct, but the correctness of this practice must be open to doubt.

Misconduct

At common law, where a juror misconducted himself before the verdict (which was and still is a common law offence) the whole jury had to be discharged, unless the accused could not have been prejudiced thereby. Thus, in *R*. v. *Ward* (1867) one juror without leave absented himself from the jury box and it was held that the whole jury must be discharged. Whether, provided the accused would not be prejudiced in the absence of the juror who has misconducted himself, the trial could now continue under the Criminal Justice Act 1965, s. 1(1), has been discussed above. Certainly there is no power to continue a trial with fewer than twelve jurors except under section 1(1).

Where the accused will not be prejudiced by the jurors' conduct and there is no question of continuing with fewer than twelve jurymen, it has been stated that the jury need not be discharged. Thus, in *R*. v. *Twiss* (1918), C.C.A., a juror conversed with a prosecution witness before the summing-up; but it was held that, on the particular facts, the accused could not have been prejudiced thereby, and the resulting conviction need not be quashed. Likewise, in *R*. v. *Box* (1964), the Court of Criminal Appeal held the fact that the foreman of the jury knew the accused's previous criminal record before the trial commenced was not a ground for quashing the conviction when, as in that case, the accused was not prejudiced thereby (although the court did stress the undesirability of a juror knowing of the accused's previous criminal record before the trial). Nevertheless, it is almost certain that in both *R*. v. *Twiss* and *R*. v. *Box*, had the juror's conduct or knowledge been brought to the attention of the trial judge before the verdict, he would have considered it advisable to discharge the jury, or that individual juror (see *R*. v. *Hood* (1968), C.A.).

Other grounds for discharge

Where evidence of the accused's previous criminal record is wrongly (or accidentally: *R*. v. *Peckham* (1935), C.C.A.) admitted, the trial judge should, if he realizes the mistake, discharge the jury. However, where such evidence is accidentally elicited the accused should normally apply at the trial for a jury's discharge, and if an application is not made a resulting conviction will not necessarily be quashed (*R*. v. *Ellis* (1961), C.C.A.). Moreover, where prejudicial evidence, other than the accused's previous criminal record, is accidentally admitted, the judge has a discretion to continue the trial, even though an application for the jury's discharge is made (*R*. v. *Weaver* (1968), C.A.).

Other grounds on which a jury have been discharged include the sudden illness of the accused (*R*. v. *Streek* (1826)) and where a witness has been kept away by collusion (though see the power to admit the deposition of the witness in such cases, Chapter 37), but the power of discharge, though discretionary, ought not to be exercised without strong reason. Thus, in *R*. v. *Lewis* (1909), where the judge had discharged the jury because certain prosecution witnesses were not ready, the Court of Criminal Appeal said that though this exercise of the judge's discretion could not be overruled he ought not to have discharged the jury merely to allow the prosecution to present a stronger case at a later trial.

Chapter Thirty-Seven

TRIAL ON INDICTMENT-EVIDENCE AND SPEECHES

Accused Given in Charge to the Jury

AFTER a full jury of twelve have been sworn in the accused will be given in charge to the jury, *i.e.*, the substance of the indictment will be read to them (excluding previous convictions which are stated in the indictment because they increase the maximum imprisonment imposable, see Chap. 33), they will be informed that the accused has pleaded not guilty and they will be told that it is their "charge to say, having heard the evidence, whether he is guilty or not." Once the accused has been given in charge to the jury, only they can return a verdict (*R.* v. *Heyes* (1951), C.C.A.).

Case for the Prosecution

Opening speech
When the accused has been given in charge to the jury, counsel for the prosecution will open the case and will state the main facts on which the prosecution rely and an outline of the evidence which they intend to call, although this will not debar the prosecution from calling further evidence.

When defence object to evidence. Although counsel for the prosecution will normally outline all the evidence which the prosecution intend to call, where it is known that the defence are intending to to object to the admissibility of particular evidence, this evidence must not be mentioned. The most common example is when the defence dispute the admissibility of a confession made by the accused, on the ground that it was not made voluntarily or, possibly, that it was obtained in breach of the Judges' Rules.

The defence know beforehand what evidence the prosecution intend to call because it is set out in the depositions or any notices of additional evidence (see below); and defence counsel, if he wishes to dispute the admissibility of any evidence, should therefore privately inform prosecuting counsel of this fact before the trial. At the stage of the trial when prosecuting counsel would otherwise call the evidence, for it is at this stage that any objection should normally be taken (*R.* v. *Cole* (1941), C.C.A.), he will inform defence counsel that he is about to adduce the evidence, and defence counsel will then inform the judge that he wishes to raise a matter in the absence of the jury. The judge, having directed the jury to withdraw, will then consider the admissibility of the evidence, and in support of their contentions the parties may call evidence, including, in the case of the defence, the accused (*R.* v. *Hammond* (1941), C.C.A.). When the judge has decided and given his decision the jury will return, and if the judge held that the evidence was not admissible the jury will hear nothing of it. In the case of a confession, however, even if the judge held that it was admissible and the jury were therefore informed of it, defence counsel may still cross-examine the prosecution witnesses in the presence of the jury in order to persuade the jury that little or no weight should be given to it (*R.* v. *Murray* (1951), C.C.A.; *R.* v. *Ovenell* (1969), C.A.).

Prosecution's evidence

When counsel for the prosecution has concluded his opening address to the jury he will call the evidence for the prosecution. This will normally be the same evidence contained in the depositions but witnesses in respect of whom conditional witness orders were made will not be called unless they have been notified to attend (for the admissibility of their depositions, see below). Moreover, the prosecution are not bound to call all the other witnesses who gave evidence (including written statements) at the committal proceedings, but the names of all such witnesses will be set out on the back of the indictment and, subject to the law as to written statements and formal admissions (see below) they must normally be present in court. The judge may then invite the prosecution to call such a witness, or, if he considers that the prosecution's discretion to refrain from calling the witness has been exercised improperly, he may call the witness himself (*R.* v. *Oliva* (1965), C.C.A.; see below). In addition the witness could be called by the defence, although the defence would then be unable to cross-examine him.

The court may always order a witness to be excluded from the court until his evidence is required.

Notice of additional evidence. The prosecution may call evidence additional to that set out in the depositions, but in this case, at least if it involves the calling of an additional witness, a rule of practice requires that notice of this additional evidence should be given to the accused, and to the court, such reasonable time before the evidence is called as in the circumstances is practicable (Lord Goddard C.J. in *R*. v. *County of London Quarter Sessions, ex p. Downes* (1954), D.C.).

Written statements. In any criminal proceedings, other than committal proceedings (although similar provisions apply to committal proceedings, see Chap. 32), a written statement by any person is admissible in evidence (either for the prosecution or the defence) to the same extent as if it were oral evidence, provided: (*a*) the statement purports to be signed by the person who made it; and (*b*) the statement contains a declaration by the maker that it is true to the best of his knowledge and belief, and that he made the statement knowing that, if it were tendered in evidence, he would be liable to prosecution if he wilfully stated in it anything which he knew to be false or did not believe to be true (Criminal Justice Act 1967, s. 9). Where the statement is made by a person under twenty-one it must also state his age (*ibid*., s. 9(3)).

Before the hearing at which it is tendered in evidence, a copy of the statement (together with a copy of any other document referred to as an exhibit therein, or information where such a document may be inspected) must have been served on each of the other parties, and the statement will not be admissible if any other party, or his solicitor, within seven days from service of the copy upon him, in writing objects (*ibid*., s. 9(2)). This means that the copy of the statement must normally be served at least seven days before the hearing, but the parties may agree to dispense with these conditions (*ibid*., s. 9(2)). Service on a party, moreover, may be effected by delivering it to, or by sending it in a registered letter or by recorded delivery service to the party or his solicitor, or by leaving it at the party's last known address (*ibid*., s. 9(8)).

The party who served the copy of the statement may still call the maker to give evidence, or the court may, of its own motion or on the application of any party (which application may have been made before the hearing) require the maker to attend before the court and give evidence (*ibid*., s. 9(4)). Where the written statement is admitted in evidence it must, unless the court directs otherwise, be read aloud and, if not read aloud, an account must be given orally of the statement (*ibid*., s. 9(6)).

Formal admissions. It may be unnecessary to prove a fact because it is the subject of a formal admission. In any criminal proceedings the prosecution or accused may make a formal admission, although it cannot be made by the accused, except at the trial itself, unless he is represented or is subsequently represented (Criminal Justice Act 1967, s. 10). A formal admission may be made in respect of any fact of which oral evidence could be given, but if made otherwise than in court it must be made in writing (and be signed by the person making it) and if made by the accused before the trial it must be approved by his counsel or solicitor (*ibid.*, s. 10(2)). Unless it is withdrawn, a formal admission is conclusive proof of the fact admitted in the proceedings in relation to which it was made and in any subsequent criminal proceedings relating to the same matter (including any appeal or retrial), but it may be withdrawn with the leave of the court (*ibid.*, s. 10).

Accused and spouse. The accused cannot be called as a witness for the prosecution with the sole exception of proceedings which are criminal in form only, for example, committing a nuisance to a public highway (Evidence Act 1877, s. 1). Moreover, one accused cannot normally be called by the prosecution to give evidence against a co-accused, although this is possible if the two accused are being tried separately or the co-accused has pleaded guilty. Nevertheless, in these cases, the accused who is to give evidence ought normally to have been sentenced before being called, otherwise evidence which he gives might be influenced by the thought that he is still to be sentenced (see *R.* v. *Pipe* (1967), C.A.).

The spouse of the accused is not normally competent to give evidence for the prosecution against either that accused or a co-accused (*R.* v. *Mount* (1934), C.C.A.). Nevertheless, there are exceptions when a spouse is either a competent, though not compellable, witness for the prosecution (see the Schedule to the Criminal Evidence Act 1898, as amended) or both a competent and a compellable witness for the prosecution (*e.g.*, offences against the person or liberty of the spouse (*R.* v. *Lapworth* (1931), C.C.A.)).

Children and young persons. A child may give either sworn or unsworn evidence in a criminal case (see below), but if he is not of sufficient intelligence to give unsworn evidence his evidence is not admissible. Where the offence charged (in any court) is one against decency or morality the court may order all persons, except the parties, their legal advisers, other persons directly concerned in the case and representatives of newspapers, to be excluded from the court during the evidence of a child or young person (Children and Young Persons Act 1933, s. 37). Moreover, in any proceedings in any court, the court may direct that no newspaper report shall reveal the name, address, school or other identifying particulars of any child or young person concerned in the proceedings, whether as the person by or against or in respect of whom the proceedings are taken, or as a witness (*ibid.*, s. 39, as amended). These provisions are in addition to those which apply in relation to juvenile courts (see Chap. 28).

Attendance of witnesses

We have already seen (Chap. 32) that a *witness order* will be made in respect of all those witnesses who gave evidence, or whose written statements were admitted at the committal proceedings, and we then considered the procedure which should be followed if a witness fails to obey the order.

If a witness did not give evidence at the committal proceedings his presence may be secured at assizes or quarter sessions by a *witness summons* (*i.e.*, a summons requiring him to attend before the trial court and to give evidence or to produce any document or thing specified in the summons), which may be issued out of the trial court or the High Court (Criminal Procedure (Attendance of Witnesses) Act 1965, s. 2(1)). Nevertheless, any person in respect of whom a witness summons has been issued may apply to the court out of which the summons was issued or to the High Court to have the summons set aside, and if the court is satisfied that he cannot give material evidence or, as the case may be, produce any document or thing likely to be material evidence, the court may direct that the summons shall be of no effect (*ibid.*, s. 2(2)). The procedure should the witness disobey the witness summons is the same as if a witness disobeys a witness order.

Where a potential witness is in prison in consequence of civil process his attendance may be procured by a writ of *habeas corpus ad testificandum*, while if he is in prison in consequence of criminal proceedings an order for his attendance may be obtained from a High Court judge.

Oath and affirmation

As a general rule each witness must either take the oath or affirm. For the cases where a witness may affirm, see Chapter 20. Nevertheless, certain witnesses may give evidence without having taken the oath or affirmed, *i.e.*, children (when they do not understand the nature of the oath but are possessed of sufficient intelligence to justify the reception of their evidence and they do understand the duty of speaking the truth: Children and Young Persons Act 1933, s. 38), witnesses called merely to produce a document, judges and counsel explaining a previous case in which they were engaged, and the Sovereign. An accused is also able to make an unsworn statement (see below).

Examination of witnesses

It is not possible within the scope of this work to deal with the examination of witnesses in detail (recourse must be had to a textbook on evidence), but each witness who gives oral evidence will be liable to be examined-in-chief by the side calling him, cross-examined by the other side and re-examined by his own side .

Admissibility of depositions

As a general rule every witness must give his evidence in person, but in the following cases a witness's deposition (*i.e.*, an oral statement made under oath which has been recorded in writing) may be admissible instead of the witness's oral evidence.

Depositions taken at the committal proceedings. By the Criminal Justice Act 1925, s. 13(3), as amended, the depositions taken at the committal proceedings (including any written statements which were tendered in evidence thereat: Criminal Justice Act 1967, s. 2(7)) may be read as evidence at the trial when the witness (1) is proved by the sworn evidence of another witness to be dead, insane, or so ill as not to be able to travel, or (2) is likewise proved to have been kept out of the way by, or on behalf of the accused or (3) is a witness in respect of whom a conditional witness order was made and he has not been notified to attend. Nevertheless, although the judge may allow the deposition to be read in these circumstances, he is not obliged to do so and he may still in his discretion exclude the deposition although the requirements outlined above have been satisfied. Thus, in *R.* v. *Linley* (1959), the prosecution's case depended to a large extent on the evidence of one witness, who was ill at the time of the trial and unlikely to recover. The judge, however, in his discretion, refused to allow the deposition of the witness to be read because the defence of the accused would have been to cross-examine the witness to try to show that he ought not be believed. If the depositions were admitted the witness's evidence would be admissible without the accused having an opportunity to cross-examine.

Where an accused at the committal proceedings admits his guilt and it is thought that he will plead guilty at the trial it is the normal practice to make a conditional witness order in respect of each of the prosecution's witnesses, because if the accused does plead guilty the witnesses will not be required. Nevertheless, even though the accused did admit his guilt before the examining justices, he need not necessarily plead guilty at the trial (although evidence of his admission will be admissible against him). If, therefore, he does not plead guilty the prosecution will, after all, have to adduce evidence against him, but, instead of using the depositions, the trial should be adjourned and the witnesses notified to attend (*R.* v. *Collins* (1938), C.C.A.).

For a deposition (though not a written statement which was tendered in evidence at the committal proceedings) to be admissible under section 13(3), it must be proved at the trial, either by a certificate purporting to be signed by the magistrate before whom it was taken (provided it is not proved to the contrary) or by the clerk to the examining justices, or by the oath of a credible witness, that the deposition was taken in the presence of the accused and that he, or his counsel or solicitor, had full opportunity to cross-examine the witness (*ibid.*, s. 13(3) (*b*)). Moreover, the deposition itself (including any written statement which was tendered in evidence at the committal proceedings) must purport to be signed by the magistrate before whom it was taken (provided, again, that it is not proved to the contrary) (*ibid.*, s. 13(3)(*c*)), or the magistrate must have signed a certificate authenticating the deposition (Criminal Justice Act 1967, s. 7).

Coroners' depositions. We have seen (Chap. 28) that in a case of murder, manslaughter and probably infanticide the coroner must put into writing the statements on oath of the witnesses at the inquest. The Criminal Justice Act 1925, s. 13(3), does not apply to these depositions but they have in practice been admitted in trials for homicide when the witness has been proved to be dead, ill or insane (*R.* v. *Butcher* (1900); *R.* v. *Cowle* (1907); *R.* v. *Black* (1910)).

Depositions of children. In any of the cases listed in the First Schedule to the Children and Young Persons Act 1933, as amended (*e.g.*, any offence involving bodily injury to a child or young person), the court may, if satisfied by the evidence of a medical practitioner that the attendance before the court of the child or young person against whom the offence is alleged to have been committed would involve serious danger to his life or health, admit a deposition of such child or young person, either for or against the accused. For the deposition to be admissible against the accused, however, he must have been served with reasonable notice that a magistrate intended to take the deposition and he, or his counsel or solicitor, must have had an opportunity to be present and to cross-examine the child or young person (ibid., s. 43).

The written statement of a child which is normally admissible at the preliminary investigation into a sexual offence (see Chap. 32) is not, however, admissible at the trial. Nevertheless, the child may make another written statement which complies with section 9 of the Criminal Justice Act 1967 (see above).

Depositions to perpetuate testimony. By the Magistrates' Courts Act 1952, s. 41, the deposition of a potential witness who is dangerously ill and unlikely to recover may be taken out of court by a magistrate. The deposition may then be admitted at the trial on indictment, either for or against the accused, provided it is proved that the potential witness has by then died, or that there is no reasonable probability that he will ever be able to travel or to give evidence, and provided also that the party against whom it is to be admitted was served with reasonable notice of the intention to take the deposition and he, or his counsel or solicitor, had an opportunity to be present and to cross-examine the potential witness (Criminal Law Amendment Act 1867, s. 6, as amended).

No case to answer

At the close of the prosecution's evidence the defence may submit to the judge that there is no case to answer, and if this submission is accepted the judge will direct the jury to return a verdict of not guilty. The judge also has power to withdraw a case from the jury (*i.e.*, to direct them to find the accused not guilty) on his own initiative (*R.* v. *George* (1908), C.C.A.).

In addition to his power to direct the jury to acquit the accused, the judge may, at any time before the summing-up (though not normally before the close of the prosecution's evidence: see *R.* v. *Middlesex Quarter Sessions, ex p. D.P.P.* (1952), D.C.), invite the jury to stop the case and return a verdict of not guilty. In this case, however, the judge merely invites the jury to stop the case if they consider that the accused cannot be convicted on the evidence, the jury being free to follow the invitation or not, and it has been said that the judge ought normally to direct them to acquit rather than merely invite them to do so (*R.* v. *Young* (1964), C.C.A.).

Defence Evidence

After the prosecution has concluded its evidence and provided the jury have not already acquitted the accused, the defence evidence and speeches will occur. The order of proceedings may, however, vary, according to whether or not the accused is represented by counsel, and the procedure when he is represented will be considered first. Nevertheless, if in fact defence counsel calls no evidence, counsel for the prosecution may immediately address the jury again (see below) (Criminal Procedure Act 1865, s. 2).

Defence opening speech

Provided defence counsel intends calling evidence on the facts (*i.e.*, not merely evidence as to the accused's character), whether or not he also intends calling the accused, he has the right to open his case to the jury before calling his evidence (*R*. v. *Hill* (1911), C.C.A.). If the only witness to the facts to be called by the defence is the accused, however, defence counsel has no such right (see below).

Evidence for the defence

The accused. The accused may give evidence for the defence, and thus be liable to cross-examination, although (excepting offences criminal in form only: Evidence Act 1877, s. 1) only on his own application (Criminal Evidence Act 1898, s. 1). One accused cannot, therefore, compel a co-accused to give evidence for him.

Where the accused is the only witness to the facts called by the defence he must be called immediately after the close of evidence for the prosecution (see also above) (Criminal Evidence Act 1898, s. 2), and in practice, even when other witnesses of fact are called, the accused should normally be called first (*per* Lord Alverstone C.J. in *R*. v. *Morrison* (1911), C.C.A.; *R*. v. *Smith* (1968), C.A.).

Accused's unsworn statement. Instead of giving evidence on oath, or presumably in addition to such evidence, the accused may still exercise his common law right to make an unsworn statement from the dock (Criminal Evidence Act 1898, s. 1(*h*)). This unsworn statement, on which the accused cannot be cross-examined by the prosecution, must be made before the prosecution counsel sums up the case against the accused (see below) (*R*. v. *Sherriff* (1903)), and, though the statement is not evidence in the sense of sworn testimony, it is more than mere comment. The judge in his summing-up to the jury should therefore tell them that they can attach such weight to the statement as they think fit (*R*. v. *Frost* (1964), C.C.A.).

Co-accused. Where there are two or more accused, then, subject to a contrary agreement between them, the evidence and speeches of each of them will take place in the order in which their names appear on the indictment. Thus, if the case is the Queen v. Smith and Brown, and both accused call evidence of fact other than themselves, Smith's counsel will normally address the court and then call his evidence, Brown's counsel will then address the court and call his evidence, then prosecution counsel will sum up the case against Smith, then against Brown, and finally Smith's counsel, then Brown's counsel, will reply (see below).

Spouse of accused. The spouse of the accused is normally a competent though not compellable witness for the defence, but can only be called on the application of the accused (Criminal Evidence Act 1898, s. 1(*c*)). The spouse could not therefore be called by a co-accused. If, however, the proceedings are criminal in form only (see above) the spouse is a compellable witness for the defence, and without the consent of the accused (see the Criminal Evidence Act 1898, s. 4(2)), and, in the cases set out in the Schedule to the Criminal Evidence Act 1898, as amended, the spouse, though only a competent witness for the defence, may be called without the consent of the accused (*ibid.*, s. 4(1)).

Other defence witnesses. Other witnesses called by the defence will be liable to be examined in chief, cross-examined and re-examined in the same way as the prosecution's witnesses.

Evidence of an alibi. The accused, at a trial on indictment, cannot, without leave of the court, adduce evidence in support of an alibi (*i.e.*, evidence which tends to show that at the time of the alleged offence he was at some particular place other than that where the offence is alleged to have been committed; see *R*. v. *Lewis* (1968), C.A.) unless he has given prior notice of the particulars of the alibi (Criminal Justice Act 1967, s. 11(1)). This notice must either be given in court during, or at the end of the committal proceedings or given in writing to the solicitor for the prosecution not later than seven days after those proceedings (*ibid.*, s. 11(3)) (see Chap. 32).

Where the accused wishes to call another witness to give evidence in support of the alibi, the notice under section 11 must include the name and address of the witness or, if he does not know them, the accused must give any information which might be of assistance in finding the witness and, thereafter, the accused must continue to take all reasonable steps to discover the witness's name or address and must supply it in writing to the solicitor for the prosecution if he does discover it (*ibid.*, s. 11(2)).

Rebutting Evidence

The prosecution cannot normally call further evidence after the close of the prosecution's case, but the judge does have a discretion to allow the prosecution to call evidence to rebut defence evidence when the defence have introduced evidence which was not foreseen and which no human ingenuity could foresee (*R*. v. *McKenna* (1956),

C.C.A.). Moreover, subject to the court's directions, where the defence adduces evidence in support of an alibi the prosecution may tender evidence in disproof of that alibi, either before or after the evidence in support (Criminal Justice Act 1967, s. 11(4)). If the court allows the prosecution to call rebutting evidence, it may allow the evidence to be called immediately after the defence evidence or even after the final speeches (*R. v. Flynn* (1957), C.C.A.), though not after the summing-up (*R. v. Owen* (1952), C.C.A.). When evidence in rebuttal is called after the final speeches, however, counsel for the defence is entitled to comment on that evidence (*R. v. Frost* (1839)).

Judge Calling a Witness

The judge himself may call a witness not called by either the prosecution or defence, and without the consent of either, if in his opinion it is necessary in the interests of justice (*R. v. Harris* (1927), C.C.A.). Nevertheless, the judge should not call a witness after the defence case has closed except where, in the course of that defence, a matter has arisen *ex improviso*, which no human ingenuity could foresee (*R. v. Harris, supra*) or the witness is called on behalf of the defence (*R. v. Tregear* (1967), C.A.; *R. v. Cleghorn* (1967), C.A.). Moreover, the judge can never call a witness to give evidence for the prosecution after the summing-up (*R. v. Owen* (1952), C.C.A.), although he can, in exceptional circumstances, call a witness for the defence after the summing-up and then deliver a supplementary summing-up with reference to that evidence (*R. v. Sanderson* (1953), C.C.A.). Once the jury have retired to consider their verdict no further evidence can be called (*R. v. Wilson* (1957), C.C.A.; *R. v. Lawrence* (1968), C.A.; *R. v. Nixon* (1968), C.A.).

Final Speeches

After the close of the evidence for the defence, counsel for the prosecution will sum up the prosecution's case against the accused (*R. v. Sherriff* (1903)). If the accused has given evidence, prosecution counsel may comment on that evidence (*R. v. Gardner* (1899), C.C.R.), but he must not comment on the fact that an accused, or his spouse, has not given evidence (Criminal Evidence Act 1898, s. 1(*b*)). (For the power of a judge to comment on the failure of an accused or his spouse to give evidence, see Chap. 38.)

After counsel for the prosecution has summed up the case against the accused, defence counsel has the right of reply (Criminal Procedure (Right of Reply) Act 1964, s. 1).

Unrepresented Accused

If the accused is not represented by counsel the order of prosecution and defence speeches and evidence will be the same as if he had been represented (the accused himself will examine the witnesses and address the court), save that if he calls no other witness than himself the prosecution will not sum up the case against him after the close of the defence evidence (if any) (Criminal Procedure Act 1865, s. 2; Criminal Evidence Act 1898, s. 3) (*R.* v. *Harrison* (1923), C.C.A.; *R.* v. *Mondon* (1968), C.A.).

Chapter Thirty-Eight

SUMMING-UP, VERDICT AND JUDGMENT

(1) The Summing-up

After the conclusion of the evidence and speeches, the judge sums up the case to the jury. In doing so he must direct them on the law, the burdens and standards of proof and, where necessary (as a matter of law or practice), on the need for corroboration. It is not possible within the scope of this work to discuss in detail the law in relation to the burdens and standards of proof and corroboration but the judge must normally tell the jury that the prosecution have the burden of proving every fact in issue (*Woolmington* v. *D.P.P.* (1935), H.L.). The prosecution, moreover, must prove the guilt of the accused beyond reasonable doubt (they must satisfy the jury so that they feel sure: *R.* v. *Hepworth* (1955), C.C.A.), although in those cases where the burden of proving a fact in issue lies on the accused (*e.g.,* his insanity) he need only prove it on a balance of probabilities (*R.* v. *Carr-Briant* (1943), C.C.A.; *R.* v. *Podola* (1960), C.C.A.).

In addition to directing the jury on the law and the burdens and standards of proof, the judge in his summing-up will usually assist the jury by reviewing the evidence on both sides, although he must make it clear to the jury that questions of fact are for them. Indeed, the judge should normally remind the jury of important evidence which is in the accused's favour, and a conviction may be quashed if he fails to do so (*R.* v. *Raney* (1942), C.C.A.). Unlike the prosecution (see Chap. 37), the judge may refer to the fact that the accused, or his spouse, did not give evidence (*R.* v. *Rhodes* (1899), C.C.R.).

Finally, the judge should direct the jury that, though the law permits him in certain circumstances to accept a majority verdict, these circumstances have not yet arisen, and he must therefore ask them to reach a unanimous verdict. Nevertheless, should the time come when it would be possible for him to accept a majority verdict, he will give them further direction (*Practice Direction* (*Crime: Majority Verdicts*) (1967)).

Retirement of jury

When the judge has concluded his summing-up the jury must decide upon their verdict. In practice juries normally retire from the jury box in order to do so.

Although the court may permit the jury to separate at any time before they retire (Criminal Justice Act 1948, s. 35(4)), once the jury have retired and before verdict they can only separate in cases of necessity, and the jurors must then remain in the custody of the court bailiffs (*R*. v. *Neal* (1949), C.C.A.). During the retirement of the jury no other person, whether an officer of the court or not, must communicate with the jury (see *R*. v. *McNeil* (1967), C.A.), although, if necessary, the judge may give the jury further assistance (*e.g.*, by answering their questions about the evidence which has been given) provided this is done in open court and in the presence of the accused (*R*. v. *Davis* (1960), C.C.A.). Nevertheless, as we saw in Chapter 37, once the jury have retired no further evidence is admissible (*R*. v. *Owen* (1952), C.C.A.).

Majority verdicts

Although it is possible for a jury in criminal proceedings to bring in a majority verdict, they cannot do so unless they have been deliberating on their verdict for not less than two hours, or such longer period as the court thinks reasonable having regard to the nature and complexity of the case (Criminal Justice Act 1967, s. 13). The jury at first must therefore attempt to reach an unanimous verdict and if they find difficulty in agreeing, the judge may endeavour to help them (*R*. v. *Chambers* (1964), C.C.A.), provided he makes it clear that it is their decision. In no circumstances should the judge try to speed up the verdict by threatening the jury (*R*. v. *McKenna* (1960): where the judge told the jury that in ten minutes he had to leave the court and that if they did not return their verdict within that time they would have to be kept together all night and resume the matter the next morning; the jury then returned a verdict of guilty within a further six minutes but the Court of Criminal Appeal quashed the conviction). Nevertheless, a judge is not bound to accept a majority verdict and he may, if the jury cannot reach a unanimous verdict, discharge them, when the accused will be liable to be tried again for the same offence (see Chap. 36 (*R*. v. *Elia* (1968), C.A.).

If the jury have not reached a unanimous verdict after two hours, or such longer period as the court has thought reasonable, they will be asked in open court to retire once more and be told that they should continue to endeavour to reach a unanimous verdict but that if they cannot, the judge will accept a majority verdict (*Practice Direction* (*Crime: Majority Verdicts*) (1967)). Nevertheless, this does not mean a bare majority, for if there are still twelve jurors, or there are eleven (one having been discharged during the course of the trial), ten of them must agree on the verdict, while if the jury have been reduced to ten jurors, nine of them must agree (Criminal Justice Act 1967, s. 13(1)). If the jury have been reduced to nine their verdict must be unanimous.

When the jury finally return they must first be asked whether at least ten (or nine as the case may be) agree upon their verdict and if the answer is yes, they will then be asked whether the verdict is "guilty" or "not guilty." If the verdict is "not guilty" the court will not inquire whether, after all, it was a unanimous verdict, or whether a majority verdict; but if the verdict is "guilty" the jury must be asked whether it was a unanimous or majority verdict and if a majority verdict the number of jurors who agreed with and dissented from it (*ibid.*, s. 13(2); *Practice Direction, supra*).

Irregularities in the juryroom

Provided there is no apparent breach of the rules an appeal court cannot quash a conviction on the ground of an alleged irregularity within the juryroom, because what transpires in the juryroom is absolutely privileged (*R.* v. *Thompson* (1962)). In this case the accused alleged on appeal that the majority of the jury had been against convicting him until the foreman of the jury produced a list of the accused's previous convictions (which had not been put in evidence), but the Court of Criminal Appeal held that they could not go into the matter. Moreover, the verdict must be returned in the presence and hearing of all the jurors and a juror who does not object at the time cannot thereafter allege on appeal that the verdict was not unanimous or was not by the majority stated (as the case may be) (*R.* v. *Roads* (1967), C.A.; and see *Boston* v. *W. S. Bagshaw & Sons* (1966), C.A.).

(2) Verdict

The verdict of the jury may be one of three kinds: (1) a *general verdict, i.e.,* guilty or not guilty on all counts (a separate verdict being taken on each count); or (2) a *partial verdict, i.e.,* guilty on some counts but not on others, or not guilty of the offence charged but guilty of some other offence by way of alternative verdict; or

(3) a *special verdict, i.e.,* where the jury decide on those questions of fact which the judge puts to them, but the judge draws the legal conclusions from the facts as found. If there are more than one accused a separate verdict will be returned in respect of each accused.

Partial verdict

Alternative counts. An indictment may sometimes charge an accused with two offences in the alternative. Thus an accused may be charged both with theft of certain goods and with "handling" the same goods. The accused cannot, however, be convicted of both offences and if he is guilty of one he cannot be guilty of the other. Nevertheless, if the jury do convict him on one of the alternative counts they will, in practice, normally be discharged from returning a verdict on the other (*R.* v. *Adair* (1958), C.C.A.). The reason is that should the accused then appeal to the Criminal Division of the Court of Appeal and the Criminal Division considers that he ought to have been convicted, not of the offence of which he was convicted, but of the alternative offence, the Criminal Division may then substitute a verdict of guilty of the alternative offence, because he was not acquitted of it (*R.* v. *Adair, supra*). If, however, the jury had brought in a verdict of not guilty of the alternative offence, the Court of Appeal would not have been able to convict him of it, even though it would have had to quash his conviction of the other offence (*R.* v. *Melvin* (1953), C.C.A.)). (See Chap. 41.)

Alternative verdict. The jury are sometimes able to find the accused not guilty of the offence charged but guilty of some other offence by way of alternative verdict, although this other offence is not charged in the indictment. These other offences will, for the sake of convenience, be called "alternative verdict offences."

By the Criminal Law Act 1967, s. 6(3), where, on a trial on indictment for any offence except treason or murder, the jury find the accused not guilty of the offence specifically charged in the indictment, but the allegations in the indictment amount to or include (expressly or by implication) an allegation of another offence falling within the jurisdiction of the trial court, the jury may find the accused guilty of that other offence or of an offence of which he could be found guilty on an indictment specifically charging that other offence. Thus, for example, if the accused is charged with burglary by having entered a building and then stolen property therein (Theft Act 1968, s. 9(1) (*b*)) he may alternatively be convicted of theft, or if charged with assault occasioning actual bodily harm he may be convicted of common assault. This is, of course, provided that in each of these cases, the facts warrant a conviction for the alternative verdict offence. Nevertheless, if an accused is charged with burglary by entering a building with intent to steal property therein (Theft Act 1968, s. 9(1) (*a*)) he cannot be convicted, by way of alternative verdict, of theft, because the count charging burglary did not include (expressly or by implication) an allegation of theft, only that the accused had intended to steal.

In addition to the general power to convict by way of alternative verdict, contained in section 6(3) of the Criminal Law Act 1967, many statutes give a particular power in relation to a particular offence. Thus the Criminal Law Act 1967, s. 6(2), provides that on an indictment for murder an accused found not guilty of murder "may be found guilty (*a*) of manslaughter, or of causing grievous bodily harm with intent to [murder]; or (*b*) of any offence of which he may be found guilty under an enactment specifically so providing, or under section 4(2) of this Act [impeding the apprehension or prosecution of the accused]; or (*c*) of an attempt to commit murder, or of an attempt to commit any other offence of which he might be found guilty; but may not be found guilty of any offence not included above." Moreover, as we have seen (Chap. 32), any accused charged on indictment with the full offence may alternatively be convicted of an attempt to commit that offence (Criminal Law Act 1967, s. 6). Other examples include the Theft Act 1968, s. 12(4) (whereby an accused charged with theft may alternatively be convicted of taking a conveyance without authority). As to a list of alternative verdicts, see Appendix III.

Special verdicts

Special verdicts, although relatively common when there is a jury in a civil case, are extremely rare in criminal cases, and they should only be obtained in the most exceptional cases (*R.* v. *Bourne* (1952), C.C.A.) (cases where a special verdict was obtained include *R.* v. *Dudley* (1884), and *R.* v. *Bourne* itself, although the use of a special verdict was criticized in the later case).

Apart from the special verdicts considered above, the verdict of not guilty by reason of insanity is also referred to as a special verdict (see the Trial of Lunatics Act 1883 and the Criminal Procedure (Insanity) Act 1964). Nevertheless, this is a quite separate use of the term "special verdict."

Receiving the verdict

Unless the jury's verdict is ambiguous (see below) the judge is normally bound to record that verdict however much he may disagree with it (*R.* v. *Crisp* (1912), C.C.A.); although most writers state the contrary, they would appear to have overlooked the comments of Channel J. in this case. However, if the jury finds the accused guilty, but the judge considers that this has not been proved, he will normally grant the accused leave to appeal and communicate his views to the appeal court. Nevertheless, if the jury returns verdicts on two counts which are inconsistent (*e.g.*, verdicts of guilty of both theft and "handling" the same goods) the judge should direct the jury to reconsider the matter (*R.* v. *Harris* (1964), C.C.A.) and if the judge fails to do so, or the jury insists on their verdicts, the conviction, in so far as it is inconsistent, must be quashed on appeal (*R.* v. *Cooper* (1947), C.C.A.).

If the jury's verdict is ambiguous the judge must endeavour to clarify the judgment and he may question the jury as to the meaning of the words used (*R.* v. *White* (1960), C.C.A.) and, if necessary, he may give the jury further directions on the law (*R.* v. *Sweetland* (1958), C.C.A.). Nevertheless, where the verdict is plain and unambiguous the judge should not question the jury about it (*R.* v. *Larkin* (1943), C.C.A.) and, as we have seen, what occurred in the juryroom is absolutely privileged, and provided there is no apparent breach of the rules the judge cannot enquire into how they reached their verdict (see *R.* v. *Hood* (1968), C.A.).

Where the jury cannot agree on their verdict by the required majority, the accused will normally be remanded for a fresh trial on the same indictment before another jury. If the second jury also cannot agree the prosecution will normally offer no evidence before a third jury or the Attorney-General will enter a *nolle prosequi*.

(3) Judgment

If the jury convict the accused of any offence, or the accused pleaded guilty, the judge, having recorded the verdict, will proceed to pass judgment, including sentence. Before judgment is passed, however, certain matters must be considered or dealt with.

Motion in arrest of judgment

At any time between conviction and judgment the accused may move the court in arrest of judgment. This can be done only on the ground of some defect in law apparent on the face of the record, and not a defect in the evidence or procedure at the trial, which should be raised on appeal. Grounds on which the accused may move the court to arrest the judgment include excessive generality in the particulars of the offence, but the motion will fail if the defect has been cured by verdict or amendment (*R* v. *Stroulger* (1886), C.C.R., where the indictment had merely charged the accused with "corrupt practices" but, on a motion to arrest judgment, it was held that this indictment had already been cured by the jury's verdict which found the accused guilty of bribery). In *Nash* v. *R.* (1864) it was held that the accused could not move in arrest of judgment on the ground of duplicity, but he could now appeal on this ground to the Criminal Division of the Court of Appeal (*e.g.*, *R.* v. *Nicholls* (1960), C.C.A.).

Formerly, when the accused was convicted of a felony he had to be asked expressly whether he wished to move in arrest of judgment (this was called the *allocutus*), but with the abolition of the distinction between felonies and misdemeanours, and with the provision that on all matters on which a distinction had previously been made the law and practice applicable should be that for misdemeanours (Criminal Law Act 1967, s. 1), the allocutus no longer occurs.

If a motion in arrest of judgment succeeds, the accused will be discharged, but this will not be a bar to a fresh indictment on the same facts.

Sentence

The sentence which the court passes will depend initially on whether or not it is one which is fixed by law.

Sentence fixed by law. A sentence fixed by law is one which the court is obliged to pass if the accused is convicted of a particular offence. Thus, if an accused is convicted of murder he must, if he has attained eighteen years, be sentenced to imprisonment for life (Murder (Abolition of Death Penalty) Act 1965, s. 1(1)), or, if he is under eighteen, he must be sentenced to be detained during Her Majesty's pleasure (Children and Young Persons Act 1933, s. 57(1), as amended). Another sentence which is fixed by law is the sentence of death on conviction of high treason (Treason Act 1814, s. 1), of piracy with violence (Piracy Act 1837, s. 2) and of setting fire to Her Majesty's ships, stores, etc. (Dockyard Protection Act 1772, s. 1) (see also Criminal Justice Act 1948, s. 80).

Sentence not fixed by law. If the sentence is not fixed by law the sentence passed will be based not only on the offence of which the accused has been convicted, but also on his background and character, including his previous convictions and any other offences which he asks the court to take into consideration (see below). After conviction, therefore, the prosecution will normally call evidence of the previous conduct and record of the accused (including matters in his favour) and in practice the strict rules of evidence are normally relaxed, so that a police officer may give evidence of the accused's previous convictions even though he has no personal knowledge of them. Nevertheless, evidence must not normally be given of matters which cannot be proved (*R.* v. *Van Pelz* (1943), C.C.A.) and if the accused challenges the prosecution's evidence or denies the previous convictions, these must be proved strictly (see below).

The accused himself (through defence counsel if there is one) may cross-examine the prosecution's witnesses, may make a plea in mitigation of sentence, and may call other defence witnesses to speak as to his character.

If the accused pleaded guilty, the procedure for determining the sentence will be basically the same as when the accused was found guilty by the jury. Nevertheless, if the accused pleaded guilty it will normally be necessary for the prosecution to outline the facts of the case and the part played by the accused. Moreover, if there were no committal proceedings or the proceedings were not fully reported, then the facts must be stated publicly in open court and in some detail, and this is so even though the sentence is one fixed by law and details of the accused's background, etc., are not therefore relevant for the purpose of fixing the sentence (*Practice Direction* (*Plea of Guilty: Statement of Facts*) (1968)).

Taking other offences into consideration. If the accused has committed offences, other than those of which he has been convicted, he may ask the judge to take these other offences into consideration in fixing the sentence. By this procedure the accused will normally avoid being charged separately with these other offences; nevertheless, he is not convicted of them and though the judge takes them into consideration in fixing the sentence for the offence of which he has been convicted (in the same way as he takes the accused's previous convictions into consideration), the sentence cannot exceed the maximum for that offence (*R.* v. *Williams* (1962), C.C.A.). In practice, therefore, the sentence which the accused receives will not normally be as great as if the offences were tried separately, but from the viewpoint of the Crown it is desirable that offences should be disclosed in this way for the expense of separate trials will be avoided and offences will be cleared up which might otherwise remain unsolved.

For a court to take another offence into consideration it must have jurisdiction over the offence (*R.* v. *Warn* (1937), C.C.A.), so that quarter sessions cannot take into consideration an offence which is triable only at assizes. Moreover, a judge is not obliged to take an offence into consideration, and he will not normally take into consideration an offence dissimilar to that of which the accused has been convicted (*R.* v. *Smith* (1921), C.C.A.). Further, although the consent of the prosecution is not normally necessary they will always be consulted, and in *R.* v. *McLean* (1911), C.C.A., where the accused was convicted of housebreaking and the judge took into consideration an offence of arson, for which the accused had already been committed for trial in another county, Lord Alverstone C.J. said that in these circumstances the consent of the prosecution is necessary, and that even if they do consent the judge ought to consider whether the public interest requires separate investigation.

Although an accused will not normally be prosecuted subsequently for an offence taken into consideration, he has not been convicted of that offence and could not plead *autrefois convict* if he were prosecuted (see Chap. 35). Thus, in *R.* v. *McLean* the charge of arson was still proceeded with and the accused was convicted of it, although the Court of Criminal Appeal reduced the sentence for the arson so that the total sentence of imprisonment was no longer than that imposed for the housebreaking, where the arson was taken into consideration. Moreover, in *R.* v. *Neal* (1949), the Court of Criminal Appeal, when it quashed the accused's conviction (on the ground that the jury should not have separated after retirement, see above), pointed out that the accused could now be prosecuted for offences taken into consideration at the time of that conviction.

As the judge cannot exceed the maximum sentence for the offence of which the accused has been convicted, he ought not to take into consideration offences which carry a type of punishment which cannot be imposed for the offence of which the accused has been convicted. Thus in *R.* v. *Williams* (1962) the accused was convicted of larceny of a motor vehicle and the judge took into consideration certain motoring offences. The Court of Criminal Appeal held that he ought not to have done so because the motoring offences carried the punishment of disqualification from driving, while the accused could not be disqualified for larceny of a motor vehicle (although an accused may now be disqualified on conviction of a similar offence).

An accused who wants an offence taken into consideration must apply to the judge personally and not merely by counsel (*R.* v. *Davis* (1943), C.C.A.). In practice, however, it is common for a list of the offences to be drawn up and the accused should then be asked by the judge whether he has received and signed this list and whether he admits the offences listed and wants them taken into consideration (*R.* v. *Nelson* (1967), C.A.).

Proving previous convictions. As we have seen, a police officer will normally give evidence of the accused's previous convictions (if any) but if the accused denies them they must be proved strictly (to the satisfaction of the judge) or ignored. Moreover, where a previous conviction is charged at the end of the indictment because it increases the maximum sentence which the court can impose (see Chap. 33) and the accused has been convicted of the offence charged, the previous conviction will be read out after the conviction and the accused will be asked whether he admits it or not. If the accused does not admit the previous conviction a jury must be sworn in to try this issue (Prevention of Crimes Act 1871, s. 9), and the conviction must be proved strictly.

There are two principal methods of proving a previous conviction strictly, under the Prevention of Crimes Act 1871, s. 18, and under the Criminal Justice Act 1948, s. 39, although by the Evidence Act 1851, s. 13, a previous conviction (or acquittal) on indictment may be proved by the production of a copy of the court record certified by the clerk of the court or other officer having custody of the records of the court, together with evidence of identity. In practice, however, it is unusual to proceed under section 13.

By the Prevention of Crimes Act 1871, s. 18, a previous conviction may be proved in any proceedings by the production of a record of such conviction and by proof that the person named in such record and the accused are the same person. In the case of a previous conviction on indictment the record should consist of a certificate containing the substance and effect of the conviction, and it should purport to be signed by the clerk of, or other officer having custody of the records of the convicting court. In the case of a previous summary conviction the record should consist of a copy of the conviction and it should purport to be signed by any magistrate having jurisdiction over the offence in respect of which the accused was previously convicted, or by the proper officer (normally the clerk) of that court, or by the clerk or other officer of any court to which such conviction has been returned. A record of any conviction made in pursuance of section 18 is admissible without proof of the signature or official character of the person appearing to have signed the same (s. 18), but it does require evidence that the person previously convicted and the accused are the same, and this proof of identity will normally be given orally, for example, by a police officer who was present in court at the time of the accused's previous conviction.

By the Criminal Justice Act 1948, s. 39, in any criminal proceedings a previous conviction may be proved against the accused by finger-print (including palm-print) evidence. This method of proof requires three certificates: one purporting to be signed by or on behalf of the Commissioner of Police of the Metropolis containing particulars relating to the previous conviction and with copies of the finger-prints of the person previously convicted annexed; a second purporting to be signed by or on behalf of the governor of a prison or remand centre in which the present accused has been detained, with the accused's finger-prints annexed; and a third purporting to be signed by or on behalf of the Commissioner of Police of the Metropolis and certifying that the finger-prints annexed to the other two certificates are of the same person (s. 39). The reason why the first and third certificates must be signed by or on behalf of the Commissioner of Police of the Metropolis is that finger-print records of all persons convicted in any part of the country are kept at New Scotland Yard. Moreover, although section 39 does not require oral evidence of identity, it can only be used when the present accused has been detained in custody. For the power of a magistrate to order a police officer to take an accused's finger-prints, see Chapter 31.

Pronouncing judgment

The judgment (including sentence) of the court is given orally by the trial judge, or chairman or recorder of quarter sessions. A court, moreover, has power to vary a sentence which it has passed so long as the court is still in session (*R.* v. *Batchelor* (1952), C.C.A.). For punishments and other methods of dealing with offenders, see Chapter 44.

Leave to appeal

If the accused has been convicted on indictment he may, after judgment, ask the trial judge for leave to appeal to the Criminal Division of the Court of Appeal on any ground of appeal which involves a question of fact alone or a question of mixed law and fact (Criminal Appeal Act 1968, s. 1). Nevertheless, in practice it is more common for an accused to apply for leave direct to the appeal court. For the whole topic of appeals, see Chapter 41.

Chapter Thirty-Nine

SUMMARY PROCEEDINGS

In Chapters 30 and 31 we discussed preliminary matters (*e.g.*, time limits: normally six months for a summary offence) and the commencement of proceedings, both in relation to trials on indictment and to summary trials. In Chapter 28 we also noticed the special rules and procedure which apply in a juvenile court.

(1) Jurisdiction to Try

The basic rule in relation to summary proceedings, like the basic rule for trial on indictment, is that the offence should normally be tried in the court for the area where the offence was committed (see the Magistrates' Courts Act 1952, s. 2(1)). Therefore, although a magistrate may issue a warrant (though not a summons) in relation to a summary offence merely on the ground that the accused resides, or is present, or is believed to reside or to be present within his area, the warrant must require the accused to be brought before a magistrates' court with jurisdiction to try the offence (see Chap. 31) and this must normally be the court of the area where the offence was committed. Nevertheless, where an offence has been committed on the boundary between two or more local jurisdictions, or within five hundred yards of a boundary, or in any harbour, river, arm of the sea or other waters lying between two or more local jurisdictions, the offence may be treated as having been committed in any of those jurisdictions (*ibid.*, s. 3(1)). Moreover, an offence begun in one court's jurisdiction and completed in another's, or committed in or on a vehicle or vessel engaged on any journey or voyage through two or more jurisdictions, may be treated as having been committed in any of those jurisdictions (*ibid.*, s. 3(2), (3)). (See also the Merchant Shipping Act 1894, s. 685: Chap. 30.)

A magistrates' court which is trying an accused for one offence also has jurisdiction to try him for any other offence, if it is a summary offence, even though it was committed elsewhere (Criminal Justice Act 1967, s. 28), and a magistrates' court has jurisdiction to try any indictable offence which is being tried summarily (see Chap. 40) whenever it would have jurisdiction as examining justices because the accused had appeared or was brought before the court (see Chap. 32) (Magistrates' Courts Act 1952, s. 2(4)). The same rule, moreover, applies if the magistrates first began to inquire into a hybrid offence as examining justices but then switched to summary trial (see Chap. 40) (*ibid.*, s. 2(4)). Further, a magistrates' court has jurisdiction to try summarily an accused, who is otherwise outside the court's jurisdiction, when it is necessary or expedient that he should be tried jointly with, or in the same place as an accused who is within the court's jurisdiction (*ibid.*, s. 2(2)).

The jurisdiction to try of a magistrates' court is, therefore, basically the same as that of assizes or quarter sessions, but a magistrates' court normally has no jurisdiction to try a summary offence merely on the basis that the accused was apprehended or is in custody within the court's area. (For the position when the accused does in fact appear before the court, see "Procedure at the trial," below.)

Ouster of jurisdiction

Although a magistrates' court may normally try any summary or hybrid offence, or any indictable offence which is triable summarily (see Chap. 40), we have seen already that a particular magistrate may not be able to try a particular case because he may be biased in that case (see Chap. 28), and there are certain other factors which may oust a magistrate's jurisdiction. Thus, the jurisdiction of a magistrates' court to try a case of assault or battery is ousted if any question arises as to the title of land or as to any bankruptcy or insolvency or execution under the process of any court (Offences against the Person Act 1861, s. 46).

Whenever it appears that any act complained of was done by the accused in the exercise of a bona fide claim of right or title to real property, the jurisdiction of the magistrates is ousted (*R. v. Holsworthy JJ., ex p. Edwards* (1952), D.C.), and the magistrates must instead hold committal proceedings with a view to the accused being tried on indictment. Nevertheless, where a statute provides that an offence may only be dealt with summarily, the magistrates' jurisdiction is not ousted (*R. v. Ogden, ex p. Long Ashton R.D.C.* (1963), D.C.). Therefore, as by definition a summary offence is an offence which a statute provides shall be tried summarily, it would seem that ouster of jurisdiction on the ground of a bona fide claim of right or title can only operate when the offence is an indictable one which is also triable summarily or a hybrid offence. Where a claim of right or title is made, the magistrates decide whether it is bona fide (*Legg* v. *Pardoe* (1860)) (as to which see further *Stone's Justices' Manual* (1969 ed.), p. 374).

An accused is also able to claim trial on indictment of certain summary offences (see Chap. 40).

(2) The Information

In Chapter 31 we saw that a summons or warrant is obtained by the laying of an information, and if an accused is tried summarily he will be tried on the information itself as recorded by the magistrate before whom the information was laid (see the Magistrates' Courts Act 1952, s. 13). Summary trial is therefore often called trial on information. Moreover, where an accused is arrested without a warrant, the police charge sheet (*i.e.*, the record of the offence with which the accused is formally charged at the police station after his arrest) is, by long custom, accepted as a sufficient information.

The information must describe the specific offence with which the accused is charged in ordinary language, avoiding as far as possible the use of technical terms, and if the offence is statutory it must state the relevant section and statute, or rule, regulation or bye-law (Magistrates' Courts Rules 1968, r. 83). An information, moreover, unlike an indictment, must charge only one offence (*ibid.*, r. 12(1): *Edwards* v. *Jones* (1947) (see also "Alternative methods of committing an offence," Chap. 33, because the law in relation to charging one offence in a count in an indictment is basically the same: *Ware* v. *Fox*; *Fox* v. *Dingley* (1967), D.C.), although if an information does charge two or more offences the prosecution may choose on which charge it will proceed and the others are struck out, provided this is done before the trial commences (*Hargreaves* v. *Alderson* (1964), D.C.: where the trial was a nullity because, although the accused was only charged at the trial with one offence, the information charged him with three offences, and the other two had not been struck out before the trial commenced). Nevertheless, again unlike trial on indictment, two or more informations may be tried together provided the accused consents (*Brangwynne* v. *Evans* (1962), D.C.: where the trial was a nullity because the magistrates tried the accused concurrently on three informations without his consent).

Several accused may be joined in the same information and be tried together when the offence charged is one in which several persons may participate; for example, trespass and assault (*Paul* v. *Summerhayes* (1878), D.C.: a case of assault). In *Macphail* v. *Jones*

(1914), D.C., a husband and wife were jointly charged in the same information with knowingly making a false representation as to their means.

(3) Summary Trial

Appearance of the parties

Where an accused does not appear in answer to a summons at a summary trial, or plead guilty by post (see below), the court may either (unlike committal proceedings) proceed in his absence (*i.e.*, by entering a plea of not guilty on his behalf) or adjourn the trial (Magistrates' Courts Act 1952, s. 15, as amended). Moreover, if the offence charged is punishable with imprisonment and the trial is adjourned, the court may issue a warrant for the accused's arrest provided that the information was substantiated on oath (*ibid.*, s. 15(2), as amended by the Criminal Justice Act 1967, s. 24(2)). Nevertheless, the court cannot proceed to try the accused in his absence nor issue a warrant for his arrest unless it is proved to the satisfaction of the court that the summons was served on the accused within a reasonable time before the trial (Magistrates' Courts Act 1952, s. 15(3)): the magistrates themselves being the judges of whether it was served a reasonable time before the trial (*Ex p. Williams* (1851)). Further, if the court does begin to try the accused in his absence, the proceedings (though not the information) will be void if the accused, at any time during or after the trial, makes a statutory declaration that he did not know of the summons or the proceedings until a specified date which is after the trial began, and the declaration is served on the magistrates' clerk within fourteen days of that date (Criminal Justice Act 1967, s. 24(3)). In practice an accused will not be tried in his absence except in minor cases where his absence is explained (see *R.* v. *Smith* (1875)).

Service of a summons on an individual accused may be effected (*a*) by delivering it to the person to whom it is directed; or (*b*) by leaving it for him with some person at his last known or usual place of abode; or (*c*) by sending it by post in a registered letter (or by recorded delivery service) addressed to him at his last known or usual place of abode (Magistrates' Courts Rules 1968, r. 82(1)). Nevertheless, if the offence is an indictable or hybrid offence and the accused does not appear at the summary trial, service of a summons under (*b*) or (*c*) cannot be treated as proved unless it is also proved that the summons actually came to his knowledge (*ibid.*, r. 82(2). There are also certain restrictions on the service of a summons on a Sunday (see Sunday Observance Act 1677, s. 6).

If the accused is a corporation, service of a summons is effected by delivering it at, or sending it by post to, the registered office of the corporation, or if there is no such office in England and Wales, to any place in England and Wales where the corporation trades or conducts its business (*ibid.*, r. 82(3)).

Where the accused, but not the prosecutor, appears at a summary trial the court may dismiss the information or adjourn the trial, or, if evidence has been received on a previous occasion (*i.e.*, the trial has previously been adjourned and this is the adjourned hearing), proceed in the absence of the prosecutor (Magistrates' Courts Act 1952, s. 16). Where neither the accused nor the prosecutor appears, the court may dismiss the information or, if evidence has been received on a previous occasion, proceed in their absence (*ibid.*, s. 17).

Both the accused and the prosecutor may, however, be represented by counsel or a solicitor, and if their counsel or solicitor is present at a summary trial they are deemed to be present unless their personal presence is required by any enactment or any condition of a recognizance (Magistrates' Courts Act 1952, s. 99). Nevertheless, unlike a trial on indictment (*R.* v. *Brice* (1819)), the prosecutor as well as the accused may appear in person and may examine the witnesses and address the court (see *Duncan* v. *Toms* (1887), D.C.).

Adjournment of the trial

A magistrates' court may at any time, whether before or after beginning a summary trial, adjourn the trial (Magistrates' Courts Act 1952, s. 14(1)). When adjourning, the court may either fix the time and place at which the trial is to be resumed, or, unless the accused is actually remanded in custody or on bail, it may leave the time and place to be notified to him later by the court (*ibid.*, s. 14(2)). Unlike committal proceedings (see Chap. 32) the magistrates may, therefore, adjourn a summary trial without formally remanding the accused, although it may remand the accused if it wishes. Nevertheless, if the magistrates are trying an indictable offence summarily, or the magistrates are trying a hybrid offence after first beginning committal proceedings (see Chap. 40) they must formally remand (*ibid.*, s. 14(4)). For the power to adjourn after conviction, see below.

Where the magistrates do adjourn a summary trial and remand an accused who has attained the age of seventeen, they must normally remand him on bail provided (1) the offence is a summary offence (which is not also an indictable offence) and is punishable with not more than six months' imprisonment (Criminal Justice

Act 1967, s. 18(1)), or (2) he is being tried summarily for a hybrid offence which is punishable on summary conviction with not more than six months' imprisonment, or (3) he is being tried summarily for an indictable offence (see Chap. 40 (*ibid.*, s. 18(2)). Nevertheless, by section 18(4), the court need not remand the accused on bail if he fails to give a proper recognizance or to produce sufficient and satisfactory sureties nor, by section 18(5), (*a*) where the offence charged is punishable on summary conviction with not less than six months imprisonment and he has been previously sentenced to imprisonment or borstal training; nor (*b*) where he has previously been released on bail and he failed to comply with the conditions of a recognizance entered into by him on that occasion; nor (*c*) where he is charged with an offence alleged to have been committed while he was released on bail; nor (*d*) where it appears to the court that it is necessary to detain him to establish his identity or address; nor (*e*) where he has no fixed abode or he is ordinarily resident outside the United Kingdom; nor (*f*) where the act or any of the acts constituting the offence charged consisted of an assault on or threat of violence to another person, or of having or possessing a firearm, an imitation firearm, an explosive or an offensive weapon. or of indecent conduct with or towards a person under the age of sixteen years; nor (*g*) where it appears to the court that unless he is remanded in custody he is likely to commit an offence; nor (*h*) where it appears to the court necessary for his own protection to refuse to remand him on bail. (For the whole topic of bail see Chap. 43.)

Attendance of witnesses

The attendance of a witness before a magistrates' court (whether for a summary trial or committal proceedings) may be secured by a witness summons (Magistrates' Courts Act 1952, s. 77). If a magistrate is satisfied that any person is likely to be able to give material evidence, or produce any document or thing likely to be material evidence, and that that person will not voluntarily attend as a witness or produce the document or thing, the magistrate will issue a summons directed to that person requiring him to attend at a stated time and place (*ibid.*, s. 77(1)). Moreover, if a magistrate is satisfied by evidence on oath that a summons would not procure the attendance of the witness, the magistrate may instead issue a warrant to arrest that witness and to bring him before the court (*ibid.*, s. 77(2)). Further, if, in any proceedings, a witness fails to obey a summons and it is proved on oath that he has been served with the summons and that a reasonable sum has been paid or tendered to him for costs and expenses, the court may issue a warrant for arrest (*ibid.*, s. 77(3)).

Procedure at the trial

The plea. If the accused has appeared, the court will state to him the substance of the information and will ask him whether he pleads guilty or not guilty (Magistrates' Courts Act 1952, s. 13(1)). Apart, however, from the power to plead guilty or not guilty (see below) the accused may raise a previous acquittal or conviction as a bar to the summary trial (*Halsted* v. *Clark* (1944), D.C., *Wemyss* v. *Hopkins* (1875)). Although this will not technically be a plea of *autrefois acquit* or *convict* (as these pleas only apply to trials on indictment), the basis of the bar and the necessary test as to whether it applies are the same (see Lord Goddard C.J., in *Flatman* v. *Light* (1946), D.C. (see Chap. 35)). For the court's power to make a hospital or guardianship order on the ground of the accused's mental condition without convicting the accused, see Chapter 44.

The mere fact that the accused has appeared before the court does not give the court jurisdiction to try the offence (*Johnson* v. *Colam* (1875), D.C.), but if the court does have jurisdiction (see above) and the accused does appear, the court may try the case even though the accused's presence was procured by an invalid summons or warrant (*R.* v. *Hughes* (1879), C.C.R.), at least if the accused does not object to the validity of the summons or warrant at the trial itself (*Dixon* v. *Wells* (1890), D.C.). Moreover, if the accused has appeared he cannot prevent the magistrates trying the case by showing any defect in substance or form in the information, or in the summons or warrant, or any variance between the information, etc., and the prosecution's evidence (Magistrates' Courts Act 1952, s. 100 (1)). Nevertheless, if the accused has been misled by the variance, the court must, on his application, adjourn the hearing (*ibid.*, s. 100(2)), and an accused cannot be tried on an information which charges the wrong offence (*Atterton* v. *Browne* (1945), D.C.). Indeed, whenever the defect is more than a technical defect the information must be amended before the trial begins (*Hunter* v. *Coombs* (1962), D.C.), the magistrates having power at common law to amend an information (see *Halsted* v. *Clark, supra*).

If the accused pleads guilty the court may convict him without hearing evidence (Magistrates' Courts Act 1952, s. 13(3)), although the court may still hear evidence if it so desires, for example, where the prosecution allege that the offence was committted in circumstances of aggravation. Once the magistrates have accepted an unequivocal plea of guilty (*e.g.*, by the entry of the conviction in the court's records or by the adjournment of the case so that inquiries may be made as to the most suitable method of dealing with the accused) they are *functi officio* and they cannot thereafter allow the accused to change his plea to one of not guilty (*R*. v. *Cambell, ex p. Hoy* (1953), D.C.; *R*. v. *Guest, ex p. Anthony* (1964), D.C.). If the plea is not unequivocal, however, the magistrates should only accept a provisional plea of guilty, and they should defer final acceptance until they have seen whether in fact the accused intended to plead guilty to the offence charged (*R*. v. *Blandford JJ., ex p. G.* (1967), D.C.). (For sentencing, see below.)

If the accused pleads not guilty, the prosecution's evidence will be called (Magistrates' Courts Rules 1968, r. 13(1)).

Prosecution's case. Before the prosecution's evidence the prosecutor may address the court (Magistrates' Courts Rules 1968, r. 13(1)). Therefore, after a plea of not guilty, a summary trial will normally continue by the prosecutor addressing the court and reveiwing the case against the accused; then the prosecution's evidence will be called. (For the examination of witnesses, see Chap. 37.)

No case to answer. At the conclusion of the prosecution's evidence the defence may submit that there is no case to answer and if the submission is accepted, the accused must be found not guilty. A submission may properly be made, and be upheld by the magistrates: (*a*) when there has been no evidence to prove an essential element in the alleged offence; or (*b*) when the evidence adduced by the prosecution has been so discredited as a result of cross-examination, or is so manifestly unreliable, that no reasonable court could safely convict upon it. Apart from these two situations, however, a magistrates' court should not in general be called upon to reach a decision as to conviction or acquittal until the whole of both sides' evidence has been placed before it, and if a submission is made the question for the magistrates is not whether they would at that stage convict or acquit but whether the evidence is such that a reasonable court might convict; if so, there is a case to answer (*Practice Direction (Submission of No Case)* (1962)). If a submission is made but rejected, the defence may then proceed to call defence evidence (*Jones* v. *Metcalfe* (1967), D.C.).

Defence case and final speeches. The defence will normally address the magistrates only once, but it may do so (at its option) either before or after the defence evidence (Magistrates' Courts Rules 1968, r. 13). Moreover, the prosecutor will not normally address the court a second time, his only address coming, as we have seen, before the prosecution's evidence is adduced. Nevertheless, in any case, either the defence or the prosecutor may be granted leave by the magistrates to address the court a second time, but where the magistrates do grant leave to one party they cannot refuse leave to the other (*ibid.*, r. 13(5)). If both the defence and the prosecutor do make two speeches, the prosecutor's second speech will come immediately before the defence's second speech (*ibid.*, r. 13(6)) or, if the prosecutor alone makes two speeches, his second speech will come immediately after the defence evidence and before the defence speech if, as is likely, it is made at this time.

Although the magistrates may allow the defence to address the court both before and after the defence evidence, they need not decide whether to grant leave until after that evidence. The defence, therefore, may have to decide whether or not to address the magistrates before the defence evidence without knowing whether, if they do so, they will be allowed to address the court a second time.

The magistrates have power, moreover, to allow the prosecution to call rebutting evidence at the conclusion of the evidence, if any, for the defence (*ibid.*, r. 13(3)), but in practice this will only be allowed when the defence disclosed evidence which no human ingenuity could have foreseen (*R.* v. *Day* (1940), C.C.A.; *Price* v. *Humphries* (1958), D.C.) (for the similar position at a trial on indictment, see Chap. 37). Apart from the magistrates' power to admit rebutting evidence, the court also has a residuary discretion to allow the prosecution to call additional evidence after it has closed its case, but in practice it rarely does so (see, *e.g.*, *Middleton* v. *Rowlett* (1954), D.C.). In the absence of special circumstances the magistrates must not, in fact, allow additional evidence to be called once they have retired to consider their verdict, and probably not after the defence has closed its case (*Webb* v. *Leadbetter* (1966), D.C.).

Verdict. After the evidence and speeches the magistrates decide whether the accused is guilty or not guilty and they normally retire from open court in order to do so (for the procedure when they desire advice on a point of law, see Chap. 28). The decision may be by a majority but (as in committal proceedings), if the magistrates are equally divided, the chairman has no casting vote; they may instead agree to acquit the accused or adjourn the case for a rehearing before a reconstituted court (*Bagg* v. *Colquhoun* (1904), D.C.). Magistrates, moreover, have no general power to convict an accused of another offence by way of alternative verdict (*Lawrence* v. *Same* (1968), D.C.). Once the magistrates have convicted the accused they are *functi officio*, and they cannot thereafter cancel their conviction and adjourn the hearing for another trial (*R.* v. *Manchester JJ., ex p. Lever* (1937), D.C.).

Sentence. If the magistrates do convict the accused (including those cases where he pleaded guilty) they will proceed to sentence him. Nevertheless, before sentencing the accused, the magistrates may adjourn the case for the purpose of enquiries being made or of determining the most suitable method of dealing with him, provided the adjournment is for not more than four weeks (or three weeks if the accused is remanded in custody) at a time (Magistrates' Courts Act 1952, s. 14(3), as amended by the Criminal Justice Act 1967, s. 30). The magistrates also have a similar power to adjourn a case, provided they also remand the accused, when the offence is punishable on summary conviction with imprisonment and the court is satisfied that the accused did the act or made the omission charged, but is of opinion that an inquiry ought to be made into his physical or mental condition before the method of dealing with him is determined (Magistrates' Courts Act 1952, s. 26(1), as amended by the Criminal Justice Act 1967, s. 30).

We have already seen that if the magistrates do adjourn a summary trial and remand the accused they must normally remand him on bail, and the same rule applies even if he is remanded after conviction. Nevertheless, the magistrates should not remand on bail if they have adjourned the case under section 26 of the Magistrates' Courts Act 1952 and it would be impracticable to obtain a medical report unless the accused were remanded in custody (Criminal Justice Act 1967, s. 18(6)). Where the trial has been adjourned after conviction and the accused does not appear at the adjourned hearing the court should not issue a warrant for his arrest unless (*a*) the offence is punishable with imprisonment, or (*b*) the court proposes to impose a disqualification on him (*ibid.*, s. 24(2)). (See also the Magistrates' Courts Act 1952, s. 15(2).) A magistrates' court cannot, however, sentence an accused in his absence to imprisonment or detention in a detention centre, or order that a suspended sentence should take effect (see Chap. 44), and it cannot disqualify an accused in his absence, unless the trial was adjourned after conviction and the notice of resumption (under the Magistrates' Courts Act 1952, s. 14(2)) stated the reason for the adjournment (Criminal Justice Act 1967, s. 26). Although the magistrates before whom any proceedings take place must be present during the whole of the proceedings (except that a magistrate may, during the proceedings, cease to act, provided that a sufficient number remains) (Magistrates' Courts Act 1952, s. 98(6)), where a trial is adjourned after conviction but before sentence the sentencing court need not be composed of the same magistrates (*ibid.*, s. 98(7)).

Before the accused is sentenced, the prosecution may adduce

evidence of his background and previous convictions and the defence may call evidence as to his character and make a plea in mitigation of sentence. The accused may also ask the magistrates to take into consideration other offences committed by him, over which the court has jurisdiction. (For the similar procedure at a trial on indictment, see Chap. 38.) If the accused is convicted of a summary offence in his absence, other than in a juvenile court, the court may take into account any of his previous convictions of summary offences provided that notice of this was served upon him not less than seven days before the conviction (*ibid.*, s. 3). Even if the magistrates, following a proper hearing, pass an invalid sentence they are *functi officio* and they cannot then substitute a proper sentence; though this could be done by a Divisional Court on an application for certiorari (see Chap. 42) (*R.* v. *Uxbridge JJ., ex p. Clark* (1968), D.C.). For punishments and other methods of dealing with offenders, see Chapter 44. For the power of magistrates to commit an accused in certain cases to quarter sessions for sentence, see below.

(4) Committal to Assizes or Quarter Sessions

With a view to Borstal training

A sentence of Borstal training, which is a form of custodial training, may be passed on an offender who is not less than fifteen years but under twenty-one years. The meaning of Borstal training and the circumstances in which it may be imposed will be dealt with in Chapter 44.

Committal by the magistrates

A magistrates' court has no power to sentence an offender to Borstal training but where an accused is convicted by a magistrates' court of an offence punishable on summary conviction with imprisonment then, if on the day of conviction he is not less than fifteen but under twenty-one years and he is an offender who, under the Criminal Justice Act 1961, s. 1(2), may be sentenced to Borstal training (see Chap. 44), the court may commit him either in custody or on bail to quarter sessions for sentence (Magistrates' Courts Act 1952, s. 28(1), as amended by the Criminal Justice Act 1961 and the Criminal Justice Act 1967, s. 20). The section applies to all offences tried summarily (whether summary, indictable or hybrid), and an offence is "punishable with imprisonment" would it have been had the accused been over twenty-one. (For the alternative, but somewhat similar, power to commit under section 29 of the Magistrates'

Courts Act 1952 when an offender over seventeen years has been convicted summarily of an indictable offence, see Chap. 40.)

Powers of quarter sessions

Where an offender is committed to quarter sessions under section 28, quarter sessions will inquire into the circumstances of the case and it may either (i) sentence him to Borstal training, or (ii) deal with him in any manner in which the magistrates might have dealt with him (Criminal Justice Act 1948, s. 20(5), as amended). Quarter sessions, therefore, need not necessarily follow the recommendation of the magistrates and sentence the accused to Borstal training, and it will reconsider the suitability of such training in relation to the accused and the offence of which he was convicted. If quarter sessions does not sentence the accused to Borstal training, however, it may only deal with him as the magistrates could have done at the time of committal to quarter sessions (*R.* v. *Hammond* (1963), C.C.A.: where an accused, who was aged sixteen at the time of committal, had turned seventeen, but quarter sessions could only sentence him as if he were sixteen). Even though quarter sessions sentences the accused to Borstal training it may, or must, also exercise any other power or duty, which the magistrates could, or should, have exercised, had they not committed the accused to quarter sessions, for example, any power or duty to disqualify the accused from driving (Criminal Justice Act 1967, s. 56(5), (6)). Nevertheless, in such cases, the magistrates may order the accused to be disqualified from driving until quarter sessions can deal with him (*ibid.*, s. 56(8)).

Appeals

Even though the magistrates committed the accused to quarter sessions for sentence, any appeal against conviction will lie in the manner normal after conviction by a magistrates' court (see Chap. 41). For the special rules as to appeals against sentence, see also Chapter 41.

Order restricting the offender's discharge

Where an offender is convicted by a magistrates' court of an offence punishable on summary conviction with imprisonment and the court is satisfied that he is suffering from mental disorder which warrants his detention in a hospital for mental treatment, the court may make an order for his detention in a specified hospital (Mental Health Act 1959, s. 60(1): see also Chap. 44). Unlike assizes and quarter sessions, however, a magistrates' court has no power to order restrictions on the release of such an offender from the hospital, but, in the case of an offender over fourteen years, if it appears to the court that if a hospital order is made an order restricting his discharge should also be made, the magistrates' court, instead of making an order under section 60(1), may commit him in custody to quarter sessions (*ibid.*, s. 67(1)). Quarter sessions should then inquire into the circumstances of the case and may (*a*) make a hospital order, with or without an order restricting his discharge; or (*b*) otherwise deal with him in any other manner in which the magistrates' court might have dealt with him (*ibid.*, s. 67(3)). For the special rules as to appeals against sentence, see Chapter 41.

Incorrigible rogue

If an accused is convicted by a magistrates' court of the summary offence of being an incorrigible rogue (see Chap. 26), he should be committed to quarter sessions, either in custody or on bail (Vagrancy Act 1824, s. 5, as amended by the Criminal Justice Act 1967, s. 20). The magistrates themselves have no power to sentence an accused for being an incorrigible rogue. Quarter sessions may then sentence the accused to imprisonment for any period not exceeding one year (Vagrancy Act 1824, s. 10, as amended; see *R*. v. *Walters* (1969), C.A.).

Although appeal against a conviction for being an incorrigible rogue lies in the manner normal after conviction by a magistrates' court (see *R*. v. *Johnson* (1909), C.C.A.), any appeal against sentence lies to the Criminal Division of the Court of Appeal because the sentence of necessity must be one which the magistrates had not power to pass (see the Criminal Appeal Act 1968, s. 10(3) and Chap. 41).

Conjunctive convictions

Where a magistrates' court is committing an accused to quarter sessions with a view to Borstal training, or for an order restricting his discharge, or as an incorrigible rogue, or for sentence after he has been convicted summarily of an indictable offence (see Chap. 40), or because he has been convicted of an offence while released on licence (see Chap. 44), or the court is committing him to either assizes or quarter sessions because he has committed a further offence while on probation or during the operational period of a suspended sentence (see Chap. 44), then the magistrates' court may also commit the accused to that court of assize or quarter sessions (1) to be dealt with in respect of another offence of which he has been convicted by the magistrates' court and which is punishable with imprisonment or which is an offence in respect of which the court has a power or duty to order him to be disqualified from driving (under s. 5 of the

Road Traffic Act 1962) or (2) to be dealt with in respect of a suspended sentence, even though that sentence could be dealt with by the magistrates' court (under s. 41(1) of the Criminal Justice Act 1967: see Chap. 44) because it was originally passed by a magistrates' court (Criminal Justice Act 1967, s. 56). Where the magistrates have power to commit an accused to assizes to be dealt with in respect of one offence and they also have power to commit him to quarter sessions to be dealt with in respect of another offence, they must, if they commit him in respect of both offences, commit to quarter sessions (*ibid.*, s. 56(7)). If the magistrates do commit an accused to assizes or quarter sessions under section 56, they may commit him in custody or on bail, as the case may require (*ibid.*, s. 56(1)).

Where an accused has been committed to a court of assize or quarter sessions under section 56, that court may, after inquiring into the circumstances of the case, deal with him in any way in which the magistrates' court might have dealt with him (*ibid.*, s. 56(5)). The court of assize or quarter sessions will exercise any power or duty which otherwise the magistrates could, or should, have exercised (*ibid.*, s. 56(5)), but the magistrates, in such cases, may order that an accused be disqualified from driving until the assizes or quarter sessions has dealt with him (*ibid.*, s. 56(8)).

(5) Pleading Guilty by Post

Although, as we have seen, an accused may be tried summarily in his absence (the court entering a plea of not guilty on his behalf), an accused could not plead guilty in his absence before the Magistrates' Courts Act 1957 (see *John* v. *Humphreys* (1955), D.C.). By section 1 of that Act, however, where a summons is issued requiring an accused to appear before a magistrates' court, other than a juvenile court, to answer to an information for a summary offence, the accused may be given the option of pleading guilty by post. The procedure is, in fact, very widely used, particularly with motoring offences. Nevertheless, an accused cannot be given the option of pleading guilty by post if the offence with which he is charged is also triable on indictment (*e.g.*, a hybrid offence), nor if the offence is one for which he will be liable to be sentenced to imprisonment for a term exceeding three months (whether or not he will be able to claim trial by jury in respect of the offence: see Chap. 40) (*ibid.*, s. 1(1)).

If the prosecutor is prepared to give the accused the option of pleading guilty by post, the prosecutor must serve on the accused with the summons (i) a notice informing the accused that he may plead guilty and setting out particulars of the procedure that will be followed if he does so (in accordance with forms prescribed by the Magistrates' Courts (Forms) Rules 1968); and (ii) a concise statement in the form prescribed of such facts relating to the charge as will be placed before the court by or on behalf of the prosecutor if the accused does plead guilty without appearing before the court (*ibid.*, s. 1(1)). The prosecutor must also inform the clerk of the magistrates' court that the documents set out above have been served upon the accused (*ibid.*, s. 1(1)).

If the accused is given the option and he does notify the clerk of the magistrates' court that he desires to plead guilty without appearing, the clerk must inform the prosecutor, and if at the trial the accused does not appear and it is proved to the satisfaction of the court that the appropriate notice and statement of facts were served upon him, the court may then either (*a*) proceed to hear and dispose of the case in his absence, whether or not the prosecutor is also absent; or (*b*) adjourn the trial for the purpose of dealing with the case as if the accused had not been given the option of pleading guilty by post (*ibid.*, s. 1(2)). Even though an accused does notify the clerk that he desires to plead guilty by post, he may withdraw that notification at any time before the trial (*ibid.*, 1(2) (i)). Moreover, as we have seen, this procedure for accepting a plea of guilty is conditional on the accused actually being absent at the time of the trial. If the accused is present in the court after all (though possibly not if he is merely present in the public gallery) the court cannot proceed to deal with him under this provision.

If the magistrates do accept a plea of guilty by post, the court must not permit any statement to be made by or on behalf of the prosecutor with respect to any facts relating to the offence charged other than the statement of facts which was served upon the accused with the summons (Magistrates' Courts Act 1957, s. 1(2) (ii)). Similarly the accused, when informed that he may plead guilty by post, must be told that he may send to the court, with notification of his plea, a written statement setting out any mitigating circumstances which he wishes to put before the court, and if he does send a statement in mitigation this must be read out before the court (*ibid.*, s. 1(2) (ii)). These provisions, moreover, must be complied with strictly, so that the prosecutor's statement of the facts and the accused's statement in mitigation must actually be read out before the court (normally by the clerk) and must not be passed to the magistrates for them to read for themselves (*R. v. Oldham JJ., ex p. Morrissey* (1958), D.C.). By this procedure it will be clear that these statements, and only these statements, have been brought to the court's attention, for no further evidence or statement on behalf of the prosecution case can be called or made, unless the trial is adjourned (*ibid.*, s. 1(2) (iii); *R.* v. *Norham and Islandshire JJ., ex p. Sunter Bros. Ltd.* (1961), D.C.). The whole of the accused's statement in mitigation must, moreover, be read out.

We have seen already that a magistrates' court cannot sentence an accused in his absence to imprisonment or detention in a detention centre or order that a suspended sentence should take effect and that it cannot disqualify an accused in his absence unless the trial was adjourned after conviction and the notice of resumption stated the reason for the adjournment (Criminal Justice Act 1967, s. 26). If, therefore, an accused pleads guilty by post, the court cannot sentence him to imprisonment, etc., but it can adjourn the trial after the plea of guilty has been accepted and recorded (see above) and, at the resumed hearing, an additional statement may be made on behalf of the prosecution and, provided the accused is present, the court may, *inter alia*, sentence him to imprisonment; etc. (although it may then disqualify him in his absence (see above). The accused must, however, be given adequate notice of the time and place of the adjourned hearing (Magistrates' Courts Act 1952, s. 14(2)) and the notice must specify (if it is so) that the reason for the adjournment is to enable a sentence of imprisonment, etc., to be imposed, if its imposition is found to be necessary or appropriate (*R.* v. *Mason* (1965)). For the court's power to issue a warrant for the arrest of the accused if he does not appear at the adjourned hearing and the offence is punishable with imprisonment, etc., see "Sentence" above.

We have seen already under "Verdict," above, the power of a magistrates' court, in the absence of the accused, to take into account the fact that he has previously been convicted of a summary offence.

Chapter Forty

ALTERNATIVE METHODS OF TRIAL

(1) Summary Trial of Indictable Offences

ALTHOUGH, as a general rule, an indictable offence will be tried on indictment, it may sometimes be tried summarily.

Indictable offences which may be tried summarily

Children. Where the accused is a child (*i.e.*, under fourteen years) any indictable offence with which he is charged, except homicide, must be tried summarily (normally in a juvenile court); provided that if he is charged jointly with an accused who is over fourteen the magistrates may commit them both for trial jointly, and the child must then be tried by whichever court is trying the other accused (Magistrates' Courts Act 1952, s. 21(1)). (For the power to remit to a juvenile court for sentence, see Chap. 28.) If the offence charged is homicide it must always be tried on indictment (*i.e.*, at assizes).

Young persons. Where the accused is a young person (*i.e.*, aged fourteen but under seventeen), any indictable offence with which he is charged, except homicide, may be tried summarily (normally in a juvenile court) (Magistrates' Courts Act 1952, s. 20(1)).

Adults. Where the accused is an adult (*i.e.*, he has attained seventeen years) and he is charged with an indictable offence, he may only be tried summarily if that offence is one which is specified in the First Schedule to the Magistrates' Courts Act 1952, as amended, for example, theft, handling stolen goods, obtaining property by deception, obtaining a pecuniary advantage by deception, abandoning or exposing a child, concealing the birth of a child and burglary (provided that the offence committed or intended in the building was itself triable summarily and that, if the offence was committed in a dwelling, entry was not obtained by force or deception or by the use of any tool, key or appliance or any person in the dwelling

301

was subjected to violence or the threat of violence: Theft Act 1968, s. 29). (See also Appendix II.)

Procedure for determining method of trial

Children. If the accused is a child the magistrates usually have no option; unless the offence charged is homicide, the accused must normally be tried summarily, and if the offence is homicide he must be tried on indictment (see above).

Adults. When an adult is charged with an indictable offence which may be tried summarily (see above), and it appears to the magistrates, having regard to any representations made in the presence of the accused by the prosecutor or made by the accused, and to the nature of the case, that the punishment that the court will have power to inflict (*i.e.*, imprisonment for a term not exceeding six months or a fine not exceeding £400 or both: Magistrates' Courts Act 1952, s. 19(6), as amended by the Criminal Justice Act 1967, s. 43(1)) will be adequate, and that the circumstances do not make the offence one of serious character and do not for other reasons require trial on indictment, the magistrates may proceed with a view to summary trial (Magistrates' Courts Act 1952, s. 19(2)). (If the court is not properly constituted for a summary trial it may adjourn and remand the accused, even for a period exceeding eight clear days: *ibid.*, s. 105(4) (*c*).) In practice the magistrates normally accede to any representation for summary trial made by the prosecution, but they need not do so (*R. v. Bodmin JJ., ex p. McEwen* (1947), D.C.).

If the magistrates are proceeding with a view to trying an indictable offence summarily, they must cause the charge to be written down, if this has not already been done, to be read to the accused, and they must tell him that he may, if he consents, be tried summarily instead of by a jury (*ibid.*, s. 19(3)). If the magistrates also think it desirable for his information, they should tell him before what court he would be tried if tried by jury, and explain what is meant by being tried summarily (*ibid.*, s. 19(3)). Moreover, the court must explain to the accused that if he consents to summary trial and he is convicted he may be committed to quarter sessions for sentence (see below) if the court, on obtaining information as to his character and antecedents, is of the opinion that they are such that greater punishment should be inflicted than the court has power to inflict (*ibid.*, s. 19(4), as amended). Failure to inform the accused of this power to commit to quarter sessions for sentence renders the proceedings void (*R. v. Kent JJ., ex p. Machin* (1952), D.C.).

It is a cardinal rule of evidence that a court must not normally know of an accused's character and previous convictions until after conviction, so that the magistrates must decide whether they are willing that he should be tried summarily without knowing of these matters. Section 19(4) then provides a procedure for dealing with an accused whose record turns out to be worse than the magistrates anticipated. Nevertheless, in cases of a serious character, the magistrates ought to refuse to try the case summarily rather than rely on their power to commit to quarter sessions for sentence (*per* Lord Goddard C.J. in *R.* v. *Norfolk JJ., ex p. Director of Public Prosecutions* (1950), D.C.).

After the accused has been informed of his right to insist on trial by jury, and of the power of magistrates to commit to quarter sessions for sentence, the court must ask him whether he wishes to be tried by a jury or consents to being tried summarily: only if he does consent to summary trial can a summary trial be held (*ibid.*, s. 19(5)). Although the consent of the prosecutor is not normally required (though he may make representations, see above), his consent is required if he is the Director of Public Prosecutions or the case is one which affects the property or affairs of the Queen or of a local authority (*ibid.*, s. 19(7)).

If the magistrates do not begin to try the indictable offence summarily they must conduct committal proceedings with a view to committing the accused for trial by jury. Nevertheless, the magistrates may change to a summary trial at any stage of the committal proceedings if they are satisfied that the requirements of section 19(2) (see above) apply and that the accused (and if necessary the prosecutor) has given consent (*ibid.*, s. 19(2)). If the magistrates do change to a summary trial, any evidence given at the committal proceedings (other than written statements admissible under s. 2 of the Criminal Justice Act 1967: s. 2(9)) shall be deemed to have been given in and for the purposes of the summary trial (Magistrates' Courts Act 1952, s. 23), but the court must recall the witnesses for cross-examination, unless they are not required by either the accused or the prosecutor (Magistrates' Courts Rules 1968, r. 19). Alternatively, if the magistrates begin to try an indictable offence summarily, the court may, at any time before the conclusion of the case for the prosecution, discontinue the summary trial and hold committal proceedings (Criminal Justice Administration Act 1962, s. 13).

Young persons. When a young person is charged with an indictable offence which may be tried summarily (*i.e.*, any indictable offence except homicide, see above), and it appears to the magistrates expedient to do so, having regard to any representations made in the presence of the accused by the prosecutor or made by the accused, and to the nature of the offence and the circumstances of the case, they may proceed with a view to summary trial (Magistrates' Courts Act 1952, s. 20(2)). As these provisions are wider than for an adult accused, the magistrates should be more inclined to agree to the summary trial of a young person than of an adult.

The rest of the procedure for determining whether a young person should be tried summarily for an indictable offence is the same as for an adult, except that a young person cannot be committed to quarter sessions for sentence, so that no question of him being told of such power can arise. (For the power to remit to a juvenile court for sentence, see Chap. 28.)

Corporations. Where a corporation is charged with an indictable offence which, in the case of an adult, may be tried summarily and the corporation appears by means of a representative, the representative must consent to summary trial (Magistrates' Courts Act 1952, Sched. 2, para. 3). Where a representative does not appear, however, the consent of the corporation to summary trial is not required (*ibid.*, Sched. 2, para. 5). Nevertheless, if the corporation is charged jointly with an individual, the magistrates cannot try either of them summarily unless each of them consents to summary trial (*ibid.*, Sched. 2, para. 9).

Summary trial

The procedure at the summary trial of an indictable offence (whether the accused is an adult, a young person or a child) is basically the same as when the offence is a summary offence: though we have seen that in the case of an adult or young person the magistrates have power to discontinue the summary trial and commence committal proceedings. If the magistrates at the summary trial of an indictable offence dismiss the charge, the dismissal has the same effect as an acquittal on indictment (Magistrates' Courts Act 1952, s. 22). Thus, the accused will be able to plead *autrefois acquit* if he is subsequently charged with an offence of which he could have been convicted by way of alternative verdict if he had been tried on indictment (*R.* v. *Gardner* (1965); though see Ch. 39 for the inability to convict by way of alternative verdict at a summary trial). As we have seen, if the magistrates convict an adult summarily of an indictable offence, he may be sentenced to imprisonment for a term not exceeding six months or a fine not exceeding £400, or both (*ibid.*, s. 19(6), as amended). If an adult is convicted summarily of two or more indictable offences the court may sentence him to consecutive terms of imprisonment, but the aggregate of the terms so imposed must not exceed twelve months (*ibid.*, s. 108(2)). A child or young person cannot be sentenced to imprisonment (see Chap. 44), but if a young person is convicted summarily of an indictable offence the court may (*a*) exercise the same powers as it could have exercised had he been convicted of an offence which was punishable with imprisonment for a term not exceeding three months; or (*b*) impose a fine not exceeding £50 (*ibid.*, s. 20(5)). If a child is convicted summarily of an indictable offence the magistrates have power, in addition to their other powers, to impose a fine (*ibid.*, s. 21(2)).

Committal to quarter sessions for sentence

Where the magistrates convict an adult summarily of an indictable offence then, if on obtaining information about his character and antecedents the court is of opinion that they are such that greater punishment should be inflicted than the court has power to inflict (see above), the court may commit him in custody or on bail to quarter sessions for sentence (Magistrates' Courts Act 1952, s. 29, as amended by the Criminal Justice Act 1967, s. 20). A magistrates' court has no power, however, to commit a corporation to quarter sessions for sentence (Magistrates' Courts Act 1952, Sched. 2, para. 7).

Where an accused is committed to quarter sessions for sentence under section 29, quarter sessions must inquire into the circumstances of the case, and may then deal with the accused in any manner in which he could be dealt with if he had just been convicted on indictment (Criminal Justice Act 1948, s. 29, as amended). Quarter sessions, moreover, must exercise or discharge any power or duty which the magistrates could, or should, have exercised had they not committed the accused under section 29 (*e.g.*, disqualifying him from driving) (Criminal Justice Act 1967, s. 56).

As quarter sessions may deal with an accused committed under section 29 as if he had been convicted on indictment, its powers are wider than if he had been committed under section 28 (*i.e.*, with a view to Borstal training), for in that case, quarter sessions, if it does not sentence the accused to Borstal training, can only deal with him in any manner in which the magistrates might have dealt with him. Moreover, if an accused has attained seventeen years but is under twenty-one, and he is convicted summarily of an indictable offence, he may be committed to quarter sessions under either section 28 or section 29. Nevertheless, because a committal under section 29 will enable quarter sessions either to sentence the accused to Borstal training or to deal with him in any other way in which it could have dealt with him had he been convicted on indictment, the magistrates ought normally to commit under section 29 rather than under section 28 (*per* Lord Parker C.J. in *R*. v. *Dangerfield* (1960), C.C.A.).

Appeals. Although the magistrates commit the accused to quarter sessions for sentence, any appeal against conviction will be in the manner normal after conviction by a magistrates' court (see Chap. 41). There are, however, special rules as to appeals against sentence and these will also be considered in Chapter 41.

(2) Trial on Indictment of Summary Offences

Summary offences which are triable on indictment

Where an accused, who has attained the age of fourteen years, is charged before a magistrates' court with a summary offence for which he is liable, or would be liable if he were an adult, to be sentenced by that court to imprisonment for a term exceeding three months, he may claim to be tried by a jury, unless the offence is an assault or an offence under section 30 (a man living on the earnings of prostitution), section 31 (a woman exercising control over a prostitute) or section 32 (solicitation by men) of the Sexual Offences Act 1956 (Magistrates' Courts Act 1952, s. 25(1), as amended). An example of an assault which is punishable on summary conviction with more than three months' imprisonment is assaulting a police officer in the execution of his duty (*Toohey* v. *Woolwich JJ.* (1967), H.L.: where it was held that the accused charged with this offence could not claim trial by jury). Moreover, if the accused will only be liable to more than three months' imprisonment should he fail to pay a fine which may be imposed on summary conviction (though this can rarely occur, see Chap. 44) he cannot claim trial by jury under section 25(1) (*Carle* v. *Elkington* (1892), D.C.).

There are not, in fact, many summary offences which are punishable with more than three months' imprisonment (though hybrid offences are often punishable on summary conviction with more than three months' imprisonment, see below). Examples, however, include: assisting a juvenile to escape from custody (Children and Young Persons Act 1963, s. 10(6)); a number of offences in relation to firearms, *e.g.* failing to comply with any condition subject to which a firearm certificate is held (Firearms Act 1968, s. 1(2)) and having a shot gun without a certificate of authorization or failing to comply with that certificate (*ibid.*, s. 2); and flying an aircraft to the danger of another (Civil Aviation Act 1949, s. 11(1)).

For the position when the accused will be liable to more than three months' imprisonment if he has previously been convicted of a like offence, see below.

In addition to the general provisions of section 25(1), a number of statutes also give an accused the right to claim trial by jury when he is charged with a particular offence. These are: Explosives Act 1875, s. 92 (when he is charged with any offence under the Act for which the penalty exceeds £100, although these offences are in fact hybrid offences, see below); Conspiracy and Protection of Property Act 1875, s. 9 (when he is charged with any offence under the Act, and for which a penalty amounting to £20 or imprisonment can be imposed); Cruelty to Animals Act 1876, s. 15 (when he is charged with any offence under the Act in respect of which a penalty of more than £5 can be imposed); and Witnesses (Public Inquiries) Protection Act 1892, s. 3 (when he is charged with any offence under the Act; in which case the prosecutor may also require trial by jury).

Procedure when accused may claim trial by jury

If the accused is charged with a summary offence and he is entitled to claim trial by jury, the procedure is the same whether he is entitled under the Magistrates' Courts Act 1952, s. 25(1), or under one of the other enactments mentioned above (*ibid.*, s. 25(2)).

To claim trial by jury the accused must have appeared in person (*ibid.*, s. 25(2)), although, if he is present, the claim may be made for him by his counsel or solicitor (*R. v. Salisbury & Amesbury JJ., ex p. Greatbach* (1954), D.C.; though the accused must be informed personally of his right: see below). If, therefore, the accused is not present, the magistrates could, in theory, proceed to try him summarily in his absence (see Chap. 39) though in practice they would normally adjourn the proceedings. Except where the prosecutor has the right to claim trial by jury (see the Witnesses (Public Inquiries) Protection Act 1892, s. 3, above), the magistrates cannot proceed with a view to the trial of such an offence on indictment unless the accused has himself claimed trial by jury (*R. v. Kakelo* (1923), C.C.A.) (for the position where the offence is a hybrid offence, see below). The accused, moreover, must make a claim for trial by jury before he pleads to the charge, and where the prosecutor is entitled to claim that the accused should be tried by jury, he must also do so before the accused pleads to the charge (Magistrates' Courts Act 1952, s. 25(2)).

Where the accused has the right to claim trial by jury, the magistrates must inform him of the right before he pleads, and if the court thinks it desirable for his information, it must tell him before what court he would be tried if tried by jury, and it must explain what is meant by being tried summarily. The magistrates must then ask the accused whether he wishes, instead of being tried summarily, to be tried by jury. (Magistrates' Courts Act 1952, s. 25(3)). Even though the accused is legally represented the magistrates must still expressly inform him personally of his right to claim trial by jury (*R.* v. *Cockshott* (1898), D.C.; *R.* v. *Kettering JJ., ex p. Patmore* (1968), D.C.; though his counsel or solicitor may then reply on his behalf: see above) and they must ask him whether he wishes to be tried "by jury," not whether he consents to summary trial (*R.* v. *Salisbury & Amesbury JJ., ex p. Greatbatch, supra*). Failure to comply with section 25(3) will render the proceedings a nullity (*R.* v. *Berkeley (Gloucestershire) JJ., ex p. Higgins* (1965), D.C.). Never-theless, in *Davis* v. *Morton* (1913), where the accused was not informed of his right before he pleaded, the magistrates allowed the prosecution to withdraw the summons when they discovered the omission during the prosecution's evidence, and a Divisional Court of the K.B.D. held that a fresh summons could then be issued (though this would have to be issued within the relevant statutory time limit for the offence, normally six months: see Chap. 30).

Corporations. Where a corporation is charged with a summary offence for which an accused may claim trial by jury and the corporation appears by means of a representative, the representative may claim trial by jury (Magistrates' Courts Act 1952, Sched. 2, para. 3). Where a representative does not appear, however, the offence must be tried summarily unless the corporation is charged jointly with an individual when the court cannot try either of the accused summarily if the other exercises his right to claim trial by jury (*ibid.*, Sched. 2, para. 9).

When claim depends on previous conviction

In a few cases the accused will only be liable on summary convic-tion to imprisonment for a term exceeding three months if he has already been convicted of a like offence. Examples include the offence of destroying a fence or wall (Malicious Damage Act 1861, s. 25) and the offences of keeping a brothel, a landlord letting premises for use as a brothel and a tenant permitting premises to be used as a brothel for prostitution (Sexual Offences Act 1956, ss. 33, 34, 35 and 36 and Sched. 2).

If an accused is charged with one of these offences he may only claim trial by jury if he has previously been convicted of a like offence, but the magistrates will not know before the trial whether or not he has previously been convicted (because, as a rule of evidence, they are not normally allowed to know until after conviction). The magistrates must, therefore, explain to the accused that he will have the right if he has previously been convicted, and they must ask him whether, if he does have the right, he wishes, instead of being tried summarily, to be tried by jury (Magistrates' Courts Act 1952, s. 25(4)). If the accused then claims trial by jury the magistrates may inquire into his previous conviction in order to verify his right to make the claim, but any inquiry which the court makes should be restricted to this purpose (Magistrates' Courts Rules 1968, r. 21). Moreover, if the accused claims trial by jury and he is subsequently committed for trial, the trial jury must not be told before conviction why he was entitled to be tried on indictment (*R*. v. *Huberty* (1906)).

Procedure when accused claims trial by jury

If the accused is entitled to and does claim trial by jury (or the prosecutor exercises his right) the magistrates must deal with the offence as if it were an offence which was punishable on conviction on indictment only (Magistrates' Courts Act 1952, s. 25(6)). Thus, the magistrates will conduct committal proceedings. Nevertheless, although section 25(6) says that the offence shall then, "as respects the accused be deemed to be an indictable offence," this only applies to the proceedings before the magistrates and not thereafter (*R*. v. *Furlong* (1962), C.C.A.). If, therefore, the accused is tried on indictment and convicted, the trial court will have no greater powers of punishment than the magistrates would have had (*R*. v. *Bishop* (1959), C.C.A.); the accused is being tried on indictment but the offence remains a summary offence (for the position when the offence is a hybrid offence, see below). In *R*. v. *Furlong, supra*, the accused was charged with three summary offences and, having claimed jury trial, he was convicted on indictment of all three. The Court of Criminal Appeal held that the accused could not be sentenced to three consecutive periods of six months' imprisonment (eighteen months' in the aggregate), because, by the Magistrates' Courts Act 1952, s. 108(1), a magistrates' court could not have imposed consecutive periods which in the aggregate exceeded six months.

Moreover, if the accused is committed for the trial of a summary offence on indictment, the indictment must not include another charge in addition to or in substitution for the offence on which the accused claimed trial by jury (*R*. v. *Phillips* (1953), C.C.A.). We saw in Chapter 33 that when the offence is an indictable offence, the indictment may charge other offences provided they are founded on facts or evidence disclosed at the committal proceedings. In *R*. v. *Brown* (1895) a Divisional Court of the Q.B.D. did hold that other offences disclosed in the depositions could be added to an indictment which charged a summary offence, but this case was decided on the basis that a summary offence tried on indictment becomes an indictable offence (see Hawkins J.). In the light of *R*. v. *Furlong, supra,* and *R*. v. *Phillips, supra,* this view is no longer tenable and the decision in *R*. v. *Brown* would appear no longer to represent the law.

If the magistrates do commit an accused, who has attained the age of seventeen, for trial on indictment of a summary offence, they must normally commit him on bail (Criminal Justice Act 1967, s. 18(3)). The conditions on which the magistrates may instead commit him in custody are the same as the conditions upon which the magistrates may remand an accused in custody when they are trying him for a summary offence (see Chap. 39). However, where the magistrates do commit the accused in custody, and either he is not represented or his counsel or solicitor so requests, the magistrates must give him a written notice stating the reason why bail was refused (*ibid.,* s. 18(8)).

(3) Trial of Hybrid Offences

Methods of trial

We noticed in Chap. 27 some of the hybrid offences which have been created. By the Magistrates' Courts Act 1952, s. 18(1), a hybrid offence is one which by virtue of any enactment is both an indictable and a summary offence, not an offence which may be tried either on indictment or summarily. Thus a hybrid offence is an indictable offence (*Hastings & Folkestone Glassworks Ltd*. v. *Kalson* (1949), C.A.; *R*. v. *Fussell* (1951), C.C.A.) but it is equally a summary offence. If a hybrid offence is tried summarily it is a summary offence, while if tried on indictment it is an indictable offence (see s. 125 of the Magistrates' Courts Act 1952 whch, for the purposes of the Act, defines "summary offence" so that it includes a hybrid offence being tried summarily, but not an indictable offence being tried summarily, and which defines "indictable offence" so that it includes a hybrid offence being tried on indictment, but not a summary offence being tried on indictment: and see *R*. v. *Furlong, supra*).

Procedure for determining method of trial

Where an accused is charged with a hybrid offence, the magistrates' court must, if the accused has attained the age of fourteen, proceed as if the offence was not a summary offence, unless the court determines on the application of the prosecutor to try the offence summarily (Magistrates' Courts Act 1952, s. 18(1)). If the accused is under fourteen the magistrates must normally try every offence (except homicide) summarily (see above). Moreover, if the prosecutor is applying for the offence to be tried as a summary offence, he must do so before any evidence is called; although if the accused fails to appear, the application may be made in his absence (*ibid.*, s. 18(2)), and in which case the summary trial itself could also, in theory, be held in his absence (see Chap. 39).

The reason why the prosecutor must make the initial application is that whether the accused ought to be tried summarily or on indictment (and thus be liable to a heavier sentence) normally depends on the details of the particular offence and on the accused's character and previous convictions. These are matters which are known to the prosecutor, not to the magistrates. Nevertheless, the prosecutor's application may be made impliedly, and if the magistrates begin to deal with the offence as a summary offence and without objection by the prosecutor, an implied application will have been made (*James* v. *Bowkett* (1952), D.C.; *Ex p. Rigby* (1958), D.C.). In practice the magistrates' clerk normally asks the prosecutor whether he wants the case tried summarily.

Prima facie the accused himself has no say as to whether the offence is tried as a summary offence or as an indictable offence, although if the prosecutor applies for summary trial the magistrates, before deciding whether to accede to the prosecutor's application, would listen to (but not necessarily follow) any representations made by, or on behalf of, the accused. Nevertheless, if the prosecutor applies for summary trial and the magistrates agree, the offence is then, for the purposes of the Magistrates' Courts Act 1952, a summary offence (see above) and if the accused will be liable on summary conviction to imprisonment for a term exceeding three months (or if he has the right to claim trial by jury under some other statute, for example the Explosives Act 1875, s. 92, see above) he is entitled to claim trial by jury under section 25 (subject to the qualifications set out therein, see above), and he must be informed of this right (s. 25(3); *R.* v. *Salisbury & Amesbury JJ., ex p. Greatbatch* (1954), D.C.) (see also *ibid.*, s. 18(6)). Many hybrid offences are, in fact, punishable on summary conviction with imprisonment for a term exceeding three months, for example, reckless and dangerous driving (maximum four months) and driving when unfit to drive through drink or drugs (maximum four months), but some are not, *e.g.*, misstatements in a prospectus (maximum three months) and having an offensive weapon in a public place (maximum three months). In the latter cases, therefore, the accused will not be able to prevent the magistrates trying the offence as a summary offence if the prosecutor has applied for summary trial.

Summary trial

If the prosecutor applies, under section 18(1), for the offence to be tried as a summary offence and the magistrates agree, the offence will, subject to any right of the accused to claim trial by jury, be tried as a summary offence. Even if the accused is an adult, the magistrates will not, therefore, have any power to send him to quarter sessions for sentence under section 29 of the Magistrates' Courts Act 1952 (*R.* v. *Norfolk JJ., ex p. D.P.P.* (1950), D.C.). As we have seen, section 29 applies when an indictable offence has been tried summarily. Nevertheless, where, under section 18(1), a magistrates' court has begun to try a hybrid offence as a summary offence, the court may, at any time before the conclusion of the evidence for the prosecution (*e.g.*, if they realize that the case is more serious than they originally thought), discontinue the summary trial and proceed to inquire into the offence as examining justices (when the offence will become an indictable offence) (*ibid.*, s. 18(5)). In this last case, moreover, neither the consent of the accused nor the consent of the prosecutor is required.

Trial on indictment

If the prosecutor does not apply for the offence to be tried as a summary offence, or the magistrates do not accede to an application which is made, the magistrates must conduct committal proceedings. The same applies when a hybrid offence is punishable on summary conviction with imprisonment for a term exceeding three months but, though the prosecutor applies for it to be tried as a summary offence and the court agrees, the accused exercises his right under section 25 and claims trial by jury. In this event the offence becomes a summary offence when the court agrees to the prosecutor's application for summary trial, but it becomes an indictable offence once the accused claims trial by jury. If the accused is then committed for trial on indictment, therefore, he will be liable on conviction to the heavier sentence which is imposable on conviction on indictment (*R.* v. *Gibbs* (1965), C.C.A.). Unlike a summary offence, which remains a summary offence although the accused does claim trial by jury (see above), a hybrid offence becomes an indictable offence (see *R.* v. *Roe* (1967), C.A.).

Committal proceedings to summary trial

Where the magistrates from the beginning inquire into a hybrid offence as examining justices, then if at any time during the inquiry it appears to the court, having regard to any representations made in the presence of the accused by the prosecutor, or made by the accused, and to the nature of the case, that it is proper to do so, the court may proceed to try the case summarily (Magistrates' Courts Act 1952, s. 18(3)). The court must have regard to any representations made by the accused (though it need not follow them), but the consent of the accused is not made a prerequisite to a change to summary trial. Nevertheless, if the accused will then be liable on summary conviction for imprisonment for a term exceeding three months (or he may claim trial by jury under some other statute, see above), section 25 will apply as soon as the proceedings become a summary trial, and the accused must then be informed of his right to claim trial by jury. Likewise, the consent of the prosecutor is not normally required, but if the prosecutor is the Director of Public Prosecutions (or the prosecution is under the customs or excise Acts : Customs and Excise Act 1952, s. 283(3)), the court cannot change to summary trial without his consent (*ibid.*, s. 18(3)) and, as we have seen (*e.g.*, under the Witnesses (Public Inquiries) Protection Act 1892, s. 3), the prosecutor very occasionally has the right to claim trial by jury for offences under a particular statute. If the magistrates do change to summary trial under section 18(3) they cannot thereafter change back to committal proceedings (*ibid.*, s. 24).

We have seen that if a hybrid offence is tried as a summary offence from the beginning, the magistrates will have no power to commit the accused for sentence to quarter sessions under section 29 of the Magistrates' Courts Act 1952. Nevertheless, if the proceedings begin as committal proceedings, but change to summary trial under section 18(3), the magistrates will have power on conviction, if the accused is an adult, to commit him to quarter sessions under section 29 (Magistrates' Courts Act 1952, s. 29). Moreover, if the accused has the right to claim trial by jury, the magistrates, before they begin to try the offence as a summary offence under section 18(3), must not only inform him of his right to claim trial by jury but they must warn him that they will have the power to commit him to quarter sessions for sentence (*ibid.*, s. 25(5)).

It is difficult to understand why the magistrates should be given this power to send the accused to quarter sessions for sentence if the proceedings are charged under section 18(3). When the summary trial is begun under section 18(3) the hybrid offence changes from being an indictable offence and becomes a summary offence, so that this is the one exception when the magistrates may commit an accused to quarter sessions under section 29 even though they have not convicted him of an indictable offence. Moreover, if the offence is not punishable on summary conviction with imprisonment for a term exceedng three months, the magistrates may change from committal proceedings to summary trial under section 18(3) without the consent of the accused, or even contrary to his wishes. Then, on conviction, he may be sent to quarter sessions under section 29 and there receive a sentence up to the maximum that can be imposed on trial on indictment. It may be that, because of the complexity of these provisions, this result was not appreciated.

Chapter Forty-One

APPEALS

(1) Offences Tried on Indictment

As we saw in Chapter 27 the method of appeal depends upon the mode of trial. Thus, if the offence was tried on indictment an appeal from the trial court will lie to the Criminal Division of the Court of Appeal, and this will be so whether the offence is an indictable offence, a summary offence or a hybrid offence. Similarly, whatever the offence, if it was tried summarily, an appeal will lie either to quarter sessions or to a Divisional Court of the Q.B.D. Nevertheless, we have also seen that in certain circumstances an appeal against sentence may lie to the Criminal Division of the Court of Appeal although an appeal against conviction lies to quarter sessions or to a Divisional Court. This may occur when the accused, having been convicted summarily, was committed to quarter sessions for sentence (under the Magistrates' Courts Act 1952, ss. 28 or 29: see Chaps. 39 and 40), or under the Mental Health Act 1959, s. 67(1) see Chap. 39), or after having been convicted of being an incorrigible rogue (see Chap. 39), or was committed to assizes or quarter sessions for sentence under the Criminal Justice Act 1967, s. 56 (conjunctive offences: see Chap. 39).

Appeals to the Criminal Division of the Court of Appeal

As we saw in Chapter 28, the Criminal Division of the Court of Appeal was established by the Criminal Appeal Act 1966 and it took over the jurisdiction of the former Court of Criminal Appeal. The powers of the Criminal Division are, however, now mainly set out in the Criminal Appeal Act 1968.

When appeals lie to the Criminal Division

Appeals lie to the Criminal Division of the Court of Appeal from a trial on indictment (which term includes a trial on a coroner's inquisition: Criminal Appeal Act 1968, s. 51(3)), at quarter sessions or assizes, but only the accused can appeal (*ibid.*, s. 1); the prosecution can never appeal from a trial on indictment. Moreover, normally

315

an accused can appeal only after conviction (*ibid.*, s. 1), but he may appeal against a verdict of not guilty by reason of insanity (*ibid.*, s. 12), or he may appeal against a finding by the trial court that he was unfit to plead or to be tried (see Chap. 35) (*ibid.*, s. 15(1)).

Appeals against conviction

An accused may appeal against his conviction (*a*) on any ground which involves a question of law alone; and (*b*) with the leave of the Court of Appeal, on any ground which involves a question of fact alone, or a question of mixed law and fact, or on any other ground which appears to the Court of Appeal to be a sufficient ground of appeal (Criminal Appeal Act 1968, s. 1(2)). However, if the trial judge grants a certificate that the case is fit for appeal on a ground which involves a question of fact, or a question of mixed law and fact, an appeal under section 1 lies without the leave of the Court of Appeal (*ibid.*, s. 1(2)).

An accused, moreover, may appeal against his conviction (as well as against the sentence) upon a plea of guilty if he did not appreciate the nature of the charge, or did not intend to admit his guilt, or upon the admitted facts he could not be guilty in law (*R.* v. *King* (1920), C.C.A.).

An accused may, therefore, appeal against his conviction as of right on any ground which involves a question of law alone, but, even if the accused's notice of appeal does allege a point of law, the appeal court must be satisfied that there is in fact a question of law before it need hear the appeal (*R.* v. *Hinds* (1962), C.C.A.). In addition, where it appears to the registrar of criminal appeals that any notice of appeal, which purports to be on a question of law alone, does not show any substantial ground of appeal, he may refer the appeal to the Criminal Division of the Court of Appeal for summary determination, and the court may then, if they consider that the appeal is frivolous or vexatious, and can be determined without adjourning it for a full hearing, dismiss the appeal summarily, without calling on any person to attend the hearing or to appear for the prosecution thereon (Criminal Appeal Act 1968, s. 20).

An accused may appeal against his conviction on any ground which involves a question of fact alone or mixed law and fact, but only with the leave of the Criminal Division of the Court of Appeal or upon the certificate of the judge who tried him (*ibid.*, s. 1(2): see above). This does not mean that the accused must apply to the trial judge for a certificate before he can apply to the Criminal Division for leave, and in practice it is normal for an accused to apply direct to the appeal court. Indeed, the Criminal Division has said that the judge ought not to grant a certificate unless the case is one where leave ought clearly to be given (*R.* v. *Boseley* (1937), C.C.A.). Nevertheless, an application for a certificate may be made to the trial judge or, if the trial judge considers it desirable to do so, he may even grant a certificate and inform the accused that in his opinion the case is fit for appeal, without an application having been made (see the Criminal Appeal Rules 1968, r. 1(2)). If an unsuccessful application is made to the trial judge, the accused may then apply for leave to the Criminal Division.

Grounds for allowing an appeal against conviction

The Criminal Division of the Court of Appeal must (subject to the "proviso," see below) allow an appeal against conviction if they think (*a*) that the verdict of the jury should be set aside on the ground that under all the circumstances of the case it is unsafe or unsatisfactory; or (*b*) that the judgment of the court of trial should be set aside on the ground of a wrong decision of any question of law; or (*c*) that there was a material irregularity in the course of the trial, and in any other case shall dismiss the appeal (Criminal Appeal Act 1968, s. 2(1)). Grounds on which the appeal court may quash the conviction therefore include defects in the indictment (*e.g.*, duplicity), the wrongful admission or exclusion of evidence, a misdirection as to the law and an inconsistency between the verdict and another verdict (*R.* v. *Andrews* (1967), C.A.).

Before the Criminal Appeal Act 1966, the appeal court could only quash the conviction when the verdict of the jury was unreasonable or could not be supported having regard to the evidence, and this was construed as meaning only if there was no evidence on which the jury could convict or there was a misdirection. If there was some evidence to support the jury's verdict and no misdirection the appeal court would not quash the conviction, even though the appeal court itself might have reached a different verdict (*per* Lord Goddard C.J., in *R.* v. *McGrath* (1949), C.C.A.). Now, however, the jury's verdict may be set aside if the appeal court is satisfied "that under all the circumstances of the case it is unsafe or unsatisfactory," and this will include cases where there was evidence on which the jury could convict (*e.g.*, evidence identifying the accused) but the Criminal Division are not themselves satisfied that this evidence was correct (see the Report of the Interdepartmental Committee on the Court of Criminal Appeal (Chairman : Lord Donovan), 1965, paras. 137-150; and *R.* v. *Cooper* (1969), C.A.).

If the Criminal Division does allow an appeal against conviction then, subject to their powers considered below, they must quash the conviction, and, except where the court orders a retrial, this will operate as a direction to the trial court to enter a verdict of acquittal (Criminal Appeal Act 1968, s. 2(2), (3)).

The proviso to section 2(1)

Although the Criminal Division is satisfied that the point raised in the appeal might be decided in favour of the accused, they may dismiss the appeal if they consider that no miscarriage of justice has actually occurred (proviso to s. 2(1) of the Criminal Appeal Act 1968). Before the Criminal Appeal Act 1966 it was necessary to show, before the proviso could be applied, that no "substantial miscarriage" of justice had occurred, and this was interpreted as allowing the appeal court to apply the proviso, and thereby uphold the conviction, only if it was satisfied "that if the jury had been properly directed they would have inevitably come to the same conclusion" (*per* Lord Sankey L.C. in *Woolmington* v. *D.P.P.* (1935), H.L.). In *Stirland* v. *D.P.P.* (1944), H.L., Lord Simon L.C. said the proviso could only be applied if "it is evident that no reasonable jury, after a proper summing up, could have failed to convict the [accused] on the rest of the evidence to which no objection could be taken." Nevertheless, provided this test was satisfied the proviso could be applied even though the irregularity in the trial was a serious one, for example, *R.* v. *Haddy* (1944), C.C.A. (wrongful comment by the judge on the accused's silence after caution) and *R.* v. *Whybrow* (1951), C.C.A. The omission of the word "substantial" in the proviso, following the Criminal Appeal Act 1966, does not, moreover, widen the circumstances in which the proviso can be applied; its effect, if any, would seem to be the reverse. It therefore seems likely that the courts will continue to interpret the proviso as set out above.

Alternative offences

Where an accused was convicted of one offence, although the jury could have convicted him of some other offence (whether the other offence was charged in an alternative count, or it was an alternative verdict offence, see Chap. 38), the Criminal Division, if it quashes the jury's verdict, may nevertheless substitute for that verdict a verdict of guilty of that other offence, provided the court is satisfied that on the finding of the jury they must have been satisfied of facts which prove the accused guilty of that other offence (Criminal Appeal Act 1968, s. 3). As we saw when we considered alternative counts (Chap. 38), the Criminal Division cannot substitute a verdict of guilty of an offence charged in an alternative count if the jury actually acquitted the accused of it (*R.* v. *Melvin* (1953), C.C.A.), nor can they substitute a verdict of guilty of an offence which is neither an alternative verdict offence nor one which was charged in the indictment. Thus in *R. v. Seymour* (1954) the Court of Criminal Appeal could not substitute a conviction of larceny for one of receiving because the accused had only been charged with receiving in the indictment.

If the Criminal Division does substitute a verdict of guilty of an offence charged in an alternative count, or of an alternative verdict offence, they may then pass such sentence in substitution for the sentence passed at the trial as is authorized by law, provided that it is not a sentence of greater severity (*ibid.*, s. 3(2)). Thus, in *R. v. Davenport* (1954) the jury had convicted the accused of larceny but the Court of Criminal Appeal held that on the facts, of which the jury must have been satisfied, the accused was guilty not of larceny but of embezzlement. The appeal court, therefore, substituted a conviction for embezzlement but they sentenced the accused to eighteen months imprisonment for the embezzlement, the same sentence as that imposed by the trial judge for the larceny. In a suitable case, of course, the appeal court will substitute a sentence of less severity than that imposed by the trial judge.

Separate counts

Where an accused appeals against conviction after having been convicted on two or more counts of an indictment, and the Criminal Division allow the appeal in respect of one or more of the counts, the Criminal Division may, in respect of any count on which he remains convicted, pass such sentence, in substitution for the sentence which was passed in respect of that count at the trial, as they think proper and which is authorized by law for the offence of which he remains convicted on that count (Criminal Appeal Act 1968, s. 4). Again, however, the sentence of the accused must not then be of greater severity than the sentence (taken as a whole) which was passed at the trial for all the offences of which he was convicted on the indictment (*ibid.*, s. 4(3)). (See, *e.g.*, *R. v. Lovelock* (1956), C.C.A.).

Substitution of finding of insanity or unfitness

Where, on an appeal against conviction, the Criminal Division consider that the proper verdict would have been one of not guilty by reason of insanity or that the accused should have been found unfit to plead or to be tried then the court must make an order that the accused be admitted to such hospital as may be specified by the Secretary of State (Criminal Appeal Act 1968, s. 6(1)).

Power to order a retrial

Where an appeal against conviction is allowed by the Criminal

Division of the Court of Appeal by reason only of evidence received or available to be received by that court under section 23 of the Criminal Appeal Act 1968 (see below), and it appears to the court that the interests of justice so require, the court may order the accused to be retried (Criminal Appeal Act 1968, s. 7(1)). If the Criminal Division is satisfied that the additional evidence is true, however, and it is conclusive of the appeal, the court will not normally order a retrial but will instead enter a verdict of acquittal. If the appeal court positively disbelieves the additional evidence it will normally treat the evidence as worthless, and will not therefore order a retrial on account of it. Nevertheless, if the appeal court is satisfied that the additional evidence is true but is not satisfied that it is conclusive, or it is not satisfied that it is true but thinks that it might be acceptable to, and be believed by a jury, then the appeal court will normally order a retrial (*R.* v. *Flower* (1966), C.C.A.). Apart from their power under the Criminal Appeal Act 1968, s. 7(1), however, the Criminal Division has no power to order a retrial, although if the first trial was a nullity they may order a *venire de novo* (see below).

If the Criminal Division does order a retrial, the accused can only be retried for the offence of which he was convicted at the trial and in respect of which his appeal has been allowed, or for any offence of which he could have been convicted at the trial by way of alternative verdict, or for an offence charged in an alternative count and in respect of which the jury were discharged from giving a verdict (Criminal Appeal Act 1968, s. 7(2)). The retrial, moreover, will be upon a fresh indictment preferred by the direction of the Criminal Division (see Chap. 33) and the accused will be tried before such court as the Criminal Division may direct (although not by a court of quarter sessions unless the offence is within the jurisdiction of quarter sessions), or otherwise before the court by which he was originally tried (*ibid.*, s. 8(1)). The Criminal Division, if it does order a retrial, may also make such orders as appear necessary or expedient for the custody or admission to bail of the accused pending the retrial (*ibid.*, s. 8(2)).

The retrial: depositions. We have seen (Chap. 37) that if a witness, who gave evidence at the committal proceedings or whose written statement was admitted at those proceedings, is unable to attend the trial on indictment (*e.g.*, because of illness) his deposition taken at the committal proceedings or his written statement may be admitted in evidence at the trial (under the Criminal Justice Act 1925, s. 13(3), as amended). Nevertheless, where a witness did give evidence at the trial but he is unable to attend a retrial, his original deposition or written statement cannot be put in evidence at the retrial. Instead, a transcript of the record of the evidence which he gave at the original trial (this should, as a general rule, always be taken at a trial on indictment: Criminal Appeal Act 1968, s. 32(1)) may, with the leave of the judge, "be read as evidence (*a*) by agreement between the prosecution and the defence [whether or not the witness could in fact attend]; or (*b*) if the judge is satisfied that the witness is dead or unfit to give evidence or to attend for that purpose, or that all reasonable efforts to find him or to secure his attendance have been made without success." (Criminal Appeal Act 1968, Sched. 2, para. 1.)

The retrial : sentence. Where an accused is again convicted on a retrial, the court before which he is convicted may pass any sentence authorized by law, provided it is not a sentence of greater severity than that passed on the original conviction (Criminal Appeal Act 1968, Sched. 2, para. 2(1)). The court before which the accused is convicted on the retrial may, moreover, if it so desires, pass such sentence on the accused as it could have passed were the accused of the age which he was at the time of the original conviction (*ibid.*, Sched. 2, para. 2(2)). Thus, for example, if the accused was twenty at the time of the original conviction but twenty-one at the time of the retrial, the court may still sentence him to Borstal training. Normally a sentence of imprisonment or other detention imposed upon an accused at a retrial shall be computed as having begun at the time of the original trial but any period during which he was on bail pending the appeal or retrial will be disregarded (*ibid.*, Sched. 2, para 2(3)).

When there was a nullity

If the Criminal Division of the Court of Appeal hold that the first trial was a mistrial (*i.e.*, a nullity) they should order that the conviction and judgment be set aside and annulled, and in addition they may order that a writ of *"venire de novo"* be issued (see below). There is some uncertainty as to what defects render a trial a mistrial rather than merely defective but in *R.* v. *Neal* (1949), C.C.A., Lord Goddard C.J. said they must be such as will render the trial a nullity from the outset, and in *R.* v. *Murphy* (1869), P.C., Sir William Erle said that cases in which a trial has been held to be a nullity include "cases of defects of jurisdiction in respect of time, place, or person [and] cases of verdicts so insufficiently expressed, or so ambiguous, that a judgment could not be founded thereon." Examples of trials held to be a nullity include the joint trial of two accused charged on separate indictments (*Crane* v. *D.P.P.* (1921),

H.L.), where the presiding deputy recorder was not properly qualified (*R.* v. *Cronin* (1940), C.C.A.), where there was no valid jury (*R.* v. *Solomon* (1958), C.C.A.), where the jury did not return the verdict (*R.* v. *Heyes* (1951), C.C.A.), where there was a fundamental defect in the committal proceedings (*R.* v. *Phillips* (1939), C.C.A.), where the consent of the Director of Public Prosecutions to the institution of the proceedings had not been obtained in a case where this was required (*R.* v. *Angel* (1968), C.A.) and where a plea of guilty was incorrectly entered on behalf of the accused (*R.* v. *Ingleson* (1915), C.C.A.; *R.* v. *King* (1920), C.C.A.); while examples of trials held not to be a nullity include cases where the jury were allowed to separate after they had retired (*R.* v. *Neal* (1949), C.C.A.; although the conviction was quashed), where there was a misnomer of a juryman (*R.* v. *Bottomley* (1922), C.C.A.) and where the judge directed the jury to acquit the accused before the prosecution had called its evidence (*R.* v. *Middlesex Quarter Sessions, ex p. D.P.P.* (1952), D.C.).

Venire de novo. If the Criminal Division holds that the first trial was a mistrial it may not only order that the conviction and judgment be set aside but that the accused should appear at the next sitting of the trial court and should there be tried for the same offence (see, *e.g.*, *Crane* v. *D.P.P.*, *supra*; *R.* v. *Solomon*, *supra*). This order is effected by a writ of *venire de novo*. The power of the Criminal Division to order the issue of a writ of *venire de novo* is derived from the similar power of the Court for Crown Cases Reserved, which was transferred to the Court of Criminal Appeal by the Criminal Appeal Act 1907, s. 20(4) (*Crane* v. *D.P.P.*, *supra*) and further transferred to the Court of Appeal by the Criminal Appeal Act 1966, s. 1(8).The appeal court, however, is not obliged to order the issue of a writ of *venire de novo* merely because the trial was a nullity (*per* Lord Parmoor in *Crane* v. *D.P.P.*, *supra*; see also *R.* v. *King* (1920), C.C.A.), only if it considers that the accused ought to be so tried again for the same offence, even though a writ of *venire de novo* were not issued (see *autrefois acquit,* Chapter 35). If the Criminal Division does order a writ of *venire de novo* to issue, they may order the accused to be remanded either in custody (*R.* v. *Baker* (1912), C.C.A.) or on bail (*R.* v. *Hussey* (1924), C.C.A.). Moreover, although the appeal court will order the accused to be tried at the next sitting of the court which originally tried him, an application may be made to the High Court under section 11(3) of the Administration of Justice (Miscellaneous Provisions) Act 1938 to try the case elsewhere (see Chap. 32) (*R.* v. *Solomon*, *supra*).

See "Venire de Novo," by R. B. Cook (1953) 71 L.Q.R. 100.

Appeals when finding of insanity

An accused who has been found not guilty by reason of insanity may appeal to the Criminal Division of the Court of Appeal on the same grounds as he may appeal against conviction, and leave is required in the same cases (see above) (Criminal Appeal Act 1968, s. 12). Moreover, subject to what is discussed below, the Criminal Division must then allow the appeal on the same grounds as they must allow an appeal against conviction (see above) (*ibid.*, s. 13(1)). If the appeal is allowed the Criminal Division must normally substitute a verdict of acquittal (*ibid.*, s. 13(4) (*b*)). Nevertheless, the court may dismiss an appeal if of the opinion that no miscarriage of justice has actually occurred (*ibid.*, s. 13(2)). Moreover, even though there are grounds for allowing the appeal, the Criminal Division may dismiss the appeal if of opinion that the accused was insane and that, but for his insanity, he should have been convicted of some other offence (*ibid.*, s. 13(3)).

The Criminal Division may allow an appeal against the verdict of not guilty by reason of insanity on the ground that at the time of the offence the accused was not insane, and in this case they may substitute a verdict of guilty of that offence or of some other offence of which the jury could have convicted him (*ibid.*, s. 13(4) (*a*)), The appeal court then has the same powers of punishment as the trial court, except that it can never sentence an accused to death but must instead sentence him to imprisonment for life (*ibid.*, s. 13).

Though the Criminal Division allow the accused's appeal against the verdict of insanity and substitute a verdict of acquittal, the court should, if they are of opinion that the accused ought to be detained in a hospital under observation (with or without medical treatment) for at least a limited period, make an order that he be admitted for observation to such hospital as may be specified by the Secretary of State (*ibid.*, s. 14(2)).

Appeals when finding of unfitness to plead or to be tried

If at the trial an accused is found unfit to plead or to be tried (see Chap. 35), he may appeal against that finding to the Criminal Division of the Court of Appeal, and the grounds of appeal and powers of the appeal court are then basically the same as an appeal against a verdict of insanity (Criminal Appeal Act 1968, s. 15). If the court allows the appeal against the finding of unfitness the accused may then normally be tried for the offence with which he was charged, and the appeal court may make such orders as appear necessary or expedient pending such trial for his custody, admission to bail or continued detention under the Mental Health Act 1959 (*ibid.*, s. 16(3)). Nevertheless, if the question of fitness to be tried was determined later than on arraignment the Criminal Division may allow the appeal on the ground that the accused should have been acquitted before the question of fitness to be tried was considered, and the court will then direct that a verdict of acquittal be recorded (*ibid.*, s. 16(2)).

Appeals against sentence

An accused who has been convicted on indictment may appeal to the Criminal Division of the Court of Appeal against any sentence (not being a sentence fixed by law) passed on him for the offence, whether passed on his conviction or in subsequent proceedings (*e.g.*, after first being placed on probation) (Criminal Appeal Act 1968, s. 9). Sentence, in this context, includes any order made by the court of assize or quarter sessions when dealing with the accused (including a hospital order, with or without an order restricting discharge: see Chap. 44) and also includes a recommendation for deportation (see Chap. 44) (*ibid.*, s. 50(1)). Where the court of assize or quarter sessions passed on the accused two or more sentences in the same proceedings (*i.e.*, they were passed on the same day or the court in passing any one of them stated that it was treating that one together with the others as substantially one sentence), and they are sentences against which an appeal can lie, then an appeal or application for leave to appeal against any one of them counts as an appeal or application in respect of all of them (*ibid.*, s. 11(2)).

An appeal against sentence, however, only lies with the leave of the Court of Appeal (Criminal Appeal Act 1968, s. 11(1)). The trial judge cannot grant an accused leave to appeal against sentence (*R.* v. *Flynn* (1963), C.C.A.) and leave is always required, even if the sentence imposed is one which by law cannot be given for the offence (*R.* v. *Biggs* (1909), C.C.A.).

If, on an appeal against sentence, the Criminal Division considers that the accused should be sentenced differently for any offence, they may quash the sentence or order and instead pass such sentence, or make such order, as they think appropriate, provided the sentence or order is one which the court below had power to make when it dealt with the accused, and provided also that, taking the case as a whole, the accused is not more severely dealt with than he was dealt with by the court below (Criminal Appeal Act 1968, s. 11(3)). Moreover, this includes power to deal with a suspended sentence previously passed on the accused even though (*a*) it was not dealt with by the court below because the accused was sentenced to Borstal training (which sentence is now being quashed), or (*b*) the court did deal with it by making no order (see Chap. 44) (*ibid.*, s. 11(4)). Where the Criminal Division does pass a fresh sentence, the sentence, unless the court otherwise directs, runs from the time when it would have begun to run if passed by the court below (*ibid.*, s. 29(4)).

The Criminal Division will only vary the sentence, however, if it was obviously excessive or wrong in principle. As Lord Hewart C.J. said in *R*. v. *Gumbs* (1926), C.C.A., "this court never interferes with the discretion of the court below merely on the ground that the court might have passed a somewhat different sentence; for this court to revise a sentence there must be some error in principle." Nevertheless, the appeal court may hear additional evidence in relation to the sentence (see below) and it may vary the sentence if, in the light of this additional evidence, it considers it right to do so (*R*. v. *Bennett* (1968), C.A.). Moreover, if the appeal court does allow an appeal against sentence it is not bound to pass another sentence and, in an appropriate case, it may simply quash the sentence passed by the court below (*R*. v. *Johnson* (1909), C.C.A.).

When accused not convicted on indictment

Where an accused, who has been convicted summarily of an offence, is committed to assizes or quarter sessions either to be dealt with for that offence (see Chaps. 39, 40: where we saw that an appeal against conviction will lie in the manner normal after conviction by a magistrates' court) or because he has committed a further offence while on probation or during the operational period of a suspended sentence (see Chap. 44), then he may appeal to the Criminal Division of the Court of Appeal against the sentence passed on him by the court of assize or quarter sessions provided (*a*) the sentence, either for that offence alone or for that offence and other offences for which sentence was passed in the same proceeding, is imprisonment for a term of six months or more, or (*b*) the sentence is one which the court convicting him (*e.g.*, the magistrates' court) had not power to pass, or (*c*) a recommendation for his deportation, an order disqualifying him from driving or an order in respect of a suspended sentence was made (Criminal Appeal Act 1968, s. 10). An appeal only lies under this section, however, with the leave of the Court of Appeal (*ibid.*, s. 11(1)). Moreover, the power to appeal, with leave, against a sentence passed in relation to one offence does not enable an accused to appeal against a sentence passed at the same time in relation to another offence if he would not otherwise be able to appeal against that other sentence (*R*. v. *Moore* (1968), C.A.).

Procedure for appealing

Notice of an appeal against conviction, or notice of an application for leave to appeal against conviction (where this is required), must be given within twenty-eight days of the date of the conviction, while notice of an appeal against sentence or against an order made by the lower court must be given within twenty-eight days of the sentence being passed or the order being made (Criminal Appeal Act 1968, s. 18). Except where conviction involved sentence of death, the time within which notice of appeal or notice of application for leave to appeal has to be given may be extended at any time by the appeal court (*ibid.*, s. 13(3), Sched. 4, para. 1). Where the conviction did involve sentence of death an extension of time cannot be granted even though the sentence of death has already been commuted (*R.* v. *Twynham* (1920), C.C.A.).

An application for leave to appeal, an application for an extension of time or an application for legal aid (see Chap. 46) may be dealt with by a single judge of the Criminal Division (*ibid.*, ss. 31, 47(3)), and in practice it normally is dealt with in this way. Nevertheless, if the single judge refuses an application, the accused may have his application determined by the court itself (*ibid.*, s. 31(3)), or the single judge may himself refer the case to the court (*R.* v. *Munns* (1908), C.C.A.).

An accused normally has a right to be present, if he desires it, on the hearing of his appeal, but where the appeal is on some ground involving a question of law alone, or on an application for leave to appeal, he is not entitled to be present, except where the court grants him leave (*ibid.*, s. 22). If an accused, who is entitled and desires to be present, is ill, the appeal must be adjourned until he may be present (*R.* v. *Dunleavey* (1909), C.C.A.). Nevertheless, where the accused has escaped from custody before the hearing of his appeal, the practice is either to adjourn the appeal or dismiss it, according to the justice of the case (*R.* v. *Flower* (1966), C.C.A.).

At any time after an accused has served notice of appeal, he may abandon his appeal by giving notice of abandonment (Criminal Appeal Rules 1968, r. 10). If an appeal has been opened before the appeal court, however, the appeal cannot be abandoned except with leave of the court (*R.* v. *De Courcy* (1964), C.C.A.). Once an appeal has been abandoned the court will not entertain an application for withdrawal of the notice of abandonment unless there was fraud or a mistake which enables the court to say that the notice of abandonment should be regarded as a nullity (*R.* v. *Moore* (1957), C.C.A.).

Where an accused does appeal to the Criminal Division the judge, chairman or recorder, etc., of the trial court will supply direct to the appeal court his notes of the trial and a report on the case.

Additional evidence

The Criminal Division of the Court of Appeal may, if it is thought necessary in the interests of justice, "order any witness who would have been a compellable witness in the proceedings from which the appeal lies to attend for examination and be examined before the court, whether or not he was called in those proceedings" or "receive the evidence, if tendered, of any witness (including the accused) who is a competent but not compellable witness" (Criminal Appeal Act 1968, s. 23(1)). Moreover, without prejudice to the generality of section 23(1), where additional evidence is tendered to the Criminal Division, the court must exercise their power to admit the evidence under that section (unless they are satisfied that the evidence if received would not afford any ground for allowing the appeal) if (*a*) it appears that the evidence is likely to be credible and would have been admissible in the proceedings from which the appeal lies on an issue which is the subject of the appeal; and (*b*) the court is satisfied that it was not adduced in those proceedings, but there is a reasonable explanation for the failure to adduce it (*ibid.*, s. 23(2)). In addition, as we have seen, the Criminal Division may order a re-trial when it allows an appeal by reason only of additional evidence.

Before the Criminal Appeal Act 1964, the Court of Criminal Appeal had put a very restrictive interpretation upon section 9 of the Criminal Appeal Act 1907 (now s. 23(1) of the 1968 Act: see above). Thus in *R. v. Parks* (1961), C.C.A., the court said that additional (or fresh) evidence was not admissible unless it was not available at the trial, it was relevant to the issues and it was credible in the sense that it was well capable of belief. Moreover, the court after considering the evidence would then go on to consider whether there might have been a doubt in the minds of the jury as to the guilt of the accused if that evidence had been given. In *R. v. Thomas* (1959), C.C.A., moreover, it was stated (*obiter*) that additional evidence was not admissible as to matters which had occurred since the trial. Nevertheless, following the Criminal Appeal Act 1964 (which first allowed the court to order a retrial; although it did not purport to amend section 9 of the 1907 Act), in *R. v. Kelly* (1965), the Courts-Martial Appeal Court (where the relevant law is the same) said that the court will now "look at each case on its merits."

In view of section 23(2) of the Criminal Appeal Act 1968 and the court's statement in *R. v. Kelly*, it would now seem, therefore, that if the additional evidence falls within the provisions of section 23(2), the Criminal Division must normally admit the evidence, and even if it does not fall within these provisions, but it does come within the terms of section 23(1) the court has a discretion whether to admit the evidence and this discretion is not fettered in the manner suggested in *R. v. Parks*, nor (possibly) in *R. v. Thomas*. Moreover, although it has been held that additional evidence is not admissible if it will re-open the main issues of fact and thereby usurp the functions of the trial jury (*R v. Rowland* (1947), C.C.A.), this rule would appear to have been abrogated by the right to order a new trial under section 7 of the Criminal Appeal Act 1968.

Computation of sentence

Where an accused who is appealing to the Criminal Division of the Court of Appeal has been admitted to bail, the time during which he was at large after being so admitted is disregarded in computing the term of any sentence that has been passed on him (Criminal Appeal Act 1968, s. 29(3)). Where he was in custody, however, pending the determination of the appeal, the time in custody, unless the Criminal Division directs otherwise, is reckoned as part of his sentence (Criminal Appeal Act 1968, s. 29(1)) and the court cannot so direct if leave to appeal has been granted by the court or by a certificate of the trial judge (see above) or where the case has been referred to the Criminal Division by the Home Secretary under section 17 of the Criminal Appeal Act 1968 (see below) (*ibid.*, s. 29(2)). Moreover, where the Criminal Division does direct that the accused's time in custody shall not be reckoned as part of his sentence, the court must state their reasons for giving this direction (*ibid.*, s. 29(2)).

Reference by the Home Secretary

By the Criminal Appeal Act 1968, s. 17, the Home Secretary, on an application made to him by an accused convicted on indictment, or without any such application having been made, may, "if he thinks fit, at any time either (*a*) refer the whole case to the Criminal Division of the Court of Appeal, and the case shall then be treated for all purposes as an appeal to the court by that person; or (*b*) if he desires the assistance of the court on any point arising in the case, refer that point to the court for their opinion thereon, and the court shall consider the point so referred and furnish the [Home Secretary] with their opinion thereon accordingly." If the Home Secretary does refer a point arising in a case to the Criminal Division the court may consider such point in private (Criminal Appeal Rules 1968, r. 16).

References under section 17(*b*) are rare in practice, but the Home Secretary not infrequently refers a case to the Court of Appeal under section 17(*a*). Examples include *R*. v. *Podola* (1960) and *R*. v. *Hinds* (1966). In *R*. v. *Sparkes* (1956), the Court of Criminal Appeal stated that additional evidence is admissible, when the case comes before the court under section 17(*a*), on a wider basis than in ordinary appeals (although additional evidence is now admitted in an ordinary appeal on a wider basis than in 1956: see above). On an appeal under section 17(*a*), however, the court will restrict itself to considering the particular ground on which the case was referred (*R*. v. *Caborn-Waterfield* (1956), C.C.A.).

Appeals to the House of Lords

Appeals lie to the House of Lords from any decision of the Criminal Division of the Court of Appeal on an appeal to that court, and at the instance of either the accused or the prosecution (Criminal Appeal Act 1968, s. 33(1)). Leave to appeal is, however, required and leave cannot be granted unless the Criminal Division has certified that a point of law of general public importance is involved in the decision (*ibid.*, s. 33(2)). Provided, however, that the Criminal Division has certified that such a point of law is involved, either that court or the House of Lords may grant leave, but only if it appears that the point of law is one which ought to be considered by the House (*ibid.*, s. 33(2)).

As it is the Criminal Division which must have certified that a point of law of general public importance is involved, should that court refuse so to certify, no appeal can lie, and the House of Lords itself has no power to certify the case in this way (*Gelberg* v. *Miller* (1961), H.L.). Nevertheless, if the Criminal Division certifies a point but refuses leave to appeal, then the accused may apply to the House of Lords for leave. In practice the Criminal Division on a number of occasions has certified a point, but refused leave. One ground for refusing leave is that, though there is a point of law of general public importance involved in the case, the point is one on which there is no uncertainty and, therefore, in the Criminal Division's opinion, it is not one which ought to be considered by the House of Lords. If a point is certified, however, the accused or prosecution must first apply for leave to the Criminal Division, and only if that court refuses leave can an application be made to the House of Lords (see below).

If the Criminal Division does certify that a point of law of general public importance is involved it should state what the point of law is (*Jones* v. *D.P.P.* (1962), H.L.). Nevertheless, if the appellant is granted leave the House of Lords is not necessarily restricted to that particular point and it may consider other points of law which arise in the case (*Att.-Gen. for Northern Ireland* v. *Gallagher* (1963), H.L.). In *Jones* v. *D.P.P.*, *supra*, however, the Court of Criminal Appeal had certified a point of law which was concerned with the conviction of the accused (*i.e.*, whether he was rightly cross-examined as to a previous offence), but the accused tried to raise a further point which was concerned with his sentence (*i.e.*, whether the trial judge had been right in law in sentencing him to imprisonment for life, to run consecutively to a term of fourteen years' imprisonment which he was already serving for another offence). The House of Lords held that the accused could not raise the further point because that was a matter of sentence: an appeal against conviction and an appeal against sentence are distinct and a point of law in relation to the sentence cannot be considered if a matter of conviction only was certified. The Criminal Division may, of course, certify a point of law which is concerned with the sentence (see, *e.g.*, *R.* v. *Verrier* (1965), C.C.A.).

Procedure for appealing

The accused or prosecution must apply to the Criminal Division for leave to appeal within fourteen days beginning with the day on which the Criminal Division decided the appeal to it from the court below. If the Criminal Division refuses to grant leave (although it did certify the case) the accused or prosecution must apply to the House of Lords for leave within fourteen days beginning with the day on which the Criminal Division refused leave (Criminal Appeal Act 1968, s. 34(1)). Nevertheless, except in a case involving sentence of death, the House of Lords or the Criminal Division may, on the application at any time of the accused (but not the prosecution) extend the time within which an application for leave may be made by him to the House of Lords or to the Criminal Division (*ibid.*, s. 34(2)).

The Criminal Division may grant bail to an accused who is appealing, or applying for leave to appeal to the House of Lords (*ibid.*, s. 36). In addition, if the Criminal Division quashed the conviction of the accused but the prosecution is appealing or applying for leave to appeal to the House of Lords, the Criminal Division may order the detention in custody of the accused or his admission to bail, so long as that appeal is pending (*ibid.*, s. 37).

Powers of the House of Lords

The House of Lords, on an appeal to it from the Criminal Division of the Court of Appeal, may exercise any powers of that court or may remit the case to that court (Criminal Appeal Act 1968, s. 35(3)). The House of Lords has therefore all the powers which we have considered in relation to the Court of Appeal, for example, to admit additional evidence, to order a new trial, to order the issue of a writ of *venire de novo* and to vary sentence.

(2) Offences Tried Summarily

An accused convicted summarily of an offence (whether a summary offence, a hybrid offence or an indictable offence) may be able to appeal either to quarter sessions or to a Divisional Court of the Queen's Bench Division. The prosecution, however, can normally only appeal to a Divisional Court.

Appeals from Summary Trial to Quarter Sessions

Rights of appeal

An accused who has been convicted by a magistrates' court may appeal to a court of quarter sessions (*a*) if he pleaded guilty, against his sentence; (*b*) if he did not plead guilty, against the conviction or sentence (Magistrates' Courts Act 1952, s. 83(1)). Leave to appeal is not required. If the accused unequivocally pleaded guilty he cannot, therefore, appeal against his conviction (*R.* v. *Durham Quarter Sessions, ex p. Virgo* (1952), D.C.), but, even though a plea of guilty was recorded, the appeal court may consider whether in fact the accused did plead guilty, and if they are satisfied that he did not, the appeal may be heard (*R.* v. *Graham Campbell, ex p. Ahmed Hamid Moussa* (1921), D.C.). Although the prosecution normally have no right of appeal to quarter sessions, a prosecutor may appeal against the decision of a magistrates' court in proceedings for an offence under the customs or excise Acts (Customs and Excise Act 1952, s. 283(4)).

For an accused to be able to appeal he must, as a general rule, have been convicted by the magistrates, but a person bound over by the magistrates to keep the peace or to be of good behaviour may appeal to quarter sessions against the making of that binding over order even though he was not convicted of an offence (see Chap. 28) (Magistrates' Courts (Appeals from Binding Over Orders) Act 1956, s. 1). Moreover, where an accused has been convicted and an order placing him on probation or discharging him absolutely or conditionally has been made, that conviction is not deemed to be a conviction for any purpose other than for the purposes of the proceedings in which the order was made, but this does not affect his right to appeal against his conviction (see Chap. 41) (Criminal Justice Act 1948, s. 12). Nevertheless, an accused cannot appeal against his sentence, whether or not he pleaded guilty, if the magistrates made a probation order or an order for his conditional discharge, and he cannot appeal against an order made in pursuance of any enactment under which the court has no discretion as to the making of the order or its terms (although there would not in fact appear to be any such enactment) (Magistrates' Courts Act 1952, s. 83(3)). The reason why an accused cannot appeal against sentence if the magistrates made a probation order or an order of conditional discharge, is that in both cases the order is not considered to be a punishment in itself and if the accused is then convicted of a further offence committed during the currency of the probation order or order of conditional discharge he will be liable to be punished for the offence for which the order was imposed (see Chap. 44), and in this case he may then appeal against the sentence imposed on him (*ibid.*, s. 83(2)).

Procedure on appeal

An accused who is appealing from a magistrates' court to quarter sessions must give notice of his appeal, within fourteen days after the magistrates' decision, to the clerk of the magistrates' court and to the prosecution (Magistrates' Courts Act 1952, s. 84(1)). The notice must be in writing, be signed by or on behalf of the accused and it must state the general grounds of appeal (Magistrates' Courts Rules 1968, r. 63(1)). Moreover, the accused may apply in writing to quarter sessions for leave to appeal after fourteen days, and quarter sessions (*i.e.*, the chairman, deputy chairman, recorder or deputy recorder) may allow the accused to appeal out of time if it thinks fit (Magistrates' Courts Act 1952, s. 84).

If the accused does give notice of appeal to the clerk of the magistrates' court, the clerk must as soon as practicable send that notice to the clerk of the peace, and he must also send to the clerk of the peace a statement of the decision from which the appeal is brought and the last known or usual place of abode of the parties to the appeal (Magistrates' Courts Rules 1968, r. 62(2)). If the accused has been granted bail pending the appeal the magistrates' clerk, in addition, must send the recognizance to the clerk of the peace before the day fixed for hearing the appeal (*ibid.*, r. 62(3)).

An accused may abandon an appeal to quarter sessions by giving notice in writing to the clerk of the magistrates' court not later than the third day before the day fixed for hearing the appeal (Magistrates' Courts Act, 1952, s. 85(1)). Provided, however, that the notice of abandonment was not a nullity (because, *e.g.*, it was made under a mistake or fraudulent inducement), a notice once given cannot be withdrawn (*R. v. Essex Quarter Sessions Appeals Committee, ex p. Larkin* (1962), D.C.).

The hearing of the appeal

Unless the appeal is against sentence only, an appeal to quarter sessions will take the form of a complete rehearing. The witnesses for both sides will be called again to give oral evidence, and fresh evidence may be introduced by either side. It is for the prosecution to prove afresh the guilt of the accused (*R. v. Leicester Quarter Sessions, ex p. Gilks* (1966), D.C.). The hearing of an appeal will differ little, therefore, from a trial itself, although an appeal is not decided by a jury (see Chap. 28). The recorder, or chairman of quarter sessions, ought not normally to have before him a transcript of the evidence given in the magistrates' court, nor a list of the accused's previous convictions (*R. v. Grimsby Borough Quarter Sessions, ex p. Fuller* (1956), D.C.) as the appeal should be decided on the evidence adduced at the appeal itself. Nevertheless, the magistrates' clerk should send to the clerk of the peace his notes on the summary trial and these may be shown to the recorder or chairman where it is necessary or desirable, for example, on an application for legal aid (*Practice Note (Appeals and Committals to Quarter Sessions)* (1956)). Moreover, on an appeal against sentence only, additional evidence may be called or the appeal may be decided solely on the evidence given in the magistrates' court (*Paprika Ltd. v. Board of Trade* (1944), D.C.).

On an appeal to it against conviction or sentence, quarter sessions may confirm, reverse or vary the decision of the magistrates or it may remit the matter with its opinion back to the magistrates' court (*e.g.*, when quarter sessions holds that a plea of guilty was wrongly entered), or it may make such other order as it thinks fit and exercise any power which the magistrates' court might have exercised (Summary Jurisdiction Act 1879, s. 31, as substituted by the Summary Jurisdiction (Appeals) Act 1933, s. 1, and amended). Quarter sessions may, therefore, reduce or increase the sentence, even though the appeal was only against conviction (quarter sessions will, in any case, have heard all the evidence again), provided the sentence imposed is one which the magistrates might have imposed. However, even if the accused is an adult and he was convicted summarily of an indictable offence, quarter sessions cannot commit him for sentence to themselves under the Magistrates' Courts Act 1952, s. 29 (*R. v. Bullock* (1964), C.C.A.).

Appeals from Summary Trial to a Divisional Court of the Queen's Bench Division

Either the prosecution or the accused may appeal from a summary trial to a Divisional Court of the Queen's Bench Division. The appeal is by way of a case stated, and the proceeding before the magistrates may be questioned on the ground that it was wrong in law or in excess of jurisdiction (Magistrates' Courts Act 1952, s. 87(1)). The prosecution or accused may appeal, moreover, even though another part of the magistrates' judgment or order was in their favour (*Burke* v. *Copper* (1962), D.C.).

Form of the case

A case stated by a magistrates' court must state the facts found by the magistrates (Magistrates' Court Rules 1968, r. 68) and it should also state the contentions of the parties, the decision of the magistrates and the questions of law which arise on the case for the determination of the Divisional court (*Downsborough* v. *Huddersfield Industrial Society Ltd.* (1942), D.C.). The only question for the Divisional Court will then be whether the magistrates were right in law in coming to the decision which they did on the facts which they found, or whether they had jurisdiction. The case must not set out the evidence on which the decision was given (*ibid.*, r. 68), unless the ground of appeal is that there was no evidence on which the magistrates' court could have come to its decision, and the appellant cannot put in the magistrates' clerk's note of the evidence, because the Divisional Court should look only at the case as stated (*McGee* v. *George* (1964), D.C.). The Divisional Court, moreover, is bound by the facts as stated in the case, and the parties cannot normally contend that the facts were different (*Musther* v. *Musther* (1894), D.C.). Nevertheless, the Divisional Court does have power, if it thinks fit, to send the case back to the magistrates for amendment (Summary Jurisdiction Act 1857, s. 7), and, before the appeal itself is heard, an application may be made for the case to be sent back, on the ground that material facts are omitted (*Practice Note* (*Case Stated*) (1953)).

Procedure for stating case

The appellant must apply to the magistrates to state a case for the opinion of the Divisional Court within fourteen days after their decision was given (Magistrates' Courts Act 1952, s. 87(2)). The application, which must be in writing, should be delivered or sent to the clerk of the magistrates' court (Magistrates' Courts Rules 1968,

r. 65) and the case may then be stated by any two or more (or one stipendiary magistrate) of the magistrates whose decision is questioned (*ibid.*, r. 66). The magistrates must, in fact, state a case if the application is made by or under the direction of the Attorney-General and they must also state a case if the application is by any other person unless they are of the opinion that the application is frivolous (Magistrates' Courts Act 1952, s. 87(5)). Should the magistrates refuse to state a case they must, if so required, give the applicant a certificate stating that they have refused to do so (although the certificate should merely state that the application was frivolous) (*ibid.*, s. 87(5)), and application may then be made to a Divisional Court of the Queen's Bench Division for an order of mandamus to compel the magistrates to state the case (see Chap. 42) (*ibid.*, s. 87(6)). If the accused does apply to the magistrates for a case to be stated, he loses his right to appeal to quarter sessions (*ibid.*, s. 87(4)).

If the magistrates state a case they must do so within three months after the application for the case to be stated (Magistrates' Courts Rules 1968, r. 67). An application may be made to the Divisional Court for an extension of this time, but an extension will not normally be granted if the failure of the magistrates was due to the fault of the applicant (*Whittingham* v. *Nattrass* (1958), D.C.). The applicant, moreover, must lodge the case in the Crown Office of the High Court within ten days after receiving it, and within four days of lodging the case he must serve on the respondent to the appeal a notice of the entry of appeal together with a copy of the case (R.S.C. Ord. 56, r. 6(1)). Again, however, the Divisional Court has power to extend the ten or four days if proper grounds are shown (*Whittingham* v. *Nattrass, supra*). Unless the Divisional Court otherwise directs, the appeal cannot then be heard sooner than eight clear days after service of the notice of the entry of appeal (R.S.C. Ord. 56, r. 6(2)).

Powers of the Divisional Court

The Divisional Court on the hearing of the appeal may reverse, affirm or amend the magistrates' decision or may remit the matter to the magistrates with its opinion thereon, or may make such order in relation to the matter, including an order as to costs, as it sees fit (Summary Jurisdiction Act 1857, s. 6). Nevertheless, the Divisional Court itself has no power to vary the sentence imposed (*Evans* v. *Hemingway* (1887), D.C.), and the court cannot order the magistrates who stated the case to pay any costs (*ibid.*, s. 6).

Appeals from Quarter Sessions to a Divisional Court of the Queen's Bench Division

Where a court of quarter sessions has determined an appeal to it from a magistrates' court (see above), though not when it has tried an accused on indictment, either the prosecution or the accused may appeal from it to a Divisional Court of the Queen's Bench Division, and this appeal will be by way of a case stated by quarter sessions for the opinion of the Divisional Court. Quarter sessions has power to state a case both under statute and under the common law.

Criminal Justice Act 1925, s. 20

After the determination by a court of quarter sessions of an appeal against a conviction by a magistrates' court or against the sentence imposed on such a conviction, either the prosecution or accused, if dissatisfied with the determination of the court of quarter sessions as being erroneous in point of law, may apply to the court of quarter sessions to have a case stated for the opinion of the Divisional Court (s. 20(1)). The application for a case to be stated must be made in writing within seven days after the determination by quarter sessions of the appeal to it, and the application should be delivered to the clerk of the peace (s. 20(1)). Before the case is delivered to the applicant, moreover, he must enter into a recognizance before a magistrate, with or without sureties (see Chap. 43), and in such sum as the magistrate considers proper, conditional upon prosecuting the appeal without delay and upon submitting to the judgment of the Divisional Court (subject to any further right of appeal) (s. 20(2)).

Like a magistrates' court, quarter sessions must always state a case under section 20 if it is applied for by or on behalf of the Attorney-General, or in any other case unless the application is frivolous, and if it refuses to state a case the clerk of the peace must, on request, deliver to the applicant a certificate of refusal, stating the reasons for that refusal (s. 20(3)). If quarter sessions does refuse to state a case the applicant may apply to the Divisional Court for an order of mandamus to compel it to do so (s. 20(4), as amended).

Under the common law

Apart from the duty of quarter sessions to state a case if the requirements of section 20 of the Criminal Justice Act 1925 are complied with, quarter sessions still retains a power under the common law to state a case. This power, moreover, is not dependent on there having been a conviction in the magistrates' court (*R. v. Somerset JJ., ex p. Ernest J. Cole & Partners Ltd.* (1950), D.C.; a town-planning action), nor need an application for the case to be stated necessarily be made within seven days of the appeal to quarter sessions having been determined (*R. v. Northumberland Quarter Sessions, ex p. Williamson* (1965), D.C.), although it should be made within a reasonable time (*Chesterton R.D.C. v. Ralph Thompson Ltd.* (1944), D.C.). Quarter sessions has a discretion whether or not to state a case under the common law, and it cannot be compelled to do so by an order of mandamus (*R. v. Northumberland Quarter Sessions, ex p. Williamson, supra*). If a party does apply under the common law for a case to be stated he must still enter into a recognizance, as under section 20(4) (R.S.C. Ord. 56, r. 1(2)).

Procedure

Whether an appeal from quarter sessions to the Divisional Court is under the Criminal Justice Act 1925, s. 20, or under the common law, notice of the appeal must normally be entered for hearing within six months of the determination by quarter sessions of the appeal to it (R.S.C. Ord. 56, r. 1(4)), but the appeal cannot be entered unless and until the case and a copy of the judgment or order, both of quarter sessions and of the magistrates' court, has been lodged in the Crown Office (R.S.C. Ord. 56, r. 1(3)). The appellant must also serve notice of the entry of appeal on the respondent within four days after the appeal has been entered (R.S.C. Ord. 56, r. 4). The powers of the Divisional Court will then be basically the same as on an appeal direct from a magistrates' court.

Appeals from the Divisional Court to the House of Lords

Appeals lie to the House of Lords from any decision of a Divisional Court of the Queen's Bench Division in a criminal cause or matter, and at the instance of either the accused or the prosecution (Administration of Justice Act 1960, s. 1(1)). The procedure is the same as for an appeal from the Criminal Division of the Court of Appeal to the House of Lords (see above), except that it is the Divisional Court which must have certified that a point of law of general public importance is involved in the decision and it is the Divisional Court, or the House of Lords, which must grant leave to appeal (ibid., s. 1(2)).

Chapter Forty-Two

ORDERS OF CERTIORARI, MANDAMUS AND PROHIBITION

ORDERS of certiorari, mandamus and prohibition are very important in relation to criminal proceedings because by them the High Court can control the conduct of inferior courts.

Certiorari is an order whereby the record of proceedings before an inferior court is to be transmitted to the High Court to be quashed. Mandamus is an order requiring an act to be performed by an inferior court, and by the Administration of Justice (Miscellaneous Provisions) Act 1938, s. 8, any power of the High Court under any enactment to require magistrates to do any act relating to their office, or to require any magistrates' court or quarter sessions to state a case, shall be exercised by order of mandamus. Prohibition is an order restraining an inferior court from exceeding its jurisdiction.

"Inferior Court"

For the purpose of orders of certiorari, mandamus and prohibition "inferior court" includes both a magistrates' court and a coroner's court (*R.* v. *Clerk of Assize of Oxford Circuit* (1897), D.C.). Quarter sessions is an inferior court when it is sitting to hear an appeal from a magistrates' court (*R.* v. *Grimsby Borough Quarter Sessions, ex p. Fuller* (1956), D.C.), and an order of mandamus may also be granted when quarter sessions is sitting as a trial court (*R.* v. *County of London Quarter Sessions, ex p. Downes* (1954), D.C.). There is some uncertainty whether an order of certiorari will lie to quarter sessions when it is sitting as a trial court, for though there are recorded cases when certiorari has been granted (*e.g., R.* v. *Norfolk Quarter Sessions, ex p. Brunson* (1953), D.C.), it has been suggested that this power was removed by an Act of 1403 (4 Hen. 4, c. 23 (see D. M. Gordon in (1953) 69 L.Q.R. 175; and also Cave J. in *R.* v. *Boaler* (1892), D.C.). A court of assize (*Ex p. Fernandez* (1861)) and the Central Criminal Court (*R.* v.

338

Central Criminal Court JJ., ex p. L.C.C. (1925), D.C.) are not "inferior courts."

Grounds on which an Order may be Granted

Certiorari

An order of certiorari may be granted on the following grounds:

(1) That there has been a defect of jurisdiction (*R.* v. *Essex JJ., ex p. Final* (1963), D.C.); and this includes the imposition of a sentence in excess of the statutory maximum (*R.* v. *Willesden JJ., ex p. Utley* (1948), D.C.). Certiorari does not lie, however, on the ground that the decision was contrary to the facts of the case or the evidence (*R.* v. *Nat Bell Liquors Ltd.* (1922), P.C.) and the High Court has no power to inquire into the evidence to see whether the facts proved warranted the conviction (*R.* v. *Mahony* (1910), High Ct., Ir.). Nevertheless, affidavit evidence may be admitted to show want of jurisdiction, even though this does not appear on the face of the record (see below) (*R.* v. *Toynbee Hall JJ., ex p. Joseph* (1939), D.C.).

(2) That there has been a breach of the rules of natural justice (*e.g., R.* v. *Wandsworth JJ., ex p. Read* (1942), D.C. (magistrates convicted without hearing defence evidence); *R.* v. *Bodmin JJ., ex p. McEwen* (1947), D.C. (magistrates heard evidence in their private room); *R.* v. *Stafford JJ., ex p. Ross* (1962), D.C. (magistrates' clerk tried to influence magistrates' decision on the facts); *R.* v. *Dorchester JJ., ex p. Giblin and Mutter* (1966), D.C. (magistrates convicted without hearing speech on behalf of defence)); or that there was a real likelihood of bias on the part of the court (*R.* v. *Grimsby Borough Quarter Sessions, ex p. Fuller* (1956), D.C.) (see Chap. 28. In practice the only way in which a denial of justice can be brought to the knowledge of the High Court is by way of affidavit (*per* Lord Caldecote C.J. in *R.* v. *Wandsworth JJ., ex p. Read* (above)).

(3) That there is an error of law apparent on the face of the record (*R.* v. *Northumberland Compensation Appeal Tribunal, ex p. Shaw* (1952), C.A.; *Baldwin & Francis Ltd.* v. *Patents Appeal Tribunal* (1959), H.L.). Nevertheless, since the Summary Jurisdiction Act 1848, only the charge, the conviction and the sentence have appeared on the face of the record of summary proceedings so that it is very rare for certiorari to lie to a criminal court on this ground (other than for an excess of jurisdiction).

(4) That the decision was obtained by fraud or perjury (*R.* v. *Recorder of Leicester* (1947), D.C.). The fraud or perjury, however, must be apparent and it must be by a party to the action or in collusion with one of the parties (*R.* v. *Ashford, Kent JJ., ex p. Richley* (1956), C.A.).

Acquittals. Certiorari will not be granted in respect of an acquittal unless the proceedings were void (*R.* v. *Justices of Galway* (1906), High Ct., Ir.; *R.* v. *Simpson* (1914), D.C.). Thus, in *R.* v. *Middlesex Quarter Sessions, ex p. D.P.P.* (1952), where the chairman of Quarter Sessions, in effect, prevented the prosecution from calling their evidence, a Divisional Court held that an order of certiorari could not be granted· because the accused had been acquitted.

Quashing written record. Certiorari only lies to quash a written record (see R.S.C. Ord. 53, r. 6), and the proceedings of the inferior court must, therefore, have been recorded in writing before they can be quashed by certiorari (*R.* v. *Newington Licensing JJ.* (1948), D.C.). As a general rule, moreover, an order of certiorari must require the record to be transmitted to the High Court to be quashed, and the court has no power to order an amendment (*per* Lord Cairns L.C. in *Walsall Overseers* v. *L.N.W. Railway* (1878), H.L.), although there is sometimes power to amend a sentence.

Sentence. Certiorari may lie in respect of the sentence only, when an inferior court has passed a sentence which is in excess of its jurisdiction (*R.* v. *Willesden JJ., ex p. Utley* (1948), D.C.). However, by the Administration of Justice Act 1960, s. 16, the Divisional Court has power to quash the sentence alone and to substitute a proper sentence.

Discretion. Certiorari is a discretionary remedy and the Divisional Court will therefore refuse to grant an order of certiorari when the circumstances make it right to do so. Circumstances in which the court may refuse an order of certiorari include, where the applicant has been guilty of delay (*R.* v. *Stafford JJ., ex p. Stafford Corporation* (1940), C.A.) (for the time limits for applying, see below), where the applicant pleaded guilty (*R.* v. *Campbell, ex p. Nomikos* (1956), D.C.), or where leave to apply was obtained by a false statement or by suppression of material facts (*per* Bray J. in *R.* v. *Barnes, ex p. Vernon* (1910), D.C.). Moreover, the Divisional Court will not grant an order of certiorari where there is some other equally convenient course open to the applicant, for example, an appeal (*per* Humphrey J. in *R.* v. *Wandsworth JJ., ex p. Read*

(1942), D.C.). But the other course must be "equally convenient," and not merely possible though with disadvantages (*R.* v. *Wandsworth JJ., ex p. Read*, above; and see *Rigby* v. *Woodward* (1957), D.C.).

Mandamus

An order of mandamus may be granted in the following cases:

(1) To compel a magistrates' court to state a case (Magistrates' Courts Act 1952, s. 87(6)) or to compel quarter sessions to state a case when it has heard an appeal from a magistrates' court (Criminal Justice Act 1925, s. 20(4), as amended) (see Chap. 41).

(2) To compel a magistrate to issue process when he has wrongly refused to do so (*R.* v. *Bennett* (1908), D.C.) (see Chap. 31).

There is, in fact, a general power to apply for an order of mandamus in all cases where a magistrate has refused to do any act relating to the duties of his office (Justices Protection Act 1848, s. 5, as amended), but mandamus will not be granted where the magistrate had a discretion whether or not to perform the act (*R.* v. *London JJ.* (1895), C.A.).

Discretion. Like certiorari, mandamus is a discretionary remedy and the Divisional Court may refuse an order, for example, where there has been undue delay (*R.* v. *Robson* (1893), D.C.), or where the matter could more conveniently have been dealt with by certiorari (*R.* v. *Owen and Others JJ., ex p. Scovell* (1907), D.C.). An order of mandamus will not be granted where the applicant had some other equally convenient course open to him (*per* Humphrey J. in *R.* v. *Wandsworth JJ., ex p. Read* (1942), D.C.).

Prohibition

An order of prohibition, which may be granted only when the proceedings are incomplete, may be issued on the following grounds:

(1) That there would be a defect of jurisdiction (*R.* v. *Chelsea JJ., ex p. D.P.P.* (1963), D.C.).

(2) That there would be a breach of the rules of natural justice, for example, there would be a likelihood of bias (*R.* v. *Farrant* (1887), D.C.), or a breach of the "*audi alteram partem*" rule (*R.* v. *North, ex p. Oakey* (1927), C.A.).

Discretion. If a defect of jurisdiction is apparent on the face of the record, the court has no discretion to refuse an order of prohibition to prevent those proceedings continuing (*Farquharson* v. *Morgan* (1894), C.A.), but otherwise an order of prohibition is discretionary (*per* Willes J. in *Mayor of London* v. *Cox* (1866), H.L.). An order of prohibition may be granted, moreover, although an appeal would have lain had the inferior court continued to deal with the case (*R.* v. *Wimbledon JJ., ex p. Derwent* (1953), D.C.).

Procedure for Applying for an Order

Application for leave to apply

An application for an order of certiorari, mandamus or prohibition (or an application for all or two of them concurrently) cannot be made unless leave to apply has been granted (R.S.C. Ord. 53, r. 1(1)).

Time for applying. An application for leave to apply for an order of certiorari in respect of any judgment, order, conviction or other proceeding must normally be made within six months after the date of the proceeding which it is sought to quash (Ord. 53, r. 2(2)). An application for leave to apply for an order of mandamus to compel quarter sessions to hear an appeal must normally be made within two months after the first day of the sessions at which the refusal by quarter sessions occurred (Ord. 53, r. 2(1)). In both cases the High Court has power to extend the time for applying (Ord. 3, r. 5), but it will not normally do so unless there are special circumstances (*R.* v. *Gloucestershire JJ.* (1890), D.C.). Apart from these cases, however, there is no fixed time limit but an application for prohibition must be made before the occurrence which it is sought to prohibit and the court always has a discretion to refuse any order after an undue lapse of time (see above).

Procedure. An application for leave to apply for an order of certiorari, mandamus or prohibition must be made *ex parte* to a Divisional Court of the Queen's Bench Division, except in vacation when it may be made to a judge in chambers (Ord. 53, r. 1(2)). The applicant must give notice of the application not later than the preceding day to the Crown Office and at the same time he must lodge a statement setting out the relief sought and the grounds on which it is sought, and affidavits verifying the facts relied upon (Ord. 53, r. 1(3)). If the High Court does grant leave it may impose such terms as to costs as it thinks fit (Ord. 53, r. 1(4)), while it may also order that the grant of leave to apply for certiorari or prohibition shall operate as a stay of the proceedings (Ord. 53, r. 1(5)).

Where a judge in chambers refuses leave to apply the applicant may make a fresh application to a Divisional Court (Ord. 53, r. 1(6)). If a Divisional Court refuses leave, an appeal may lie to the House of Lords (Administration of Justice Act 1960, s. 1).

Application for an order

If leave to apply for an order of certiorari, mandamus or prohibition is granted, the application must be made by originating motion to a Divisional Court of the Queen's Bench Division, except in vacation when it may be made by originating summons to a judge in chambers (Ord. 53, r. 3(1)). The motion must be entered for hearing within fourteen days after such leave was granted (Ord. 53, r. 3(2)) and the notice of motion or the summons, and copies of the statement accompanying the application for leave, must be served on all persons directly affected, for example, on the clerk of the court against whose decision the order is sought, and on the other parties (Ord. 53, rr. 3(3) and 4(1)). There must normally be eight clear days between service of the notice or the summons and the day named therein (Ord. 53, r. 3(1)).

The hearing. On the hearing no grounds other than those contained in the statement can normally be relied upon, although the court has power to grant leave to the contrary (Ord. 53, r. 4). The magistrates themselves may give their reasons by affidavit together with any facts which they consider material (Review of Justices Decisions Act 1872, s. 2). The court in deciding on the application must then take into consideration the matters set forth in the affidavit, even though the magistrates do not appear (*ibid.*, s. 3).

Appeals

An appeal may lie to the House of Lords at the instance of either side from any decision of a Divisional Court of the Queen's Bench Division in a criminal cause or matter (Administration of Justice Act 1960, s. 1). This includes a decision by a Divisional Court on an application for an order of certiorari, mandamus or prohibition and the law and procedure is the same as for appeals from a Divisional Court which has heard an appeal by case stated (see Chap. 41).

Chapter Forty-Three

BAIL

The Nature of Bail

BAIL is the name given to a process whereby an accused person, instead of being kept in custody to await his trial, appeal or other hearing, is released on a written agreement (called a recognizance) that if he does not attend the trial, etc., he will be liable to have to pay to the Crown the amount of money fixed in the recognizance (*i.e.*, to have his recognizance estreated). Certain other persons (called sureties) may also be, and normally are, required to enter into recognizances whereby they undertake to see that the accused does appear at the trial, etc., and if he fails to do so they are also liable to have to pay to the Crown the amount fixed in their recognizances. Where an accused is unable to produce the required sureties immediately he may be remanded in custody until they are produced (see the Magistrates' Courts Act 1952, s. 95), although subsequently the magistrates may vary or dispense with the requirement as to sureties (*ibid.*, s. 94). In addition, where bail is granted, such conditions may be imposed which appear to the court granting the bail to be likely to result in the accused's appearance at the time and place required, or to be necessary in the interests of justice or for the prevention of crime (Criminal Justice Act 1967, s. 21(1)). The accused cannot, however, be required to find sureties in respect of these additional conditions (*ibid.*, s. 21(2)).

If, therefore, an accused is released on bail, whether with or without sureties, no money is paid or lodged in the court, but if he fails to appear at the time and place stipulated in the recognizance, or he breaks any other condition of the bail, then the accused (and, if he fails to appear, his sureties, if any were required) will be liable to have to pay to the Crown the amount fixed. Nevertheless, the court has a discretion whether to order that the recognizances of the accused or his sureties be estreated, and if so whether in whole or in part.

344

Sureties

As we have just seen, the duty of sureties (or "bail" as they are sometimes misleadingly called) is to see to the attendance of the accused. If a surety believes that the accused is likely to break the condition that he should attend at a stipulated time and place, the surety may notify a police officer in writing of his belief and state that he wishes to be relieved of his obligations as a surety. The police officer may then arrest the accused and bring him before a magistrate as soon as practicable, and in any event within twenty-four hours of the arrest, or, if the accused is required by the condition of the bail to appear before a court within twenty-four hours of his arrest, he must be brought before that court (Criminal Justice Act 1967, s. 23). In addition, a police officer, without being requested by a surety, may similarly arrest an accused if the police officer has reasonable grounds for believing that the accused is likely to break (or is breaking or has broken) any condition on which he was admitted to bail (*ibid.*, s. 23(1) (*a*)). Where an accused is brought by a police officer before a magistrate, the magistrate may, if of opinion that the accused has broken or is likely to break any condition, remand or commit him to custody or alternatively release him on his original recognizance or on a new recognizance, with or without sureties, and, if not of that opinion, shall release him on his original recognizance (*ibid.*, s. 23(3)).

As the sureties will be liable to pay to the Crown the amount of their recognizances, should the accused fail to attend the trial, etc., they should be of sufficient ability to pay this amount if called upon to do so, and normally only householders are accepted. The proposed sureties may be examined upon oath as to their means and, in addition the police may object to any of those proposed. The grounds of objection may include that the surety is himself a convicted person (*R.* v. *Edwards* (1791)), and a surety must not be an infant or a person in custody.

If the accused does not appear at the trial, etc., the sureties will be liable to have their recognizances estreated but, as we have seen, the court will have a discretion whether to estreat the recognizances, and if so whether in whole or in part. Thus, in *R.* v. *Doyen* (1899) where the accused, who was a Frenchman, had gone to France and had then been unable to return for the trial because of mental illness, the court refused to estreat the recognizances, while in *R.* v. *Sangiovanni* (1904) it was said that the recognizances of the sureties would not normally be estreated if they had taken reasonable steps to secure the attendance of the accused.

Whether Bail should be Granted

We have seen that in certain cases the magistrates must grant bail to an accused (Chaps. 39, 40). Apart from these cases, however, the basic rule is that a person should not be deprived of his liberty without just cause, so that an accused awaiting trial should be released on bail unless there is good cause to the contrary. The refusal or delay to grant bail in a suitable case is an offence against the liberty of the subject and a violation of the Habeas Corpus Act 1679 and of the Bill of Rights 1689 (see Archbold *Criminal Pleading, Evidence & Practice*, 37th ed., para. 202). Where the accused has already been convicted, however, and been sentenced to imprisonment or other detention, the reverse is the rule and a court has no inherent jurisdiction to grant him bail (*Ex p. Blyth* (1944)) (see below).

Although the basic rule is that before conviction an accused ought to be granted bail unless there is good cause to the contrary, whether or not the case is a suitable one for bail is a matter for the court's judicial discretion (*R. v. Phillips* (1920)). There has been some doubt as to whether there was a discretion to refuse bail in cases of misdemeanours (which would now apply to all offences except treason: Criminal Law Act 1967, s. 1(2)) (see Roscoe's *Criminal Evidence*, 16th ed., p. 245; and see *R. v. Phillips* (1947), C.C.A.), but it would seem that there is now a discretion in all cases (see Archbold, *op. cit.*, para. 202). Nevertheless, in *Ex p. Thomas* (1956), where the magistrates granted bail but fixed the amount of the recognizances at so high a figure that the accused could not avail himself of it (which is in itself contrary to the Bill of Rights 1689), the High Court held that this was, in effect, a denial of bail and that the correct procedure was an application by the accused for a writ of habeas corpus.

The major consideration in deciding whether bail should be granted is whether it is probable that, if the accused is released on bail, he will appear to take his trial (*Re Robinson* (1854)), and in considering this matter the court may have regard to the nature of the offence charged, the nature of the evidence and the possible punishments. Nevertheless, although it is very rare to grant bail in, for example, a case of murder, it is not unknown. Other matters which the court may consider in deciding whether to grant bail are whether witnesses may be interfered with and whether or not, if the accused is released on bail, a repetition of the offence is likely (*R. v. Phillips* (1947), C.C.A.). It is normal for the court, when it is considering whether bail should be granted, to be informed of the previous convictions and record of the accused and bail will not normally be granted to an accused who has a bad criminal record (*R*. v. *Wharton* (1955), C.C.A.). The previous convictions (of which the court is normally informed in writing) should not, however, be mentioned in any newspaper report of the proceedings (*R*. v. *Fletcher* (1949), C.C.A.) and a magistrate who is informed of any previous convictions for the purposes of considering bail cannot then try the guilt of the accused (Criminal Justice Act 1967, s. 19). In deciding on the amount of the recognizances the court will also have regard to the wealth of the accused and this will include consideration of whether or not the accused will be able to indemnify the sureties (see *R*. v. *Porter* (1910), C.C.A.).

Where a magistrates' court refuses to remand or commit on bail an accused who has attained seventeen years the court must, if he is not represented by counsel or a solicitor, inform him that he may apply to a High Court judge for bail (see below) (Criminal Justice Act 1967, s. 18(7)).

When Bail may be Granted

On arrest with a warrant
A warrant for arrest may be endorsed with a direction that the accused shall on arrest be released on bail on his entering into such a recognizance, with or without sureties, as is specified in the endorsement (Magistrates' Courts Act 1952, s. 93(1)). If the warrant were endorsed in this way, the accused, after being arrested on the warrant and after being taken to a police station, should be released on bail by the officer in charge of that station in accordance with the endorsement on the warrant (*ibid.*, s. 93 (2)).

If a child or young person is arrested with a warrant (which is not endorsed for bail), or without a warrant, and he cannot be brought before a magistrates' court forthwith, a police officer not below the rank of inspector, or the officer in charge of the police station to which the accused is brought, must inquire into the offence and must release the accused on bail on a recognizance entered into by the accused or his parent or guardian (with or without sureties), unless the offence is homicide or other grave crime or it is necessary in the accused's interest to remove him from his associates, or the officer has reason to believe that his release would defeat the ends of justice (Children and Young Persons Act 1933, s. 32(1), as amended). The recognizance may, in fact, be conditioned not only for the attendance of the accused but of his parent or guardian as well (Children and Young Persons Act 1963, s. 25(2)) (see "Juvenile courts," Chap. 28).

On arrest without a warrant

In addition to the provisions in relation to children and young persons, any accused after arrest without a warrant may be released on bail (with or without sureties) by a police officer not below the rank of inspector, or the officer in charge of the police station to which the accused is brought, and, unless the offence is a serious one, the accused must be released on bail if it will not be practicable to bring him before a magistrates' court within twenty-four hours after his arrest (Magistrates' Courts Act 1952, s. 38(1)). Where further inquiries into the case have to be made the accused may be released on bail on entering into a recognizance conditioned for his appearance at a police station, instead of before a magistrates' court (*ibid.*, s. 38(2)). (See also the Children and Young Persons Act 1933, s. 13.)

On remand

If the magistrates adjourn committal proceedings they must remand the accused either in custody or on bail, while if they adjourn a summary trial they may (subject to those cases where they must remand on bail: see Chap. 39) remand either in custody or on bail. If the accused is remanded on bail the magistrates may do so with or without sureties and the recognizances may be conditioned for the appearance of the accused at the end of the fixed period of remand or (where the proceedings may be adjourned again and to save the sureties the necessity of attending every adjourned hearing) at every adjourned hearing of the case (Magistrates' Courts Act 1952, s. 105).

On committal for trial

If the examining justices commit an accused for trial on indictment, unless the charge is treason, they may (subject to those cases where they must commit on bail: see Chap. 40), commit him either in custody or on bail (with or without sureties) (Magistrates' Courts Act 1952, s. 7(2)). If the accused is charged with treason, however, he cannot be admitted to bail except by order of a High Court judge or Secretary of State (*ibid.*, s. 8). In view of the time that may elapse between a committal for trial and the trial itself, it is at this stage that the question of bail is probably most important and the matters which we have considered as to whether bail should be granted are particularly relevant here.

Even though the examining justices first commit an accused in custody they have power, at any time before the first sitting of the trial court, unless the charge is treason, to release him on bail (*ibid.*, s. 7(3)).

For the power of a coroner to grant bail to an accused committed for trial on a coroner's inquisition, when the offence charged is manslaughter or infanticide, see Chapter 28.

For the procedure when an accused who has been committed for trial on bail fails to surrender to his bail, see Chapter 34.

By the High Court

Where, in connection with any criminal proceedings, an inferior court (*i.e.*, quarter sessions, a magistrates' court or a coroner) has power to admit an accused to bail, but either refuses to do so, or does so, or offers to do so, on terms unacceptable to him, the High Court (*i.e.*, a judge of the High Court) may admit him or direct his admission to bail or, where he has been admitted to bail, may vary any conditions on which he was so admitted or reduce the amount in which he or any surety is bound, or discharge any of the sureties (Criminal Justice Act 1967, s. 22). Nevertheless, the High Court cannot impose conditions as to the time and place of appearance of the accused which the inferior court would not have had power to impose (*ibid.*, s. 22(2)).

We have already seen that a magistrates' court must sometimes inform an accused that he may apply for bail to the High Court, but the power of the High Court to admit to bail extends to all cases where the inferior court could admit to bail, including where the accused has appealed to the High Court or to quarter sessions (see below). The High Court also has power to admit an accused to bail who has applied to that court for an order of certiorari (see below).

An application to the High Court for bail is made to a judge in chambers. It must be made by summons supported by an affidavit and it is for the prosecutor, on whom the summons must be served at least twenty-four hours before the day named for the hearing (R.S.C. Ord. 79, r. 9), to show cause why bail should not be granted.

If the High Court refuses to grant bail a further application cannot, however, be made to the Court of Appeal or to the Lord Chancellor (see *Re Kray* (1965), L.C.).

By the trial court

Where an accused has been committed for trial on indictment, the trial court itself has power to grant bail and it may do so, for example, if the trial is adjourned, particularly if the accused was committed for trial on bail by the examining justices. For the position when the accused is not tried at the next session of the trial court, see the Assizes Relief Act 1889, s. 3, and the Habeas Corpus Act 1679, s. 6.

Bail

On appeal

From trial on indictment. Where an accused, who has been convicted on indictment and sentenced to imprisonment or other form of detention, is appealing to the Criminal Division of the Court of Appeal, there is no inherent jurisdiction to grant him bail (see above) but bail may be granted by the appeal court or by a judge of the appeal court under section 19 of the Criminal Appeal Act 1968. Thus, the trial judge may grant him bail provided he is a judge of the Queen's Bench Division of the High Court (Criminal Appeal Act 1966, s. 1(4)). Nevertheless, the accused will not be granted bail without good cause, and in practice bail is rarely granted (for a case where bail was granted, see *R. v. Tarran* (1947), C.C.A.).

If the Criminal Division of the Court of Appeal orders a retrial, it may make such orders as appear to be necessary or expedient for the custody or admission to bail of the accused pending the retrial (Criminal Appeal Act 1968, s. 8(2)).

From summary trial. Where an accused has given notice of appeal to a court of quarter sessions against the decision of a magistrates' court or he has applied to a magistrates' court to state a case for the opinion of the High Court, then, if he is in custody, the magistrates' court may release him on bail on his entering into a recognizance, with or without sureties, conditioned (*a*) if he has given notice of appeal, for his appearance at the hearing of the appeal; (*b*) if he has applied for the statement of a case, for his appearance before the magistrates' court within ten days after judgment of the High Court, unless conviction has been quashed by the High Court (Magistrates' Courts Act 1952, s. 89(1)). The magistrates' court cannot, however, grant the accused bail under this section if he has been committed in custody to quarter sessions for sentence under sections 28 or 29 of the Magistrates' Courts Act 1952 (*ibid.*, s. 89(2)). Nevertheless, the magistrates may have committed him on bail to quarter sessions for sentence, when no question of bail on a concurrent appeal will arise, because the accused will not be in custody. Likewise, if the accused has been committed in custody to quarter sessions for sentence, the High Court may grant him bail in relation to that committal even though he has also appealed against the conviction (see above).

On appeal to the House of Lords. The Criminal Division of the Court of Appeal or a Divisional Court of the Queen's Bench Division may also grant bail to an accused who is appealing, or is applying for leave to appeal, from that court to the House of Lords (Criminal Appeal Act 1968, s. 36; Administration of Justice Act 1960, s. 4, as amended). In addition, when the prosecution is appealing to the House of Lords the Criminal Division or the Divisional Court has power to make an order providing for the detention of the accused, or directing that he shall not be released except on bail, pending that appeal (Criminal Appeal Act 1968, s. 37(2); Administration of Justice Act 1960, s. 5(1)).

On application for an order of certiorari

Neither the magistrates nor a High Court judge has any inherent jurisdiction to grant bail to a convicted person who is applying for an order of certiorari (*Ex p. Blyth* (1944)), but bail may be granted by a judge of the High Court under the Criminal Justice Act 1948, s. 37(1) (*d*).

Chapter Forty-Four

PUNISHMENTS AND OTHER METHODS OF DEALING WITH OFFENDERS

(1) In General

Death

Sentence of death (*i.e.*, death by hanging), which was historically, the normal punishment for all felonies and, more recently, for murder, can now be awarded only on conviction for high treason (Treason Act 1814, s. 1), piracy with violence (Piracy Act 1837, s. 2) and setting fire to any of Her Majesty's ships, stores, etc. (Dockyards Protection Act 1772, s. 1). Moreover, an offender can never be sentenced to death if he was under eighteen years at the time the offence was committed (Children and Young Persons Act 1933, s. 53, as amended by the Murder (Abolition of Death Penalty) Act 1965, s. 1(5)) (see also below), nor can a woman who is pregnant be sentenced to death (Sentence of Death (Expectant Mothers) Act 1931, s. 1).

Imprisonment

Before the Criminal Justice Act 1948 there was a distinction between imprisonment and penal servitude, and imprisonment could be inflicted with or without hard labour. By section 1 of that Act, however, penal servitude and hard labour were abolished and there is now only one form of imprisonment. Where an old enactment confers power to pass a sentence of penal servitude it is to be construed as conferring power to pass a sentence of imprisonment for a term not exceeding the maximum term of penal servitude (*ibid.*, s. 1(1)).

Imprisonment is expressly provided by many statutes as a possible punishment for the offences therein mentioned, but in addition imprisonment can be imposed for any common law offence not subject to special statutory punishment and for any statutory offence for which no specific statutory punishment is prescribed (Archbold, *Criminal Pleading, Evidence & Practice* (37th ed.), para. 659). Nevertheless, no court may sentence an offender under the age of seventeen to imprisonment (Criminal Justice Act 1961, s. 2(2)) and generally no court may sentence to imprisonment an offender who is of an age for Borstal training (*i.e.*, he is under twenty-one, see below) unless it is for a term of at least three years (eighteen months if the offender has already served a sentence of Borstal training (see *R.* v. *Hughes* (1968), C.A.), or a sentence of imprisonment for at least six months) or unless it is for a term not exceeding six months (*ibid.*, s. 3). The reason for this provision is that if the court considers that the sentence should be for more than six months but for less than three years the court should sentence the offender to Borstal training. Consecutive sentences of imprisonment which in the aggregate (though not individually) amount to or exceed three years may, however, be passed (*R.* v. *Scully* (1966), C.C.A.).

No court should, in fact, sentence an offender under twenty-one years to imprisonment unless no other method of dealing with him is appropriate, and if the sentencing court is quarter sessions or a magistrates' court it must state the reason for its opinion that no other method is appropriate (Criminal Justice Act 1948, s. 17: Magistrates' Courts Act 1952, s. 107). Likewise, a magistrates' court should not pass a sentence of imprisonment on a first offender (*i.e.*, one who since attaining the age of seventeen has not been convicted of an offence punishable with imprisonment) of twenty-one years or over unless no other method is appropriate, and, if it is not appropriate, the reason must be specified (First Offenders Act 1958, s. 1).

Alternatively, a magistrates' court, where it could have passed a sentence of imprisonment, may instead order an offender to be detained for any period not exceeding four days in a suitable place (*e.g.*, a police cell) certified to be so by the Home Secretary (Magistrates' Courts Act 1952, s. 109), or the court may order detention during the day when the order is made within the precincts of the court or at any police station (*ibid.*, s. 110).

These provisions as to imprisonment are, however, subject to the court's power or duty to pass a suspended sentence (see below), and section 57 of the Criminal Justices Act 1967 (which is to come into force on a day to be named) provides that the Home Secretary may make rules requiring courts to consider a social inquiry report on the accused before they sentence him to imprisonment, Borstal training or detention in a detention centre (see below).

Maximum term of imprisonment. In the case of most statutory offences the statute states the maximum sentence of imprisonment which can be imposed. If, however, an offender is convicted on indictment of a statutory offence and he is liable to imprisonment, but the maximum term imposable is not stated by any enactment or expressed to extend to imprisonment for life, the offender is liable to imprisonment for not more than two years (Criminal Law Act 1967, s. 7(1)). If the offence is a common law offence and no statute provides a maximum punishment for that offence there is no limit to the term of imprisonment which can be imposed, provided the sentence is not inordinate. Thus in *R.* v. *Wilson* (1965) a sentence of twenty-five years imprisonment was imposed for the common law offence of conspiracy to rob a mail train. In the case of a summary or hybrid offence (which must be statutory) the maximum sentence will be laid down by statute (for the maximum when a magistrates' court is composed of a single magistrate or is sitting in an occasional court-house, see Chapter 28). Where an indictable offence is tried summarily the maximum term of imprisonment imposable is six months (Magistrates' Courts Act 1952, s. 19(6)) or where two or more sentences of imprisonment for indictable offences tried summarily are to run consecutively, the aggregate of the terms cannot exceed twelve months (*ibid.*, s. 108(2)) (see Chap. 40)). Otherwise the magistrates cannot impose consecutive terms of imprisonment which in the aggregate exceed six months unless they have power to impose more than that term for any of the offences, when the aggregate maximum is equal to the maximum for that one offence (*ibid.*, s. 108).

Persistent offenders. Before the Criminal Justice Act 1967, persistent offenders could be dealt with by means of orders of preventive detention or corrective training, but these were abolished by section 37(1) of that Act. Nevertheless, the Act introduced a new system of *extended sentences*.

Where an offender is convicted on indictment of an offence punishable with imprisonment for two years or more and

(*a*) the offence was committed before the expiration of three years from a previous conviction of an offence punishable on indictment with such a sentence or from his final release (including a release on licence: see below) from prison after serving a sentence of imprisonment, corrective training or preventive detention passed on such a conviction; and

(*b*) he has been convicted on indictment (or been sentenced to imprisonment, corrective training or preventive detention by quarter sessions after being convicted by a magistrates' court of an indictable offence) on at least three previous occasions since he attained twenty-one years of offences punishable on indictment with such a sentence; and (*c*) the total length of the sentences of imprisonment, corrective training or preventive detention to which he was sentenced on those occasions was not less than five years and—

(i) on at least one of those occasions a sentence of preventive detention was passed on him;

(ii) on at least two of those occasions a sentence of imprisonment (other than a suspended sentence which has not taken effect) or of corrective training was so passed, and of those sentences one was a sentence of imprisonment for three years or more in respect of one offence or two were sentences of imprisonment each for two years or more in respect of one offence

then, if the court is satisfied, by reason of his previous conduct and of the likelihood of his committing further offences, that it is expedient to protect the public from him for a substantial time, the court may impose an extended term of imprisonment (Criminal Justice Act 1967, s. 37(2), (4)).

The extended sentence imposed need not exceed the normal maximum sentence authorized for that offence (*R*. v. *Ottewell* (1969), H.L.) and if the offence of which the accused has now been convicted is punishable with more than ten years' imprisonment, the extended term of imprisonment which the court may impose can never exceed that maximum. Otherwise, however, if the offence is punishable with at least five years, the extended term of imprisonment may be up to ten years or, if the offence is punishable with less than five years, the extended term of imprisonment may be up to five years (*ibid.*, s. 37(3)). Where, moreover, an extended term of imprisonment is imposed, the court must issue an "extended sentence certificate" stating that the term was so imposed (*ibid.*, s. 37(5)).

To enable the court to take a previous conviction or sentence into account for the purpose of imposing an extended sentence, notice must be given to the offender that it is intended to prove the previous conviction or sentence at least three days before the extended sentence is imposed (*ibid.*, s. 38(3)).

Length of imprisonment. Subject to the matters which we have just considered, and unless the sentence is one fixed by law (see Chap. 38), the general rule is that the trial court may sentence an offender to any term of imprisonment up to the maximum imposable. Nevertheless, a magistrates' court cannot impose imprisonment for less than five days (Magistrates' Courts Act 1952, s. 107(1): though see the power of a magistrates' court to order detention in, *e.g.*, a police cell, above). The length, moreover, of any sentence of imprisonment is normally treated as reduced by any period during which the offender was in custody in relation to those proceedings (Criminal Justice Act 1967, s. 67).

Where an offender is serving a sentence of imprisonment, other than imprisonment for life, the Home Secretary, if recommended to do so by the Parole Board (a board set up for the purpose of advising the Home Secretary on such matters), may release him on licence after he has served not less than one-third of his sentence or twelve months thereof, whichever expires the later (Criminal Justice Act 1967, s. 60(1)). Conditions, moreover, with which the offender must comply, may be specified in the licence (*ibid.*, s. 60(4)). If he is recommended to do so by the Parole Board, the Home Secretary may also release on licence an offender serving a sentence of imprisonment for life, but cannot do so in this case, or where the offender was sentenced to detention during Her Majesty's pleasure, except after consultation with the Lord Chief Justice together with the trial judge, if available (*ibid.*, s. 61(1)). The trial judge, in fact, when sentencing an offender convicted of murder to imprisonment for life, may recommend a minimum perod which should elapse before the Home Secretary releases that offender (Murder (Abolition of Death Penalty) Act 1965, s. 1(2)).

In addition to these powers of the Home Secretary to release on licence, up to a third of any sentence of imprisonment, which is for a term of more than one month (other than a sentence of imprisonment for life), may be remitted on the ground of the offender's industry and good conduct, although the term of imprisonment cannot be reduced thereby to less than thirty-one days (Prison Act 1952, s. 25; Prison Rules 1964, r. 5). However, where an offender has been sentenced to an extended term of imprisonment, or to a sentence of imprisonment for eighteen months or more and he was under the age of twenty-one when sentenced, he may, instead of being granted remission (and without prejudice to the Home Secretary's powers to release him on licence as considered above), be released on licence at any time when he could otherwise have been discharged on remission (Criminal Justice Act 1967, s. 60(3)).

Where an offender has been released on licence the licence, unless previously revoked, remains in force until, in the case of an offender who was sentenced to an extended term of imprisonment or who was under twenty-one years when sentenced, the date of the expiration of the sentence or, in the case of any other offender, the date on which he could have been discharged from prison on remission of part of his sentence (*ibid.*, s. 60(6)). Nevertheless, the Home Secretary (normally on the recommendation of the Parole

Board) may revoke a licence and recall an offender to prison (*ibid.*, s. 62). Moreover, if an offender subject to a licence is convicted by a magistrates' court of an offence punishable on indictment with imprisonment, the court may commit him in custody or on bail to quarter sessions for sentence (when quarter sessions will have the same powers as if he had been convicted summarily of an indictable offence: see Chap. 40), and in this case, or if, while subject to a licence, he is convicted on indictment of an offence punishable with imprisonment or is committed to quarter sessions under section 29 of the Magistrates' Courts Act 1952 (see Chap. 40), the court of assize or quarter sessions may, whether or not it passes any other sentence upon him, revoke the licence (Criminal Justice Act 1967, s. 62(7)).

Where an offender, who is serving a sentence of imprisonment for a term of less than eighteen months, was under the age of twenty-one when the sentence was passed, he is subject after his release from prison to supervision as if he had been released from a detention centre (see below) (*ibid.*, s. 63).

The prisons. The prisons themselves are under the control of the Home Office and the Home Office decides on the type of prison to which an offender is sent. The treatment, discipline and training of prisoners is also under the control of the Home Office, but a committee of visiting justices will inquire into any grave offence against prison discipline with which a prisoner is charged (*e.g.*, escaping from prison or assaulting a prison officer) and they will punish the prisoner if they find the matter proved (*e.g.*, by loss of remission or forfeiture of privileges). Minor offences are dealt with by the prison governor.

The purpose of imprisonment. The primary purpose of imprisonment is traditionally prevention and deterrence, but in recent years the period of imprisonment has, so far as possible, been used more for the reformation of the prisoner by appropriate training and treatment. Nevertheless, the training and treatment otherwise desirable are not always compatible with necessary security and imprisonment is increasingly coming to be regarded as the sentence to be imposed only where other methods of treatment have failed or are considered inappropriate. (See *The Sentence of the Court*, a Home Office publication.)

Suspended sentences of imprisonment

Where a court passes a sentence of imprisonment of not more than two years for an offence, it may order that the sentence shall not take effect unless, during a period specified in the order (called the "operational period"), being not less than one year or more than three years from the date of the order, the offender commits in Great Britain another offence punishable with imprisonment and, thereafter, a court orders that the original sentence shall take effect (Criminal Justice Act 1967, s. 39(1)). If a court does pass a suspended sentence, it must explain to the offender in ordinary language his liability if he commits a further offence punishable with imprisonment during the "operational period" (*ibid.*, s. 39(7)). Moreover, a court which has passed a suspended sentence for one offence, cannot make a probation order in respect of another offence (*ibid.*, s. 39(2)), and where a suspended sentence has been passed and the offender is subsequently sentenced to Borstal training for another offence, he ceases to be liable to be dealt with in respect of the suspended sentence (*ibid.*, s. 39(8)).

A court which passes a sentence of imprisonment of not more than six months in respect of any one offence is normally obliged to pass a suspended sentence (*ibid.*, s. 39(3); *R.* v. *Flanders* (1969), C.A.). Nevertheless, the court need not pass a suspended sentence if (*a*) the act, or any of the acts, constituting the offence consisted of an assault on, or threat of violence to another person, or of having or possessing a firearm, an imitation firearm, an explosive or an explosive weapon, or of indecent conduct with or towards a person under sixteen years; or (*b*) the offence is one in respect of which a probation order or order for conditional discharge was originally made (but the offender has broken the conditions of the order; see below) or the offender was subject to such an order at the time of committing the present offence; or (*c*) the court, on the same occasion, is sentencing the offender to immediate imprisonment for another offence; or (*d*) the offender is serving, or, since the commission of the present offence, has served a sentence of imprisonment or Borstal training previously passed for another offence; or (*e*) the offender has, at any time before the commission of the present offence, been sentenced to corrective training, imprisonment or Borstal training or been subject to a suspended sentence (*ibid.*, s. 39(3)).

If convicted of further offence. Where an offender is convicted of an offence punishable with imprisonment, and it was committed during the "operational period" of a suspended sentence, that offender will be dealt with in respect of the suspended sentence. If the later conviction is by a court of assize or quarter sessions that court may deal with the offender in respect of any suspended sentence, but a magistrates' court may only deal with him if the suspended sentence was itself passed by a magistrates' court (Criminal Justice Act 1967, s. 41(1)). Where an offender is later convicted by a magistrates' court and the suspended sentence 'was passed by a court of assize or quarter sessions, the magistrates' court may either (*a*) commit him in custody or on bail to the appropriate court of assize or quarter sessions (which will be the court which originally passed the suspended sentence unless, having regard to the time and place, it would be more convenient for him to be dealt with by some other court, and he would not suffer hardship thereby), or (*b*) give written notice of the conviction to the clerk of the court by which the suspended sentence was passed (*ibid.*, s. 41(2), (3)). Moreover, in reliance on a notice served under section 41(2), above, or in any other case where it appears to a judge or magistrate of a court which has passed a suspended sentence (*e.g.*, in the case of assizes, any judge of the High Court or in the case of quarter sessions or a magistrates' court, any magistrate of that court's area) that the offender has been convicted of an offence punishable with imprisonment committed during the "operational period" of the suspended sentence, the judge or magistrate may issue a summons or warrant directing the offender to appear, or be brought, before that court (*ibid.*, s. 42). Nevertheless, unless he is acting on a notice served under section 41(2), a magistrate cannot issue a summons except on information and cannot issue a warrant except on information in writing and on oath (*ibid.*, s. 42(4)). Further, in any case where a warrant is issued but the appropriate court of assize or quarter sessions is not then being held, the offender must be brought before a magistrates' court for the place where he was arrested and that court will commit him in custody or on bail to that court of assize or quarter sessions unless, having regard to the time and place, it is more convenient for him to be dealt with by some other court, and he will not suffer hardship thereby (*ibid.*, s. 42(5)).

Where a court deals with an offender in respect of a suspended sentence because he has been convicted of an offence punishable with imprisonment which was committed during the "operational period," the court may (*a*) order that the suspended sentence shall take effect with the original term unaltered (*i.e.*, that the offender shall now serve the sentence of imprisonment which was originally passed, but suspended); or (*b*) order that the sentence shall take effect with the substitution of a lesser term for the original term; or (*c*) continue the suspended sentence but substitute for the original period a new "operational" period" expiring not later than three years from the date of this variation; or (*d*) make no order with respect to the suspended sentence (*ibid.*, s. 40(1)). Nevertheless, the court must make an order under (*a*) above (rather than under (*b*),

(c) or (d)) unless it is of the opinion that it would be unjust to do so in view of all the circumstances which have arisen since the suspended sentence was passed, including the facts of the subsequent offence, and in this case it must state its reasons (*ibid.*, s. 40(1)). Where a court does order that a suspended sentence shall take effect (with or without any variation of the term) the court may order that the sentence shall take effect immediately or that it shall commence on the expiration of some other term of imprisonment to which the offender has been sentenced by that or some other court (*ibid.*, s. 40(2)).

If an offender is dealt with in respect of a suspended sentence by a court of assize or quarter sessions, any question whether he has been convicted of an offence punishable with imprisonment committed during the "operational period" of the suspended sentence is determined by the court and not by the verdict of a jury (*ibid.*, s. 40(6)). Moreover, for the purpose of any appeal, any order made by the later court is to be treated as a sentence passed by that court for the original offence (*ibid.*, s. 40(9)).

A fine

Where an accused is convicted on indictment of any offence, other than an offence for which the sentence is fixed by law, the court has a general power to impose a fine in lieu of or in addition to dealing with him in any other way (though see "Probation", below) (Criminal Law Act 1967, s. 7(3)). A magistrates' court may also fine an offender as the whole, or part of a sentence if they have summarily convicted him of an indictable offence (Magistrates' Courts Act 1952, ss. 19(6), 21(2)) and they have power to fine an offender whom they have convicted of any statutory offence (maximum £100: Criminal Justice Act 1967, s. 43(2)) unless the statute was passed after 1879 and it expressly provides to the contrary (Magistrates' Courts Act 1952, s. 27(3)). In addition, a fine is expressly provided as a possible punishment instead of, or in addition to, any other punishment for many statutory indictable offences and for almost all hybrid and summary offences, and the statute often (and in the case of hybrid and summary offences almost always) states the maximum amount imposable.

There is no general limit to the amount of a fine, although Magna Carta 1215 and the Bill of Rights 1689 provide that a fine shall not be excessive and unreasonable. Many statutes, however, limit the amount of the fine in relation to a particular offence, and by the Magistrates' Courts Act 1952, s. 19(6), as amended, the maximum fine that may be imposed when an adult (*i.e.*, one aged seventeen or over) has been convicted summarily of an indictable offence is £400 (for the maximum under s. 27(3) see above). The maximum when a young person (*i.e.*, one aged fourteen and under seventeen) is convicted summarily either of an indictable offence or of a summary offence is £50 (Magistrates' Courts Act 1952, s. 20(5); Criminal Justice Act 1961, s. 8), although in the case of a summary offence the enactment creating the offence may provide a lower maximum. In the case of a child (*i.e.*, one aged under fourteen) the maximum fine that the magistrates may impose (whatever the offence) is £10 (Magistrates' Courts Act 1952, s. 32, as amended by the Criminal Justice Act 1961, s. 8(1)). Moreover, where a child or young person is fined the court may (and in the case of a child normally must) order the fine to be paid by his parent or guardian (Children and Young Persons Act 1933, s. 55(1)).

A court of assize or quarter sessions when imposing a fine may allow time for payment of it and/or direct payment by instalments (Criminal Justice Act 1948, s. 14(1)). Moreover, the court must make an order fixing a term of imprisonment (not exceeding twelve months) which the offender will be liable to undergo if the fine is not paid (*ibid.*, s. 14(1), as amended), but an offender cannot be committed to prison without being allowed time for payment unless (*a*) in the case of an offence which was also punishable with imprisonment, he appears to the court to have sufficient means to pay the fine forthwith; or (*b*) it appears to the court that he is unlikely to remain long enough at a place of abode in the United Kingdom to enable payment of the sum to be enforced by other means; or (*c*) he is also being sentenced for that offence or some other offence to immediate imprisonment or detention in a detention centre or he is already serving a term of imprisonment or detention (Criminal Justice Act 1967, s. 47(2)). Otherwise, the collection, enforcement and remission of the fine will be enforced as if the fine had been imposed by a magistrates' court (see below) (which will be the magistrates' court which committed the offender for trial or sentence unless some other court is specified by the assizes or quarter sessions), save that the magistrates' court cannot remit the whole or any part of the fine (see below) without the consent of the judge of the assizes or quarter sessions (*e.g.*, in the case of assizes, any judge of the High Court, or, in the case of quarter sessions, the chairman or deputy chairman or the recorder or deputy recorder) (Criminal Justice Act 1967, s. 47). Where a fine is imposed by the Criminal Division of the Court of Appeal (on appeal thereto) or by the House of Lords (on appeal from the Criminal Division) the fine is treated for the purposes of collection, etc., as if imposed by the court of assize or quarter sessions from which the appeal lay (*ibid.*, s. 47(9)).

A magistrates' court, like a court of assize or quarter sessions, cannot commit an offender to prison without allowing him time for payment except in the three cases outlined above (*ibid.*, s. 44(2)). Moreover, a magistrates' court must not make an order fixing a term of imprisonment in default of payment unless it can commit the offender to prison forthwith, but does instead allow him time for payment (*ibid.*, s. 44(3)). Indeed, the court cannot subsequently commit him for failure to pay unless he is already serving a term of imprisonment or detention, or the court has, in his presence, inquired into his means and (*a*) in the case of an offence punishable with imprisonment, he has the means to pay forthwith; or (*b*) all other methods of enforcing the payment are inappropriate or unsuccessful (*ibid.*, s. 44(4), (5)). The court may also, on inquiring into the offender's means, remit (*i.e.*, cancel) the whole or a part of the fine if it is just to do so having regard to any change in his circumstances since the conviction (*ibid.*, s. 44(10)).

Where an offender is committed to prison by a magistrates' court on failure to pay a fine the maximum periods are, where the fine did not exceed £2—seven days, exceeded £2 but not £5—fourteen days, exceeded £5 but not £20—thirty days, exceeded £20 but not £50—sixty days, exceeded £50—ninety days. However, where the offence in relation to which the fine was imposed related to Her Majesty's revenue under the control of the Commissioners of Inland Revenue then the maximum periods of imprisonment are, where the fine exeeded £50 but not £100—ninety days, exceeded £100 but not £250—six months, exceeded £250 but not £500—nine months, exceeded £500—twelve months. Moreover, if the defaulter has paid part of the fine he will be liable to be imprisoned for such proportion of the normal maximum imposable as the amount unpaid bears to the total fine imposed, although the maximum period cannot be reduced to less than five days. (See the Magistrates' Courts Act 1952, Sched. 3, as amended by the Criminal Justice Act 1967, s. 93.) For the power to commit a young person to a detention centre or a remand home in default of paying a fine, see below.

Apart from imprisonment or detention, a fine may be enforced in the High Court or a county court (other than by issue of a writ of *fieri facias* or other process against goods or by imprisonment) as if the sum were due to the clerk of the magistrates' court under a judgment of the High Court or a county court, although the clerk cannot take proceedings to recover the sum unless authorized by the magistrates' court after inquiry into the offender's means (Criminal Justice Act 1967, s. 45). In addition, if it appears to a magistrates' court that the offender has defaulted in payment and he is in receipt of earnings, the court may, after inquiring into his means, make an attachment of earnings order within the meaning of the Maintenance Orders Act 1958 (*i.e.*, an order directing his employer to pay part of his earnings direct to the clerk of the magistrates' court) (Criminal Justice Act 1967, s. 46).

Probation

The making of a probation order by the court (which normally requires the offender's consent, see below) means that the offender is put under the supervision of a probation officer (a number of whom are appointed for each area) for a period specified in the order, or not less than one year nor more than three years (Criminal Justice Act 1948, s. 3(1)). The order will normally impose other conditions to secure the good conduct of the offender and for preventing a repetition by him of the same offence and the commission of other offences (*ibid.*, s. 3(3)); for example, that he should be of good behaviour and lead an industrious life, and that he should keep in touch with the probation officer in accordance with such instructions as the probation officer may from time to time give. In a suitable case, moreover, the order may require the residence of the offender in a specified institution (*e.g.*, in a probation hostel) for a period not exceeding twelve months, but such an order can only be made after the court has considered the home surroundings of the offender (*ibid.*, s. 3(4)). The court also has power, if it is satisfied on the evidence of a duly qualified medical practitioner that the mental condition of an offender is such as requires, and may be susceptible to, treatment (though not as to warrant a "mental health order," see below), to make a condition of the probation order that the offender submit for a specified period, not exceeding twelve months, to treatment as a resident patient in a hospital, or as a non-resident patient, or otherwise under the direction of a specified medical practitioner (*ibid.*, s. 4).

Although the court may make an award of costs against the accused, it cannot make, as a condition of a probation order, a requirement for the payment of damages for injury or of compensation for loss (*ibid.*, s. 3(3)), but such an order may be made as a separate order, although this is normally limited to £100 when the order is made by a magistrates' court (*ibid.*, s. 11(2)). Moreover, a court cannot impose a fine in addition to a probation order (*R.* v. *Parry* (1951), C.C.A.) and if the offender is convicted of more than one offence a probation order ought not to be made in respect of one of the offences if a sentence of imprisonment (or other form of detention) is to be made in respect of the other offences (*R.* v. *Evans* (1959), C.C.A.). Nevertheless, in addition to making a probation order, the court may disqualify an offender from driving or endorse his licence (Criminal Justice Act 1967, s. 51).

Any court may make a probation order in respect of any offender convicted of any offence, except where the sentence for that offence is fixed by law (Criminal Justice Act 1948, s. 3(1)). Where the offender is not less than fourteen years of age, however, his consent is required (*ibid.*, s. 3(5)). The court before making the order (and before obtaining the offender's consent, when this is required) must explain to him in ordinary language the effect of the order and that if he fails to comply therewith, or commits another offence while the order remains in force, he will be liable to be sentenced for the offence for which he is being placed on probation (*ibid.*, s. 3(5)).

"A conviction." Although a probation order can only be made following a conviction for an offence, that conviction is not to be deemed to be a conviction for any purpose other than for the purposes of the proceedings in which the order is made (Criminal Justice Act 1948, s. 12). Thus, the conviction will be a conviction for the purpose of allowing the accused to appeal against conviction (*ibid.*, s. 12(3)), but it will not be deemed to be a conviction, for example, for the purpose of subsequently empowering a court to pass a heavier sentence, when this is possible, provided the accused has a previous conviction (*R.* v. *Stobbart* (1951), C.C.A.). Nevertheless, even though the court makes a probation order, the conviction will operate as a bar to subsequent proceedings for the same offence (*e.g.*, the offender may plead *autrefois convict*) (*ibid.*, s. 12(3)).

Discharge, amendment and review of probation orders. Where a court has made a probation order, the court (*i.e.*, the supervising court: see the Criminal Justice Act 1948, s. 80) may, on the application of the probation officer or of the offender, discharge the order (*ibid.*, s. 5(1) and Sched. 1) or make, in substitution therefor, an order of conditional discharge (*i.e.*, for the unexpired probation period) (Criminal Justice Act 1967, s. 53: see below). The court also has power, upon the application of the probation officer or the offender, to amend a probation order by cancelling any of the requirements thereof or by inserting therein (normally only with the offender's consent, see above) any requirement which could be included if the order was then being made by that court (Criminal Justice Act 1948, s. 5(1) and Sched. 1).

Breach of probation order. If an offender who has been placed on probation fails to comply with any of the conditions of the probation order, a magistrate may, on information being laid, issue a summons requiring the offender to appear before a magistrates' court at a specified time and place or, if the information was in writing, and on oath, he may issue a warrant for the offender's arrest (Criminal Justice Act 1948, s. 6(1)). The magistrates' court may then impose on the offender a fine not exceeding £20, or, in a suitable case, it may make an attendance centre order in respect of the offender (see below), but the probation order will remain in force (*ibid.*, s. 6(3), as amended).

As an alternative, however, the magistrates, if the probation order was made by a magistrates' court, may deal with the offender, for the offence in respect of which the probation order was made, in any manner in which they could have dealt with him if they had just convicted him of that offence (including putting the offender on probation again: *R*. v. *Havant JJ., ex p. Jacobs* (1957), D.C.; *R*. v. *Thompson* (1968), C.A.), or, if the probation order was made by a court of assize or quarter sessions, commit him in custody or on bail (with or without sureties) to that court (*ibid.*, s. 6(3); and see the Criminal Justice Act 1967, s. 54(4)). The court of assize or quarter sessions, provided that it is satisfied that the offender has failed to comply with any of the conditions of the probation order, may then deal with him for the offence in respect of which the probation order was made, in any manner in which the court could have dealt with him if it had just convicted him of that offence (Criminal Justice Act 1948, s. 6(4)) or, alternatively, it may impose on him a fine not exceeding £20 (Criminal Justice Act 1967, s. 54(5)). Nevertheless, as the court of assize or quarter sessions must itself be satisfied of the breach of the probation order, details of the original conviction, of the probation order and of the alleged breach must be put to the offender when he appears before the court and he should be asked whether he admits them. If he does not do so evidence of these matters must be led and the offender himself may give evidence and call witnesses (*R*. v. *Holmes* (1965), C.C.A.), although the issue will not be tried by a jury (Criminal Justice Act 1948, s. 11(4)).

If the offender is dealt with for the offence in respect of which the probation order was made, by either a magistrates' court or a court of assize or quarter sessions, the original probation order is thereby terminated (though not a separate order for damages for injury or compensation for loss: *R*. v. *Evans* (1963), C.C.A.), but if a court of assize or quarter sessions imposes a fine under section 54(5) of the Criminal Justice Act 1967 the probation order will continue.

Commission of further offence. When an offender who has been placed on probation commits a further offence during the currency of the probation order he will be liable, in addition to being punished for the later offence, to be punished for the original offence for which he was placed on probation. Where the offender has already been convicted and dealt with for the later offence, a magistrate or (where the probation order was made by an assize court) a High Court judge may issue either a summons requiring the offender to appear at a specified time and place or a warrant for his arrest (although a magistrate cannot issue a warrant except on information in writing and on oath) (Criminal Justice Act 1948, s. 8(1)), and the court before which the offender is to appear must normally be the court by which the probation order was made (*ibid.*, s. 8(3)).

Where an offender who has been placed on probation is convicted of a further offence by the same court which placed him on probation, that court may then go on to deal with him for the offence for which he was placed on probation (*ibid.*, s. 8(5)), but separate sentences should be passed, and if the offender is sentenced to imprisonment for both offences the terms of imprisonment should normally be consecutive (*R.* v. *Webb* (1953), C.C.A.). Moreover, if the probation order was made by a magistrates' court and the offender is convicted of the later offence by a different magistrates' court, that magistrates' court may normally deal with the original offence as well (*ibid.*, s. 8(7)), while if the probation order was made by a magistrates' court and the offender is convicted of the later offence by a court of assize or quarter sessions, or he was committed to the court for sentence, the court of assize or quarter sessions may (and normally should: *R.* v. *Calvert* (1963), C.C.A.) deal also with the original offence (*ibid.*, s. 8(6)). Where, however, the probation order was made by a court of assize or quarter sessions and the offender is convicted of the later offence by a magistrates' court, that court should commit him in custody or on bail (with or without sureties) to the court of assize or quarter sessions which made the probation order (*ibid.*, s. 8(4)).

Where an offender is dealt with by a magistrates' court for an an offence for which he was originally placed on probation, or he is dealt with by a court of assize or quarter sessions for an offence for which he was placed on probation by that court, he may be dealt with as if he had just been convicted by that court of the original offence (*ibid.*, s. 8). Where, however, a court of assize or quarter sessions deals with an offender who was originally placed on probation by a magistrates' court, it may only deal with him in any manner in which a magistrates' court could deal with him (*ibid.*, s. 8(6)). If an offender has been committed to be dealt with to the court which originally made the probation order, the procedure will be the same as if he had been brought before that court for failure to comply with the terms of the order (see above) (*R*. v. *Holmes* (1965), C.C.A.).

Binding over

To come up for sentence. Except where the sentence is one fixed by law, a court may, in lieu of sentence, require a convicted offender to enter into recognizances, with or without sureties, to come up for judgment if and when called upon to do so (in practice a maximum time limit is always fixed : see, *e.g.*, *R*. v. *David* (1939), C.C.A.). It is normal in such cases for the court to insert a clause in the binding over order that the offender during such period shall be of good behaviour and the court may also impose special clauses, for example, that the offender shall reside in a specified hospital (see, *e.g.*, *R*. v. *Green-Emmott* (1931), C.C.A.) or that he shall return to another country (*R*. v. *Flaherty* (1959), C.C.A.). If an offender then fails to come up for judgment if called upon to do so, or he breaks the conditions of the recognizances, the recognizances may be estreated. If called upon to come up for judgment, moreover, the offender will be sentenced for the original offence. A binding over order, however, unlike a probation order, does rank as a conviction.

In substitution for or in addition to some other sentence. In addition to the power of a court to bind over a person to keep the peace and to be of good behaviour where there has been no conviction (see Chap. 28), a court may do so, with or without sureties, in respect of an offender convicted of any common law or statutory misdemeanour (and therefore, since the Criminal Law Act 1967, s. 1, of any offence), and in addition to, or in substitution for any other punishment (except where the sentence is one fixed by law). This power was, at least in part, originally derived from the Justices of the Peace Act 1361 (*R*. v. *Ayu* (1958), C.C.A.), but the Offences against the Person Act 1861, s. 71, and corresponding provisions in the other criminal law consolidation Acts of 1861, as amended, also make express provisions for offences punishable under the respective Act, although the offender cannot then be imprisoned for more than one year for not finding sureties. An offender may, therefore, be sentenced to imprisonment and may also be bound over to keep the peace and to be of good behaviour for a fixed period (*R*. v. *Edgar* (1913)) commencing on the termination of that imprisonment (*R.* v. *Hart* (1808); *Dunn* v. *R.* (1848)), and even though the imprisonment was for the maximum time allowed by the statute (*R.* v. *Trueman* (1913), C.C.A.).

Absolute and conditional discharge

Where a court convicts an offender of an offence (other than one for which the sentence is fixed by law) and it is of opinion, having regard to the circumstances, including the nature of the offence and the offender's character, that it is inexpedient to inflict punishment and that a probation order is not appropriate, it may discharge the offender absolutely or conditionally (*i.e.*, subject to the condition that he commits no offence during the period, not exceeding three years from the order, as may be specified therein) (Criminal Justice Act 1948, s. 7(1), as amended by the Criminal Justice Act 1967, s. 52). In addition, the court has power to award costs against the offender or to order him to pay damages for injury or compensation for loss (the same as with a probation order: see above) (Criminal Justice Act 1948, s. 11(2)), but, as an order of discharge can only be made when the court considers it unwise to inflict punishment, a court cannot both fine an offender and make an order of absolute or conditional discharge (*R.* v. *McClelland* (1951), C.C.A.). For the power to substitute an order of conditional discharge for a probation order, see above.

If an offender, who has been conditionally discharged, is subsequently convicted of an offence committed during the period of conditional discharge he may also be sentenced for the original offence (*ibid.*, s. 8), and this must be explained to him by the court before it makes an order for conditional discharge (*ibid.*, s. 7(3)). If the offender is sentenced for the original offence, however, the order for conditional discharge ceases to have effect (*ibid.*, s. 7(4)).

Like a probation order, an order for absolute or conditional discharge can only be made following a conviction for an offence, but that conviction is not to be deemed to be a conviction for any purpose other than for the purposes of the proceedings in which the order is made (*e.g.*, for the purpose of allowing the offender to appeal against the conviction) (*ibid.*, s. 12).

Mental health order

By the Mental Health Act 1959, s. 60, a court may make an order for the detention of an offender in a specified hospital (*i.e.*, "a hospital order"), or it may make an order placing him under the guardianship of a local health authority (*i.e.*, "a guardianship order").

A court of assize or quarter sessions may make such an order when the offender has been convicted of any offence, other than one for which the sentence is fixed by law, and when (*a*) the court is satisfied, on the written or oral evidence of two medical practitioners (as specified in the Act): (i) that the offender is suffering from mental illness, psychopathic disorder, subnormality or severe subnormality (as defined in the Act); and (ii) that the mental disorder is of a nature which warrants his detention in a hospital for medical treatment, or his reception into guardianship under the Act; and (*b*) the court is of the opinion, having regard to all the circumstances including the nature of the offence and the character and antecedents of the offender, and to the other available methods of dealing with him, that the most suitable method of disposing of the case is by means of such an order (*ibid.*, s. 60(1)). Where a hospital order is made by a court of assize or quarter sessions, and it appears to the court, having regard to the nature of the offence, the antecedents of the offender and the risk of him committing further offences if set at large, that it is necessary for the protection of the public so to do, the court may further order that the discharge of the offender from the hospital shall be restricted (as specified by the Act) either without limit of time or during such period as is specified in the order (*ibid.*, s. 65).

A magistrates' court has power to make a hospital or guardianship order provided the offence of which the offender was convicted is punishable on summary conviction with imprisonment (*ibid.*, s. 60(1)). It may also make an order without convicting an accused, when he has been charged with an act or omission as an offence and the court is satisfied that he did the act or made the omission charged and the court could have made an order had it convicted him (*e.g.*, when an accused is unfit to be tried) (*ibid.*, s. 60(2)). A magistrates' court has no power, however, to make an order restricting an offender's discharge, but it may instead commit him to quarter sessions and quarter sessions may then make such an order (see Chap. 39).

Recommendation for deportation

Any court which has convicted an *alien* of an offence, which is punishable (or which would be if the offender were of full age) with imprisonment, may make a recommendation that the offender should be deported. Whether or not the offender is deported, however, is a matter for the Home Secretary (Aliens Order 1953, art. 20). By the Commonwealth Immigrants Act 1962, s. 7, a court may make a similar recommendation for deportation in respect of a *Commonwealth citizen* who has attained the age of seventeen and who is convicted of an offence punishable with imprisonment, but the section does not apply to certain classes of Commonwealth citizens (*e.g.*, those born or naturalized in the United Kingdom or the spouses of such citizens and those who are ordinarily resident in the United Kingdom at the date of the conviction and who have been continuously so resident for a period of at least five years), and a notice (describing the class of persons in respect of whom a recommendation may and may not be made) must have been given to a Commonwealth citizen at least seven days before a recommendation for deportation may be made. A court may make a recommendation for deportation, whether of an alien or a Commonwealth citizen, in addition to any other punishment which it imposes (even when the offender has been sentenced to life imprisonment: see the Criminal Justice Act 1967, s. 58) and though the Home Secretary, if he makes a deportation order, may do so before the expiration of the other sentence, his normal practice is to wait until the sentence has been served (*R.* v. *Singh* (1963), C.C.A.).

If a recommendation for deportation is made by a court of assize or quarter sessions the accused may appeal against the recommendation to the Criminal Division of the Court of Appeal (Criminal Appeal Act 1968, ss. 9, 10, 50; Commonwealth Immigrants Act 1962, s. 8(4)), but if the recommendation is made by a magistrates' court there is no provision for an appeal.

(2) Young Offenders

Borstal training

Borstal training was introduced by the Prevention of Crime Act 1908. Under this Act a number of Borstal institutions were set up where young offenders might receive a period of training with a view to making them useful and law-abiding members of society. Moreover, as a court cannot usually sentence an offender under twenty-one years to imprisonment (see above), Borstal training is normally the gravest form of punishment that can be imposed on a young offender.

When an offender is convicted on indictment of an offence punishable with imprisonment, then, if on the day of his conviction he is not less than fifteen but under twenty-one years of age, the court may, in lieu of any other sentence, pass a sentence of Borstal training (Criminal Justice Act 1948, s. 20(1), as amended by the Criminal Justice Act 1961, s. 1). The court may exercise its power to pass a sentence of Borstal training in any case where it is of opinon, having regard to the circumstances of the offence and after taking into account the offender's character and previous conduct, that it is expedient that he should be detained for training for not less than six months, but a sentence of Borstal training must not be passed on an offender under seventeen years of age unless the court is of opinion that no other method of dealing with him is appropriate (Criminal Justice Act 1961, s. 1(2)). Moreover, in the case of an offender of any age, a court, before sentencing him to Borstal training, must consider any report made in respect of him by or on behalf of the Home Secretary (*ibid.*, s. 1(3)). A magistrates' court has no power to pass a sentence of Borstal training but it may instead commit an offender to quarter sessions with a view to Borstal training (Magistrates' Courts Act 1952, s. 28, as amended) (see Chap. 39).

The maximum period of Borstal training is two years and an offender cannot normally be released before the expiration of six months, but within these limits the actual period of Borstal training for a particular offender will be decided by the Home Secretary and not by the sentencing court (Prison Act 1952, s. 45, as amended by the Criminal Justice Act 1961, Sched. 4). The length of sentence will, in fact, depend on how quickly and successfully the offender responds to the training provided in the Borstal institution. After release, moreover, and until two years from the date of his release, the offender is under the supervision of such society or person as may be specified by notice by the Home Secretary (normally a probation officer) and if, during those two years, the offender fails to comply with any requirement specified in the notice at the time of his release, or as subsequently modified, the Home Secretary may by order recall him to a Borstal institution and the offender is then liable to be detained until the expiration of two years from his sentence or six months from his being recalled, whichever is the later (Prison Act 1952, s. 45, as amended).

Detention centre

Detention centres were first introduced by the Criminal Justice Act 1948 and the intention was to provide an institution to which young offenders might be sent for a comparatively short period, but where they might be given what has been described as "a short sharp shock." Thus the purpose of a detention centre order is primarily deterrent, and during his period at the centre the young offender will be subject to rigorous training and discipline.

Any court may send an offender under twenty-one but not less than fourteen years of age to a detention centre if he has been convicted of an offence which is punishable with imprisonment (or which would be if the offender were of full age), provided that the court has been notified by the Home Secretary that a detention centre is available for the reception from that court of offenders of his class or description (Criminal Justice Act 1961, s. 4). Nevertheless, an order cannot be made in respect of an offender who has already been imprisoned for at least six months or undergone Borstal training unless the court, after considering a Home Office report on him, considers that there are special circumstances (whether relating to the offence or to the offender) which warrant the making of such an order in respect of him (*ibid.*, s. 4(4)). For the power of a court to send an offender to a detention centre instead of to prison when he has been convicted of a further offence during the "operational period" of a suspended sentence, see the Criminal Justice Act 1967, s. 40(3), (4).

The normal period of detention ordered is three months but if the offender has attained the age of seventeen or is convicted before a court of assize or quarter sessions, and the maximum imprisonment which could be imposed for the offence exceeds three months, the detention ordered may be not less than three nor more than six months (Criminal Justice Act 1961, s. 4(2)). Moreover, if the offender has attained the age of seventeen and he is convicted of two or more offences for which detention centre orders may be made, he may be sentenced to consecutive periods of detention not exceeding six months in the aggregate, while if he has already been sentenced to detention he may be sentenced to a further consecutive period, not exceeding nine months in the aggregate (*ibid.*, s. 7). After release from a detention centre an offender is also subject to supervision (as after Borstal training: see above), normally for twelve months, but if recalled he can only be detained for a maximum period of fourteen days (*ibid.*, Sched. 1).

An offender under seventeen but not less than fourteen years of age may also be committed to a detention centre for from one to six months in default of paying a fine when, but for his age, he could have been sent to prison (see above) (*ibid.*, s. 5).

Remand home

A remand home is primarily for accommodating juveniles who have been remanded in custody to await trial, but any court may send to a remand home an offender aged ten but under seventeen provided he has been convicted of an offence which is punishable with imprisonment (or which would be if he were of full age) (Children and Young Persons Act 1933, s. 54(1), as amended by the Criminal Justice Act 1961, Sched. 4). The court must, however, consider that no other method of dealing with him is suitable and if the offender is aged not less than fourteen he must instead be sent to a detention centre if one is available (*ibid.*, s. 54(1), as amended). The maximum term for which an offender may be committed to a remand home is one month, but the term cannot exceed the maximum term of imprisonment imposable for the offence of which he was convicted if that is less than one month (*ibid.*, s. 54(2), as amended).

An offender under seventeen but not less than fourteen may also be committed to a remand home for up to one month in default of paying a fine when, but for his age, he could have been sent to prison (see above) (*ibid.*, s. 54(3), as amended).

Approved school

Approved schools, which were first set up in the nineteenth century, are independent residential establishments (often under a religious or charitable organization) but which, as the name implies, are approved and indeed very largely controlled by the Home Office. They are not solely penal institutions, for juveniles may be sent to an approved school who are in need of care, protection or control, but a court may send a young offender to an approved school when it considers that he (or she) needs not only removal from the undesirable influences which are present in his home but also a substantial period of residential training.

Any court may send an offender under seventeen but not less than ten years to an approved school, provided that he has been convicted of an offence which is punishable with imprisonment (or which would be if he were of full age) (Children and Young Persons Act 1933, s. 57). The period of detention, if the offender is a child, is three years or until the expiration of four months after he ceases to be of compulsory school age (at present fifteen), whichever is the later; or if the offender is a young person the period of detention, if he has not attained the age of sixteen, is three years, or, if he has attained the age of sixteen, is until he attains the age of nineteen (Children and Young Persons Act 1933, s. 71, as amended by the Criminal Justice Act 1948, s. 71). Nevertheless, an offender may be released from an approved school before the end of such period, although the managers of the school cannot release him during the first six months without the consent of the Home Secretary (Criminal Justice Act 1961, s. 14). After release, moreover, whether before the end of the normal period of detention or not, the offender will be under the supervision of the managers of the approved school for a period normally two years, or until he attains twenty-one years, whichever is the earlier (Criminal Justice Act 1961, Sched. 2, Pt. 1).

Where a court could send an offender to an approved school, it may instead commit him to the care of *a fit person,* whether a relative or not, who is willing to undertake the care of him, and in this case a probation order may also be made in respect of that offender (Children and Young Persons Act 1933, s. 57).

Attendance centre

A magistrates' court may send an offender aged under twenty-one but not less than ten years to an attendance centre, provided that he has been convicted of an offence which is punishable with imprisonment (or which would be if he were of full age), or he has failed to comply with the requirements of a probation order (Criminal Justice Act 1948, s. 19(1), as amended by the Criminal Justice Act 1961, s. 10). Nevertheless, an offender cannot be sent to an attendance centre unless the court has been notified by the Home Secretary that a centre is available for persons of the offender's class or description, and an order cannot be made if the offender has previously been sentenced to imprisonment, Borstal training or detention in a detention centre, or has been sent to an approved school (*ibid.,* s. 19(1), as amended).

The aggregate number of hours for which an offender may be required to attend at an attendance centre is usually twelve, but it may be less if the offender is under fourteen years, and it may be for up to twenty-four if there are special circumstances (Criminal Justice Act 1961, s. 10). Attendance at an attendance centre will normally entail attendance for sessions of two hours each (maximum of three hours: Criminal Justice Act 1948, s. 19(2), as amended) on successive, or alternate, Saturday afternoons. The court, however, which made the order, has power to discharge the order or vary the day or hour specified therein for the offender's first attendance at the centre (Criminal Justice Act 1948, s. 19(3)).

Attendance centres, which were established by the Criminal Justice Act 1948, are usually organized by the police. An attendance centre order is designed to have a deterrent effect both on the offender and on others, and the instruction given to the offender at the centre and the influence of the attendance centre staff is designed to teach him to respect the law and the property of others. See *The Sentence of the Court,* a Home Office publication.

Other methods of dealing with young offenders

We have already considered the powers of a court to sentence a young offender to death, to imprison him or fine him, or to make a probation order in respect of him. Probation orders are, in practice, very common in the case of young offenders and, as we have seen, the consent of an offender under fourteen years is not required before a probation order can be made.

Where a child or young person is convicted on indictment of any offence punishable in the case of an adult with imprisonment for fourteen years or more (unless the sentence is one fixed by law), and the court is of opinion that none of the other methods of punishment is suitable, the court may sentence him to be detained for such period, not exceeding the maximum term of imprisonment with which the offence is punishable, as may be specified in the sentence (Children and Young Persons Act 1933, s. 53, as amended by the Criminal Justice Act 1961, ss. 2, 41). The Home Secretary will then direct the place in which the offender is to be detained (Children and Young Persons Act 1933, s. 53(2)) and, if recommended to do so by the Parole Board, he may subsequently release the offender on licence (Criminal Justice Act 1967, s. 61(1)). The licence then remains in force until the date of the expiration of the sentence (*ibid.*, s. 61(3)) and it may contain such conditions and be revoked in the same way as a licence granted to an adult offender after imprisonment (see above).

Where an offender under eighteen years is convicted of murder, he must be sentenced to be detained during Her Majesty's pleasure, *i.e.*, in such place and under such conditions as the Home Secretary may direct (Children and Young Persons Act 1933, s. 53(1), as amended by the Murder (Abolition of Death Penalty) Act 1965, s. 1). The Home Secretary, if recommended to do so by the Parole Board, may also subsequently release such an offender on licence but he cannot do so except after consultation with the Lord Chief Justice together with the trial judge if available (Criminal Justice Act 1967, s. 61).

Chapter Forty-Five

REWARDS, COMPENSATION AND RESTITUTION

(1) Rewards

WHERE it appears to a court of assize or quarter sessions that any person was active in or towards the apprehension of an accused charged with an arrestable offence, the court may order that there should be paid to that person such sum of money as seems to the court reasonable and sufficient to compensate him for his expenses, exertions and loss of time in or towards such apprehension (Criminal Law Act 1826, s. 28, as amended by the Criminal Law Act 1967, Sched 2). The reward is then paid by the Treasury.

(2) Compensation

Where a man is killed in endeavouring to apprehend an accused who is now charged with an arrestable offence, the court before whom the accused is tried may order the payment of compensation to his widow or his children (if he does not leave a widow), or his parents (if he leaves neither widow nor children) of such sum as the court thinks fit (Criminal Law Act 1826, s. 30, as amended). The compensation is paid by the Treasury. In addition, any court of assize or quarter sessions which has convicted an accused of any offence tried on indictment may, immediately after such conviction and upon the application of any person aggrieved, award any sum of money, not exceeding £400, by way of compensation for any loss, or damage to property suffered by the applicant through or by means of the offence of which the accused has been convicted (Forfeiture Act 1870, s. 4, as amended by the Criminal Law Act 1967, Sched 2). The magistrates have a similar power to award compensation when they have convicted an accused of an indictable offence (Magistrates Courts Act 1952, s. 34, as amended). In these cases the compensation must be paid by the accused, although, subject to the Criminal Appeal Act 1968, s. 50(1) (see Chap. 41), it is not part of the sentence: *R. v. Dorset Quarter*

Sessions, ex p. Randall (1967), D.C.), and it may be enforced against him like an order for the payment of costs (see Chap. 46) (Forfeiture Act 1870, s. 4).

As we have seen (Chap. 44) a court which has made a probation order in respect of an accused may, as a separate order, make an order for the payment of damages for injury or of compensation for loss, although this is normally limited to £100 when the order is made by a magistrates' court (Criminal Justice Act 1948, s. 11(2)). Again the compensation is payable by the accused and may be enforced against him like an order for the payment of costs (*ibid.*, s. 11(3)), but if the accused is a child or young person the court may instead order that the compensation should be paid by his parent or guardian (Children and Young Persons Act 1933, s. 35; Criminal Justice Act 1961, s. 8(4)).

There are also certain other statutory provisions which allow an order for compensation to be made in relation to particular offences. Thus, for example, a magistrates' court may order an accused to pay compensation to the party aggrieved if it has convicted him of malicious damage to property (Criminal Justice Administration Act 1914, s. 14(1)), or, where any court has ordered the restitution of any stolen goods to the owner, the court may order that any innocent purchaser of those goods from the accused should be compensated out of any money found on the accused when he was arrested (Theft Act 1968, s. 28(3)).

Criminal Injuries Compensation Board

In addition to the powers of a court to make an order for compensation, there has been set up a Criminal Injuries Compensation Board which may make *ex gratia* payments to victims of crimes of violence. Compensation may be paid to almost all who suffer personal injuries in direct consequence of a criminal offence or trying to arrest an offender or prevent a crime. If the injuries are fatal the victim's dependants may apply. The Board was created in 1964 and its powers have been used extensively. (For further details see "Compensation for Victims of Crimes of Violence," 1964, Cmnd. 2323.)

(3) Restitution

Where goods have been stolen, and an accused has been convicted of any offence with reference to the theft, the goods should be restored to the owner and normally the court may make an order accordingly (Theft Act 1968, s. 28(1)). These "restitution orders" have been considered already in Chapter 16.

Chapter Forty-Six

COSTS AND LEGAL AID

(1) Costs

IN a criminal case the basic rule is that unless the court makes an award of costs each party will bear its own costs. In the case of the prosecution, however, since most prosecutions are conducted by the police, this will normally mean that the costs are paid by the local authority, but if the prosecution is being conducted by a private prosecutor it will mean that he will have to pay the costs of the prosecution personally. The accused, unless he has obtained legal aid (see below), will pay his own costs personally.

If a criminal court does make an award of costs it may order the accused to pay the costs of the prosecution, or the prosecutor to pay the costs of the defence, or it may order the costs of either the prosecution or the defence or both of them to be paid out of local funds, *i.e.*, normally out of the funds of the county or county borough where the offence, or alleged offence, was committed (Costs in Criminal Cases Act 1952, s. 7).

Magistrates' courts

Local funds. A magistrates' court dealing summarily with an indictable offence or inquiring into any offence as examining justices, may order the payment out of local funds of the costs *of the prosecution* (Costs in Criminal Cases Act 1952, s. 5(1)), and in practice the court will normally do so. These costs will be such as appear to the court reasonably sufficient to compensate the prosecutor for the expenses properly incurred by him and to compensate any witness for the prosecution for the expense, trouble or loss of time properly incurred in his attendance (whether or not he gave evidence) (*ibid.*, s. 5(3)).

Where a magistrates' court has dealt summarily with an indictable offence and has dismissed the information, or has inquired into any offence as examining justices and has determined not to commit the accused for trial, it may order the payment out of local

funds of the costs *of the defence* (*ibid.*, s. 5(2)). In this case, however, mere acquittal or discharge is not in itself a ground for the
exercise of the court's discretion and each case must be considered
on its own merits: whether the prosecution have acted unreasonably and whether the accused by his conduct has in effect brought
the proceedings on himself are among the matters to be taken
into consideration (*Practice Direction* (*Costs in Criminal Cases*)
1959)). Nevertheless, even if the court does not order the general
defence costs to be paid out of local funds, it may order the costs
of any defence witness, or of any witness attending or called at the
instance of the court, to be so paid (*ibid.*, s. 5(4)). If an order for
payment of defence costs is made, the basis of the costs will be the
same as that for the prosecution, considered above (*ibid.*,
s. 5(3)).

In addition, a magistrates' court may also make an order for the
payment of costs out of local funds when it has dealt with an
offender for breach of a probation order or of a conditional discharge, or for having committed a further offence during the
"operational period" of a suspended sentence or has dealt with a
breach of a recognizance, etc., which was made on conviction of
an indictable offence (Criminal Justice Act 1967, s. 31). Moreover,
except where it has dealt with a breach of a recognizance, a magistrates' court, in these cases, may also make an award of costs to
be paid between the parties (see below) (*ibid.*, s. 31).

Between the parties. If an accused is convicted at a summary trial,
the magistrates' court has power to order him to pay *to the prosecution* a specified sum in costs (Costs in Criminal Cases Act 1952,
s. 6(1)). In practice the magistrates often do make such an order
but while the amount of these costs is, in this case, also in the
discretion of the magistrates they should be such as the court
thinks just and reasonable (*ibid.*, s. 6(1)) and they must not be a
penalty in the guise of costs (*R.* v. *Highgate JJ., ex p. Petrou* (1954),
D.C.). Moreover, where the court orders payment of any sum as a
fine or compensation, and the sum so ordered does not exceed five
shillings, the court must not order the accused to pay any costs
unless in the particular case it thinks fit to do so (*ibid.*, s. 6(1)). If
the accused is a young person the court may, or if a child the court
normally must, order the costs to be paid by his parent or guardian
(Children and Young Persons Act 1933, s. 55(1)), but if an accused
under seventeen years is ordered to pay the costs personally they
cannot exceed the amount of any fine ordered to be paid (Costs in
Criminal Cases Act 1952, s. 6(1)).

If the accused is acquitted at a summary trial the magistrates' court has power to order the prosecutor to pay *to the accused* such sum in costs as it thinks just and reasonable (*ibid.*, s. 6(1)), but in practice the court rarely exercises a discretion to award such costs unless the conduct of the prosecutor is seriously in question (see *Criminal Costs* (2nd ed.) by Graham J. Graham-Green, p. 5). Where examining justices decide not to commit the accused for trial and they consider that the charge was not made in good faith, they may order the prosecutor to pay the whole or any part of the costs of the defence (*ibid.*, s. 6(3)). This discretion is, however, limited to where the charge was not made in good faith and if the amount so ordered exceeds twenty-five pounds the prosecutor may appeal to quarter sessions against the order (*ibid.*, s. 6(4)). It is, therefore, comparatively rare for a magistrates' court to award costs against the prosecutor.

Where a magistrates' court orders costs to be paid by the accused the order may be enforced in the same manner as a fine (see Chap. 44 (*ibid.*, s. 10(3)). Moreover, if an accused is committed to prison for failure to pay costs, the period of imprisonment will depend on the amount of the costs awarded (Magistrates' Courts Act 1952, s. 64 and Sched. 3). Payment of costs by the prosecutor may be enforced like a civil debt (Costs in Criminal Cases Act 1952, s. 10(3)).

Assizes and quarter sessions

Local funds. A court of assize or quarter sessions before which an accused has been tried on indictment or inquisition may order the payment out of local funds of the costs of the prosecution or, if the accused was acquitted, it may order the payment out of local funds of the costs of the defence (Costs in Criminal Cases Act 1952, s. 1(1)). Moreover, where the accused was legally aided (see below), the court in all cases must order the payment of defence costs out of local funds (Poor Prisoners' Defence Act 1930, s. 3(1)). Again, costs ordered to be paid out of local funds will be such as appear to the court reasonably sufficient to compensate the prosecutor, or the accused, for the expenses properly incurred by him and to compensate any witness for the prosecution, or the defence, or who is attending or was called at the instance of the court, for the expense, trouble or loss of time properly incurred in his attendance (whether or not he gave evidence) (Costs in Criminal Cases Act 1952, s. 1(2); see *Practice Direction* (*Crime: Costs*) (1968)), but, unless the court otherwise directs, no sum shall be payable in respect of any witness for the prosecution or defence who is a witness to character only (*ibid.*, s. 1(4)).

Like a magistrates' court, a court of assize or quarter sessions will normally order the costs of the prosecution to be paid out of local funds but the fact that the accused was acquitted is not in itself a sufficient ground for ordering the defence costs to be so paid. Nevertheless each case is in the discretion of the court, and, though the fact that the prosecution has acted unreasonably or the accused by his conduct has in effect brought the proceedings upon himself are matters to be considered, the accused need not necessarily show some fault on the part of the prosecution before he can be awarded costs (*Practice Direction (Costs in Criminal Cases)* (1959). Again, however, the costs of any defence, or court witness, may be ordered to be paid out of local funds even though no order as regards the defence costs in general is made (*ibid.*, s. 1(3)).

Where an accused is committed for trial but not ultimately tried, the court to which he was committed has the same powers to order the payment of costs as if he had been tried and acquitted (*ibid.*, s. 13).

These provisions as to costs also apply when an accused has been committed to a court of quarter sessions for sentence, under the Magistrates' Courts Act 1952, ss. 28 or 29, or has been committed with a view to a hospital order with an order restricting his discharge, or when he has been committed after being convicted of being an incorrigible rogue (see Chaps. 39, 40) (Costs in Criminal Cases Act 1952, s. 14). In addition a court of assize or quarter sessions may make an order for the payment of costs out of local funds when it has dealt with an offender for breach of a probation order, or of a conditional discharge, or for having committed a further offence during the "operational period" of a suspended sentence, or for breach of a recognizance to keep the peace, etc., made on conviction of an indictable offence (Criminal Justice Act 1967, s. 31). Quarter sessions has no power, however, to order payment out of local funds when it has sat in its appellate capacity (except for an appeal under the Vagrancy Act 1824) (see Costs in Criminal Cases Acts 1952, s. 14(3), (4)).

Between the parties. A court of assize or quarter sessions before which any person is prosecuted or tried on indictment or inquisition (*a*) may, if the accused is convicted, order him to pay the whole or any part of the costs incurred in or about the prosecution and conviction, including any proceedings before the examining justices; or (*b*) may, if the accused is acquitted, order the prosecutor to pay the whole or any part of the costs incurred in or about the defence, including any proceedings before the examining justices (Costs in

Criminal Cases Act 1952, s. 2(1), as amended by the Criminal Justice Act 1967, s. 32(1)). If the accused is a child or young person, the court (like a magistrates' court) may, and in the case of a child normally must, order any costs which are awarded against that accused to be paid by his parent or guardian (Children and Young Persons Act 1933, s. 55(1)), but there is no statutory limit on the costs which a court of assize or quarter sessions may order a child or young person to pay.

These provisions also apply when an accused has been committed for trial but not ultimately tried (Costs in Criminal Cases Act 1952, s. 13: see above), or when an accused has been committed by a magistrates' court to quarter sessions for sentence, or with a view to a hospital order with an order restricting his discharge, or when he has been convicted of being an incorrigible rogue (*ibid.*, s. 14). In addition, a court of assize or quarter sessions may order one party to pay costs to the other when it has dealt with an offender for breach of a probation order, or of a conditional discharge, or for having committed a further offence during the "operational period" of a suspended sentence (Criminal Justice Act 1967, s. 31). Moreover, when a court of quarter sessions has heard an appeal from a magistrates' court it may also make such order as to costs, to be paid by either party, as it thinks fit (Summary Jurisdiction Act 1879, s. 31(1), as amended by the Summary Jurisdiction (Appeals) Act 1933, s. 1), but this discretion must be exercised judicially, and while an unsuccessful appellant is normally ordered to pay costs, it has been said that the prosecution should rarely be ordered to pay costs to a successful appellant (*David* v. *Commissioner of Metropolitan Police* (1962), D.C.).

Costs awarded against a party under the Costs in Criminal Cases Act 1952 are taxed (*i.e.*, ascertained by the clerk of the trial court (Costs in Criminal Cases Act 1952, s. 2(3)), and they are then recoverable in the same manner as costs ordered to be paid in a civil High Court action (*i.e.*, by process of execution) or like a civil debt (*ibid.*, s. 10(1)). Moreover, if an accused, having been convicted, is ordered to pay costs, the court may direct that money taken from him on arrest should be paid for this purpose (*ibid.*, s. 10(1)). Where quarter sessions makes an order for costs on an appeal to it, the court may order the costs to be taxed or, in lieu of directing a taxation, it may fix the sum to be paid, although the court must then have regard to the means of the party (Summary Jurisdiction (Appeals) Act 1933, s. 5(1)). Costs awarded by quarter sessions on an appeal to it may only be recovered as a civil debt (*ibid.*, s. 5(2)).

Criminal Division of the Court of Appeal

Local funds. The Criminal Division of the Court of Appeal may, when they allow an appeal against conviction or against a verdict of insanity or a finding that the accused was unfit to plead or to be tried, order the payment to the appellant (*i.e.*, the accused) out of local funds of such sums as appear to the court reasonably sufficient to compensate him for any expenses properly incurred in the prosecution of his appeal, including any proceedings preliminary or incidental thereto (*e.g.*, an application for leave to appeal), or in carrying on his defence (Criminal Appeal Act 1968, s. 24). Except where they are for a specific amount, these costs must be ascertained as soon as practicable by the registrar of criminal appeals (*ibid.*, s. 28(2)). Moreover, where an appellant who is not in custody appears before the Criminal Division, either on the hearing of his appeal or in any proceedings preliminary or incidental thereto, the court may direct that there be paid to him out of local funds the expenses of his appearance; and these must also be ascertained as soon as practicable by the registrar of criminal appeals (*ibid.*, ss. 27, 28(2)). There is no provision, however, allowing an order for the payment out of local funds of the prosecution's costs (see Costs in Criminal Cases Act 1952, s. 3(4)).

Between the parties. The Criminal Division of the Court of Appeal may, when they dismiss an appeal, or application for leave to appeal, order the appellant to pay the whole or any part of the costs of the appeal or application (Criminal Appeal Act 1968, s. 25(1)). Except where they are for a specific amount, these must also be ascertained as soon as practicable by the registrar of criminal appeals (*ibid.*, s. 28(2)). There is no provision for an order against the prosecution (see *ibid.*, s. 28(1)).

Divisional Court of the Queen's Bench Division

On an appeal to a Divisional Court by case stated, that court may make such orders as to costs as it sees fit (Summary Jurisdiction Act 1857, s. 6). A Divisional Court cannot, however, make an order for costs to be paid out of local funds. In practice the court normally awards costs to the successful party, and these may include the costs of appearing in the magistrates' court (*Turner & Son Ltd.* v. *Owen* (1956), D.C.).

The costs of proceedings for orders of certiorari, mandamus and prohibition are basically in the discretion of the court (Supreme Court of Judicature (Consolidation) Act 1925, s. 50(1)), but they should normally follow the event (R.S.C. Ord. 62, r. 3(2)). Nevertheless, in exceptional cases, costs may not be awarded to the successful party and the general rule is that costs should not be awarded against a party who does not appear to resist a successful application, although the court will award costs against him when that party materially contributed to the error giving rise to the application (*R.* v. *Liverpool JJ.*, *ex p. Roberts* (1960), D.C.). Even the magistrates may be ordered to pay costs, at least if they appear (*R.* v. *Llanidloes Licensing JJ.*, *ex p. Davies* (1957), D.C.) although the Lord Chancellor may defray out of money provided by Parliament any costs awarded against a magistrate, magistrates' clerk or clerk of the peace (Administration of Justice Act 1964, s. 28).

On the trial of an indictment or inquisition at bar in the Queen's Bench Division, the court has the same powers as a court of assize or quarter sessions to order costs to be paid between the parties (Costs in Criminal Cases Act 1952, s. 15(1)), but the court has no power to order costs to be paid out of local funds.

House of Lords

Local funds. Where an appeal to the House of Lords (from either the Criminal Division of the Court of Appeal or a Divisional Court of the Queen's Bench Division) is determined in favour of the accused, the House of Lords may, if it thinks fit, order the payment to him out of local funds of such sums as appear to it reasonably sufficient to compensate him for any expenses properly incurred in that appeal or (if the appeal is from the Criminal Division) the prosecution of his appeal to the Criminal Division or in carrying on his defence (Criminal Appeal Act 1968, s. 39; Costs in Criminal Cases Act 1952, s. 4(1), as amended). The Criminal Division or the House of Lords may also award costs out of local funds to an accused when the prosecution has unsuccessfully applied to that court for leave to appeal to the House of Lords (Criminal Appeal Act 1968, s. 39).

Between the parties. Where the Criminal Division of the Court of Appeal or the House of Lords dismiss an application by an accused for leave to appeal from the Criminal Division to the House of Lords they may order him to pay the whole or any part of the costs of the application (Criminal Appeal Act 1968, s. 40). Apart from this provision, however, costs cannot be awarded against a party on any appeal from the Criminal Division to the House of Lords (*ibid.*, s. 41(1)). There is no express provision allowing the House of Lords to order one party to pay costs when the appeal is from a Divisional Court of the Queen's Bench Division, but the

House of Lords may have this power under the Administration of Justice Act 1960, s. 1(4) (which allows the House to exercise any powers of the court below).

(2) Legal Aid

Legal aid in almost all criminal proceedings is now governed by Part 4 of the Criminal Justice Act 1967 and the rules made thereunder.

Magistrates' courts

A magistrates' court may order that a person shall be given legal aid when he is charged before that court with an offence (including one who has been summoned or arrested for an offence but has not yet appeared before the court, or one who is before the court with a view to him being bound over to keep the peace, etc.) or when he is before the court to be dealt with for breach of a probation order or for a suspended sentence or for having failed to comply with a recognizance to keep the peace, etc. (Criminal Justice Act 1967, s. 73(2)). The legal aid will be granted by means of a *legal aid order*, and the order will be for representation by a solicitor only, except where the offence charged is an indictable offence and the court considers, because of circumstances which make the case unusually grave or difficult, that representation by both counsel and a solicitor would be desirable (*ibid.*, s. 74(2)). Where applicable, a legal aid order will extend to the solicitor giving advice as to a possible appeal and giving notice of that appeal (*ibid.*, s. 74(5)).

An application for a legal aid order may be made either to the magistrates' clerk in the appropriate form or orally to the court (Legal Aid in Criminal Proceedings (General) Regulations 1968, reg. 1). A magistrates' court (including the clerk), moreover, must make a legal aid order whenever it appears to them that it is desirable to do so in the interests of justice and that the accused's means are such that he requires assistance in meeting the costs which he may incur (*ibid.*, s. 75(1), (2)). The accused must furnish a written statement of his means (*ibid.*, s. 75(4)) and the court may request the Supplementary Benefits Commission to inquire into his means and report on the matter (*ibid.*, s. 77). Nevertheless, any doubt as to whether legal aid should be granted must be resolved in favour of the accused (*ibid.*, s. 75(5)).

If legal aid is granted to an accused he may thereafter be ordered to make contribution towards the costs incurred on his behalf, or even to pay the whole amount of those costs (*ibid.*, s. 76(1)). Where the legal aid was granted by a magistrates' court and the accused was not committed to a court of assize or quarter sessions for trial or sentence, the order for contribution may be made by the magistrates' court which disposed of the case, but where the accused was so committed it should be made by the court of assize or quarter sessions (*ibid.*, s. 76(4)). Nevertheless, an order will not be made unless it appears to the court reasonable having regard to his resources and commitments, and any resources and commitments of his spouse will be considered for this purpose (*ibid.*, s. 78).

Where, moreover, it appears to a court which is making a legal aid order that it is likely that the accused will subsequently be required to make a contribution, the court may order him to make a payment on account of that probable contribution at the time it makes the order (*ibid.*, s. 75(3)). Otherwise any contribution may be recovered summarily as a civil debt, or be enforced in the High Court or a county court as if it were an order of that court, or be secured by an attachment of earnings order (*ibid.*, s. 79).

Whether or not a legally aided accused is ordered to pay a contribution, any costs which he recovers in the proceedings must be paid into the legal aid fund up to the amount of the legal aid payment on his behalf (*ibid.*, s. 79).

Assizes and quarter sessions

Where an accused is committed to or appears before a court of assize or quarter sessions for trial or sentence, either the court which committed him or the court of assize or quarter sessions may grant him legal aid (Criminal Justice Act 1967, s. 73(4)). Likewise, where he has been convicted or sentenced by a magistrates' court and he desires to appeal to quarter sessions, either of those courts may grant him legal aid, and, if an accused does appeal to quarter sessions, the prosecutor may be granted legal aid (*ibid.*, s. 73(3)). Further, where an accused appears before a court of assize or quarter sessions to be dealt with for a breach of a probation order or for a suspended sentence or for breach of a recognizance to keep the peace, etc., that court may grant him legal aid (*ibid.*, s. 73(4)).

The legal aid order will be for representation by a solicitor and counsel except that, in cases of urgency where there is no time to instruct a solicitor, the order may be for representation by counsel only, or, where any proceedings are before a court of quarter sessions before which solicitors have a right of audience, it may be for representation by a solicitor only (*ibid.*, s. 74). Where applicable, the order will extend to advice which may be given as to a possible appeal and giving notice of that appeal (*ibid.*, s. 74).

A legal aid order under these provisions must be made where it appears to the court desirable to do so in the interests of justice and that the applicant's means are such that he requires assistance in meeting the costs which he may incur and, subject to the accused's means, an order must also be made where he is committed for trial on a charge of murder (*ibid.*, s. 75(1), (2)).

In practice legal aid ought always to be granted to an accused, unless he has adequate means, whenever he is pleading "not guilty" or the offence is a serious one or a heavy sentence will be called for (*R.* v. *Howes* (1964), C.C.A.; *R.* v. *Serghiou* (1966), C.A.; *R.* v. *Green* (1968), C.A.).

Otherwise, the provisions in relation to legal aid which apply to proceedings before magistrates' courts, including those relating to contribution, apply also to proceedings before courts of assize or quarter sessions.

Dock briefs

Apart from legal aid, an accused who is not represented may select any member of the Bar present in the court of assize or quarter sessions and who is not already engaged in the case to represent him, and this practice is known as a dock brief. A barrister who accepts a dock brief is normally entitled to a fee of two guineas (and half-a-crown for his clerk). With the wider provisions for legal aid which are now available, however, it is likely that the procedure relating to dock briefs will become less and less used.

Criminal Division of the Court of Appeal

When an accused is convicted or sentenced by a court of assize or quarter sessions and he desires to appeal to the Criminal Division of the Court of Appeal, the Criminal Division may order that he be given legal aid for the purpose of the appeal and any proceedings preliminary or incidental thereto (Criminal Justice Act 1967, s. 73(5)). Where, moreover, the Criminal Division orders a retrial, that court, or the court of assize or quarter sessions by which he is to be retried, may grant him legal aid for the purpose of the retrial (*ibid.*, s. 73(8)).

The legal aid order will be for representation by a solicitor and counsel except that where the accused is appealing to the Criminal Division the order may be for representation by counsel only (*ibid.*, s. 74). Moreover, the order may provide, in the first instance, for advice by counsel or solicitor on the question whether there appear to be reasonable grounds of appeal (*ibid.*, s. 74(8)). Otherwise, the provisions in relation to legal aid which apply to proceedings before magistrates' courts, including those relating to whether legal aid ought to be granted, apply also to proceedings before the Criminal Division or on a retrial.

Divisional Court of the Queen's Bench Division

The special provisions for legal aid in criminal cases do not apply to criminal proceedings in a Divisional Court of the Queen's Bench Division. However, the normal civil provisions do apply and an applicant who is able to show that he has reasonable grounds, for example, for appealing to a Divisional Court by case stated may be granted legal aid under the Legal Aid and Advice Act 1949, s. 1. It is not possible within the scope of this work to state these provisions in detail but the applicant's income and capital must not exceed the prescribed limit and he may be required to pay a contribution (see s. 1, as amended).

House of Lords

Where either party to an appeal to the Criminal Division of the Court of Appeal desires to appeal to the House of Lords, the Criminal Division may order that the accused be given legal aid for the purpose of the appeal and any proceedings preliminary or incidental thereto (Criminal Justice Act 1967, s. 73(7)). The order will be for representation by a solicitor and counsel (*ibid.*, s. 74(1)).

A legal aid order must be made where it appears to the Criminal Division desirable to do so in the interests of justice and that the applicant's means are such that he requires assistance in meeting the costs which he may incur and, subject to the accused's means, an order must be made where the prosecutor appeals, or applies for leave to appeal, to the House of Lords (*ibid.*, s. 75). Otherwise, the provisions in relation to legal aid which apply to proceedings before magistrates' courts apply also to these apeals to the House of Lords.

When there is an appeal from a Divisional Court of the Queen's Bench Division to the House of Lords the normal civil provisions apply (see above).

Appendix I

OFFENCES WHICH ARE TRIABLE, OR NOT TRIABLE, AT QUARTER SESSIONS

Criminal Law Act 1967

Schedule 1

LIST A Division I: *Offences triable by all courts of quarter sessions*

1. Offences against section 17 of the Malicious Damage Act 1861 (arson of stacks of corn etc.).
2. Offences against sections 53 and 55 to 58 of the Post Office Act 1953 (certain offences in connection with mails).
3. Offences against section 5 of the Perjury Act 1911 in relation to statements in statutory declarations.
4. The following offences against the Forgery Act 1913: —

(*a*) offences against section 2(2) (*a*) in relation to any document, being an authority or request for the payment of money or for the delivery or transfer of goods or chattels, where the amount of the money or the value of the goods or chattels does not exceed £100; and

(*b*) offences against section 7 (*a*) where the amount of the money or the value of the property in respect of which the offence is committed does not exceed £100; and

(*c*) uttering any forged document the forgery of which is an offence triable by the court in question.

5. Offences against the Public Bodies Corrupt Practices Act 1889.
6. Unlawful combinations and conspiracies to cheat and defraud.

LIST A Division II: *Offences triable by courts of quarter sessions other than courts with restricted jurisdiction [because they do not have a legally qualified chairman, etc.]*

1. *Repealed by the Theft Act 1968, s. 33.*
2. Offences under section 14 of the Malicious Damage Act 1861 (destruction of textiles during manufacture or of textile machinery).
3. Offences against the Coinage Offences Act 1936, other than

offences against sections 1(1) (*a*), 2, 9(1) and (2) and 10 (certain offences in relation to coinage of higher denominations, to coining implements and to removal of coining implements, coin or bullion from the Mint).

4. Offences against the following provisions of the Perjury Act 1911: —

(*a*) section 2 (false statements on oath made otherwise than in judicial proceedings);

(*b*) section 3 (false statements etc., with reference to marriage);

(*c*) section 4 (false statements etc., as to births or deaths);

(*d*) section 5 (false statutory declarations and other false statements without oath);

(*e*) section 6 (false declarations etc., to obtain registration etc., for carrying on a vocation).

5.—(*a*) Offences consisting of the forgery of any document or thing, being offences triable on indictment or alternatively by a magistrates' court, except offences against section 1 of the Official Secrets Act 1920;

(*b*) Offences against section 13 of the Stamp Duties Management Act 1891 (frauds in connection with stamps and dies);

(*c*) The following offences against the Forgery Act 1913: —

(i) offences which would before the passing of that Act have constituted offences against section 13 of the Stamp Duties Management Act 1891;

(ii), (iii) *Repealed by the Criminal Justice Act 1967, s. 103.*

(*d*) Offences against section 36 of the Criminal Justice Act 1925 (forgery of passport and false statement to obtain passport).

6.—(*a*) Bigamy and offences against the marriage laws.

(*b*) Offences, and attempts to commit offences, against section 6 of the Sexual Offences Act 1956 (intercourse with girl under 16), and offences against section 13 of that Act (indecency between men) and attempts to procure the commission by a man of an act of gross indecency with another man.

7. Offences against section 60 of the Offences against the Person Act 1861 (endeavouring to conceal birth of child).

8. Offences against section 9 of the Night Poaching Act 1828 (poaching at night by armed gangs).

9. Conspiracies to commit offences punishable on summary conviction.

LIST B: *Offences excluded (subject to List A) from jurisdiction of all courts of quarter sessions*

1. Any offence for which a person may be sentenced to death.

2. Any offence for which a person may under or by virtue of any enactment be sentenced to imprisonment for life.

3. Misprision of treason.

4. Offences against the Queen's title, prerogative, person or government, or against either House of Parliament .

5. Blasphemy and offences against religion.

6. Composing, printing or publishing blasphemous, seditious or defamatory libels.

7. Administering or taking unlawful oaths.

8. Perjury and subornation of perjury, offences against the Perjury Act 1911, and offences which under any enactment are declared to be perjury or to be punishable as perjury or as subornation of perjury.

9. Forgery, offences against the Forgery Act 1913 and offences which under any enactment are declared to be forgery or to be punishable as forgery.

10.—(*a*) Bigamy and offences against the marriage laws;

(*b*) Abduction of women and girls, and offences against sections 1 to 13, 17 to 27 and 29 of the Sexual Offences Act 1956;

(*c*) Attempts to commit offences against the following provisions of the Sexual Offences Act 1956, namely, sections 2, 5, 6, 7, 9, 10, 11, 22 and 23, and attempts to procure the commission by a man of an act of gross indecency with another man.

11.—(*a*) Bribery;

(*b*) Offences under the Prevention of Corruption Act 1906;

(*c*) Corrupt practices within the meaning of the Representation of the People Act 1949 (including any provision of that Act as applied by section 67(5) of the Licensing Act 1964).

12. Unlawful combinations and conspiracies, other than conspiracies or combinations to commit offences which the court in question has jurisdiction to try when committed by one person.

13. *Repealed by the Theft Act 1968, s. 33.*

14. Offences against section 9 of the Night Poaching Act 1828 (poaching at night by armed gangs).

15. Offences under the Official Secrets Acts 1911 to 1939.

16.—(*a*) Attempted murder, and attempts to commit offences against section 1 of the Infant Life (Preservation) Act 1929 (child destruction).

(*b*) Offences against section 60 of the Offences against the Person Act 1861 (endeavouring to conceal birth of child).

17. Offences against section 1 of the Geneva Conventions Act 1957.

18. Offences against section 1 of the Road Traffic Act 1960 (causing death by reckless or dangerous driving).

19. Offences against section 2 of the Suicide Act 1961 (aiding and abetting suicide).

Appendix II

INDICTABLE OFFENCES BY ADULTS WHICH MAY BE TRIED SUMMARILY

Under the Magistrates' Courts Act 1952, Sched. 1, as amended

1. Setting fire to crops, trees, etc. (Malicious Damage Act 1861, s. 16).

2. Maliciously damaging trees, shrubs, etc. (Malicious Damage Act 1861, ss. 20, 21).

3. Malicious damage exceeding £5 (Malicious Damage Act 1861, s. 51).

4. Maliciously wounding or inflicting grievous bodily harm (Offences against the Person Act 1861, s. 20).

5. Assault occasioning actual bodily harm and indictable common assault (Offences against the Person Act 1861, s. 47).

6. Disclosing telegrams (Telegraph Act 1868, s. 20).

7. Offences under section 13 of the Stamp Duties Management Act 1891.

8. Offences under sections 53 and 55 to 58 of the Post Office Act 1953 (which include unlawfully taking away or opening a mail bag).

9. Making a false statement in a statutory declaration (Perjury Act 1911, s. 5).

10. Forgery with intent to defraud, in relation to any document being an authority or request for the payment of money or for the delivery or transfer of goods and chattels, where the money or the value of the goods or chattels does not exceed £100 (Forgery Act 1913, s. 2(2) (a)).

11. Forgery of valuable securities, in relation to any document being an accountable receipt, release, or discharge, or any receipt or other instrument evidencing the payment of money, or the delivery of any chattel personal (Forgery Act 1913, s. 2(2) (a)).

12. Forgery of documents in general (Forgery Act 1913, s. 4).

13. Demanding money or property on forged documents, where the money or the value of the property does not exceed £100 (Forgery Act 1913, s. 7 (a)).

14. Offences under section 36 of the Criminal Justice Act 1925 (certain offences relating to passports).

15. Offences under section 11 of the Agricultural Credits Act 1928 (frauds by a farmer in relation to an agricultural charge).

16. Defacing and uttering defaced coins (Coinage Offences Act 1936, s. 4).

17. Uttering, and possessing with intent to utter, counterfeit coin (Coinage Offences Act 1936, s. 5(1)-(4), (6)).

18. Exporting counterfeit coins (Coinage Offences Act 1936, s. 7(1) (*b*)).

19. Making, possessing and selling medals resembling gold or silver coin (Coinage Offences Act 1936, s. 8).

20. Gross indecency between men (Sexual Offences Act 1956, s. 13).

21. Procuring another man to commit with a third man an act of buggary which is not an offence (Sexual Offences Act 1967, s. 4(1)).

22. Any indictable offence under the Theft Act 1968 except—

(*a*) robbery, aggravated burglary, blackmail and assault with intent to rob; and

(*b*) burglary comprising the commission of, or an intention to commit, an offence which is not triable summarily under this Schedule; and

(*c*) burglary in a dwelling if entry to the dwelling or the part of it in which the burglary was committed, or to a building or part of a building containing the dwelling, was obtained by force or deception or by the use of any tool, key or appliance, or if any person in the dwelling was subjected to violence or the threat of violence; and

(*d*) handling stolen goods from an offence not committed in the United Kingdom.

23. Committing an indecent assault upon a person, whether male or female.

24. Offences in relation to stamps issued for the purpose of national insurance under the provisions of any enactments as applied to those stamps.

25. Uttering any forged document, the forgery of which is an offence which is itself triable summarily in the case of an adult.

26. Assisting an offender guilty of an arrestable offence, or inciting a person to commit such an offence, where that offence is triable summarily under this Schedule.

27. Concealing an arrestable offence or not disclosing information concerning it, where that offence is triable summarily under this Schedule.

28. Aiding, abetting, counselling or procuring the commission of any of the aforementioned offences; attempting to commit any such offence and attempting to commit any hybrid offence.

29. Any offence consisting in the incitement to commit a summary offence or to commit any offence mentioned in paragraphs 1 to 25 above.

Under the Criminal Justice Administration Act 1962, Sched. III, Pt. 1

1. Abandoning or exposing a child (Offences against the Person Act 1861, s. 27).

2. Concealing the birth of a child (Offences against the Person Act 1861, s. 60).

Appendix III

ALTERNATIVE VERDICTS

IN addition to the general provisions of section 6 of the Criminal Law Act 1967 (see Chap. 38), some statutes allow an accused to be convicted by way of alternative verdict of specified offences. Some of these offences are listed below.

Offence charged	Alternative Verdicts	Statutory Authority
Murder	(1) Manslaughter	Criminal Law Act 1967, s. 6(2)
	(2) Causing grievous bodily harm with intent to do so	Criminal Law Act 1967, s. 6(2)
	(3) Infanticide	Infanticide Act 1938, s. 1(2)
	(4) Child destruction	Infant Life (Preservation) Act 1929, s. 2(2)
Manslaughter	Child destruction	Infant Life (Preservation) Act 1929, s. 2(2)
Infanticide	Child destruction	Infant Life (Preservation) Act 1929, s. 2(2)
Abortion	Child destruction	Infant Life (Preservation) Act 1929, s. 2(2)
Child destruction	Abortion	Infant Life (Preservation) Act 1929, s. 2(3)
Rape	(1) Procurement of a woman by threats	Sexual Offences Act 1956, s. 37 and Sched. II, para. 1 (a)
	(2) Procurement of a woman by false pretences	Sexual Offences Act 1956, s. 37 and Sched. II, para. 1 (a)
	(3) Administering drugs to obtain or facilitate intercourse	Sexual Offences Act 1956, s. 37 and Sched. II, para. 14 (a)
Incest by a man	(1) Intercourse with a girl under 13	Sexual Offences Act 1956, s. 37 and Sched. II, para. 14 (a)
	(2) Intercourse with a girl under 16	Sexual Offences Act 1956, s. 37 and Sched. II, para. 14 (a)
Theft	Taking a conveyance without authority	Theft Act 1968, s. 12(4)

Appendix IV

SOME EXAMPLES OF INDICTMENTS

[Not including the Commencements]

Common law offences

1. STATEMENT OF OFFENCE
   Murder.
   PARTICULARS OF OFFENCE
A.B., on the . . ., in the county of . . ., murdered X.Y.

2. STATEMENT OF OFFENCE
   Manslaughter.
   PARTICULARS OF OFFENCE
A.B., on the . . ., in the county of . . ., unlawfully killed X.Y.

3. STATEMENT OF OFFENCE
   Assault occasioning actual bodily harm.
   PARTICULARS OF OFFENCE
A.B., on the . . ., in the county of . . ., assaulted X.Y., thereby occasioning him actual bodily harm.
[*Note: this offence is sometimes charged under section 47 of the Offences against the Person Act 1861.*]

4. STATEMENT OF OFFENCE
   Common assault.
   PARTICULARS OF OFFENCE
A.B., on the . . ., in the county of . . ., assaulted X.Y.
[*Note: this offence is sometimes charged under section 47 of the Offences against the Person Act 1861.*]

5. STATEMENT OF OFFENCE
   Libel.
   PARTICULARS OF OFFENCE
A.B., on the . . ., in the county of . . ., published a defamatory libel concerning X.Y., knowing it to be false, in the form of a letter addressed to P.Q., which contained the following defamatory matters concerning the said XY.:
   [*Details of the defamatory matters.*]

Under the Malicious Damage Act 1861

1. STATEMENT OF OFFENCE
   Arson, contrary to section 2 of the Malicious Damage Act 1861.
395

PARTICULARS OF OFFENCE

A.B., on the . . ., in the county of . . ., maliciously set fire to a dwelling-house, one *X.Y.* being therein.

2. STATEMENT OF OFFENCE

 Arson, contrary to section 3 of the Malicious Damage Act 1861.

 PARTICULARS OF OFFENCE

A.B., on the . . ., in the county of . . ., maliciously set fire to a house with intent to injure or defraud.

Under the Offences against the Person Act 1861

1. STATEMENT OF OFFENCE

 Wounding with intent, contrary to section 18 of the Offences against the Person Act 1861.

 PARTICULARS OF OFFENCE

A.B., on the . . ., in the county of . . ., wounded *X.Y.*, with intent to do him grievous bodily harm, or to resist the lawful apprehension of the said *A.B.*

2. STATEMENT OF OFFENCE

 Causing grievous bodily harm with intent, contrary to section 18 of the Offences against the Person Act 1861.

 PARTICULARS OF OFFENCE

A.B., on the . . ., in the county of . . ., caused grievous bodily harm to *X.Y.*, with intent to do him grievous bodily harm, or to resist the lawful apprehension of the said *A.B.*

3. STATEMENT OF OFFENCE

 Wounding, contrary to section 20 of the Offences against the Person Act 1861.

 PARTICULARS OF OFFENCE

A.B., on the . . ., in the county of . . ., maliciously wounded *X.Y.*

4. STATEMENT OF OFFENCE

 Bigamy, contrary to section 57 of the Offences against the Person Act 1861.

 PARTICULARS OF OFFENCE

A.B., on the . . ., in the county of . . ., married *X.Y.* during the life of his wife *P.Q.*

5. STATEMENT OF OFFENCE

 Administering poison with intent to procure miscarriage, contrary to section 58 of the Offences against the Person Act 1861.

 PARTICULARS OF OFFENCE

A.B., on the . . ., in the county of . . ., with intent to procure the miscarriage of a woman named *X.Y.*, unlawfully administered to [*or* caused to be taken by] her a poison or other noxious thing, namely ————— [*or* the nature of which is unknown].

6. STATEMENT OF OFFENCE
   Using an instrument to procure miscarriage, contrary to section 58 of the Offences against the Person Act 1861.
   PARTICULARS OF OFFENCE
A.B., on the . . ., in the county of . . ., with intent to procure the miscarriage of a woman named *X.Y.*, unlawfully used an instrument or some other unknown means.

7. STATEMENT OF OFFENCE
   Endeavouring to conceal birth, contrary to section 60 of the Offences against the Person Act 1861.
   PARTICULARS OF OFFENCE
A.B., on the . . ., in the county of . . ., endeavoured to conceal the birth of a child of which she had been delivered, by secretly disposing of the dead body of the child.

Under the Forgery Act 1913

1. STATEMENT OF OFFENCE
   Forgery, contrary to section 2(1) of the Forgery Act 1913.
   PARTICULARS OF OFFENCE
A.B., on the . . ., in the county of . . ., with intent to defraud, forged a certain will purporting to be the will of *X.Y.*

2. STATEMENT OF OFFENCE
   Forgery of document, contrary to section 4(1) of the Forgery Act 1913.
   PARTICULARS OF OFFENCE
A.B., on the . . ., in the county of . . ., with intent to defraud, forged a certain document purporting to be [*description of the document*].

3. STATEMENT OF OFFENCE
   Uttering forged document, contrary to section 6(1) (2) of the Forgery Act 1913.
   PARTICULARS OF OFFENCE
A.B., on the . . ., in the county of . . ., uttered a certain forged document purporting to be [*description of the document*] knowing it to be forged and with intent to defraud.

4. STATEMENT OF OFFENCE
   Demanding money on a forged instrument, contrary to section 7 of the Forgery Act 1913.

PARTICULARS OF OFFENCE

A.B., on the . . ., in the county of . . ., with intent to defraud, demanded from *X.Y.* the sum of £50 under or by virtue of a forged bill of exchange knowing the same to be forged.

Under the Sexual Offences Act 1956

1. STATEMENT OF OFFENCE

   Rape, contrary to section 1(1) of the Sexual Offences Act 1956.

   PARTICULARS OF OFFENCE

A.B., on the . . ., in the county of . . ., had sexual intercourse with *X.Y.*, without her consent.

2. STATEMENT OF OFFENCE

   Sexual intercourse with a girl under thirteen, contrary to section 5 of the Sexual Offences Act 1956.

   PARTICULARS OF OFFENCE

A.B., on the . . ., in the county of . . ., had sexual intercourse with *X.Y.*, a girl of the age of twelve years.

3. STATEMENT OF OFFENCE

   Sexual intercourse with a girl under sixteen, contrary to section 6(1) of the Sexual Offences Act 1956.

   PARTICULARS OF OFFENCE

A.B., on the . . ., in the county of . . . had unlawful sexual intercourse with *X.Y.*, a girl of the age of fourteen years.

4. STATEMENT OF OFFENCE

   Incest, contrary to section 10(1) of the Sexual Offences Act 1956.

   PARTICULARS OF OFFENCE

A.B., being a male person, on the . . ., in the county of . . ., had sexual intercourse with *X.Y.*, who is, and was to his knowledge, his daughter.

5. STATEMENT OF OFFENCE

   Indecent assault, contrary to section 14(1) of the Sexual Offences Act 1956.

   PARTICULARS OF OFFENCE

A.B., on the . . ., in the county of . . ., indecently assaulted *X.Y.*

Under the Road Traffic Act 1960

1. STATEMENT OF OFFENCE

   Causing death by reckless driving, contrary to section 1(1) of the Road Traffic Act 1960.

PARTICULARS OF OFFENCE

A.B., on the . . ., in the county of . . ., caused the death of *X.Y.* by driving a motor-vehicle on a road recklessly, having regard to all the circumstances of the case.

2. STATEMENT OF OFFENCE

Reckless driving, contrary to section 2(1) of the Road Traffic Act 1960.

PARTICULARS OF OFFENCE

A.B., on the . . ., in the county of . . ., drove a motor-vehicle on a road recklessly, having regard to all the circumstances of the case.

3. STATEMENT OF OFFENCE

Driving a motor-vehicle when unfit to drive through drink, contrary to section 6(1) of the Road Traffic Act 1960.

PARTICULARS OF OFFENCE

A.B., on the . . ., in the county of . . ., when driving a motor-vehicle on a road named ————, was unfit to drive through drink.

Under the Theft Act 1968

1. STATEMENT OF OFFENCE

Theft, contrary to section 1 of the Theft Act 1968.

PARTICULARS OF OFFENCE

A.B., on the . . ., in the county of . . ., stole a book, the property of *X.Y.*

2. STATEMENT OF OFFENCE

Robbery, contrary to section 8 of the Theft Act 1968.

PARTICULARS OF OFFENCE

A.B., on the . . ., in the county of . . ., robbed *X.Y.* of a watch.

3. STATEMENT OF OFFENCE

Assault with intent to rob, contrary to section 8 of the Theft Act 1968.

PARTICULARS OF OFFENCE

A.B., on the . . ., in the county of . . ., assaulted *X.Y.* with intent to rob him.

4. STATEMENT OF OFFENCE

Burglary, contrary to section 9(1) (*a*) of the Theft Act 1968.

PARTICULARS OF OFFENCE

A.B., on the . . ., in the county of . . ., entered as a trespasser a building known as —————, and with intent to steal therein.

5. STATEMENT OF OFFENCE

Burglary, contrary to section 9(1) (*b*) of the Theft Act 1968.
PARTICULARS OF OFFENCE
A.B., on the . . ., in the county of . . ., having entered as a trespasser a building known as —————, stole therein a camera, the property of *X.Y., Limited.*

6. STATEMENT OF OFFENCE
   Aggravated burglary, contrary to section 10(1) of the Theft Act 1968.
   PARTICULARS OF OFFENCE
A.B., on the . . ., in the county of . . ., entered as a trespasser a building known as —————, and with intent to do unlawful damage therein, and at the time of the said entry had with him a firearm, namely an air pistol.

7. STATEMENT OF OFFENCE
   Removing article from place open to the public, contrary to section 11(1) of the Theft Act 1968.
   PARTICULARS OF OFFENCE
A.B., on the . . ., in the county of . . ., without lawful authority, removed from the *National Gallery*, a building to which the public had access in order to view a collection of paintings housed therein, a painting forming part of the said collection, and which collection was intended for permanent exhibition to the public.

8. STATEMENT OF OFFENCE
   Taking conveyance without authority, contrary to section 12(1) of the Theft Act 1968.
   PARTICULARS OF OFFENCE
A.B., on the . . ., in the county of . . ., without having the consent of the owner or other lawful authority, took a conveyance, namely a ————— motor car index number —————, for his own use.

9. STATEMENT OF OFFENCE
   Abstracting electricity, contrary to section 13 of the Theft Act 1968.
   PARTICULARS OF OFFENCE
A.B., on the . . ., in the county of . . ., dishonestly used without due authority a quantity of electricity, the property of the ————— *Electricity Board.*

10. STATEMENT OF OFFENCE
    Obtaining property by deception, contrary to section 15(1) of the Theft Act 1968.
    PARTICULARS OF OFFENCE
A.B., on the . . ., in the county of . . ., dishonestly obtained from *X.Y.* one gold watch by deception, namely by falsely pretending that

a certain cheque which he, the said *A.B.*, then produced and delivered to the said *X.Y.* was a good and valid order for the payment of £50, and that he, the said *A.B.* had authority to draw a cheque for the payment of £50 upon the London Bank, Limited, situate at ———, in the said county of ———.

11. STATEMENT OF OFFENCE

Obtaining pecuniary advantage by deception, contrary to section 16(1) of the Theft Act 1968.

PARTICULARS OF OFFENCE

A.B., on the . . ., in the county of . . ., dishonestly obtained the opportunity to earn remuneration as a teacher at the ——— School, ———, in the county of ———, by a deception, namely that he had a Master of Arts degree from the University of ———.

12. STATEMENT OF OFFENCE

Blackmail, contrary to section 21(1) of the Theft Act 1968.

PARTICULARS OF OFFENCE

A.B., on the . . ., in the county of . . ., with a view to gain for himself, made an unwarranted demand of a watch from *X.Y.*, with menaces.

13. STATEMENT OF OFFENCE

Handling stolen goods, contrary to section 22(1) of the Theft Act 1968.

PARTICULARS OF OFFENCE

A.B., on the . . ., in the county of . . ., did handle a clock, the property of *X.Y.*, knowing or believing the same to have been stolen.

14. STATEMENT OF OFFENCE

Going equipped for burglary, contrary to section 25(1) of the Theft Act 1968.

PARTICULARS OF OFFENCE

A.B., on the . . ., in the county of . . ., not being at his place of abode, had with him an article for use in the course of burglary, namely a screwdriver.

Under other Acts

1. STATEMENT OF OFFENCE

Perjury, contrary to section 1(1) of the Perjury Act 1911.

PARTICULARS OF OFFENCE

A.B., on the . . ., in the county of . . ., being a witness upon the trial of an action in the Queen's Bench Division of the High Court of Justice in England in which one *X.Y.* was plaintiff and one *P.Q.* was defendant, knowingly falsely swore that he saw one *S.T.* in the street called Chancery Lane, London, on the —— day of ——,

2. STATEMENT OF OFFENCE

> Child destruction, contrary to section 1 of the Infant Life (Preservation) Act 1929.

PARTICULARS OF OFFENCE

A.B., on the . . ., in the county of . . ., with intent to destroy the life of a child capable of being born alive, wilfully inserted an instrument into the womb of *X.Y.* and thereby caused the death of her child before it had an existence independent of her.

3. STATEMENT OF OFFENCE

> Infanticide, contrary to section 1(1) of the Infanticide Act 1938.

PARTICULARS OF OFFENCE

A.B., on the . . ., in the county of . . ., caused the death of her child, being a child under the age of twelve months, by a wilful act, that is to say, by stabbing it with a knife, but at the time of the act she had not fully recovered from the effect of giving birth to such child and by reason thereof the balance of her mind was then disturbed.

INDEX

403